INSIGHT GUIDES

Texas

D0066940

APA PUBLICATIONS

Part of the Langenscheidt Publishing Group

INSIGHT GUIDE
Texas

Editorial
Project Editor
Jeff Evans
Editorial Director
Brian Bell

Distribution

UK & Ireland
GeoCenter International Ltd
The Viables Centre, Harrow Way
Basingstoke, Hants RG22 4BJ
Fax: (44) 1256 817988

United States
Langenscheidt Publishers, Inc.
36–36 33rd Street 4th Floor
Long Island City, NY 11106
Fax: 1 (718) 784 0640

Australia
Universal Publishers
1 Waterloo Road
Macquarie Park, NSW 2113
Fax: (61) 2 9888 9074

New Zealand
Hema Maps New Zealand Ltd (HNZ)
Unit D, 24 Ra ORA Drive
East Tamaki, Auckland
Fax: (64) 9 273 6479

Worldwide
**Apa Publications GmbH & Co.
Verlag KG (Singapore branch)**
38 Joo Koon Road, Singapore 628990
Tel: (65) 6865 1600. Fax: (65) 6861 6438

Printing

Insight Print Services (Pte) Ltd
38 Joo Koon Road, Singapore 628990
Tel: (65) 6865 1600. Fax: (65) 6861 6438

©2006 Apa Publications GmbH & Co.
Verlag KG (Singapore branch)
All Rights Reserved
First Edition 1986
Fourth Edition 1999
Updated 2003. Reprinted 2006

CONTACTING THE EDITORS
We would appreciate it if readers
would alert us to errors or outdated information by writing to:
**Insight Guides, P.O. Box 7910,
London SE1 1WE, England.
Fax: (44) 20 7403 0290.
insight@apaguide.co.uk**
NO part of this book may be reproduced,
stored in a retrieval system or transmitted
in any form or means electronic, mechanical, photocopying, recording or otherwise, without prior written permission of
Apa Publications. Brief text quotations
with use of photographs are exempted
for book review purposes only. Information has been obtained from sources
believed to be reliable, but its accuracy
and completeness, and the opinions
based thereon, are not guaranteed.

www.insightguides.com
In North America:
www.insighttravelguides.com

ABOUT THIS BOOK

The first Insight Guide pioneered the use of creative full-colour photography in travel guides in 1970. Since then, we have expanded our range to cater for our readers' need not only for reliable information about their chosen destination but also for a real understanding of the culture and workings of that destination. Now, when the internet can supply inexhaustible (but not always reliable) facts, our books marry text and pictures to provide those much more elusive qualities: knowledge and discernment. To achieve this, they rely heavily on the authority of locally based writers and photographers.

Texas lends itself especially well to Insight Guides' approach. As the writer John Steinbeck, in his book *Travels With Charley,* observed: "Texas is a state of mind, Texas is an obsession."

How to use this book
The book is carefully structured both to convey an understanding of the state and its culture, and to guide readers through its sights and activities:

◆ To understand Texas today, you need to know something of its past. The first section covers the state's past and culture in

◆ The photographs are chosen not only to illustrate geography and attractions but also to convey the many moods of Texas and its people.

The contributors

The original edition of *Insight Guide: Texas* was edited by **Diana Ackland** and **Janie Freeburg**. They assembled a team of fine Texas writing talent, including **John Smith**, **Paul Powell**, **Mel McCombie**, **A.C. Greenze**, **Lisa Jones**, **Sue Winton Moss**, **Winston Derdon**, **John Minton**, **Gary Taylor**, **Michael Murphy**, **Pamela Jantzen**, **Fernando de Luna**, **Lisa Germany** and **Louis Dubose**. That edition was taken over by Insight's editor-in-chief of North American titles, **Martha Ellen Zenfell**, who also did the picture edit for this new edition.

In 2000 the guide was revised and re-organized by **Jeff Evans**, a freelance journalist who specializes in guidebooks and leisure-activity writing and whose books have covered such subjects as beer and television. **John Wilcock**, an Insight Guides stalwart, provided new essays and was assisted by two Texas-based writers, **Ann Mills** and **Christopher Walters**.

But a guidebook is only as good as its most recent incarnation, and Jeff Evans fully updated all the information in this current edition. It was edited by **Alyse Dar**, a native Texan now working as an editor for Insight. Many of the book's wonderful photographs were specially commissioned from **Jack Hollingsworth**.

lively, authoritative essays written by specialists. This section includes essays on the state's **History** and **Features** on its culture today.
◆ The main **Places** section gives a full run-down of all the attractions worth seeing, divided by geographic areas. The principal places of interest are coordinated by number with full-color maps.
◆ The **Travel Tips** listings section provides comprehensive information on travel, hotels, restaurants, sports and festivals. Facts may be located quickly by using the index printed on the back cover flap.

Map Legend

— ·· —	International Boundary
– – – –	State Boundary
⊖	Border Crossing
— ·—·—	National Park/Reserve
✈ ✛	Airport: International/Regional
🚌	Bus Station
🅿	Parking
❶	Tourist Information
✉	Post Office
🕆 ✝ ✟	Church/Ruins
✝	Monastery
☾	Mosque
✡	Synagogue
🏰 🏚	Castle/Ruins
∴	Archeological Site
∩	Cave
⚊	Statue/Monument
★	Place of Interest

The main places of interest in the Places section are coordinated by number with a full-color map (e.g. ❶), and a symbol at the top of every right-hand page tells you where to find the map.

CONTENTS

Maps

El Capitan
Peak,
Guadalupe
Mountains
National
Park

Information panels

Insight on ...

Places

WHERE BIG IS BEAUTIFUL

*The myths are magnificent but so is the reality. What appeals
most about Texas – and Texans – is the huge diversity*

There's one word people use more than any other to describe Texas: "big." Big ranches, big cities, big money, big sky, big smiles, big mountains, big fun and, above all, big hearts. Plain and simple – Texas is a big place, and its image in the American mind has always been larger than life. It's been said that the US is a frontier nation and that distinctly American notions like "rugged individualism" were shaped by the vast wilderness that beckoned at the country's western border. Possibly more than any other state, Texas epitomizes this frontier ethic. And, as some people see it, the American spirit has blossomed here more fully than anywhere else.

For many people, Texas *is* America – the one place where the American dream is still alive, where the values and traditions that helped build the nation are still a viable part of the culture. Think, for example, of all the American icons that come from Texas: the cowboy, the sheriff, the six-shooter, the 10-gallon hat, the maverick, the oil baron, the longhorn and the open range, just to name a few. And how many times have you seen the big-hearted, drawling Texan used to represent Americans as a whole, slapping the world on the back and inviting it in for a barbecue? Distortions they may be, but they evoke an image of an America recognized around the world.

Getting to know a place that is as broadly mythologized can be difficult because often we mistake myth for reality, settling for stereotypes or caricatures. So it's important for travelers to strip away their preconceptions and try to pry the real Texas away from its image. Sometimes they are the same thing, but usually not.

The best way to approach the state is to forget about "Big Texas" and concentrate on something smaller. Texas isn't a single place, after all, and Texans aren't a single people. There is as much diversity here as there is anywhere else in the country and when you begin to focus on specific people, towns or places, the stereotypes will quickly fall away. Yes, there are cowboys and wealthy oilmen. Also ranchers, Native Americans, Latinos and plenty of horse traders. But there are also things that you never expected: a Vietnamese fishing community along the Gulf Coast, a Czech farming town out on the plains, or a community of artists in a dusty border town.

"Texans want to believe they're different, a reverberating quality that other places don't have," said the late author James Michener, who made the state the subject (and the title) of his 32nd novel and then came to live here. "Texas has a rather logical pull on the imagination of the creative artist. I have great respect for the Texas legend. How you specify that it is a legend and how it became a legend and so on is a tough artistic problem. But I have great respect for it." ❏

PRECEDING PAGES: "Big Tex" at Texas State Fair; western festival at Fort Worth Stockyards; painted pump jacks at Post; Houston skyline from Tranquility Park. **LEFT:** cowboy in contemplation.

THE LONE STAR STATE

Cultural traditions, economic realities and the sheer distances involved mean

that Texas could actually be five different states under its Lone Star

Texas is a world in itself. To understand this, one starts with size. With 267,000 sq. miles (692,000 sq. km) in land area, Texas is larger than many nations of the world, including every country in Europe. Size creates space, space makes for distance, and distance creates differences. These are the basic ingredients that have helped make Texas and Texans outstanding in the eyes of the world. Although sometimes treated as a kind of international joke, the truth is that Texas is enormous and its inhabitants inordinately proud of it.

These facts go to explain not only the wide geographic choices for the visitor but how diversified are its peoples and their cultures: there is no such thing as "a Texas" or "a Texan." These are collective names.

Distance and difference

Because of its size, traveling the entire state takes a good deal of time. It is not the kind of place that can be covered in a day or two. There are 940 highway miles (1,500 km), for example, between Texline on the northern border of the Texas Panhandle, and Brownsville at the mouth of the Rio Grande across from Mexico. From Texarkana in the northeast corner, beside the Arkansas border, to El Paso at the state's extreme western tip is 810 miles (1,300 km).

As one crosses this vast surface, everything changes: the configuration of the earth, the economy, time zones, and even the seasons. It is feasible to be snowbound in Amarillo one day and the next day to be sunbathing on the beaches of South Padre Island. Out west, in the mountain areas of the Big Bend and around Fort Davis, the torrid summer endured in most of the state is pleasantly tempered by altitude. It takes only a little traveling around to understand why Texans never think of their province as one place, one thing or one society.

PRECEDING PAGES: Cadillac Ranch – a pop art monument to the open road, Amarillo.
LEFT: Hispanic Texan all dressed up in San Antonio.
RIGHT: a big welcome to big Texas.

Cattle and oil

It was cattle and then oil that originally fueled the state's economy and made it what it is, and both can be found, or have thrived, in almost every part of the state. In the early days, land and cattle were pretty much the only assets of the fledgling republic, which wasted no time

in converting them into money, selling land to the Federal government and longhorn steers by the millions to buyers in the north and west.

Oil and gas, of course, are almost everywhere in the state with only 34 of Texas' 254 counties not having found oil or natural gas within their boundaries. Texas is the largest petroleum-producing state in the US, and it has been estimated by economists that, if Texas were an independent nation, it would rank as the world's fifth-largest petroleum-producing country. The diminishing oil, however, is getting more and more expensive to pump out of the ground and no major new wells have been discovered for half a century or more.

Though one's sense of the past comes from human works – the buildings, roads and other monuments resulting from centuries of creative efforts – what is under the land has often been more important in Texas than what is on top. Faults, folds, intrusions and other geological movements, beginning 250 million years ago, formed the hidden reservoirs and basins that contain the great supplies of petroleum, natural gas, coal, salt, sulfur and other minerals.

Not only has Texas increased in wealth and importance because of its subsurface minerals, but, in its most important agricultural regions, the High Plains, water pumped to the surface

farm, and their attitude toward their own and other people's customs, religions and traditions.

Boundaries

The exact boundaries of North, South, West, East and Central Texas may vary, but the inhabitants of each seem to accept the fairly general definitions. For example, when a Texan mentions "West Texas," it is not just the geographical portion of the state that is being described: it is also a collection of traditions associated with that part of Texas and attached to its residents. And each major region contains its subregions, which are also recognizable to most

from underground aquifers has transformed a "desert" into one of the world's great cotton- and food-producing areas.

Five states

When the old Republic of Texas joined the United States a century and a half ago, it retained the right to divide itself into as many as five states, should it so decide. And, although this option has so far been eschewed, it still lurks at the back of some minds. Certainly it would make this huge behemoth more manageable. The so-called "Five States of Texas" are recognizable by the manner in which the inhabitants earn their living, the crops they

Texans, such as the Gulf Coast, the Rio Grande Valley, the Panhandle and the High Plains, although these subregions have not acquired their own unique cultural patterns in the way the larger "states" have.

Plenty of time

West Texans are considered highly individualistic, quick to react but free with their purse and time. In West Texas one is seldom told, "I don't have time to see you now." Because so many of the region's leaders have associated themselves with ranching and the oil business, West Texans are seen as people willing to gamble – forced to gamble by the nature of their enterprises.

Ranching, whether cattle or sheep and goats, is a very cyclical undertaking, dependent on the fluctuations of both the weather and the market.

Oil is famous for not always being where the prospector drills, but it can also reward its finder, and the landowner, with instant wealth. Most West Texas ranches today depend on oil and gas from their vast acres for economic survival. But all over Texas, the sight of the "horsehead" pump is common, some towering as high as a three-story building, pulling oil from those ancient reefs and seabeds many meters below the surface. One is bound to see more pump jacks than cowboys even in West

"Coonier" folk

East Texas natives, especially old timers, are held by the rest of Texas to be shrewder, more Southern-rural, often gifted with a special kind of earthy humor and wisdom. Or, as one may still hear in certain parts of East Texas, they're "coonier," a tribute to the clever tactics of the raccoon, an animal quite prevalent in the region. This was the part of Texas most like the Old South, with cotton plantations and slow, unhurried ways back in the time of its agricultural dominance. Here one finds dense forests, humid swamps and wide, slow-moving rivers, while, at its western edges, some 500 miles

Texas, which was once informally known as "Big Ranch Country." The stark flatness of the area, the open spaces that seem to go on forever, and the huge sky are often startling to newcomers, who will immediately understand the meaning of the term "high lonesome." Natives insist on the distinction between West Texas, which stretches from the western edge of Hill Country to El Paso, and the northwestern Panhandle, which includes the cities of Lubbock and Amarillo.

LEFT: Jefferson is full of historic homes.
ABOVE: the 1841 cabin of John Neely, the founder of Dallas.

(800 km) away, there are arid deserts, barren mountains and streams that, although furious when full, are often dry.

Even today, East Texas is a region of mostly smaller towns and many rural communities of the crossroads variety, consisting of a general store, a service station, a couple of churches (usually Protestant) and maybe a schoolhouse, left empty when the country schools were consolidated years ago. East Texas, incidentally, has produced some of Texas' better-known writers and other artists, many of them working from the strong sense of tradition that seems to come with the land. The late William Goyen's writings were filled with East Texas imagery.

Alvin Ailey, the renowned choreographer, was born in East Texas. And sculptor James Surls is based in East Texas and uses woods found in the area as his main medium.

Down to the border

South Texas starts (in the Texas mind) at San Antonio and continues southward to the Rio Grande. Along its edges it supports two separate cultures: the long, well-populated curve of the Gulf Coast and that other world of mostly Hispanic Texans along the river border with Mexico. South Texas was the birthplace of the Texas cowboy, who began as a Mexican

vaquero (origin of the Western term "buckaroo"), and of the 19th-century trail drives made famous in story, film and song. It remains a spread out, sparse land containing several of the state's major ranches, including the famous 825,000-acre (334,000-hectare) King Ranch.

Owing to the centuries-old Hispanic influence (some land deeds in South Texas go back to the Spanish kings), South Texans have the reputation of being easy-going, and are passionate and fiercely loyal to their families and political leaders. The lower Rio Grande Valley, called simply "The Valley" by Texans, furnishes a significant percentage of the citrus fruit and vegetables for sale in the US.

Selling the goods

North Texans share fewer traditional traits, probably because of the region's long-time role as merchant to all the rest of Texas and the Southwest. Storekeepers have always had to learn to be all things to all customers, and North Texas has found customers all over the world for everything from clothing to electronics. Because Dallas and Fort Worth are its key metropolises – their combined areas go by the name "The Metroplex" – North Texas assumes more sophistication than other parts of Texas, although the statement meets fierce and determined resentment if repeated too often. Citizens of Austin and Houston are not known for their high opinion of Dallas, though almost everyone praises Fort Worth for its old-fashioned charm.

An atmosphere of promotion and display has influenced an unusual number of film and theatrical figures to come out of North Texas, including two Dallas playwrights: the late Preston Jones, with his *Texas Trilogy*, and Don Coburn, whose *Gin Game* won a Pulitzer Prize in 1978. Larry L. King's musical *Best Little Whorehouse in Texas* was one of the most durable theatrical productions of the 1970s and 1980s. Not to be overlooked are the screenwriter Robert Benton from Waxahachie, and the Oscar-winning film actress Sissy Spacek from Quitman.

In the middle

Central Texas is not as well-defined geographically as the other sections, often overlapping them. But the folklore of its people is strong. Perhaps from the fact that it contains Austin, the state capital and hotbed of liberalism, or because it has had to learn political compromise with its bordering regions, Central Texas has contributed a large proportion of political figures to the lore of the Lone Star State.

The foremost example, of course, is Lyndon Johnson, US president from 1963 to 1969. He was born in the Hill Country, to the north and west of the capital, yet he never attempted to pull up those roots during his rumbustious journey to the White House.

Central Texas is also home to large German and Czech populations, which moved into the state during the 19th century. ❑

LEFT: Cowboy of the West.
RIGHT: Texas' highest point, Guadalupe Peak.

Decisive Dates

1519 Spain lays claim to the region comprising the present state of Texas.

1685 La Salle lands in Matagorda Bay and sets up a short-lived French colony.

1718 The *presidio* (president) San Antonio de Bexar and the mission San Antonio de Valero (the Alamo) are established on the San Antonio river.

1754 Construction is started on the present Alamo chapel.

1793 San Antonio de Valero mission is closed and its lands are divided up among Indian families.

GEN. ANTONIO LOPEZ DE SANTA ANNA.

1801 A Spanish cavalry unit from San Carlos del Alamo de Parras occupies the mission as a garrison.

1822 Stephen F. Austin brings the first 300 families to help Mexico settle Texas.

1824 Mexican constitution promises Texas statehood.

1830 Law of April 6 toughens restrictions on immigration from the US into Texas, heightening tensions between Anglo settlers and Mexico.

1834 Santa Anna is elected president after the Mexican Revolution and starts to centralize the Mexican government.

REVOLUTION

1835 Texas revolt begins; San Antonio is occupied. The Texas Rangers are officially instituted.

1836 Santa Anna invades. Texas declares independence. Siege and battle of the Alamo. All defenders of the mission are killed. Santa Anna is later defeated at San Jacinto. Texas becomes an independent republic.

1839 Austin, formerly the village of Waterloo, is established as the new nation's capital.

1841 Republic of Texas' President Mirabeau Lamar sends a small armed force to New Mexico in a vain attempt to seize territory from Mexico.

1842 Santa Anna retaliates by twice seizing San Antonio, leading to an expedition by mutinous Texas volunteers which ends in disaster at Mier.

1844 US Senate rejects annexation treaty with the Republic of Texas, dashing hopes until the election of US President James K. Polk, who revives the annexation effort.

1846 Ending almost a decade of independence, Texas joins the US. War breaks out between Mexico and the US.

1848 War ends. The Rio Grande becomes a permanent international boundary in the Treaty of Guadalupe Hidalgo.

1850 US Army repairs the Alamo.

1853 The Buffalo Bayou Brazos and Colorado – the first railway chartered by Texas – begins operating.

1854 The state establishes two Indian reservations.

1858 The army imports camels for use in the arid western part of the state.

1861 Texas secedes from the Union in favor of the Confederacy. The Alamo is used by the Confederate Army during the war between the states.

1865 Final battle of the Civil War. Announcement at Galveston that slavery has been abolished.

1866 Large-scale cattle drives to the north begin.

1870 Texas is readmitted to the Union.

1873 Record rainfall (109 ins/279 cm) at Clarksville.

1875 Comanche Chief Quanah Parker loses his last fight and is forced onto a reservation, effectively ending Indian wars in Texas.

1876 Charles Goodnight founds the J.A. Ranch at Palo Duro Canyon, the first cattle ranch in northwest Texas.

1884 Fence cutting wars; new laws ban the practice.

1888 The Alamo chapel, having been used as a warehouse, is sold by the Catholic church to the state.

1894 Oil is discovered at Corsicana.

EARLY 20TH CENTURY

1900 Hurricane destroys half of Galveston and kills 6,000 people.

1901 Mining engineer Captain A.F. Lucas discovers the Spindletop gusher near Beaumont.

1905 State of Texas grants custodianship of the Alamo to the Daughters of the Republic of Texas.

1907 Neiman-Marcus department store opens in downtown Dallas.

1910 First military airflight in a Wright Brothers plane at Fort Sam Houston.

1916 Pancho Villa and his men cross the border to raid Texas communities.

1917 Race riots occur in Houston. Texas legislature votes to impeach Governor Jim Ferguson for mismanagement of state funds.

1920 Border skirmishes between Mexico and Texas come to an end.

1925 Miriam "Ma" Ferguson, wife of impeached Governor Jim Ferguson, becomes the first female Governor of Texas. She is re-elected for a second term in 1933.

1930 Oil strike by C.M. 'Dad' Joiner 100 miles (160 km) east of Dallas becomes the East Texas Oil Field, the largest petroleum deposit on earth at that time.

1932 Texas Babe Didrikson Zaharias wins three Olympic gold medals.

1933 Texan Wiley Post makes first solo flight around the world.

1934 Career of Depression-era bank robbers Bonnie Parker and Clyde Barrow ends in a hail of bullets, after a 102-day manhunt led by Texas Ranger Frank Hamer.

POST-DEPRESSION TEXAS

1947 Fiery chain explosions demolish much of the coastal refinery town of Texas City, killing 408 and injuring almost 2,000.

1953 Dwight D. Eisenhower becomes the first Texas-born President of the US.

1956 George Stevens' movie of Edna Ferber's novel *Giant* is released to wide popularity, forever fixing the myth of tough Texas oilmen in American folklore.

1958 Texas Instruments' Jack Kilby ushers in the electronics age with his revolutionary development of the silicon chip.

1959 Lubbock-born rock 'n' roll singer Buddy Holly dies in an airplane crash.

1962 NASA opens Manned Spacecraft Center at Houston.

1963 President John F. Kennedy is assassinated while touring Dallas in a motorcade with Texas Governor John Connally. Kennedy's Texan-born Vice-President, Lyndon B. Johnson, is elevated to presidency.

1964 Lyndon B. Johnson wins election for the presidency in the largest landslide in US history.

1969 Apollo 11 commander Neil Armstrong calls Houston from the moon.

PRECEDING PAGES: the storming of the Alamo.
LEFT: Antonio Lopez De Santa Anna.
RIGHT: Republican Governor of Texas, George W. Bush, Jr is elected President of the US.

1976 Houston Democrat Barbara Jordan becomes the first African-American woman to deliver a keynote address at a party conference.

1978 *Dallas* TV drama series begins and is soon screened all over the world.

1985 Larry McMurtry's novel *Lonesome Dove*, about a Texas cattle drive, is published to immense popular and critical acclaim; TV adaptation follows.

1988 Sometime Houstonian George Bush is elected President of the US.

1992 Texas billionaire Ross Perot makes an unsuccessful bid for the presidency.

1993 Federal agents storm the compound of the Branch Davidians near Waco, resulting in more than

80 deaths. El Paso author Cormac McCarthy wins the National Book Award for *All the Pretty Horses*, a novel set in West Texas during the 1940s.

1998 Governor George W. Bush, Jr refuses to grant reprieve for convicted murderess Karla Faye Tucker, who becomes the first woman to be executed in Texas since 1863.

2001 Texas Governor George W. Bush, Jr is sworn in as the 43rd President of the US. Tropical Storm Allison claims 23 lives. Thousands lose their jobs as Houston-based energy company, Enron, collapses.

2003 Fifty House Democrats and 11 Senate Democrats attempt to thwart electoral redistricting bills by fleeing to Oklahoma and New Mexico. Hurricane Claudette triggers heavy flooding in central and south Texas. ❑

SIX FLAGS OVER TEXAS

Control of Texas has been handed from one external power to another,

but independence and self-determination remain the watchwords of its people

A Texan's love of, and zeal for, Texas is stronger and more important than any regional affiliation. And the thing that binds Texans tightest is history.

Pass through a few Texas towns large enough to have an independent school system, and the names on the schools will begin to take on a familiar sound: Austin, Crockett, Fannin, Bonham, Lamar, Travis, Houston. Every town will have buildings or streets carrying one or more of those names, too.

Schoolchildren, taught Texas history by legislative decree, grow up on stories about its legendary heroes. Today, with thousands of Hispanic and black students, schools are beginning to be called by the names of ethnic heroes such as Benito Juárez, Emiliano Zapáta or Martin Luther King. Historical mythology is strong in all ethnic groups.

Unlike New England or the Atlantic seaboard states, Texas had no single source of settlement. White men came quite early to some parts of the state and arrived 350 years later to the others. The famous "Six Flags Over Texas" theme is rooted in historical fact. Each flag – those of Spain, Mexico, France, the Republic of Texas, the Confederacy, and the United States – represented a separate, if brief, period of the state's history.

The Texan coast may have been sighted by Amerigo Vespucci as early as 1497, but there is evidence of much earlier inhabitants – some possibly as far back as 37,000 years. Archeological studies have revealed no grand past civilizations in Texas such as were found in Mexico and Central and South America, but there were interesting cliff dwellers in the Texas Panhandle, and cave dwellers left traces of their fascinating paintings for us to ponder throughout western Texas. The Caddo confederations encountered in eastern Texas by the first Europeans were an agricultural people.

LEFT: three of the flags to have flown over Texas – the Mexican, the Spanish and the French.
RIGHT: trading with the natives.

The natives

Along the Gulf Coast lived the nomadic Karankawas, who used simple farming methods and were not given to nomadic movement. Practitioners of ceremonial cannibalism, and always incredibly fierce, they had been wiped out by the white man's diseases and bullets by

the 1850s. The Native Americans that the Texas settlers battled against were Plains tribes who rode in from the north on horses descended from those brought to the New World by early Spanish explorers.

One of these, Alvar Núñez Cabeza de Vaca, was cast ashore on what is believed to have been Galveston Island, working his way across Texas for eight years before finally reaching Spanish Mexico in 1536. He and three other shipwrecked survivors of the Narvaez expedition were enslaved by the Karankawas, but, after escaping, gained such reputations as medicine men that, when they approached a strange tribe, everyone turned out to welcome them.

When Cabeza de Vaca returned to civilization with tales of cities of gold and pearl "to the north," the myth of the Seven Cities of Cibola became the motive for several Spanish expeditions to Arizona, New Mexico and Texas. These golden cities and the equally mythical Gran Quivira were never found, of course, but the search for them led to Spanish colonization of the Southwest.

It was France laying claim to the area around Matagorda Bay that caused the Spanish to

---

FRIENDS

The Native American cry "*tejas*" ("friend"), from which the state derived its name, has been translated over the years into the Texas state motto: "friendship."

Spanish heritage

Despite owning Texas for nearly three centuries, the Spanish settled it only for protection, in narrow strips along the coast and the rivers. Even San Antonio, the major Spanish settlement, was more important militarily and as a mission than as a commercial center.

Spain's mark, however, is still strong in Texas, with many of the outstanding geographical features and major rivers bearing Spanish names. Numerous Spanish missions still stand, at least partly

begin settling Texas. In 1685, French explorer René Robert Cavelier, Sieur de La Salle, had landed on the Texas coast and built a fort. By the time Spanish authorities in Mexico heard of the French intrusion, La Salle had been killed by his own men and the colony wiped out by Native Americans. Nevertheless, the nervous Spanish began to build missions on the border between French Louisiana and Spanish Texas.

In East Texas, they met Native Americans who greeted them with the cry "Tejas!." Thinking this was the name of a large tribe, the Spanish explorers called the area Tejas, or Texas. Later, settlers realized the word was a widely used greeting meaning "friend."

restored, and various Spanish legal terms and property laws survive as Texas statutes.

Perhaps the most important Spanish inheritance was passed to cattle ranching. Almost every practice and piece of equipment used by ranchers has a Spanish name and origin. These range from *chicote*, a rawhide whip, to *tumbador*, someone who throws calves ready for branding.

The older regions of greatest Spanish colonization, from San Antonio and Laredo south, especially those along the Rio Grande river, still show evidence of this influence in their architecture, language, religion and everyday customs.

Between 1811 and 1821, Spain found itself continually putting down rebellions in Texas. In 1811, the young Santa Anna, later to be the scourge of the Alamo but then still a junior officer, was in one of these disciplinary forces. At the same time, the Spanish authorities recognized that the sparsely occupied parts of Texas were always under threat unless developed, so they encouraged immigration. Moses Austin was among the men who applied for an *empresario* grant but, when he died just after receiving it, his son, Stephen Fuller Austin (today known as the "Father of Texas"), renegotiated it in his own name and brought in 300 settlers.

The Texas nation

"Texians" (as they were then called) never learned to get along well with the Latin laws, religion and political practices of Mexico. Aggravated by the unpopular Law of April 6 1830, which aimed to restrict Anglo immigration, the inevitable break came in 1835 when the Anglo-American majority in Texas led a rebellion against what were considered despotic governmental practices. In reality, the despotism was mainly created by Mexican dictator Santa Anna.

The Texas Revolution lasted only eight months, but it gave Texas the myth and image

Those first colonists are to Anglo-Texas what the passengers of the *Mayflower* are to Massachusetts: the proudest blood lines go back to "The Old 300." In 1821, Mexico gained its independence from Spain and, within the next decade, 41 *empresario* contracts were signed, permitting the arrival of nearly 14,000 Anglo-Americans to supplement the original Spanish population. Eventually hundreds more settlers joined the Austin colonists.

FAR LEFT: Sam Houston, Governor and Senator of Tennessee, involved in the Texas Revolution.
LEFT: Congressman Davy Crockett.
ABOVE: Texas battle flag in Austin's State Capitol.

which Texans are exhorted to live up to. It was this short but successful period of rebellion that created the Texas Valhalla, with such heroes as Ben Milam, James Fannin, Jim Bowie, William B. Travis, James Bonham, Davy Crockett with his fellow Tennesseans, and General Sam Houston.

From the Texas Revolution came the stories of the Alamo, those 13 fateful days in 1836 when 189 patriots held out against the fierce onslaught of 4,000 Mexicans, who eventually overran the fort, killing all its defenders, save a few women, children and slaves.

Minimizing his losses, Santa Anna said: "It was but a small affair," and ordered the bodies of the heroes to be burned. His aide, noting that he took many casualties, losing many of his best men, muttered: "Another such victory and we are ruined."

Forty-six days later, the Texans got their revenge. Along with a group of American volunteers, and led by General Sam Houston, they gained vengeance at San Jacinto.

Taking Santa Anna and his 1,500 men by surprise, Houston's force, though greatly outnumbered, routed the Mexicans within minutes. "Remember the Alamo," they shouted to each other as they charged, and it has never been forgotten. Santa Anna was captured, 600 of his

troops were killed, and Texas was free. A new republic was born.

The period that followed was the seedbed for the feelings of loyalty for which Texans are so famous. And no matter how diverse their lives, or how far from Texas they may wander, all Texans hold the Alamo in common ownership.

From 1836 to 1845, the Republic of Texas was an independent nation with its own flag, its own ambassadors, its own President and Congress, and, after some moving around, its own specifically designed national capital at Austin. It is true that millions of Texans today may recall the Republic only occasionally, but they have never entirely forgotten it.

Their self-reliance and fierce loyalty (which has not always endeared Texans to their fellow American citizens) comes from that decade of independence. The state seal and the Lone Star flag, which is still displayed as frequently as the national banner, remain from that independent government.

First president

Commander of the army Sam Houston was elected as first President of the new Republic of Texas, his 5,199 votes far outnumbering the total votes of his rivals (Henry Smith, 743; Stephen F. Austin, 587).

The Mexicans were still to cause major trouble in the next decade, when, in 1842, they invaded Texas and briefly captured San Antonio before withdrawing. And there was also the Indian problem.

Houston had lived among the Cherokees, and understood the Indian mentality more than most. He wanted to stabilize the situation, and proposed a guarantee of Indian rights through legal title to Indian lands. But he found that he was unable to keep the promises he made to the Cherokees. When Houston's term expired, the new president, Mirabeau Lamar, proposed that all Indians be expelled from Eastern Texas: "Nothing short of this will bring us peace and safety," Lamar thundered, "the white man and the red man cannot live in harmony together… Nature forbids it…"

The republic expanded rapidly, tripling its population, but the influx of slaves – brought by southerners settling on the Gulf Coast to develop the cotton crop – was to prove disputacious when Texans voted to join the Union in 1845.

As part of the annexation arrangement, the Federal Congress assumed the Texas Republic's $5 million in debts and allowed Texas to retain possession of all undistributed land (although, in the 1840s and 1850s, much of it was still in the possession of the Comanches). There were no federal taxes in effect but Texas had no wealth, only land. It sold to the US its rights to New Mexico and Colorado, and Sam Houston and other conservatives supported the Boundary Act on the grounds that the state had more desert land than it could use.

Pressing for funds for frontier defense, Texas persuaded Congress to give it an extra $7.75 million in 1855. With the money, the state launched a major building program of state structures, courthouses, schools, transportation systems – all of which was achieved without imposing taxes. This then conditioned Texas to look for sources other than taxes to finance its activities.

By 1860, when Sam Houston was elected Governor for a second term, Texas was again in debt. The following year, when the Civil War broke out, Houston was forced to resign after he refused to swear allegiance to the Confederacy.

THE LAND IS OURS

Unusually, Texas still owns all its public lands. If the Federal government wishes to create a park, or cut a stand of timber, it has to ask the state's permission.

so little ideology other than a profound belief in the American nation and its destiny…"

Three months after Houston's burial, in 1863, the Confederate legislature of Texas passed a resolution: "His public services through a long and eventful life, his unblemished patriotism, his great private and moral worth, and his untiring, devoted and zealous regard for the interests of the state of Texas command our highest admiration, and should be held in perpetual remembrance by the people of this state."

American giant

"In retirement and isolation at Huntsville, Houston was a tragic figure. He did not live out the war," wrote historian T.R. Fehrenbach. "He was a giant of the American 19th century who had outlived his time and the full understanding of his countrymen. Houston confused men; he had the politician's knack of listening attentively to everything brought before him, saying little and always giving the impression he might go along with every argument. He had

LEFT: the capital of Texas in Austin.
ABOVE: a cowboy at an annual western festival at Fort Worth Stockyards.

Newcomers

During the period of revolution, resettlement and republic, thousands of people came to Texas to get away from whatever their life had been "back home." They weren't always fleeing from the law. More often, the new Texans came west to escape failure or some sort of unhappiness that could be left behind. This is very much a continuing tradition as, even today, Texas becomes home for thousands who leave other parts of the nation every month to seek new opportunities in the Lone Star State. When one recalls that a high percentage of the dead at the Alamo, and a majority of the unfortunates who were slaughtered earlier at Goliad, were recent arrivals in Texas, and that even Davy Crockett, the superhero of the Alamo, had only been in Texas for a few weeks, the tradition of the newcomer hero becomes understandable.

At the time of the Civil War, most Texas settlers were from the agricultural South. A plantation economy, with its accompanying slavery, controlled East Texas and the Coastal Plains, where cotton was a profitable crop. Thus, Texas was overwhelmingly drawn into the Civil War on the side of the Confederacy. It was never torn by any major battles, and, after the war, sectional wounds healed quicker in Texas than in any other southern state. Within a decade,

newcomers from northern states were not only arriving in great numbers but were assuming positions of business and economic leadership.

Opportunity frontier

When the Union blockaded the Gulf Coast during the Civil War, Texas managed to smuggle some cotton across the Rio Grande for shipment to world markets, but the blockade was serving another purpose, then unknown. Unable to export its cattle even to the Confederate Army, Texas' herds built up during the Civil War to more than 3 million. Once the war was over, there was tremendous demand for this beef in northern and western states.

Texas went through relatively little of the sorrow and desperation of the Reconstruction period. And because it was the only ex-Confederate state that offered its southern sister states hope of a new beginning, southerners flocked there. The 15 years that followed Appomattox saw Texas emerge as the opportunity frontier of the whole nation, north and south alike. It has retained that position, and has continued to uphold that reputation.

Families from every social level picked up and moved to Texas, bursting the old frontier boundaries until, like a flooding river, they swept out onto the prairies and battled with Native Americans for the wealth of grass and soil which was once thought to be the "Great American Desert." This movement to the frontier created two new Texas myths: one was the frontiersman and his sturdy pioneer wife, and the other was the cowboy.

Texas was readmitted to the Union in 1870 and, with the 1875 surrender of Comanche Chief Quanah Parker at Fort Sill, Oklahoma, the far western portion of the state was finally ready for ranching on a large scale. Barely a decade later, though, the wide open spaces were being fenced and confined as settlers and sheep farmers fought to contain the open range.

Oil was discovered at Corsicana in 1894 by workers drilling for water. With the discovery of the major gusher at Spindletop in 1901, Texas entered the new century with an economic boom.

The Texas style

The state's tradition of independence has had a direct influence on both the business climate and the political philosophy of modern Texas, creating a sense of self-sufficiency which, critics say, amounts at times to the conviction of Divine Destiny in the minds of some residents.

Whether embodied in the bygone wildcatter oilmen or contemporary computer magnates who amass fortunes at breakneck speed, the old ethos of resourcefulness and individual initiative still holds sway in Texas. Everyday life is infused with a dramatic tension between the legacy of the frontier past and the imperatives of the urban present. ❏

LEFT: Houston's Ship Canal, vital access to the sea.
RIGHT: the historic Strand district, Galveston, survivor of the mighty 1900 hurricane.

Jared L. Brush.

Charles Lux.

R. G. Head.

John H. Iliff.

Thos. H. Lawrence.

John W. Snyder.

John T. Lytle.

THE TALE OF THE LONGHORN

With hardy livestock and even hardier cowboys, life

on the great cattle trails was no picnic

The first cattle known to have entered Texas were 500 cows brought in by Coronado in 1541. Subsequent explorers also brought cattle, which gradually wandered into the wilderness. By 1757, Reynosa (pop. 269) had 18,000 head of cattle.

A fat cow was worth four pesos in 1779, with hides and tallow more valuable than beef. Mission Espiritu Santo, on the banks of the winding Guadalupe river, between present-day Victoria and Mission Valley, was the first great cattle ranch in Texas. Around 1770, it claimed 40,000 head of cattle.

Ideal trail cattle

The definitive Texas cow was the longhorn – a hybrid breed from Spanish *retinto* (criollo) stock and English Hereford and Bakewell cattle that were brought in from Ohio, Kentucky and other southern and midwestern states in the 1820s and '30s. These longhorns had a spread of 5 or 6 ft (1.5 or 2 meters), with some spanning a full 8 ft (2.5 meters) from tip to tip. They were apparently "tough to eat and tougher to handle" but, with their long legs and hard hooves, were ideal trail cattle which gained weight even on the way to market.

"No animal of the cow kind will shift and take care of itself under all conditions as will the longhorns," declared a veteran rancher, Charles Goodnight. "As trail cattle, their equal has never been known. They can go further without water and endure more suffering than others."

By the mid-19th century, great hordes of Texas longhorns that had been roaming freely, and shaped by nature and environmental conditions, were being gathered into herds for the trail drive north. "No other industry in the Southwest had such an economic significance or such picturesque aspects. The driving of

herds caused towns, customs and a distinctive type of people to grow up beside the trails," was the assessment of a 1930s writer for the *WPA Guide*.

Cattleman Edward Piper made what may have been the first northern drive in 1846, moving a herd from Texas to Ohio. He was fol-

lowed almost immediately by many other contractors, especially after the end of the Civil War. Eight to 20 hands were needed to trail a herd of 2,000–3,000 cattle, about one man per 250–350 animals, with crews including a trail boss and cook plus a horse wrangler (usually a young boy), to handle the six or eight mounts needed for each man.

The boss

The all-important trail boss had "as many duties as the captain of a steamboat." He arose early to wake and assign the men, ensured there were always enough provisions, settled all disputes, kept counting the cattle to see none had been

PRECEDING PAGES: cattle and cowboy nostalgia for Fort Worth's Stock Yards.
LEFT: a gallery of Texas cattlemen.
RIGHT: Chisholm Trail round-up, Fort Worth.

lost and rode ahead to check on water supplies. "A boss," explained one, "rides about three or four times as far as the herd goes." Exploring ahead, the boss would ride part way back and, from some hilltop, wave his hat to indicate which direction the herd should take.

Points and drags

The herd itself was usually a mix of beeves – mature steers – and cows (who walked with a less steady stride). It had a head (point) and feet (drag), with swing men watching the "shoulders" and flank men watching the "hips." Riders bringing up the drag, sometimes physically pushing the laggards ahead, were enveloped in dust, especially on the alkali flats, and kept a "wipe" across their faces. The best place to learn cuss words, recalled one veteran, was always on the drag. "There is a Homeric quality about the cowboys' profanity and vulgarity that pleases rather than repulses," concluded John A. Lomax, the music historian: "He spoke out plainly the impulses of his heart."

It was crucial to keep the herd moving, although the trick to successful trail herding was to keep the cattle from knowing they were under restraint. One drawback to mixed herds was the almost daily arrival of new calves,

which usually had to be shot or abandoned, as they could rarely keep up with the demanding pace of their elders.

Branding

Cattle drives began in early spring when new grass was emerging but before the rivers were swollen with heavy run-offs. In the north, drives had to be completed before the autumn snowfalls.

As the hundreds of cattle bore the brands of many different owners, they would be fed through a chute where each beast would be lightly slashed with a road brand, on the left side behind the shoulder. The owner's brand

NEVER CROSS A COOK

After the trail boss, the cook held the most authority and, for obvious reasons, it paid to stay on his good side. In addition to driving the chuck wagon, serving up grub and acting as doctor to both men and animals, a cook might also serve as a custodian for personal belongings, a stakeholder for bets and even be ready to pull a tooth. As for what he cooked, the mainstays were fluffy sourdough biscuits, accompanying pork and beans or the inevitable steak, with occasionally son-of-a-gun stew, which appeared to contain everything except horns, hide and hooves. Accompanying this came six-shooter coffee, strong enough to float a pistol.

would have been applied by the *marcador* when, as a calf, it was flanked, mugged or bull-dogged, each of which methods "throws" the animal on its right side, leaving its left side upwards for branding. Branding required skill and experience because, if the irons were pressed too hard, the mark would go too deep and leave sores. There were other preliminaries too: the male calves had to be castrated (the roasted testicles were a much-prized snack), and horns had to be trimmed to prevent the animals injuring each other.

Brands were not widely used by Spanish and Mexican ranchers because their *ranchos* oper-ated on the *patrón* system. The *patrón*, in the manner of a feudal lord, owned all the cattle and land within the "fiefdom" of his *rancho*, so there was very little need to establish his ownership by branding. If the cattle were on his land, they were his.

Each Texas ranch had its own distinctive brand, which was registered with the Cattle-man's Association, and established brands were recognized by their distinctive pattern every-where on the range. Before the Civil War, it was not uncommon for a South Texas rancher to start a herd by rounding up unbranded cattle and giving them his brand. "Mavericks," or unbranded cattle, are said to have gotten their name from Samuel Maverick, the Matagorda County entrepreneur of the 1840s.

On the move

Once underway, the trail drive would cover up to 16 miles (26 km) per day, although a herd making only 10 or 12 miles (16 or 19 km) could take a leisurely lunch by grazing and thus put on some weight en route. The easiest part of each day was the afternoon, when the thirsty cattle were eager to reach water – the basic secret of successful trailing being the grazing and watering: well-fed cattle were less likely to stampede.

At night, the foreman would bed down the animals in some cool, dry spot well away from woodland (that might hide Indians) or ravines (into which they might stampede) and the two men on watch would ride slowly around the herd, usually humming or crooning softly, which the cattle appeared to find soothing.

The watchmen, judging time by the stars, changed every two hours – a pot of coffee was kept hot on the coals all night – and the guard waking his successor always made sure

LEFT: branding a cow.
ABOVE: contemporary engraving of a longhorn cattle drive to Abilene, Kansas, in the 1870s.

Samuel Maverick

S amuel Maverick, born in South Carolina in 1803 to a prosperous family, arrived in South Texas at Matagorda Bay in 1835. He had been a lawyer back home and planned to start a new career as a land speculator in this promising new territory, but almost immediately he found himself caught up in frontier politics and the Mexican War. At one point he was almost executed by the Mexicans as a spy, but, after an appeal by the wife of a fellow prisoner, all were reprieved.

Before long, Maverick was busy selling his prop-

erties back East and buying land at 15¢ per acre. By 1842, he was said to have become the biggest landholder in the state and his stated ambition was to travel on his own land all the 600 miles (960 km) from San Antonio to El Paso. Later that year, Maverick was caught during the invasion of San Antonio and imprisoned in Mexico for seven months. On his return, he reluctantly accepted 400 cattle from a neighbor in lieu of a debt, thus becoming a rancher.

His spread was amidst the tall grass and wild clover of the Matagorda Peninsula, a 70-mile (112-km) long sandbar off the Gulf Coast as much as 5 miles (8 km) wide, with an irregular grass-covered prairie running down the center. Without much inter-

est, he placed the cattle under the indifferent care of his black slaves, who are said to have reported that their boss was not enthusiastic about applying a burning iron to flesh. The slaves branded about one-third of the growing herd, many of which eventually strayed to the mainland.

Charlie Siringo, who in 1885 published the first cowboy biography, referred to Maverick as "being a chickenhearted old rooster," who "wouldn't brand or earmark any of his cattle." Another story, however, says that he had just too many cattle to brand. There did exist an "MK" brand but it was never extensively used.

At one meeting of neighboring cattlemen, Maverick supposedly told them that if they all made sure their own cattle were branded then the ones left over would clearly be his, a naive attitude one might think, except that naive might not be the precise word to describe the largest landowner in the entire state.

Stray cattle were hardly a rarity but, in those parts, when cowmen came across unbranded ones, it was usually assumed they were Samuel Maverick's. Naturally, many of Maverick's unmarked herd were seized by other, less scrupulous ranchers, who stamped them with their own brand. It being the custom of the times, nobody regarded it as stealing: if cattle were unbranded or the brand was unregistered, there was simply no recourse in law, although it was widely accepted that suckling cows belonged to their mothers and shared the same brand. Some heartless but enterprising "maverickers" were not averse to slitting a calf's tongue so that it could not suckle nor cry for its mother. According to an old saying all it took to make a cowman was "a rope, nerve to use it and a branding iron."

Some ranchers hired "maverickers" to brand as many as 18 "mavericks" per day, at 50 cents to a dollar apiece. Eventually, in 1854, Samuel Maverick sent a party of *vaqueros* to round up his herd, which numbered several hundred, and move it to Rancho Conquista, a spread he'd acquired on the San Antonio river, 50 miles (80 km) from the city.

More than ever disenchanted with the cattle business, Maverick later sold his herd, but the use of his name to describe stray cattle spread beyond the state of Texas and lives on today to signify people who make their own way in life, independent of the crowd. ❑

LEFT: Samuel Maverick, the unconventional rancher and one-time biggest landowner in Texas.

to call him by his name. "No one liked to touch a sleeping man," wrote historian Wayne Gard, "lest he become so startled that involuntarily he would reach for his six-shooter."

The drive cost the herd's owner about $500 per month, worked out on the basis of about 75¢ per head of cattle for three months.

Breaking the ban

When shipping began to California and New Orleans (after the cattle had been driven to the

MAKING BIG MONEY

In 1884, the cattle-driving Pryor brothers were contracted to deliver 45,000 head in 15 separate lots, earning themselves a handy net profit of around $20,000.

in Chicago. He sent 35,000 head the first year and kept doubling the figure until 1871, in which year cowboys pushed about 600,000 animals north from Texas. Over the next 20 years contractors drove 5–10 million cattle out of Texas, becoming the state's first big income producer. Longhorns with their stamina and endurance became a symbol of the state.

After the slaughter of the buffalo herds, and after the Indians (who, anyway, usually preferred to eat buffalo rather than beef) had been

nearest railheads in Kansas and Missouri – some 1,000 miles/1,600 km away), cows were fetching only three or four dollars a head in Texas, while they were worth upward of $30 apiece in the North. In 1867, defying a ban by several neighboring states (imposed because local ranchers feared the spread of the deadly Texas tick fever), Illinois cattle dealer Joseph G. McCoy managed to persuade Kansas Pacific officials to lay a siding to Abilene in Kansas, at the edge of the quarantine area. From there, he began shipping cattle to the Union Stockyards

confined, the ranches spread north onto the Great Plains, where windmills and wells solved the problem of water supplies.

Ranchers claimed as much land as they needed and enforced their "property rights" with six-shooters.

Barbed reply

By the 1880s, with the state trying unsuccessfully to ban foreign ownership, would-be ranchers from all over the world were flocking to Texas, but overstocking, followed by a severe drought, led to the inevitable bust.

New procedures were desperately needed; people believed that stock had to be both con-

ABOVE: re-creating a trail ride at Gainesville, near the Texas-Oklahoma border.

served and contained. Such fencing as there had been in the past in Texas had been constructed primarily from the osage tree, but this changed in 1874, when an Illinois man, Joseph F. Glidden, was granted a patent for new fencing material which consisted of barbs wrapped around a single strand of wire. There were hundreds of competing designs but Joseph Glidden's was the one which eventually predominated. It was praised as being "light as air, stronger than whisky and cheap as dirt."

> **ART ON THE TRAIL**
>
> Charles M. Russell was the major painter of the longhorn's "fire, muscle and movement," while Frederick Remington specialized in depicting trails and stampedes.

Fence cutting

Battles between cattlemen and the "nesters" (small farmers, sheep ranchers, etc.) broke out, with thousands of incidents of wire cutting – a Fence Cutting War that soon embroiled the Texas Rangers. Nevertheless, sheep ranching persevered and, by early in the 20th century, Texas had become the major state for wool production, a $23 million crop from several million sheep.

When fencing began there were other problems. For instance, those with legal title to land were prone to fencing it off and thus barring others' cattle from grass and water. Compromises eventually had to be made, such as openings for public roads every 3 miles (5 km) and amending English common law to recognize that, in arid country, all people living in a watershed had rights to flowing water. Similarly, individual preferences had to be taken into account in a state so large, where different counties held different views of segregation, alcohol and carrying arms. "It was firmly established in the Texan mind that men make laws to their need and satisfaction and for no other reason," wrote the historian T.R. Fehrenbach, explaining that trying to impress a Texan with a notion of a higher law was like impressing a Comanche with the wisdom of the Great White Father in Washington.

Last of the longhorns

With the end of unlimited free range grass, it became more economical to raise cattle that developed faster than longhorns, which, by the 1920s, had been almost bred out of existence. Shorthorns and Herefords predominated.

Longhorns were saved from probable extinction by Will C. Barnes and other Forest Service men, who collected a small herd of breeding stock for Oklahoma's Wichita Mountains Wildlife Refuge. A few years later, oilman Sid W. Richardson financed the acquisition of small herds for Texas state parks. Eventually, cattlemen rediscovered the longhorn's longevity, its resistance to disease, fertility, ease of calving, ability to thrive on marginal pastures, and also the fact that its leaner beef was in tune with the times.

One result of the cattle drives was that ranches were established not only in the uninhabited parts of Texas but also on the hitherto remote plains of the Middle West and in the Indian Territory that is now the state of Oklahoma. As the Indians were pushed further and further back, even the mountains and desert plains in the far-Western parts of the state, beyond the Pecos river, became valuable property. Indeed, these are the major cowman's strongholds today, and they contain some of the largest ranches in the state. ❏

LEFT: pioneering rancher Charles Goodnight.
RIGHT: longhorn at the enormous King Ranch in southern Texas.

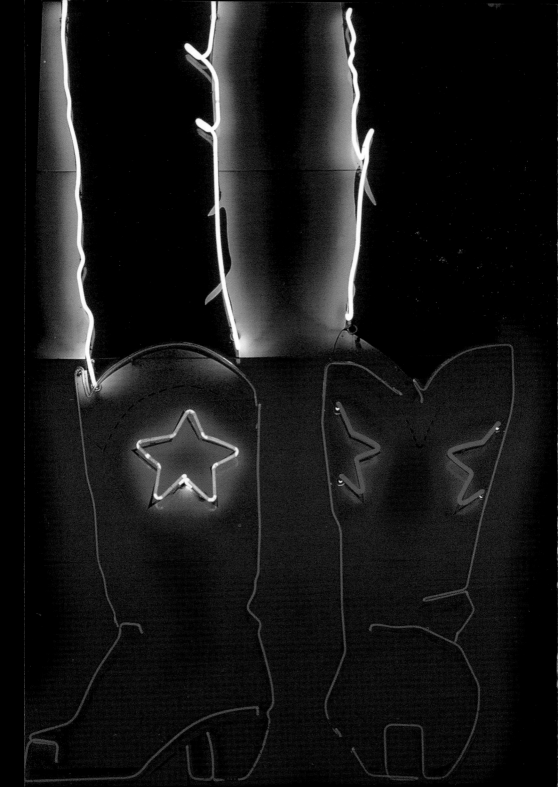

MODERN TIMES

After the legacy of the longhorn came the bounty of black gold,
and with it an increasingly urban sophistication for the rural state of Texas

Although at least a dozen western states contributed to the cowboy legend, Texas has done more than its share to make the cowboy an American icon. Several thousand cowboys can still be found doing all the traditional cowboy chores, except fighting Native Americans – which was never a cowboy chore in the first place. The traditional garb of the cowboy is also seen today in hundreds of Texas cities, towns and villages, although not every pretender wearing high-heeled boots and a cowboy hat will be a cowboy.

"The first sign that someone is becoming a real Texan," said the author James Michener, appears to be "that first big purchase of cowboy hat and boots… then you're on your way."

Boots, oversized buckle belts, denims and rodeo shirts are everyday wear for millions of Texans – not a costume – and a visitor who wishes to dress in the same manner should feel perfectly free to do so. Unlike some areas of the world where the traditional national dress is held sacred, Texans not only accept but encourage visitors to wear traditional clothes.

Frontier heritage

In a sense, the frontiersman and his mate survive, although the conditions and the times that made them have long since passed. It is the frontier that still provides so much of the motivation for today's Texas: self-sufficiency, a sense of obligation to one's fellow citizen, openness, mutual trust and a sense of sharing by people living under the same pressures. A lot of Texas business, including big business deals, is conducted on the basis of a handshake or a telephone conversation; that is rare in any part of the globe and, sadly, is rapidly becoming rarer even in Texas.

The frontier was a mutually dependent society: if someone was lazy, weak or careless, everyone might be hurt and thus all were

PRECEDING PAGES: bait shop on the Bolivar peninsula.
LEFT: cowboy boots come in all guises in Texas.
RIGHT: not-so-lonesome cowboy.

expected to shoulder their share of community work and duty. Hard work and shrewdness were valued over the creative arts and purely intellectual pursuits. Today, most Texans are still deeply influenced by these values, although by now they are far more receptive to intellectual and artistic accomplishment.

The great oil rush

The greatest change in the way Texas lived and viewed itself began in 1901, when the Spindletop oil field near Beaumont, in the southeastern corner of the state, blew in with billions of barrels of oil each year. Spindletop was where the world's modern petroleum industry was born. No field like it had been dreamed of before and, with the later development of the East Texas oilfield in Rusk County, it ensured that Texas, and the world, would never be the same again.

With the Spindletop discovery, the state had jumped from an agricultural economy to a financial-industrial economy. At first, Texans were slow to recognize change and many still haven't fully accepted it. To this day, the struggle between rural and urban values continues to divide the state. In the 1960s, the trend toward suburbanization increased, as more and more farmers preferred to live in town and visit their fields by car. Indeed, most Texans now live in urban areas, a fact not always apparent from the many movies and novels about the state that turn on the romance of the past.

Since Spindletop, Texas has rarely failed to lead the US in petroleum production. In the early days, it led the world. This added to the state's tendency to measure itself not against sister states but against the world.

Recent decades

The 1960s produced a series of events bigger even than the state itself. The traumatic assassination of President John F. Kennedy in Dallas in 1963 was followed by the succession of the vice president, Lyndon B. Johnson – a Texan – as the 36th US President. The year before had seen the opening of NASA's Manned Spacecraft Center at Houston, and, before the decade was over, Apollo 11 astronaut Neil Armstrong was transmitting the first words from the surface of the moon: "Houston, Tranquility Base here. The Eagle has landed." Somehow, it seemed appropriately Texan in style.

A TEXAS PRESIDENT

Lyndon Baines Johnson (1908–73) was born into a Texas Hill Country farming family. Ruthlessly ambitious, he became a senator in 1948 and John F. Kennedy's Vice-President in 1960. Three years later, aboard Air Force One, he was sworn in as US President, just 99 minutes after Kennedy's assassination in Dallas.

In the 1964 election, Johnson had a landslide victory but his years at the White House, dedicated to creating "the Great Society," were darkened by the shadow of the Vietnam War. Vociferous domestic opposition to the conflict persuaded "LBJ" to step down in 1968 and he retired, with his wife, Lady Bird, to their Texas ranch.

In the 1970s, while price freezes, gas shortages and minority rights became as familiar concepts to Texans as to the rest of the country, the state continued to grow. In 1973, it became the fourth most populous state in the Union.

The Arab oil embargo increased domestic production in Texas oilfields. Towns such as Lubbock, Abilene and Odessa doubled in size. But no big new fields have been discovered for 50 years now and, with the cost of bringing up existing supplies double what it was in the 1970s, the state has increasingly found itself supplying oil equipment to other producers, such as Mexico. Texas crews now operate offshore oil rigs all over the world.

In the 1990s, Texas replaced Democratic Governor Ann Richards (1991–94) with the future US President, the Republican George W. Bush. However, through Mrs Richards, women had finally cracked the political glass ceiling, and, in 1993, Texas elected its first woman senator, Kay Bailey Hutchison.

Superlative Texas

Texas facts and figures are seldom expressed in other than superlative terms: *The* biggest; *The* best. And Texas planners tend to think along the same lines. That's one of the reasons why such a high percentage of recent US build-

Dallas is a perfect example: it is a city legendary the world over for its involvement in the oil business, but it is located in a section of Texas that has never produced any.

However, Texas' rich oil resources are a double-edged sword. On the one hand, oil has brought immeasurable wealth to the state, especially now that domestic sources of energy are so highly valued. But Texans' reliance on oil has also made the state vulnerable. The crash in world oil prices caused a great deal of hardship in Texas in the early 1980s and was followed by the shock of the Savings and Loan crisis of the late 1980s, when over a million Texans lost

ing and real estate development has taken place in cities such as Dallas, Houston and Austin. Some Texas cities have experienced the disadvantages of uncontrolled growth. But this fact has not discouraged Texas developers.

Today, despite the abrupt price plunge in the 1980s, the oil industry is more than an important part of the economy. It brings the state together. Even in the 34 non-producing counties, oil plays a vital part in local business.

FAR LEFT: John F. Kennedy, assassinated in Dallas.
LEFT: Ann Richards, Governor in the 1990s.
ABOVE: poster produced by Lubbock schoolchildren for Texas' sesquicentennial celebrations.

their homes. Now, state leaders recognize the importance of economic diversification and go out of their way to attract high-tech firms. Computer chip fabrication and software development have found a receptive home in Austin.

The new economy

Everything – from the fashion industry to movie and television production – is currently taking root in Texas, and all of these new players are challenging the oil industry's long tenure at the head of the state's economic pyramid. The new economy is based on a more general and sounder combination of manufacturing and finance.

Movies in Texas

For a long time after William Wellman cast the big sky near San Antonio as a featured lead in his seminal airplane drama *Wings* (1927), major movie production in Texas was a rare event. Notable movies made in Texas were virtually unheard of during the glory days of the Hollywood studio era, when even Howard Hawks' *Red River* (1948), the saga of a Texas cattle drive, employed Arizona locations. The lonely house on the West Texas plain in George Stevens' *Giant* (1956), filmed near Marfa, echoed that movie's solitary eminence

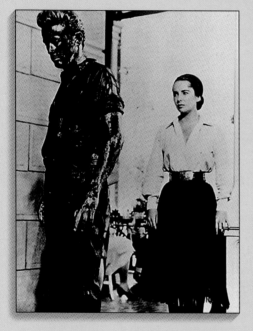

among film stories about Texas that were actually shot in the state.

A case can be made for Texas novelist Larry McMurtry as author of the soaring popularity Texas now enjoys as a film location. The adaptation of a McMurtry novel, *Hud* (1963), was the first major hit movie shot in Texas since *Giant*, and was followed by Warren Beatty's *Bonnie and Clyde* (1967), shot near Dallas. Peter Bogdanovich's film of another McMurtry novel, *The Last Picture Show* (1971), shot in and around McMurtry's hometown of Archer City in West Texas, created an even bigger stir.

Despite accelerating activity throughout the 1960s, 1970s and 1980s, the dream of a film industry to match Texas' increasing opinion of its importance was still a chimera, when another Larry McMurtry yarn rode to the rescue. His big mid-career best-seller, *Lonesome Dove*, an elegiac epic about a cattle drive, became an enormously popular TV mini-series in 1989.

The timing was probably coincidental and its significance more symbolic than real, but after *Dove* came the deluge: Oliver Stone's *JFK* (1991), Clint Eastwood's *A Perfect World* (1993), *What's Eating Gilbert Grape* (1993), *Dazed and Confused* (1993), *The Underneath* (1995), *Lone Star* (1996), *The Whole Wide World* (1996), *Michael* (1996), *Suburbia* (1997), *The Newton Boys* (1998) and *Hope Floats* (1998) – all but the Stone picture shot in or near Austin. Notable television movies include *The Good Old Boys* and a sequel to *Lonesome Dove*, *Streets of Laredo* (both 1995).

Lonesome Dove was adapted by Austin screenwriter William Witliff and most of it was shot near the capital city. It was Austin's charms that finally attracted enough stars for a permanent movie colony in Texas. Houston and Dallas could match Austin's non-union labor costs and exceed its technical facilities, but they could not compete with its easygoing hedonism and plentiful live music – both appealing to movie folk – nor the diversity of nearby locations.

Pine forests, scrubby hills, vast prairies, small town squares, and, during the odd rainy year, lush pastures and sparkling creeks can all be found within striking distance of the capital city. And a typical winter in Austin is sunny and agreeable.

A base of competent film crew personnel developed in Austin, many of whom cut their teeth on independent features such as Richard Linklater's *Slacker* (1990), made for milk money and entirely devoted to a ramble through everyday Austin bohemia. Linklater's decision to remain in Austin while he pursued his career gave heart and employment to other young filmmakers, and, within a few years, Hollywood producer Lynda Obst chose the area for a second home.

By the turn of the millennium, Dallas was generating the greatest sums of money as the base for two popular TV series, *Walker Texas Ranger* and *Barney*, while feature filmmakers virtually tripped over each other in Austin, where Hollywood features were regularly in progress.

Dallas money versus Austin cachet: a vintage Texas state of affairs that is likely to endure. ❑

LEFT: James Dean and Elizabeth Taylor on the set of *Giant*, filmed at Marfa.

Texas has taken over national leadership in many phases of the chemical industry (not just petrochemicals). It has remained an important aerospace center, and is attracting more and more technological manufacturing firms. But, still a major farm and ranch center, it contains the most farmland of any American state and ranks third among the states in total agricultural income. It is first in the production of cotton, cattle, sheep, goats and, in most years, rice.

Its location in the US "sunbelt" is also enticing. All kinds of corporations are shifting their headquarters to the Lone Star State, not just for its more favorable climate but also for its access

a pragmatic people, and they are willing to make changes in the name of progress. Even the Alamo, the sacred shrine of Texas liberty, had to be rescued from commercial development in 1905. In most cases, historical and sentimental concerns take a back seat when they involve anything less than the biggest and the best. This attitude might strike some observers as rather hard-hearted, but Texans are so frank that most people find it endearing.

Friendliness and hospitality

Friendliness and hospitality are Texan traditions that are quickly adopted by new residents.

to world markets, its central location and its eagerness to acquire fiscal and industrial families. Major international corporations, too, have opened branches in Dallas and Houston.

Tradition and pragmatism

Despite their strong sense of history, Texans have always been receptive to new ideas, never holding on to some outdated asset for sentimental or historical reasons. Although they quite clearly appreciate tradition, they are also

ABOVE: Southfork Ranch, home of the feuding, oil-rich Ewing family in the long-running television drama series *Dallas*, and now open to the public.

Visitors will find Texans, in general, helpful and gracious. They are never too busy to answer questions, give directions or help out people in need. The smaller the town, the more likely you are to receive this personal attention, but even the big cities of Texas have more public heart than most other big cities.

Most Texans show a great deal of public respect for the elderly and for women. Even street urchins use such terms as "ma'am" and "sir" to adults. Many Texans see themselves as the highest expression of the American character. To them, Texas epitomizes the American dream, and is valid in every way. They believe in Texas in a way more often found in older, more chauvinistic cultures. But Texas is also maturing, taking on an international viewpoint as more and more of its young people travel outside its borders.

Sporting artists

Texas is growing swiftly and coming of age, socially and artistically, with a speed to match its technology. Although artists are often not given the respect and support they receive in other societies, Texas is beginning to accept more responsibility for supporting the arts in their varied forms. And

there are few visitors who will not find some expression of their native or national tradition honored in one of the Texas museums, galleries or parks.

Texas also plays a lot and is dedicated to sports, particularly baseball and American football, although soccer has become popular with younger Texans, more and more of whom are playing the game. Texas athletes of both sexes have established themselves as stars and record-holders in track and field, swimming, gymnastics, golf, baseball, basketball, tennis, motor and horse racing, sailing and polo. There is scarcely a Texas town that cannot volunteer the name of some native son or daughter who

> **ALL EYES ON DALLAS**
>
> The TV series *Dallas* first aired in the US in April 1978 and ran until May 1991. The drama topped ratings charts all over the world.

has gone on to receive national or international sporting acclaim. And visitors who participate in such activities as golf or tennis will find doors opened to them.

Increasingly urban

Although in the eyes of the United States, as well as the rest of the world, the prevailing image of Texas remains rural, it is solidly urbanized by a ratio of 10 to one. Life today in the larger Texas cities has scant connection with the Texas of history and romance. Nevertheless, these metropolitan people were fascinated, along with everybody else, by the TV drama series *Dallas,* which – despite the cast working in high-rise offices – pictured the ranch as the center of Texas family life, even if the Ewings were not exactly an average family.

The depiction of sophisticated shopping centers and cosmopolitan boutiques as typical of Texas, as some recent films and television dramas have done, violates some of the world's most precious preconceptions (or misconceptions). Yet the urbanity is all true, and in the major cities one can find virtually every famous retail name and designer label offered in the capitals of Europe and Asia, or in New York or Los Angeles.

As a matter of fact, many Europeans and glamorous figures from the rest of the US come to Texas to shop in such exclusive stores as the world-renowned Neiman-Marcus. Few people realize that Dallas ranks as the second- or third-largest fashion marketing center in the country. But, of course, as Texas has grown, it has acquired the vices and problems it long scorned as "big city" or "foreign." It houses three of the largest US cities, so slums, pollution and traffic are a part of the urban scene.

A mini-US

Texas is said to be modern America in microcosm, bowing to changes while proclaiming a rugged individualism.

Perhaps this is the best way for personal independence in the US to survive – honoring traditions while, at the same time, regarding them with a flexible state of mind. ❑

LEFT: Market Square color, San Antonio.
RIGHT: the mustang sculptures of Las Colinas, Irving, near Dallas.

TEXANS

Peoples from all over the world have made Texas – the land of opportunity – their home, bringing with them their own individual cultures and traditions

One of the saddest sights in New Orleans or Galveston is the daily arrival of hundreds of refugees from the older Southern states, seeking homes on the Texan prairies. The flood of emigration from South Carolina, Alabama and Georgia is formidable... Old men and little children, youths and maidens clad in homespun, crowd the railway cars, looking forward eagerly to the land of promise. The ignorance of these people with regard to the geography of the country in general, is dense. "I never travelled so much befo'," is a common phrase; "is Texas a mighty long ways off yet?"
— Edward King, 1874

Anglo immigrants established the overall trends of the state's cultural development, when they wrested the area from Mexico in the 19th century. But there have been other cultural influences: Texas is cross-hatched with a complicated pattern of regional and ethnic divisions.

"Anglos" who settled in Texas before annexation were mainly from the American South, although, even within this group, there were major cultural differences. Immigrants from the deep South, where slavery was deeply rooted, tended to settle east of San Antonio. Those from the upper South, where slavery was less pervasive, tended to settle to the west. Like Southerners today, these settlers held a wide range of political, religious and moral views, some of them in direct opposition to each other. And yet, despite their differences, early Southern settlers established the powerful Anglo-Southern or Anglo-Celtic-Southern culture in contrast to, and often at odds with, those of other immigrants.

The cowboy image

For a long time, the Anglos east of San Antonio set the tone for the whole state. East Texas was

PRECEDING PAGES: cowboy culture past and present, Fort Worth.
LEFT: Mexican-American, Rio Grande City.
RIGHT: Tyler Rose Festival Queen, East Texas.

not just Southern – it was an extension of the deep South. In the oil-rich 20th century their influence waned, while the West, with its powerful icons, became more influential. Denim overalls and cotton growing gave way to cowboy boots and cattle raising as essential elements in the international image of Texas.

Non-Southern dishes like chicken-fried steak, tortillas and chili have by and large replaced the traditional offerings of grits, greens and cornbread on the Anglo table.

Today, Texas is identified much more readily with the American West than with the South, and recent immigrants seem to prefer the state's "cowboy image" to its connection with the Confederacy. Even long-time Texans seem to be giving up their claim to the Old South and their nostalgic attachments to the heyday of Southern culture. Although, for the most part, cowboys are a thing of the past, the "cowboy image" seems more in keeping with the state's vitality than the cultivation of Southern memories. And, because being a cowboy was never an exclusively Anglo experience, it tends to run right across Texas' many ethnic boundaries.

Anglo-Southerners are not just being Westernized, they are disappearing. Whites of Old Southern descent make up less than half the population, especially after heavy immigration from California, the Midwest and the Northeast during the mid-1990s boom years. And, due to the large number of Mexican-Americans in Texas, white non-Hispanics form a smaller percentage of the population here than in the country as a whole.

HUGO THE RED

Even though Hugo O'Conór was a Spanish governor, it was clear he was not of Hispanic origin – he was called the "Red Captain" for the distinctive color of his hair.

day and age, but, if the great-great-grandparents of typical Texas blacks could be assembled, some of them would be black, but a number would, in fact, be white.

Irish or Spanish

The Irish were among the first Europeans in Texas. In fact, Hugo O'Conór was a Spanish governor of Texas in the late 18th century. Where O'Conór came from and how he ended up in the employ of the Spanish are questions to which the answers are lost. More Irish arrived in Texas in

form a smaller percentage of the population here than in the country as a whole.

The composition usually called "Anglo" is likely to consist of several European and possibly some non-European elements. Texas was the location of the earliest Polish community in the United States and some of the first Irish ones. The largest group of immigrants to come directly from Europe was German.

Intermarriage between Anglo-Southerners and recently arrived continental colonists, and later between this mixed group and Hispanics, occurred as soon as they began to live within sight of each other. The taboo against Anglo-black marriages is rarely broken even in this

the 1820s and 1830s, when the Spaniards granted what are now the counties of Refugio and San Patricio (St Patrick) to Irish settlers. The Mexican government evidently wanted an Irish Catholic buffer between the areas of Protestant-born Anglo settlements and the Spanish-speaking Catholics.

After the Republic of Texas was declared in 1836, the Europeans viewed the area as more stable politically than when it was part of Mexico. Leaders of the Republic encouraged immigration more actively than had the Mexican government. Whether Texas would be annexed by the United States was then unknown, but these factors combined to open Texas up to a flood of Europeans whose imagination had been captured by the Texas Revolution.

From the beginning, the Texas government saw to it that new settlers received land, and immigrant aid groups, like the Adelsverein, organized migration to Texas. However, it was not well-administered and ran short of badly needed relief funds.

The Germans

The Germans' first permanent settlement was Industry, in Austin County, west of Houston, so-called for its cigar factory. Many Germans settled in the port cities of Galveston and Indi-

urban ports, while others settled for a while in the interior where there were friends and relatives. After they had found their bearings, they proceeded to establish daughter communities. Constrained by the settlement patterns of previous groups and the threat of Comanche raids farther west, most Germans made their homes in a 10-county strip north of San Antonio which, in fact, became the center of German influence in the state.

The German immigrants came from all walks of life. Some were peasant farmers, while others were well-educated. Some brought with them libraries that were extensive for the time

anola. Typically, they wrote home an "America letter" that described – often with exaggerated, if not downright false, hopefulness – the human happiness, fertility and wonderful climate of Texas. Their letters were shared among a village or other group of acquaintances from which more brave Germans, despite the danger, would set out. German immigrants tried to bring along an entire support group, motivated in varying degrees by wanderlust, political idealism and the desire for social and economic improvement. Some stayed in the relatively

Left: airforce cadet and his date.
Above: German Texans in Fredericksburg.

and place, and they belonged to learned organizations such as the Goethe Society.

In *Journey Through Texas,* Frederick Law Olmsted, who traveled throughout the South from 1850 to 1859, wrote with surprise and admiration about the intellectual attainments of the German colonists in Texas. He described their primitive but neat log cabins, plastered and stuccoed, and their books, musical instruments and paintings. Olmsted hoped their liberal influence would move Texas out of the Old Southern sisterhood of slave states.

Frederick Law Olmsted recorded: "One of the party said to me: 'I think if one or two of the German tyrants I could mention could look in upon us now, they would display some chagrin at our enjoyment, for there is hardly a gentleman in this company whom they have not condemned to death, or to imprisonment for life.'... Laboring like slaves (I have seen them working side by side, in adjoining fields), their wealth gone; deprived of the enjoyment of art, and, in a great degree, of literature; removed from their friends, and their great hopeful designs so sadly prostrated. I have been assured, I doubt not, with sincerity, by several of them, that never in Europe had they had so much satisfaction – so much intellectual enjoyment of life, as here."

Most of the Germans disliked slavery. Nor did they wish to annihilate the Native American, who considered Germans a distinct tribe, superior to the loathsome Spaniards, Mexicans and Anglo-Americans. Today, after Britain, Germany is the origin of most non-Hispanic whites in Texas.

Latin colonies

In the German agricultural villages of Sisterdale, Bettina and Comfort, Latin was spoken in everyday life; the communities are remembered as "Latin colonies," and, understandably, they mystified their Anglo neighbors at the

BARBECUES AND SCHNITZELS

German settlers often gathered on market days and holidays to sell their produce or celebrate. On these occasions, whether revisiting a large market city such as San Antonio or just celebrating at one of their villages, they roasted a calf, sheep or goat. This custom may well be the origin of that typically Texan food, the barbecue. Some people also believe another unique Texas preparation, chicken-fried steak, is of German derivation. They point to its obvious similarities with the German *schnitzels*, which are also breaded and pan-fried cuts of meat. To make genuine chicken-fried steak, a typically Southern cream-style gravy is added.

time. It is just as well that the neighbors understood little of what the Germans had to say, for their beliefs were on the whole very different from those of the Anglo-Southerners.

Not only were many of them opposed to slavery, as Olmsted the Abolitionist noted, but several communities – Sisterdale and its daughter village of Comfort, in particular – were the centers of free thought and agnosticism. Many of the German settlers were Lutheran, and a few Catholic, but their free-thinking may have been unique on the frontier.

Broad German influence continues to this day in certain parts of Texas. Until the 1950s, the Tex-Deutsch dialect, an amalgam of English and German, was spoken in many settlements of San Antonio. Today it has almost disappeared, and the Germans of the Texas Hill Country are becoming more like the Anglo majority and less like a true minority group.

Deliberate attempts to preserve German festivals have resulted in the regular celebration of the Fredericksburg Easter Fires and the *Wurstfest* in New Braunfels. The Easter Fires are lighted on the hills surrounding Fredericksburg on the Saturday before Easter. While local legend holds these fires were originally set by Comanche Indians, scholars have demonstrated that they were probably a custom brought from southern Germany which can be traced to pagan roots. The *Wurstfest* in New Braunfels usually comes in fall, at more or less the same time as the German *Oktoberfest*. Sausage and beer consumption, and a *gemütlich* sociability, link this New World celebration to the boisterous beer halls and *kellers* of Munich.

The Slavs

The Texas State Historical Marker at Serbin, Texas, makes interesting reading: "Trilingual (Wendish-German-English) community founded in 1854 by 588 Wends under the leadership of the Rev. John Kilian. The Rev. Kilian (Evangelical Lutheran) named the place Serbin because the Wends were descendants of Lusatian Serbs (or "Sorbs"). A thriving town 1865–1890; had grocery, dry goods, jewelry, drug and music stores, shops of wagon maker, blacksmith, saddler, post office, three doctors, two dentists. On Smithville-Houston Oxcart Road – sending out cotton, other produce, and hauling in staples. Decline began about 1890 as railroads bypassed settlement by several miles."

Just as German communities have adapted more and more to the dominant Anglo culture, other small groups, have been similarly absorbed. A group of Polish Catholics followed their priest southeast of San Antonio in 1854 to set up the first Polish colony in the US, Panna Maria. Later, several more Polish towns were established in Texas.

Two other major Slavic groups in the state are the Czechs and Wends. Together, several central and eastern counties still have the largest rural populations of Czechs in the US. Czech settlements are generally agricultural, and most Texas Czechs have made their names and fortunes as farmers. Not as numerous as the Germans, the Czechs have nevertheless preserved their culinary traditions – their jam-filled rolls called *kolaches* are especially popular.

Several Czech communities hold celebrations to honor their heritage. Annual festivals in West, Taylor and Ennis draw city-dwellers from Dallas, Austin and Houston to eat sausage and sauerkraut and dance the polka.

Wends are a German-speaking group who left their homes in Prussia in the 1840s. Those

in Texas settled in two counties east of Austin, Lee and Fayette. The church and farm were the centers of Wendish life. Today most Wends have left the smaller towns for the city, but their colony in Texas was the only such community located in North America.

The Cajuns

French colonization of Texas was sporadic. While La Salle and other French explorers were among the early visitors to Texas, and Jean Lafitte and his pirate band established an early enclave in Galveston, the French influence seen today in the state has mainly come from a group of French-American settlers. The

---

LEFT: German biergarten in Fredericksburg.
RIGHT: Treue der Union Monument in Comfort honors German Texans killed by Confederate soldiers.

Cajuns are descendants of the Acadians, who were removed from their Canadian homeland in the 19th century. After resettling in French-owned Louisiana, they developed their own culture, combining French, Spanish, Indian and black elements.

In the early 20th century, the discovery of oil in East Texas lured Cajuns to the area. The Texas Cajuns tend to blend into other ethnic groups and be considered either Anglo or black, but their Gallic love of good food and good times lends a distinctive flavor to the East Texas areas where they have settled. Jambalaya, gumbo, and crawfish *étouffé* are eaten through-out the bayou country of East Texas. Cajun music is also enjoying renewed popularity. Usually played on accordions and guitars, and sung in the Cajun French *patois*, this music brings many an East Texas dance hall alive and kicking on a Saturday night.

Hispanics

"Here are fine stone mansions," the *New York Tribune* wrote of San Antonio in 1879, "that would not be out of place in the loveliest suburbs of Philadelphia, and here are Mexican huts thatched with cornstalks, beside which the dwellings Stanley saw in Uganda were models

ADDITIONAL ANGLOS

Other smaller groups have blended into the Anglo culture. A substantial Scandinavian population immigrated to the hot climate of Texas; Greeks settled along the coast, particularly around Galveston; and a small Italian contingent lived in the larger cities but also had agricultural settlements in the Brazos Valley.

The Jews' principal migration took place in the 19th century, when German and Eastern European Jews came to Texas. Today, Jews are an urban group in the state, but synagogues in small towns like Brenham and Corsicana are reminders that they have been in Texas as long as many other European settlers.

of comfort. Fine modern churches, with carpeted aisles and cushioned pews, stand in sight of a venerable Spanish cathedral where swarthy penitents, muffled in shawls, crouch on the stone floor and tell their beads. Here are spacious stores, filled with as costly goods as can be found in Eastern cities, daily newspapers, banks, water works, gas works, telegraph offices, a club and a theatre; and there are quaint and dirty little Mexican shops, adobe buildings with loop-holed battlements, scarred with bullet marks, alongside wagon trains from Chihuahua and Monterrey bringing silver and taking back cotton, soldiers, priests, nuns, negroes, greasers, half-breed Comanches, dirt, dogs and fleas."

In his book of essays, *In a Narrow Grave*, Larry McMurtry put forward the view that Texas cities are always improved when the Hispanic influences the Anglo. If this is true, Texas cities must be improving: their Hispanic populations are increasing steadily. San Antonio, Houston and El Paso are among the top US metropolitan areas in total Hispanic population, and Texas follows only California in the number of Hispanics: people with Spanish surnames make up more than a quarter of its population. In big cities like Dallas and Houston, where blacks used to be the largest minority, Hispanics are gaining on, or surpassing, them. In the state as a whole, Hispanics overtook blacks as the dominant minority group in the late 1940s.

Spanish-speaking peoples are gradually re-Hispanicizing the state, following much the same immigration patterns as Anglos. This is ironic, as it was the inability of the Mexican government to induce Spanish-speakers to move to Texas that was one of the reasons Mexico could not hold on to the area. Hispanics are no longer confined behind the imaginary boundary that once kept them west and south of the San Antonio river. Today there are *barrios* in the cities of Dallas and Fort Worth, and even in the Texas Panhandle, bringing Mexican-American customs, traditions and color as far north as the lonely, windswept High Plains.

The Hispanics were the first non-Native American Texans, or *Tejanos* , and descendants of these original settlers form a small, stable and often wealthy core of the Spanish-speaking population of Texas. Sometimes intermarrying with wealthy Anglos, these *Tejanos* have succeeded in preserving a culture distinct even from the rest of the Spanish-speakers.

LEFT: German Texans.
ABOVE: chorus of Hispanic women at the Las Posadas Hispanic Festival, San Antonio.

Hispanic influence is strongly felt at the dinner tables and snack bars of Texas. More than any other minority group, Spanish-speaking Texans have made their cuisine part of the mainstream of Texas life and, increasingly, that of the rest of the nation. *Tacos, enchiladas, fajitas* and all the rest of the Tex-Mex menu are found as often on the Texas table as chuck roast and ice-tea. While chili may be an Englishman's attempt to reproduce curry in Texas, and the barbecue may have originated with German Texans, neither of these staples of Texas cooking would taste the way they do without their Hispanic spices. The very word "barbecue" is probably of Spanish origin.

The Blacks

But the more he... learned about the blues, the more he discovered why the secret was so well-kept. "The Rollin' Stones, Eric Clapton and Cream... all my idols fell apart before my very eyes. They were nothing but low-down, dirty thieves! They steal the music from these cats and then carry on like they are something... They can't be big enough to ...say, "Hey, if you like me, you should check out the masters, the men who made this music first."

— Austin nightclub-owner Clifford Antone to Ed Ward in the *Austin American-Statesman*, 1980

The other major minority group, African-Americans, have not been absorbed by the Anglo culture as the Germans and Czechs have, but they have lived in Texas as long as the Spaniards. When Cabeza de Vaca was shipwrecked on the Gulf Coast in 1528, an African slave named Esteban, or Black Stephen, was with him. He was eventually killed by Native Americans, probably in Sonora, Mexico. Blacks, enslaved or free, were found in subsequent Spanish settlements, and intermarriage resulted in a significant *mulatto* population in Spanish Texas.

The first large infusion of blacks came after the Republic of Texas was established. The Mexican stand against slavery had made owners reluctant to import their human chattels, and the absence of slavery had created a haven for free blacks. But, after independence, it became legal, and former deep Southerners began to bring in slaves. Slavery tended to be concentrated east of the Texarkana-San Antonio line, where the Anglo "masters" were settled.

Following Emancipation, and into the 20th century, blacks often lived a rural life on scattered farms or in small black communities. Today, as they move to cities within Texas and elsewhere, the rural communities that preserved black culture are dying out.

Black migration to cities outside the state is responsible for the decline in the share of the general population that is Afro-American, and Hispanics have now overtaken blacks as the largest minority group. Geographer Terry Jordan believes that Texas' transition from a Southern to a Western self-image is linked to this shift in the most visible minority. Blacks are part of the Southern tradition, while Hispanics seem to belong to later 19th-century frontier history.

The popularly accepted idea that blacks were not an important part of western frontier life ignores some significant black history. Many runaway slaves and free blacks joined the Native Americans and lived with them, not just on the frontier but beyond it.

The black soldiers of the ninth and 10th Cavalry and the 24th and 25th Infantries who fought the Native Americans were called "buffalo soldiers" by the tribes. Despite this role played by black soldiers in the Indian wars, most Texans continue to associate blacks only with the Southern strands of Texas' history.

Blacks themselves are more often urban now, so that their political and cultural influence is most strongly felt in the cities.

The Native Americans

Texans tend to think their Native American population was simply dispersed to other states. In fact, many Texas tribes were totally destroyed, including the Tejas who gave the state its name. For many years, it was commonly believed that the only unassimilated Native Americans in the state were the Alabama and Coushatta, two Southern tribes who migrated to East Texas where they lived on one of the state's three reservations.

Other important groups include the Tiguas, who preserved their culture almost in secret in the *barrio indio* of El Paso, and the Kickapoos, who migrate annually from Mexico across the Rio Grande to Eagle Pass in South Texas.

Recently, Native Americans have been staging a comeback in Texas. Oklahoman and New Mexican Indians, especially Cherokee and Navajo, have moved to the larger cities. In Dallas and Houston, which have the largest Native American populations, they live in distinct communities, but not along tribal lines. When this new wave of immigration is added to all the Texans who have at least some Indian blood, Native Americans in Texas may be better represented than first thought.

> **KICKAPOOS CROSSING**
>
> Kickapoo Indians enjoy special dispensation from both US and Mexican governments, allowing them to roam freely across the border between the two countries.

The Asians

Asians were the last large group to be added to the Texas mix, although they first came to the state on their eastward trek after the California gold rush. Chinese laborers worked on the railroad, but were frequently abandoned by the rail companies when the tracks were finished. Isolated in a strange world, the Chinese were then usually hired as cheap labor to undercut emancipated blacks.

The first wave of Chinese immigrants did not have much lasting impact on Texas, since US immigration laws banned most Chinese women from the country. Some agricultural laborers in Robertson County intermarried with local women, producing the "Black Chinese" of Calvert. More or less permanent Chinatowns were formed in El Paso, and later in San Antonio, but restrictive immigration policies kept the Asian population to a low level in Texas until fairly recent times.

In the early 20th century, Japanese settlers started experimental rice-farming communities along the coast, while Chinese and Japanese merchants set up small businesses in San Antonio and other cities. Until recently, Asian-run groceries served the black community, but a new influx of Southeast Asians has made Asian products more profitable.

The latest Asian migration, the result of the Vietnam War, has included Vietnamese, Cambodians and others. Many have settled on the Texas Gulf Coast where they fish in areas traditionally harvested by other groups, particularly Anglos.

Misunderstandings and prejudice at first resulted in several killings and other ugly incidents that involved the influence of the Ku Klux Klan. However, the coast is now fairly calm, and Texas seems ready to add another piece to its mosaic of cultures.

While a distinctive Vietnamese culture might seem most likely to thrive in fishing settlements along the coast, not all Vietnamese live in these areas, nor do they all earn a living by fishing. Many of the latest immigrants are technicians and other highly trained people who have settled in Texas' urban areas (the Asian populations of Austin and Houston more than doubled in the 1980s and 1990s). Others are found in rural communities as professional workers, farmers and ranchers.

The Southeast Asians are reminiscent of other Texas immigrant groups – that is, most Texans – in the value many of them place on family life and hard work. ❑

LEFT: African-American Texan serving barbecue at Buffalo Gap, Abilene.
RIGHT: Asian Texan at an assembly plant, Amarillo.

THE TEXAS RANGERS

Efficient, tough and uncompromising: the Texas Rangers are a remarkable band of law enforcers, a legion of heroes with a reputation second to none

To the average person, the name Texas Rangers conjures up an image of the Dallas baseball team. But, for most of the first century of Texas history, the Texas Rangers were almost synonymous with that history. No police force in the country had the high prestige of the Texas Rangers. The WPA *Guide* noted in 1940: "The man in the tan trousers and shirt, wide-brimmed Western hat, black tie, leather holster and sidearms not only commands respect but admiration."

Texas Rangers were "one of the most colorful, efficient and deadly bands of irregular partisans on the side of law and order the world has ever seen," one historian noted… "called into being by a society that could not afford a regular army." Many of these adventurers were famous before reaching their thirties, men who showed "an utter absence of fear," superb psychologists at understanding not only the enemy but also the men around them.

When Frederick Law Olmsted made his *Journey Through Texas* in the 1850s, he found "men and officers on terms of perfect equality, calling each other by their Christian or nicknames." Rations were being issued to all ranks every four days: hard bread and pork, flour, rice, sugar and coffee, with fresh beef.

In the 1880s, Texas Ranger Captain Bill McDonald (who was known for his readiness "to charge hell with a bucket of water") confronted three gunmen who'd tried to ambush him. He dropped one, and, after taking bullets through his left side and right wrist, was busy cocking his pistol with his teeth when the other two outlaws fled. "No man in the wrong can stand up against a man in the right who keeps on a-coming," was the romantic (and somewhat optimistic) assessment of this episode by a fellow Texas Ranger.

PRECEDING PAGES: custom-made saddles at Capitol Saddlery in Austin.
LEFT: "bank robber" in action during a Frontier Days Celebration, Bandera.
RIGHT: star of the Texas Rangers.

Origins of the force

The genesis of this fearsome force was in 1823, when Stephen F. Austin hired 10 experienced frontiersmen as "rangers" for a punitive expedition against the Indians. But it wasn't until 12 years later that the Texas legislature instituted the Texas Rangers as an official body: 56

men in three companies, each with a captain and two lieutenants.

The Head Ranger, a major, was subject to the army's commander-in-chief. Earning the same pay as the army, Rangers supplied their own mounts and rations and had to be equipped with "a good horse (and) one hundred rounds of powder and ball" at their own expense. They protected the frontier against raiding Mexicans, and fought against outlaws and Indians.

Rangers in the Republic

During the years of the Republic of Texas (1836–45), the Rangers at first worked as scouts and couriers during the first presidency of Sam Houston, who fostered friendship with the Indians. The Rangers retrieved cattle and helped passage over "muddy roads and swollen streams." But, from December 1838, under the presidency of Mirabeau B. Lamar, five new Ranger companies were commissioned, which spent the next three years fighting Indians.

The army and the Rangers were often at odds, due to conflicting sets of rules and orders; the former sought to police the frontier and keep peace, while the Rangers rode to push back and punish the Indians.

When Sam Houston was re-elected in 1841, he realised that the Rangers were the most

battling guerrillas, they earned a fearsome reputation as *los diablos Tejanos* (Texan devils). Between 1845 and 1875, Rangers fought in the big and little wars against Indians and Mexicans, as well as tracking down robbers and horse thieves. As late as 1849, 200 Texans were killed or carried off by Indians.

Revolver revolution

In 1851, when a 21-year-old former sailor by the name of Samuel Colt began manufacturing the first .34-caliber six-shooter weapon, nobody seemed particularly interested. Then one of the revolvers found its way into the hands of a vet-

effective and economical way of protecting the frontier, which became a flash point the following year, when Captain John Coffee 'Jack' Hayes and 150 Rangers helped repel an invasion. Sent into Laredo, then a Mexican town, Hayes boldly rode off with some horses, returning them a few days later with an admonition to the Mexicans to stay in their place. When, nevertheless, a wagon train was attacked by brigands, he hunted down the culprits.

A few years later, the Mexican War of 1846 brought the Rangers worldwide fame. "Armed to the teeth," they successfully guided the US Army to Monterrey and were at home in the remote deserts of northeastern Mexico, where,

eran Ranger, Captain Samuel Walker, who saw its potential for a man fighting on horseback. At his suggestion, Colt designed a heavier .44-caliber gun (later .47), which became the standard weapon for US cavalrymen.

The first to use Colt's new six-shooter on the Plains Indians was the aforementioned Captain Jack Hayes, a 23-year-old former Tennesseean who had arrived in Texas as a surveyor, before he was appointed by President Lamar to be Chief of Rangers at San Antonio. All the ideal requirements for a Texas Ranger seemed to come together in this handsome, quiet "gentleman of purest character," and, by the time he ended his service, at 34, he was the model which all Rangers aspired to emulate. One Commanche war chief swore never to confront the Colt-equipped Jack Hayes, "who has a shot for every finger on his hand." Largely thanks to Hayes and his men, the revolver became the symbol of power in Texas at a time when many Mexicans were still fighting with lances and ropes.

PISTOL PACKING

Texas Rangers are allowed to choose their own weapon. Many prefer to use a Colt .38 or a .357 Magnum.

the Rangers were regenerated. Its Special Force unit gained a fearsome reputation, on one occasion stacking a dozen dead rustlers "like cordwood" in a Brownsville square "as a lethal response to the death of one Ranger." Among the 3,000 desperadoes they "thinned out" were the multiple killer John Wesley Hardin, who was fatally shot before he could finish his autobiography, and bank robber Sam Bass, whose gang they ambushed.

Taking out the bad men

After the end of the Mexican War (February 2 1848), the Rangers went into a decline and

After some busy years trying to enforce the laws that prompted the Fence Cutting War

were little used. One Ranger captain, arriving to help a community fight off the Indians, said that all he was doing afterwards was hearing complaints from farmers about Rangers killing their hogs. At the onset of the Civil War (1861), many joined the Confederate forces.

State Democrats, back in power in 1874, declared Texas was "overrun with bad men," and, to counter these, plus Indian attacks on the western frontier and border raids by Mexicans,

LEFT: inside the Texas Rangers Hall of Fame, Waco.
ABOVE: Samuel Colt, gun-manufacturer.
RIGHT: John Wesley Hardin, one of the outlaws gunned down by Rangers.

(when the use of barbed wire became widespread), the Rangers endured another lean period at the beginning of the 20th century, when the force was trimmed down to just four 20-man companies.

But the 1910 revolution against Mexico's president Porfirio Diaz created unrest at the border. Then the onset of World War I, with its need to counter German intrigues and American draft dodgers, was followed by Pancho Villa's raid on Columbus, New Mexico, in 1916.

Executed without trial

In responding to these challenges, sometimes, critics charged, the Texas Rangers' actions were high-handed and they were not being held accountable. If an ethnic Mexican was found armed, he was often accused of banditry and killed outright. In 1915, a group of Rangers, having captured a carload of Mexicans suspected of robbing a train near Brownsville, took them into the bushes and shot them. In the ensuing scandal, one local politician alleged that 200 Mexicans had been similarly executed without trial, and that 90 percent of them had been innocent. The indiscriminate killing of hundreds of Hispan-

RANGERS' REPUTATION

One early writer once said of the Texas Rangers that they "could ride like Mexicans, shoot like Tennesseeans and fight like the very devil."

ics during the war became a source of "scandal and embarassment" and, in 1919, prompted a legislative investigation which discredited Ranger tactics. The force was overhauled by recruiting "men of high moral character." Higher salaries – as well as more restraints – were introduced.

The Prohibition years

Prohibition found Rangers patrolling the border against tequila smugglers, protecting Federal farm inspectors, monitoring labor and Ku Klux Klan demonstrations, and taming the lawless oil boom towns. During Prohibition years, the Rangers were often at odds with local lawmen, who preferred to leave gambling casinos and illegal drinking joints alone.

In 1932, the Rangers ill-advisedly backed the wrong candidate, Governor Ross Sterling, in the Democrat primary, and, when his opponent, Miriam "Ma" Ferguson, took office, all 44 Rangers were fired. Salaries were slashed, a new force of 32 was recruited and Texas became a haven for the likes of George "Machine Gun" Kelly and Bonnie (Parker) and Clyde (Barrow). Parker and Barrow were eventually hunted down by renowned Ranger Frank Hamer.

New qualifications

In 1935, under Governor James Allred, the Rangers became part of a larger force which included the Highway Patrol and Headquarters Division. New qualifications were laid down for Rangers, who had to be between 30 and 45 years of age (later extended to 50), 5 ft 8 ins (1.74 meters) in height and "perfectly sound" in mind and body.

Each Ranger was required to be "a crack shot" and underwent extensive training in ballistics and investigation techniques. An "intelligent" weekly report was demanded from each man, summarizing his activities.

Rangers were spread throughout the state, becoming plain-clothes officers and sometimes a sort of rural constabulary. When World War II arrived, they were kept busy rounding up enemy aliens and helping protect vulnerable sites. Their attitude toward America's Mexican neighbors changed, as a new era of friendship between the two countries began.

The job of the Rangers widened enormously in the 1960s, when the 8,000 cases they had been dealing with annually almost doubled, due to increasing urbanization and, more particularly, the numerous civil rights demonstrations. Some of the old complaints began to resurface, as the Rangers again began to hear accusations about their attitude to citizens.

Today's Rangers (about 100 men and women) are supplied by the Department of Public Safety with powerful cars and sophisticated weapons and communications equipment. ❏

LEFT: Lieutenant Clete Buckaloo, Texas Ranger, Waco.
RIGHT: the Texas Rangers Hall of Fame in Waco.

DON'T FENCE ME IN

A real Texas cowboy bore little resemblance to the Indian-fighting,

songs-around-the-campfire hero created by Hollywood

American and European humorists had been getting a laugh out of the rough-and-tumble American frontiersmen long before the frontier reached the plains of Texas. When Texas became the frontier, the larger-than-life characteristics of Daniel Boone, Davy Crockett and Mike Fink, the riverboat man, were grafted onto the cowboy.

In the popular imagination, he became the Tall Texan, who could outshoot, outdrink and outlive any living creature on two legs or four. Because he lived on the last American frontier – in a country that revered its frontier experience – the Texas cowboy has captured more attention than any other cowboy, from Italy to the pampas of Argentina and the prairies of Canada.

The cowboy, as he is known best, is primarily a creation of movie-makers and novelists. The real working cowboy inspired writers like Ned Buntline *(The Black Avenger, The Comanche's Dream)* and Owen Wister *(The Virginian),* who immortalized him in the dime novels written in the 1880s and 1890s. They made the cowboy into a romantic hero at about the time the frontier was being closed by the progress of civilization. Other novelists, like Zane Grey *(The Riders of the Purple Sage)* and Louis L'Amour *(Hondo),* have kept the cowboy hero alive for later generations.

Cowboy stars

Movie directors, among them John Ford *(Stagecoach, Fort Apache)* and Howard Hawks *(Red River, Rio Bravo),* put a heroic version of the West on film, helping to make stars of actors such as John Wayne, Gary Cooper and Jimmy Stewart. These "serious" western stars shared the screen in the pre-television era with singing cowboys like Roy Rogers and Gene Autry, who starred in popular western serials.

PRECEDING PAGES: working cowboy at the Goodnight Stables, Palo Duro Canyon.
LEFT: modern-day cowboy enjoys a gallop.
RIGHT: saddle and rifle, timeless cowboy icons.

The working cowboy

Underneath all the storybook and movie glitter, there was always a real working cowboy, and there still is today. The working cowboy did not fight nearly as many Indians as we see him fighting in the movies. Most of the Native Americans were gone when the cowboy

arrived. Like the Indian, the cowboy came to be seen as a noble hero.

The cowboy lived out under the stars. He supplied his own strong code of frontier ethics in a land with no established law, and he enforced it with a gun. And he did all his work on horseback. The cowboy's closeness to nature, his strong defense of his honor, and his horse made him the image of the modern knight. Of course this heroic image has always appealed to the popular imagination.

The history of the working cowboy begins with the introduction of cattle into the New World by Spanish explorers as early as the 16th century. Most of the details of cattle ranching had been worked out by the Spaniards in northern Mexico and southern Texas by the time the first Anglos came into the area in the 1820s.

The Spanish cattle ranching vocabulary was assimilated by the early Texas cattlemen, along with the rest of Spanish cattle culture. Words like *lariat* (rope), *remuda* (string of riding horses) and *corral* (holding pen for cattle) are still in use today. Words for unique western land forms, such as *mesa* (high plateau) and *arroyo* (dry wash), were also adopted.

No Fancy Boots

The boot was one of the cowboy's tools: he had no need of the exotic leathers and elaborately stitched tops seen on today's fashionably macho and expensive footwear.

was "saddle music" to the cowboy. While the *vaquero* usually wore spurs only for work, many a Texas cowboy felt naked if he had to take them off.

For a long time, cowboys wore a very characteristic pair of striped breeches. These gave way in the 1870s to the blue denims manufactured by the Levi-Strauss Company of San Francisco.

A cowboy covered his breeches with heavy leather leggings, called chaps, when he rode through brushy country. "Chaps" is a corrup-

Cowboy costume

Much of the Texas cowboy's costume came from the *vaquero*, as the Spanish cowboy was called. High-heeled boots helped to keep a cowboy's feet in the stirrups when he was riding his horse. The narrow toes of the boots were designed to slide easily into the stirrup, while the boot tops were 12–16 inches (30–40 cm) high and perfectly plain in design. The leather was good quality and durable.

Being generally concerned with the well-being of his animals, the Texan cowboy replaced the sharp, roweled spurs favored by the *vaquero* with larger, blunt wheels, in order to protect his horse's flanks. The jingle of spurs

tion of the Spanish word *chapparal*, meaning heavy brush.

Head and neck wear

The bandana, an oversized neckerchief, was invaluable to cowboy and *vaquero* alike. It kept the hot sun off the back of their necks and mopped the sweat from their faces. It could be a sling for a broken arm or a mask to filter the acrid dust of the trail. Wrapped around a couple of biscuits, a bandana could serve as a lunchpail for a cowboy riding night-watch on his herd.

The tall-crowned, wide-brimmed *sombrero* worn by the *vaquero* was never favored by the Texas cowboy. Nor was the fabled ten-gallon hat ever worn by anyone but the movie cowboys. There was a wide variety of headwear among real cowboys, from the cavalry-style fedora to the shapeless farmboy's hat, but, by the 1870s, the hats made by John B. Stetson of Philadelphia had become standard western wear. Cowboys who worked for a dollar a day would pay $10 to $20 for a good hat and $20 to $30 for a good pair of boots. They were that important to his job.

Shirts were widely varied, some no more than homemade flour sack affairs. As likely as not, they were covered with a vest. The sleeveless vest gave warmth and protection, but did

drive years from the mid-1860s through the 1880s. Prior to this time, the cattle business in Texas was rather low-key. It centered on Spanish-style ranches that were loosely run and generally unfenced – prime conditions for creating "mavericks" in the rich South Texas grasslands where the hardy longhorn cattle could easily survive on their own.

After the Civil War, a flood of immigrants from the South entered Texas, many of them young single men looking for a new life. They found it as cowboys.

The price of cattle in the industrial cities of the North was up to as much as $40 a head,

not bind the cowboy's arms while he worked. For cold weather, a cowboy wore a blue denim jacket or a fleece-lined leather shortcoat. An oilcloth slicker kept off the rain. A cowboy rarely carried more than one change of clothes, which he packed into a bedroll.

Trail driving days

The cowboy's life was a hard one. As many a "greenhorn" quickly learned, a cowboy had to have common sense and a head for survival. The heyday of Texas cowboying was the trail

whereas, in South Texas, longhorns could be bought for $4 apiece. Thus, there was plenty of work for cowboys old and new, driving cattle from Texas to the railheads in Kansas, from where beef was then shipped to city markets.

A cowboy's work began in spring with the cattle roundups or "cow hunts," as old-time cowboys called them. Nursing calves followed their mothers as the cattle were herded into holding pens. There the animals were separated by their brands and claimed by their owners.

Young calves were marked with the same brand as their mothers. They came to be known on the trail as "dogies," from the short rope that tethered the new-born calf to its mother.

LEFT: western mural, Fort Worth.
ABOVE: a cowboy works long hours!

As herds became larger and cattle thieves began to alter brands, some ranchers took to cutting notches in the ears of their cattle as a secondary form of identification.

Trail ballads

After all the rounding up and branding, the trail drive began. Many a cowboy ballad was composed on the open trail, as the cowboys sang to comfort their cattle and keep them from stampeding. Cowboy ballads were usually laments about loneliness, lost love, and the hard life on the trail. "The chief contribution made by white men of America to the

folksongs of the world," observed J. Frank Dobie, are "the cowboy songs of Texas and the West... rhymed to the walk, the trot and the gallop of horses."

Hollywood western stars like the late Gene Autry and Roy Rogers capitalized on this aspect of cattle trail life, making their careers as "singing cowboys." But historians are scornful about this excess of song, pointing out that a hard day's drive more usually ended with conversation around the fire, or perhaps a game of poker. Few cowboys would have had room in their saddlebags for musical instruments of any kind, much less something as bulky as a guitar or a banjo.

Beginning the drive

To start a drive, small herds of cattle, rounded up in South Texas by four or five cowboys, would be driven toward a pre-arranged point where a trail herd was formed. The trail drives then followed well-known routes that were determined more by general directions, involving designated passes or river fords, than by specific paths. Small operators with only 10 or 12 cowboys went up the same trails used by big outfits with 50 or more cowhands.

With the sale of the cattle in Abilene, the cowboys were paid for the first time on their long ride from Texas. For many of them, all the long nights of sleeping on the ground and long days of herding cattle over the open plains were erased in wild drinking and carousing in houses of ill-repute. When the last dust of the trail drive had been washed away, the cowboys mounted up for the long ride home. Some were broke, some were hungover, and a few who had been indiscreet with their revolvers were shot.

Not all cowboys wasted their money in the saloon and the bordello for, as often as not, the wages of the trail drive were used to buy cattle back in South Texas or in Mexico. A cowboy might also take his pay in cattle when he returned home, driving them north as part of a larger herd the following summer. In this way some cowboys became ranchers. They invested their profits in land and cattle, building up small spreads of their own. Some land was also available through homesteading, but cowboys were cattle workers and not much for farming.

The fenced range

By the 1890s, with most of the open rangeland between Texas and Kansas claimed by private owners and fenced with wire, the trails to the railheads were blocked. At the same time, the railroad was expanding. In Texas, Fort Worth became the major railhead. Slaughterhouses and packing companies were built in Fort Worth and San Antonio, making it unnecessary to drive cattle to Kansas. Amarillo and Abilene became active markets in Northwest Texas.

With the closing of the open range, cowboys settled down to work on ranches throughout all but the wooded eastern third of Texas. Some cowboys became ranch owners by working up from smallholdings, or through marriage into cattle-ranching families. Others decided to sign on as hired hands with larger outfits.

It was not uncommon for a rancher to marry a woman much younger than himself, his own younger years being given to building up a ranch that would support a family. This practice left many women widowed and in charge of ranches, since their husbands generally died first. Some women, who would not be confined to the home, took an active part in the management of Texas ranches and still do so today.

Hard work was still a major part of life for the ranch cowboy. In addition to the spring for repairing saddles, bridles and other pieces of important ranch equipment.

KING OF RANCHES

The enormous King Ranch in southern Texas was modeled so closely on the Spanish *rancho* that *Patrón* King even led an entire village out of Mexico to work on it.

Gigantic spreads

It was in the era of the open range that the great ranches of Texas began to form. The King Ranch in South Texas is the largest in the state. Boastful as ever, Texans measure the ranch's current size as 1.23 RIs (Rhode Islands), or 823,000 acres (333,000 hectares). It was founded in 1853 by a former Rio Grande steamboat captain, Richard King.

round-up and branding, the ranch cowboy had to look after his cattle year-round. Cowboys gave up sleeping out under the stars for the bunkhouse, and the chuckwagon of the trail drive was replaced by the ranch kitchen. Cowboys still practiced their riding and roping, but now they worked in the corral or inside the fences of the ranch. In the fall and winter, cowboys rode the fencelines in order to mend them, even though fences were the ultimate insult to a range-bred cowboy. Winter was also a time

LEFT: strong coffee fortified cowboys on the long trail rides.
ABOVE: faces of the west.

Even though the original boundaries of the ranch are no longer the same, the King Ranch is substantially intact and still family owned. There are organized tours, and any highway that goes to Kingsville will cut through some part of it.

The celebrated XIT Ranch in the Texas Panhandle was started, not by Texans, but by northeastern land and cattle syndicates. In the 1870s and 1880s, the state sold the land to the syndicates to finance the present State Capitol in Austin. Originally a monstrous 4.54 RIs (more than 3 million acres or 1.25 million hectares), the XIT was split up in later years as the out-of-state investors went their separate ways.

Black Cowboys

Although it is a little-known fact, some of the best young cowboys to come into Texas were black Americans leaving the war-ravaged states of the South.

Blacks in the West often met the same prejudice they faced elsewhere. Few acquired property or social distinction. But, to a cowboy, a man was as much a man as he could prove himself to be. A black drover who could show his dependability to the outfit was accepted with little regard for his color. It was estimated that about one-quarter of

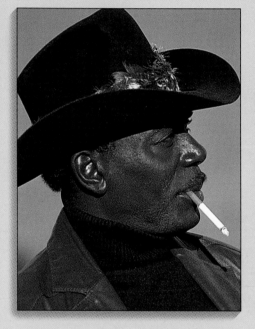

the cowboys on the northbound traildrives between 1866 and 1895 were black, with 63 percent of the others being white and the remainder Mexican.

Many of the early black cowboys had been born as slaves and eventually found more freedom on the open ranges than in urban areas. After the Civil War, when some ranches east of the Trinity river had all-black crews, many became horsebreakers, but very few achieved the elevated status of foremen or managers, although a handful became Federal peace officers or took up careers as rodeo performers. One Texas-born Afro-American cowboy, Bill Pickett, claimed to have invented steer wrestling.

Bose Ikard, a slave born in Mississippi in 1843, was brought to Texas by his master in 1852 and learned the cowboy trade on a ranch near Weatherford. Freed as a result of the Civil War, he went to work for the famed Western rancher Charles Goodnight, eventually becoming not only his chief detective but also his banker.

Ikard helped Goodnight and his partner Oliver Love blaze the early northwards trail that bore their names. "He surpassed any man I had in endurance and stamina," Goodnight once said of him. His story was among those told in the novel and TV mini-series *Lonesome Dove*.

Afro-American slaves were also working as horse wranglers on rancher Abel Pierce's spread in 1853 but were too valuable to use when the boss was breaking horses, especially the most dangerous mounts, because, he said, "those Negroes are worth a thousand dollars apiece."

Another former slave, Isom Dart – who was born Ned Huddleston in Arkansas in 1849 – had an early career stealing horses in Mexico and swimming them across the Rio Grande to sell in Texas. Later his gambling and fighting in Northwest Colorado entangled him with the law. He joined a gang of rustlers in 1875 but was lucky to make his escape when the rest of the gang was ambushed. After that, he changed his name to Isom Dart, bought a ranch and tried to go straight but was tracked down and killed, at the age of 51, by bounty hunter Tom Horn.

The 1993 made-for-television movie *Return to Lonesome Dove* featured a fictional character named Isom Picket, who was a composite of the real life Dart and Bill Pickett.

Another black cowboy of the 19th century, Daniel W. Wallace, rode the cattle trails from adolescence and accumulated enough money to buy a 1,200-acre (485-hectare) ranch near Loraine, with 500–600 cattle. In 1877, he sat down to write a pulp novel about Deadwood Dick which was so successful that it spawned 30 more such novels by the time of his death in 1885. A cowboy named Nat Love was one of many who claimed to have been the original model for Deadwood Dick, saying he had acquired the nickname by winning a roping contest in Deadwood, Arizona in 1876.

Several movies have featured black cowboys, among them being Mel Brooks's parody Western, *Blazing Saddles* (1974), and Clint Eastwood's Oscar-winning *Unforgiven* (1993), in which Morgan Freedman played sidekick Ned Logan. ❑

LEFT: the Black Cowboy was much respected by his Anglo peers.

With the changing times, Texas ranches have become more mechanized. The only contemporary ranch of any size doing business in the traditional way is the Kokernot 06, between Fort Davis and Balmorhea in Davis County.

Longhorn revival

On the ranches, exotic breeds of heavy beef cattle like the Hereford, the Angus, and the Charolais have replaced the stringy old longhorns of trail drive days. Longhorns, though, are making a comeback with some modern breeders, because of their longevity, high calf yield and resistance to disease.

informal gatherings of locals who all pitched in to provide the livestock, riders and entertainment. Nowadays, rodeo is controlled by the Professional Rodeo Cowboys Association (PRCA), which sanctions more than 650 rodeos each year all over the United States – even in places such as New York City. There are National Finals held annually in mid-December in Oklahoma City, and the top rodeo cowboys make six-digit salaries competing in as many as 125 competitions a year.

The events are bull riding, bare-back bronco riding, calf roping, steer wrestling, saddle bronco riding and, for women, barrel racing. In

Today, veterinarians freeze semen from championship bulls and artificially inseminate prize cows. Some even transplant embryos from artificial matings into surrogate mothers, who carry the calf to term. In recent years, up to a million dollars have been bid for breeding rights to champion bulls. The cattle ranch has become scientific and mechanized.

Cowboy spectaculars

Rodeo is the sport of cowboys, devloping naturally out of their skills and tasks as they worked with livestock. Early rodeos were just

ABOVE: bulldoggin' a calf at a rodeo.

the 1930s and 1940s, there was an extensive women's rodeo circuit. Women competed in the same events as men and added gymnastic trick-riding, too. However, during World War II, women's rodeo was discontinued and never regained popularity.

Rodeo contests can be held indoors or out, but the basic requirement is a large, dirt-floored corral or arena, with chutes along one side and escape gates for the livestock opposite them. The arena is surrounded by stands, and behind the stands are barns and holding pens, where the stock is kept before entering the arena. Bull and bronco riders mount up in small pens that open directly into the arena.

When the gate swings open, a rider tries to stay on the bucking animal for eight seconds. Half of the points scored in a ride come from the total time the rider stays mounted; the other half are then awarded for the competitor's style and daring.

Like bullfighting, rodeo can be a very dangerous sport. The animals are wild, and often attempt to trample or gore dismounted riders. The rodeo cowboy's best friend is the clown, who runs into the arena to distract the mount while the rider is on the ground.

Whether local, regional or national, modern rodeo almost always awards prize money to the

top riders. Elaborately inscribed belt buckles, displaying the cowboy's name and the event he won, are presented as trophies.

Cowboy heritage

The world of the cowboy and the Wild West has been preserved in several modern museums dedicated to its memory.

One of the finest collections can be found in the Panhandle-Plains Museum in Canyon, Texas. The T-Anchor Ranch Headquarters, built in 1877 and still intact, is on the museum grounds. Another fine collection is in the Longhorn Museum in Pleasanton, which claims to be "the birthplace of the American cowboy."

Exhibits in this museum document the cowboy and his Indian and Spanish antecedents. San Antonio has not only The Trail Drivers Association, but also the Institute of Texan Cultures, both displaying collections of cowboy – and cowgirl – memorabilia.

The XIT Museum in Dalhart chronicles the history of that famous old ranch, while the National Cowgirl Museum and Hall of Fame in Fort Worth has a collection celebrating women in rodeo.

The Ranching Heritage Center on the campus of Texas Tech University in Lubbock is the home of 20 buildings representing ranch housing from the Spanish days to the large family ranch houses of 1890s cattle barons. Almost any county historical museum in any town in cattle country (South and West Texas) preserves some artifacts from the trail driving and cowboy era.

Lost skills

The visitor looking for working cowboys today is at something of a loss. Modern equipment has made many of the cowboy's traditional jobs obsolete. Contemporary cowboys still using traditional methods, like those on the Kokernot 06 in Hereford, operate in isolation on the back pastures of large ranches. The best ranch to visit is the YO Ranch near Kerrville. Dude ranches in the Bandera area also offer a taste of ranch life. But, all in all, a rodeo is the most accessible form of cowboy life available today.

Beware of imposters

Not all the folks you see strolling around in boots and jeans are cowboys. People who *look* like cowboys may have never even been astride a horse. Cowboy hats, western-cut shirts with pearl snaps, big buckles on tooled leather belts and exotic leather boots are standard fashion for many modern Texans.

Find a fellow who takes things too far by adding a swagger and some big talk to this costume and you have what's popularly referred to as a "drugstore cowboy," or, more facetiously, a "Rexall ranger." He's the cowboy who spends more time at the drugstore lunch counter than he ever does astride a horse. ❑

LEFT: a face of the West at Fort Worth Stock Yards.
RIGHT: fancy cowboy boots – as *not* worn by the trail riders, who preferred plainer, more functional styles.

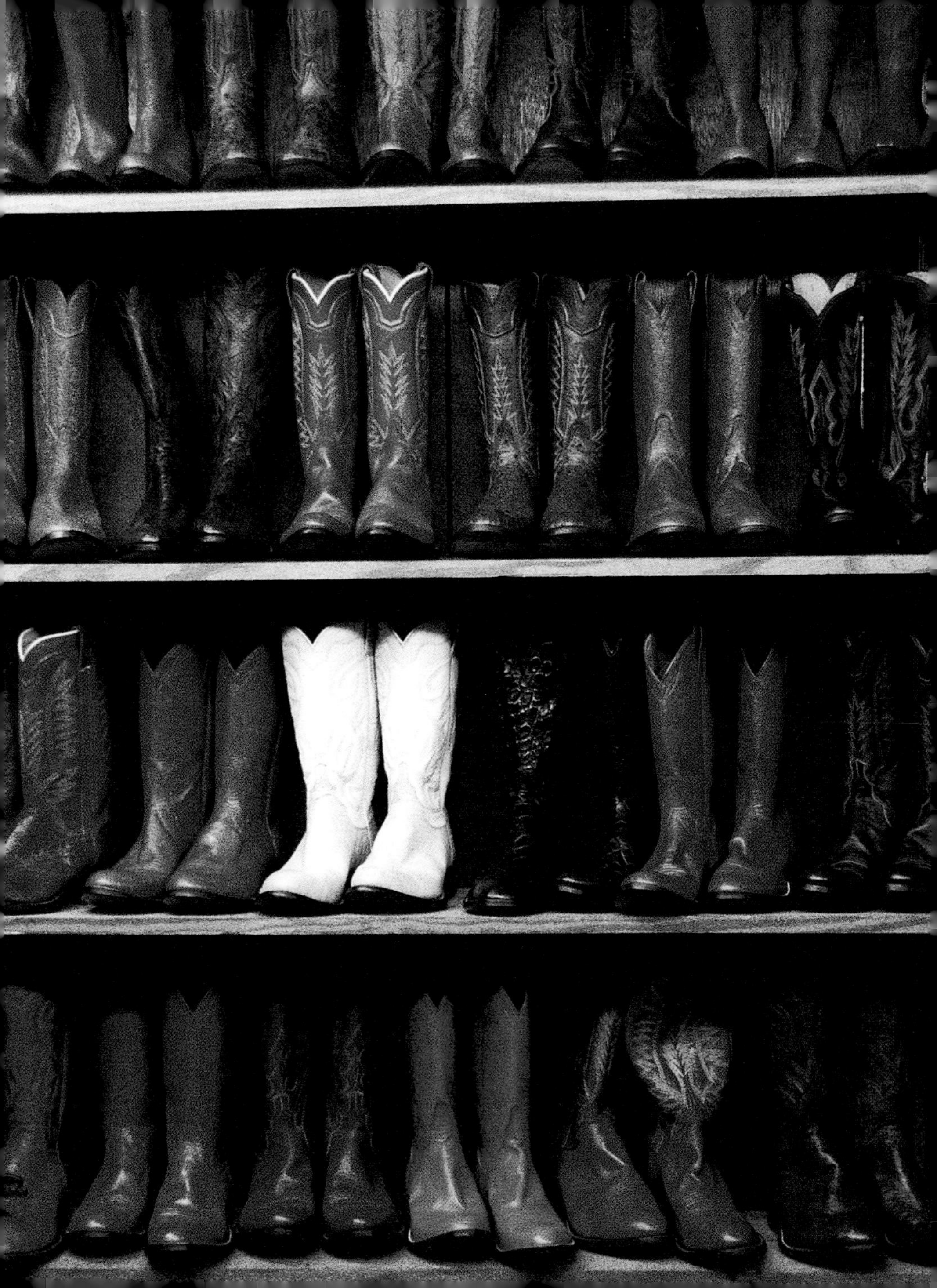

MUSICAL TRADITIONS

From country, blues and folk to conjunto, Western Swing and
good ol' rock 'n' roll – musically, Texas has it all

While Texas is associated in most people's minds with country music, especially cowboy songs, the state has a rich and varied musical tradition to which most of its important immigrant groups, notably the Anglo-Irish, African-Americans, Latinos and Czechs, have contributed. None of these groups existed in a vacuum. The constant cross-fertilization of distinct ethnic sources accounts for both the diversity and the similarity of traditional Texas music.

Home of country

The tendency to think of Texas as the home of country-and-western and cowboy music is understandable. Texans have made some of the most important contributions to the development of country music, from its beginnings in the late 19th century to the present.

When they came to the South, the early Anglo-Irish settlers brought with them a vigorous heritage of folksongs, ballads and fiddle music. In Texas and the surrounding region, unique Southwestern forms soon developed, like the cowboy songs that were documented extensively in the early 20th century by the Texan John A. Lomax, one of America's earliest and most prodigious folk song collectors.

Texans also developed distinctive instrumental styles, like the highly ornamented and fluid Texas fiddle style that can be heard at the many annual fiddle contests. Held throughout the state during the spring and summer, particularly in East Texas where the popular annual gatherings at Crockett and Athens take place, these contests allow fiddlers to display their skills and compete. One of the Texas fiddle style's earliest practitioners, the legendary A.C. Eck Robertson, was also one of the first country musicians to record. In the 1920s, he waxed such classics as *Sally Gooden* and *Brilliancy*.

PRECEDING PAGES: musical parade in Fort Worth.
LEFT: jazz festival at Dallas Museum of Art.
RIGHT: early picture of Texan country music legend Willie Nelson, with Kris Kristofferson.

The continued vitality of country music in Texas is seen in the ongoing popularity of small country-and-western dance halls that are dotted throughout the state and, of course, in the revolving cast of larger nightclubs in the major cities. The 1970s saw the emergence of the Outlaws, led by native Texans Willie Nelson and

Waylon Jennings, who fled the Nashville status quo and reinvented themselves in Austin.

Austin City Limits

The capital of Texas continues to supplement Nashville as the country music capital of the United States.

There is a wide audience for the television series *Austin City Limits*, filmed on the University of Texas campus and aired since 1974 by PBS stations across America. During this time, the widely popular show has featured more than 300 musicians, including virtually every important name in post-war American country and roots music.

Willie Nelson likewise achieved the status of American institution long ago, his weathered visage a national icon, his laconic vocal style and fluid guitar playing still refreshing and instantly recognizable. Nelson is so comfortable on the road that he prefers sleeping in his bus even when it is parked outside a first-class hotel.

FIFTY YEARS OF SWING

Pioneer of Western Swing, Bob Wills was one of Texas' most durable musicians. His career stretched from the 1920s all the way into the 1970s.

Unconventional

While Texas continually generates conventional country stars who succeed in logging the big

Western swing

Perhaps Texas' most original contribution to country music is the musical style known as Western Swing. It was originally developed by Milton Brown and his Musical Brownies, and the Light Crust Doughboys, the latter being one of the longest-running of all Western Swing bands. However, most people agree that the genre was perfected by Bob Wills and his Texas Playboys. Milton Brown's Brownies, with whom Bob Wills played before leaving to start his own

chart hits – including George Jones over three decades ago, and George Strait more recently – it is the iconoclasts who make the most compelling music.

Grandfathered by the *sui generis* rock 'n' roll ancestor Buddy Holly of Lubbock, they make a kind of Texas music that belongs to no one genre while at times sounding like all of them. Joe Ely, Jimmie Dale Gilmore and their favorite songwriter, Butch Hancock, all from Lubbock as well, each have memorable work to their credit and can summon high lonesome poetry on command. From further south, San Antonio-reared Steve Earle became one of the toughest Nashville rockers.

band, might have achieved the stature of Wills and the Playboys had it not been for Brown's untimely death in a car wreck at the beginning of his career in 1936.

While Western Swing drew heavily on the Anglo-American repertoire of folk songs and fiddle music, most groups deployed a small instrumental line-up to achieve a full sound similar to that of the Benny Goodman and Duke Ellington big bands. Wills was one of the few who included brass in his line-up.

Western Swing shares important cross-pollinated traits with African-American, Tex-Mex and Czech music and is still in the repertoire of contemporary groups.

The blues

"Blues came to Texas, lopin' like a mule," sang the famous Texas bluesman Blind Lemon Jefferson. The line has caused some scholars to speculate that the blues may even have originated in Texas. While it is now recognized that the blues developed gradually throughout the southern United States, Texans were certainly indispensable to the style's development.

The blues put the freely structured melodic wail of the field holler (the song of a person laboring alone in the fields) into the densely structured, rhythmic polyphony of the work songs that coordinated the movements of con-

Aaron "T Bone" Walker, went on to become one of the first performers to play blues in a modern style on the electric guitar.

Making a living

Even after national labels began issuing large numbers of "race records" (the industry term for records made by black people) in the 1920s, most performers were unable to make a living from their music. Still others, particularly songsters like Ragtime Henry Thomas, another 1920s recording artist, made a specialty of playing at country dances, picnics and suppers for both blacks and whites. These

vict gangs, and the religious songs that united church congregations. All of these influences can be heard in the work of important early Texas bluesmen like the aforementioned Jefferson and Alger "Texas" Alexander, who both began recording in the 1920s. So did another important progenitor, the guitar evangelist Blind Willie Johnson, whose guitar playing masked the fact that he never recorded a single secular song. Their Texas contemporary,

LEFT: fiddle and guitar – the basis of most Texas music.

ABOVE: the fiddles, guitars and horns of a *mariachi* band performing at San Juan.

songsters featured some blues, but they also sang and played folk songs, ballads, dance pieces and even the popular Tin Pan Alley songs, all of which were the common heritage of black and white Texans. They drew from a tradition that preceded the blues.

The Texas songster tradition persisted into the 1960s and 1970s, when young whites "rediscovered" the blues. Mance Lipscomb, who died at the age of 80 in 1976, was one of these rediscovered African-American songsters. The country blues were also being performed by Sam "Lightnin'" Hopkins (died 1982), a cousin of "Texas" Alexander, and Weldon "Juke Boy" Bonner. Texas' next generation of players, including the late Albert Collins (another cousin of Lightnin' Hopkins), continued to produce exciting electric blues, a tradition kept alive today by Clarence "Gatemouth" Brown and his peers.

From blues to rock

Texas has also been home to younger white artists who draw their inspiration from the blues, a trend which stretches from the late Janis Joplin – who was part of Austin's folk revival scene in the 1960s before moving on to California, where her rapid rise to stardom ended in a tragic death – right through currently

of the 13th Floor Elevators in the 1960s to the avant-punk noise of the Butthole Surfers in the 1980s, with the hard rock of The True Believers, Austin's best 1980s combo, occupying the esthetic middle range. Though all of those bands are now gone, their inheritors can still be found playing urban clubs.

Conjunto

Like their Anglo-American counterparts, the settlers who immigrated to Texas from Mexico brought with them a vast store of folk songs and ballads – or *corridos* – which have been comprehensively documented, largely

popular products of Austin's music scene, notably Lucinda Williams.

Two brothers based in Austin, Jimmie and Stevie Ray Vaughan, amassed an international reputation as electric blues guitarists of the first order, Jimmie with the Fabulous Thunderbirds and Stevie Ray with his Texas Tornadoes, a hugely successful act at the time of his untimely death in 1990. His brother carries on solo.

Also emerging from the blues-rock scene of the 1970s was ZZ Top, for many years one of the strongest and strangest bands in America. This Texas rock tradition deserves special mention as a wellspring of raucous, often bizarre music, stretching from the psychedelic anthems

through the efforts of the late Texas folklorist, Professor Americo Paredes.

Texas-Mexicans were also innovators and helped develop a distinctive Mexican-American dance music called *conjunto*. While the distinguishing feature of conjunto, the accordion, was introduced to Texas-Mexicans by the Germans in the 1840s, by the late 19th century they had developed an accordion style all their own.

Conjunto was not insulated from other ethnic traditions. The early performer Narciso Martinez, whose first recording was released in 1935 and who is sometimes called "the Father of Conjunto Music," even recorded a version of the Bob Wills standard *San Antonio Rose*.

Conjunto has also had an interesting influence on Texas rock 'n' roll, which could be heard through the 1980s in the Tex-Mex rock 'n' roll of the Sir Douglas Quintet, or the frantic *"nuevo wavo"* dance tunes of Joe King Carrasco and the Crowns (actually Tex-Mex rock played fast and loud). Denton's Brave Combo, which debuted in 1980 as a "nuclear polka" band, assimilates conjunto as well as Scandinavian and a little bit of everything else into its infectious, eclectic dance music.

Tejano and Czech

Tejano, a genre of Tex-Mex pop closely related to conjunto, received national attention when its brightest young star, Selena Quintanilla Perez, was killed by a deranged employee in 1996. While a clear successor to Selena has yet to emerge, Tejano's popularity has continued to grow.

Most visitors will be unaware of Texas' long tradition of Czech dance music. Like the conjunto bands, Czech brass bands, such as the famous Baca family, who recorded in the 1920s and 1930s, played polkas predominantly, the two types of music, conjunto and polka, being mutually reinforcing. Czech music in Texas has not attracted as much attention as it deserves.

Clubs and festivals

There are clubs throughout the state that offer fine live music. However, the club scene is volatile, with venues opening and closing, or changing ownership or location, continuously. An Austin club, Antone's, is a good example. It opened at a fourth location in 1997, this time near the 6th Street entertainment district, the latest in over 20 years of on-again off-again existence. Antone's, which seems likely to endure, offers fine blues by both local acts and nationally touring ones.

Texas' annual fiddle competitions and other musical events are usually well-advertised. The Texas Folklife Festival, sponsored every June by the University of Texas Institute of Texan Cultures at San Antonio, offers a fairly comprehensive sampling of authentic traditional Texas music, as well as revival forms.

For folk music fans, the Kerrville Folk Festival in May is mandatory, and every kind of global and regional pop music can be found at Austin's gigantic South By Southwest festival, which overwhelms the capital city every March.

An essay like this can hardly exhaust the many and diverse musical components of Texas culture. The southeastern Gulf Coast, for example, shares a tradition of Cajun (French-Acadian) music with the neighboring state of Louisiana. And other ethnic populations have equally intriguing musical histories, which are well worth discovering. ❑

TEXAS ON DISC

Recordings by most of the artists mentioned here, especially the country-and-western, blues and rock musicians, are readily available. Most record dealers should have them in stock, or will be able to order them. The Folklyric label has issued an excellent 16-album series of Texas-Mexican border music. In addition, in connection with the Bicentennial, the Library of Congress issued a 15-record series, *Folk Music in America*. While these albums contain music of immigrant groups from throughout the United States, they are especially rich in Texas music and contain examples of all the types discussed in this feature.

LEFT: music after Mass at the San José Mission, San Antonio.
RIGHT: the influential Buddy Holly, Lubbock's most famous son.

TEXAN ARCHITECTURE

From adobe huts and primitive log cabins to glistening glass towers, the state's architecture is a fascinating mix of the functional and the inspired

In Texas today, the words "Remember the Alamo" also have a special relevance to Texas architecture. For most of the 20th century, and especially in recent years, a battle has been waged between people who want new Texas architecture to reflect native values and styles and those who want to move beyond regionalism to the very cutting edge of international design.

It's an issue that is not likely to be resolved soon, because, at a deeper level, it is a struggle over the image of Texas itself. The conflict between regional design and international design isn't just about architecture. It's part of an ongoing struggle between rural and urban Texas, between native architects and outsiders, and between the mythical Lone Star State and the real, contradictory, contemporary Texas.

Beginning with adobe

To remember the Alamo in San Antonio is, of course, to remember the Spaniards – Texas' first European settlers. The Spaniards gave architectural life to the creamy white limestone of Central Texas, and introduced skill and efficiency to the simple adobe technique of the Native Americans. Although the late 19th-century Spanish architect, Antonio Gaudí, would have approved of the tribes' method of globbing one handful of mud on top of another to make a wall, the 18th-century Spanish friars taught them to mold heavy, regular adobe bricks in wooden frames.

Adobe, together with wood and stone, was used by the Native Americans, and later the Spaniards, all along the lower Rio Grande river. It was easier to make adobe bricks than to quarry stone, and an adobe wall protected the interior of a house or church from the heat just as well as stone. Not only is adobe sturdy and well-suited to the hot, dry Southwestern cli-

mate, it is a sensuous material that affords all sorts of stylistic features. For instance, because the walls are so thick, all windows have window seats; and because steps and oven hoods are also made of adobe and plastered over, in the same manner as the walls, the interiors have a sculpted all-of-a-piece quality.

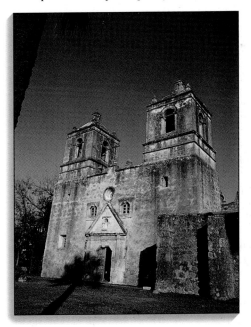

Remember the Alamo

The Spanish missionaries in Texas, used to the Renaissance churches of their homeland, took pains to create an architecture that went beyond function. They wanted their buildings to express beauty in the wilderness. The Alamo is remembered as the bloody place where early Texans sacrificed their lives for freedom, but the building itself, in the heart of downtown San Antonio, is the image of quiet repose. The stone arches and carved niches suggest that the Alamo deserved a different kind of fame. The bell tower and "rose window" of San Antonio's San José Mission are proof that the Spaniards intended not just to survive, but to glorify, too.

PRECEDING PAGES: Town Lake, formed by the Colorado River, in downtown Austin.
LEFT: the Dallas skyline.
RIGHT: Mission Concepción, San Antonio.

Farmhouse style

Such a claim can hardly be made for the early Anglo-American settlers of the 1820s and 1830s. When farmers from Tennessee, Kentucky, Mississippi and Alabama rolled into Texas, they brought with them the only architecture they knew – the plain log house and its cousin, the functional frame house of roughly hewn boards. There was nothing extra in these houses, nothing to make life on the Texas frontier a little sweeter or softer.

And yet, as is often the case with architecture, function led people to design structures that were, if not beautiful, still comfortable in

the landscape. The deep porch offered protection against the sun, the dog or possum "trot" (an open breezeway between two essential rooms or cabins) was used for such things as curing meat and for sleeping outdoors, and the steeply pitched gable roof protected the house from the pounding rain. These features not only eased the hardships of frontier life, they created a simple, graceful, appealing style.

Even the Germans who emigrated to Texas from the 1840s onwards modified their age-old method of building stone and timber *(Fachwerk)* houses in order to incorporate elements of the Anglo farmhouse. Their hewn frameworks were joined with mortise and tenon

joints, secured by wooden pegs. In the 1850s, Frederick Law Olmsted, traveling to San Antonio, slept in New Braunfels in a "small cottage of a single story, having the roof extended so as to form a verandah, with a sign hanging before it, *Guadalupe Hotel, J. Schmitz.*"

Formality and grace

Before the Civil War, most people in Texas did not live in houses as snug and pleasant as those of the Germans in Central Texas. They were only too glad to leave behind their relatively crude houses when life grew easier, and when the classic Greek Revival and later Victorian

styles were brought into the eastern, central and southern parts of the state.

The Greek Revival put classical columns on the porches of even the simplest log houses, and gave a touch of Southern formality and grace to larger buildings. Greek Revival is found in Austin (for instance, in the Governor's Mansion), but it flowered in East Texas. Crockett, Jefferson, Marshall, Tyler and Houston all have charming and varied examples of the Greek Revival, which remained popular into the 1870s when Victoriana became all the rage. The Victorian buildings of Nicholas Clayton of Galveston, and the Richardson-Romanesque courthouses of James Riley Gordon in many of the county seats (look for his buildings in such places as San Antonio, Waxahachie, La Grange, Stephenville, Sulphur Springs, Giddings and New Braunfels) are evidence of the growing influence of gentility. When Texans began to concern themselves with porticoes and turrets, high culture had clearly arrived.

VICTORIAN GENTILITY

One of the most elegant Victorian buildings in Texas, Austin's Driskill Hotel, designed by Frederick E. Ruffini, is still open for business.

Modern Texas

Beaux-arts eclecticism held sway in Texas briefly, just long enough to influence some public and university buildings. The trickle-

Not many skyscrapers were built in Texas in the 1920s and 1930s. The few that did go up, like Houston's Esperson Building, were in the then-popular eclectic style.

Within a period of about 50 years, roughly between 1870 and 1920, domestic architecture in the state was seen to mature. Indeed, wealthy Texans systematically demonstrated that what was fashionable in Paris or London was fashionable in Houston, or even on the ranch. The set for the 1956 film *Giant* (about a Texas rancher and oilman) captured this spirit of

down popularity of the Arts and Crafts Movement in Britain found expression in thousands of Texas bungalows.

During the Great Depression, courthouses and other public buildings were built by government labor. Their blocky, repetitive shapes and flat reliefs in the Art Moderne style make it easy to date such monumental buildings as the Fort Worth City Hall and the distinctive courthouses of Travis, Brazoria and Eastland Counties to this period.

FAR LEFT: ornate column at Rice University, Houston.
LEFT: Bishop's Palace, Galveston.
ABOVE: German-style architecture, Fredericksburg.

brashness, while the movie's Second Empire mansion, silhouetted against endless West Texas ranchland, carried it to absurd limits.

Self-conscious insecurity

Some of the houses in Houston's River Oaks section are only a little less self-conscious. Even when the stylistic adaptations are imaginatively and tastefully handled, and local stone, such as pink granite, has been used, there is often a feeling of insecurity about the homes of newly rich Texans. Sometimes those who made it felt the need to rise above their architectural roots – sullied as they were by poverty, struggle and, not infrequently, illiteracy.

Exterior influences

In the 1920s and 1930s, small groups of architects abroad – in California, New York and
Spring Green, Wisconsin (at Frank Lloyd
Wright's Taliesin compound) – formulated new
ideas about Modern architecture that would
eventually make it acceptable for Texans to
look upon their architectural heritage without
shame. Their new ideas ranged from the
"organic naturalism" of Wright's "Prairie Style"
to the "machines for living" of the Frenchman
Le Corbusier, but all of them respected what
was functional in architecture – and opposed
what was merely applied and decorative. In this

them. Ford's own Trinity University campus in
San Antonio (begun in 1949), a group of brick
buildings that beg comparison with Italian hillside villages, is faithful to the nature of the hilly
Texas landscape. His Johnson City Post Office
(1970) is a modified ranch house of limestone
blocks with a wide front porch and a sloping
roof. His Cowboy Artists of America Museum
in Kerrville (1983) is both a fortress built of
creamy limestone and a gallery of near-forgotten
building techniques. Throughout his life (he
died in 1982), Ford had great influence on
Texas architects. His teachings still form the
basis of the regionalist school of thought.

light, the functional and formal aspects of missions and ranch houses were re-evaluated. If
early Texans had allowed form to "follow"
function out of necessity, a later generation of
Texans made a conscious choice to do so. The
result was the flowering of Texas architecture in
the mid-20th century.

It was at this time that Texas buildings began
to show not contempt, but deference to their
older neighbors. San Antonio architect O'Neil
Ford, who, along with others, became interested in the accurate restoration of Spanish
colonial architecture, taught Texans to respect
the scale and character of indigenous buildings,
and to appreciate the native materials used in

Boxy towers

Ironically, the Modern emphasis on function,
which prepared the way for a new appreciation
of Texas' early buildings, was also responsible
for giving birth to the attitude that the architecture of the past did not stack up well against
the box. When the German Bauhaus architects
sold Americans on their philosophy in the
1940s, cities like New York and San Francisco
began to build boxy skyscrapers.

Texas cities were still young at that time, and
possessed a few fine old buildings and almost
no tradition of urban architecture. Thus, when
cities like Houston and Dallas began to expand,
much of their growth took the logical form of

the Modern glass box. Their new urban buildings delivered a message as honest as that conveyed by the early settlers' houses: unadorned simplicity was still at home in Texas. Later, the boxes were criticised for their brutality.

Early Texas structures were admired for their utility and for their rural beauty, but they certainly didn't influence high-rise architecture in the heyday of the box. A golden sunset reflected by the limestone facades of Central Texas could evoke the memory of Coronado and his search for the Seven Golden Cities; or a lonely wind whistling through a broken windmill near an isolated ranch house could conjure up romantic images of the hard frontier life. But what, after all, did rough-cut limestone blocks or pitched roofs have to do with multi-story, steel-framed buildings?

In the years when the glass box dominated, Houston architecture came into its own. The Tenneco skyscraper (1963), with its exposed steel frame, and One Shell Plaza (1965), with its clean white facades, were as sophisticated and current as any new buildings, anywhere.

Philip Johnson set the stage for his Houston breakthroughs with his Amon Carter Museum in Fort Worth (1960), which has the stately order of a Greek temple. Later, by breaking up the rigidity of the Bauhaus box with the trapezoidal towers of his Pennzoil Place and his round-cornered Post Oak Central buildings (both 1976), Johnson drew international eyes to Texas architecture. The state that was famous for its rugged individualism at last had a Modern architecture that expressed it. Even the more conservative Dallas received oddly shaped, shimmering, reflective glass buildings and a City Hall (dedicated 1978) which broke out of the box completely. I.M. Pei's design, which took the form of an immense triangle balancing on one edge, sent cantilevered floors of offices precariously (it seemed) out over a plaza. O'Neil Ford was outspokenly annoyed by the City Hall, believing its effectiveness depended on playing tricks with the viewer's expectations. It was intentionally unnerving. Ford and his opinions are relevant to the shift in taste in skyscraper design in the early 1980s.

PEI IN THE SKY

Chinese-born architect I(eoh) M(ing) Pei, responsible for some of the most distinctive modern buildings in Texas, is also famous for the Louvre's glass pyramid in Paris.

LEFT: the Kimbell Art Museum, Fort Worth.
ABOVE: Texan architecture flowered in the 20th century with a bold use of color.

Once again, with his Houston skyscrapers, Philip Johnson led the way for developer Gerald Hines, but this time he did more than break out of the box. His designs now referred openly to the architectural styles of the past. His lighthouse-like Transco Tower, with Art Deco setbacks, and his Gothic Republic Bank tower were the world's first postmodern skyscrapers.

And that wasn't all. By sheathing Republic Bank in red granite, Johnson made an oblique reference to Texas' many granite public buildings. His 1983 plan for The Crescent in Dallas (offices, hotel and shopping court), was said to draw inspiration from early Texas architecture.

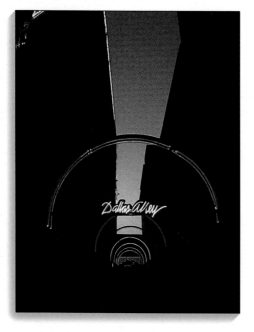

DON'T FORGET THE KIMBELL

Fort Worth's much-admired Kimbell Museum, opened in 1972, draws from the past in subtle ways. Its barrel vaults, which allow light to stream down along interior walls, may recall the silos that architect Louis Kahn admired in the Texas landscape, but this is, at best, conjecture. What makes the Kimbell appropriate to Texas are its strength, tranquility and aura of permanence. It looks back to the years before Texas dressed its buildings up in the styles of the East, beyond the Victorian and Greek Revival periods to the simple, functional early Texas buildings. It is regional in the finest sense of the word. Remember the Alamo, but don't forget the Kimbell.

Suddenly, the regional architecture that pragmatists like O'Neil Ford had championed became popular with postmodern architects, interested in its romantic connotations.

Muddying the waters

A thin sheath of limestone or granite on a steel-framed skyscraper does not, however, make a regionalist building. If anything, it only serves to muddy the water between the opposing regional and international camps. For the most part, regionalist architecture is still practiced by Texas architects on a small scale in rural areas. Many large urban commissions still go to outsiders. In recent years, for instance, the green glass Allied Bank Building, by Skidmore, Owings and Merrill; the steel and glass Four Leaf Towers, by Cesar Pelli; and the silvery granite needle of I.M. Pei's Texas Commerce Bank have been added to Houston's skyline.

Dallas, meanwhile, is becoming somewhat more daring. The designs for new office towers have not been innovative – most go no farther than the now-clichéd sawtooth edge – but things are changing. I.M. Pei has designed two 60-story rockets of glass docked in a water garden downtown, and Philip Johnson plans a postmodern building whose arches allude to the work of the Italian architect Palladio.

The challenge

As Texas keeps growing, its architecture will continue to change. Houston has attracted attention as a center of new architecture by the country's best-known architects. But, in days ahead, the cities to watch may be San Antonio – the controversial library is particularly noticeable – and Austin, where local architects are at last being given important commissions, instead of imported "talent". Already in Austin – a town rich in Victorian structures – one of the new office buildings on Congress Avenue, which leads to the pink granite Capitol, is made of granite from the same quarry and has a gable roof. Several other buildings with early-Texas pretensions are planned or in progress.

The challenge for architects is to keep these buildings honest and original – learning from Texas' past, but anticipating a new Texas. ❏

LEFT: skyline view from Tranquility Park, Houston.
RIGHT: Wise County Courthouse, Decatur, built by James Riley Gordon from pink granite in 1895.

OUR·CONFEDERATE·SOLDIERS

ERECTED BY THE
DAUGHTERS OF THE

IN MEMORIAM
THEIR NAMES BRAVED

PLACES

*A detailed guide to the entire state, with principal sites
clearly cross-referenced by number to the maps*

Texas has it all: sophisticated cities, beautiful beaches, colorful deserts, sleepy border towns, wide open plains and dramatic mountains. In both geography and culture, it is a microcosm of the entire country. Texas contains as much diversity and internal contradictions as any other part of the United States. You'll find wild rodeos and honky-tonks, but also fine museums and elegant restaurants; towering glass skyscrapers and bustling sidewalks, but also quaint Victorian homes and old-time country fairs.

Texas is a place where all sorts of social, economic and geographic boundaries intersect, and each part of the state has a distinct character. You'll notice the influence of the Old South in East Texas, and the vital mix of Mexican and American cultures along the Rio Grande. You'll find that Texans are still struggling with the conflict between rural and urban values, and that there are more "cowboys" walking the streets of Houston or Dallas than there are on the range.

Tours of Texas generally start in the Dallas-Fort Worth Metroplex, two cities that have grown into a single bustling metropolitan area. The Metroplex has been a major business center for years, but recently the cities have made strides in the cultural arena as well. Fort Worth's museum district houses some of the finest collections in the state and the new Dallas Arts District is quickly becoming a hub of culture and entertainment.

To the east, Houston is Texas' largest city, and with its rich ethnic mix, great wealth, exciting architecture and thriving arts community, it is also one of the liveliest. People don't often think of Texas as a coastal state, but Texans have been enjoying the warm breezes, glorious sunshine and brilliant blue waters of the Gulf of Mexico since the early 1900s. America's "Third Coast" has over 300 miles (500 km) of white, powdery beaches, quaint Victorian villages, modern resorts, bustling fishing towns and major ports.

As you travel south, toward the Rio Grande, Texas' Hispanic roots become apparent. San Antonio is the urban capital of Hispanic politics and culture in Texas – as well as the home of the Alamo – but it is in the small towns along the Rio Grande that the Tex-Mex blend of *la frontera* is most distinct.

The scene changes dramatically as you travel west. In Central Texas, the land begins to open up and the towns grow farther apart. In the state's westernmost corner, the plains give way to desert. El Paso, this region's largest city, has more in common with its New Mexican neighbors than it does with its sister cities to the east. ❏

PRECEDING PAGES: Lajitas in the Trans-Pecos region; "El Capitán", Guadalupe Mountains National Park; East Texas lakes. **LEFT:** Denton County Courthouse.

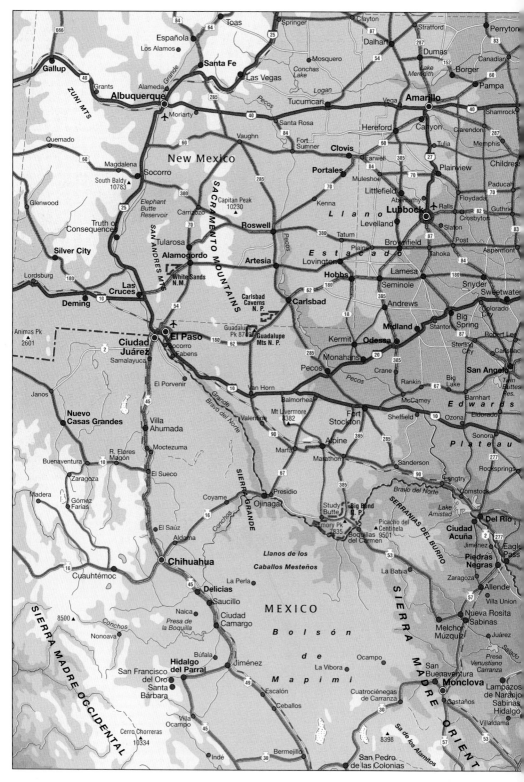

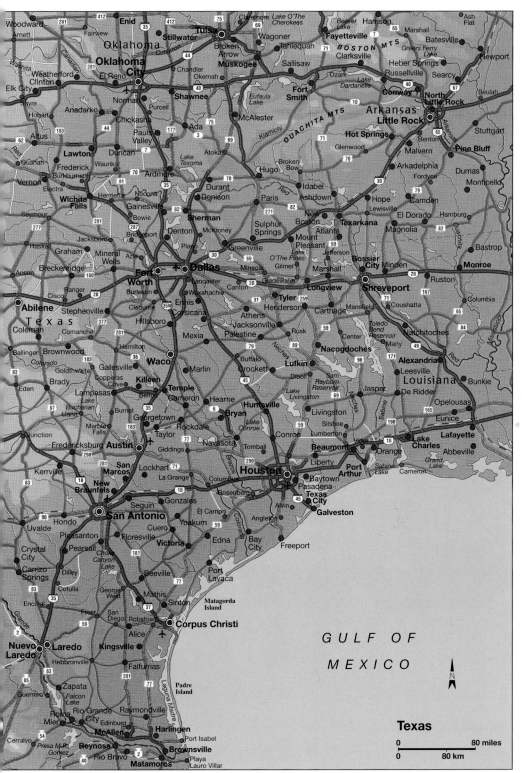

Texas

DALLAS

Map on page 120

The city is a good-living, skyscraper settlement with a penchant for the arts and some of the best shopping in the land, but it remains scarred by the events of November 22, 1963

I t's no accident that the famous television series was called *Dallas* and not, say, *Houston*. Echoing the inter-city rivalry of other places, sophisticated Dallasites are confident about proclaiming their superiority. "Houston? Why would anyone want to go there?", asks a Dallas tourist official with puzzled disdain, an attitude bolstered by her home town's world-class architecture, unrivaled art collections and glittering shopping malls that lure big spenders from around the world.

Downtown

The easiest way to explore downtown Dallas is via the expanding light rail system which runs predominantly on the west side of town. This rail system (DART) shares Union Station with Amtrak and here, beside the Stemmons Freeway in the southwest corner of town, is a good place to begin.

Four stepped, perpendicular glass boxes house the **Hyatt Regency Hotel**, connected to which is the 560-ft (172-meter) **Reunion Tower ❶** (open daily; entrance fee; tel: 214-651-1234). Topped by a geodesic dome with 260 lights, the tower adds a dramatic night-time star to the city's skyline. An observation deck, revolving restaurant and lounge are accessible via fast elevators and the views, understandably, are the best in Dallas. **Reunion Arena**, just to the south, was the home of the Dallas Mavericks basketball team and the Dallas Stars hockey team until they moved to the American Airlines Center in 2001. Reunion Arena is now mostly used for rock concerts and as home base for the Dallas Sidekicks soccer team.

The city began in this area, in the **Cabin of John Neely Bryan ❷** beside the nearby Trinity river, which Bryan mistakenly believed to be navigable for trade all the way to the Gulf of Mexico. An earlier colony, La Reunion, founded by French settlers, had failed, largely because the colonists had been artisans in Europe, not farmers. Bryan, however, survived and lived long enough to welcome, in 1872, the first passengers arriving on the Houston and Texas Central Railroad. This was the beginning of the city's major expansion. Between 1880 and 1890 Dallas' population tripled to 38,000, the mule cars that transported passengers around town were replaced by electric trams, the *Dallas Morning News* began publication, and the forerunner of the annual State Fair of Texas began. Bryan's reconstructed cabin now sits on a grassy sward across from the Old Red Courthouse on Houston Street.

Just east of the Reunion Tower is the city's huge **Convention Center ❸**, flanking a grassy hillside which is home to a herd of longhorns. This exhibit, which shares **Pioneer Plaza ❹** with an ancient cemetery, is the

PRECEDING PAGES: Dallas skyline. **LEFT:** "Big Tex" towers over the Texas State Fair. **BELOW:** Dallas Farmers Market.

world's biggest collection of bronze sculptures. Dozens of longhorns and three cowboys by Texan sculptor Robert Summers sprawl down a realistic cattle trail in a setting enhanced by native plants and a stream that cascades over a miniature limestone cliff. Beyond the Plaza, facing the public library, the futuristically stepped-back **City Hall ❺** is the work of international architect I.M. Pei.

From the Reunion Tower's observation deck, it is easy to be impressed by Dallas' architecture. This tangible display of big-money investment began way back in 1908, when Texas law demanded that every insurance company doing business in the state should keep a substantial part of its assets in Texas. Insurance remains essential to the city's economy, along with banking, merchandising, and, most recently, high technology. For many years Dallas was the world's largest inland cotton market, and all the farmers of North Texas did their banking here. But it was after World War II that the city began its most accelerated growth. Two large aircraft factories were built in the suburbs, and, for a time in the 1950s, Dallas was headquarters for more than 450 oil companies. At least 17

The Pioneer Plaza exhibit covers over 4 acres (1.6 hectares) and pays tribute to the Texas trail-driving days. It was unveiled in 1994.

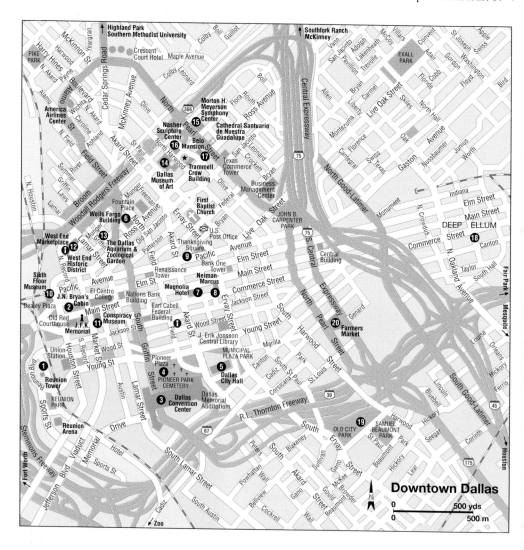

Downtown Dallas

Fortune 500 companies, including Exxon, J.C. Penney, GTE and Kimberly Clark, currently have their headquarters in the Dallas area.

Northeast, on Main Street, is the **Nations Bank Building**, a 72-story giant outlined with 2 miles (3 km) of green neon; while the sharp angles of I.M. Pei's 60-story **Wells Fargo Building** (Field Street and Ross Ave) near Fountain Place, catch one's eye from everywhere in the city. Also distinctive are the octagonal Thanksgiving Tower (Elm and Ervay) and the Texas Commerce Tower (Pearl and San Jacinto), whose slit tower had to be modified to cut down its wind tunnel effect. Almost hidden by the huge behemoths surrounding it is Pegasus, the flying red horse trademark (reconstructed in 1999) atop the **Magnolia Hotel** ❼ (formerly Magnolia Petroleum) at Main and Akard streets. This was the tallest building in the South when it went up in 1922. Behind it, at Main and Ervay, is the **Neiman-Marcus** ❽ department store and, two blocks north, close to the light-rail line, is **Thanksgiving Square** ❾. This tranquil oasis, by architects Philip Johnson and John Burgee, incorporates a spiral-shaped chapel with stained-glass ceiling, a reflecting pool, waterfalls, a copse of sweet gum trees and a tower with bells. In the square is one of the entrances to Dallas' **Underground City** – 3 miles (5 km) of subterranean shops and restaurants.

"Big Tex" – mascot of the Texas State Fair – personified.

JFK Memorial

The liveliest area to walk around is just north of the Reunion Tower: the **West End**. With many of the city's oldest buildings restored as shops and cafés, the area is filled with arts and crafts, pushcart traders, clubs and boutiques. If walking is too much trouble, visitors can take horse-drawn carriage rides around the area.

Head up Houston Street, past the unmistakable Old Red Courthouse (behind which, at Main and Market, is the simple **John F. Kennedy Memorial**, designed by Philip Johnson), and ahead on the left is the most-visited site in Dallas: the former Texas School Book Depository building, from which Lee Harvey Oswald shot President Kennedy. Here, the **Sixth Floor Museum** ❿ (open daily; entrance fee; tel: 214-747-6660) overlooks Dealey Plaza, through which the President was riding in a motorcade on November 22 1963 when he was assassinated. Oswald – later arrested and murdered on live television while in police custody – fired the fatal shots from a corner window on the building's sixth floor, a site roped off in the museum.

Don't underestimate the time needed to see the museum: it is immensely interesting (and moving), and, to the uninitiated, serves as a quick course about a significant era in US history. Among the messages in the visitors' book is one from a child who observed it was the first time he had seen his father cry. The museum, which gets an average of 1,000 visitors each day, houses exhibits about JFK's campaign; his social and economic programs; the space race; and the "Red Threat". Reproductions of newspaper stories from around the world are on show, including the full-page advert in the *Dallas Morning News* on the day of his visit to the city, in which his right-wing enemies accused him of communist sympathies. Cameras used by spectators watching the motorcade can be seen, as can the famous Zapruder

BELOW: President John F Kennedy remembered.

camera and some of the footage it recorded of the assassination. A videotape of the dramatic events of that day includes a tearful Walter Cronkite announcing the President's death.

Conspiracy theories

President John F. Kennedy was on his way to make a speech at the Dallas World Trade Center when he was assassinated. The shots rang out at 12.30pm; the President was pronounced dead in hospital at 1pm.

Kennedy's assassination understandably spawned endless speculation about who was to blame, with the skeptics ranging from those who felt that Oswald had been a patsy for the Cubans, or the Mafia, to dyed-in-the-wool conspiracy theorists who believed it to be the latest chapter in a chain of events masterminded by unspecified secret forces. Despite the conclusions of four major investigations into the crime, almost four out of five Americans believe that the killing was the result of a conspiracy.

Opposite the Kennedy Memorial, at 110 Market Street, **The Conspiracy Museum ⓫** (open daily; entrance fee; tel: 214-741-3040) serves as a focus for all who reject the findings of the Warren Commission, which named Oswald as the sole assassin. "We just want people to think", says museum director Tom Bowden. "Maybe that way we can correct the textbooks so that they contain information about the larger conspiracy."

BELOW: the building from which JFK was assassinated.

The West End continues north of the DART rail line, whose station at Pacific and Lamar (shared with a bus transfer station) is almost surrounded by parking lots, which accommodate visitors to the neighboring streets. Here bars, saloons, restaurants and cafés keep pedestrian traffic constantly on the move. Crowds are always gathered on the steps outside the **West End Marketplace ⓬** (open daily), inside which are cinemas, nightclubs and outlets for Western clothing, holographic gifts and Texan wine, plus eating places of all kinds.

Map on page 120

Bringing new business to the West End is the striking **American Airlines Center** (2500 Victory; tel: 214-665-4797), a state-of-the-art sports stadium that has superseded the Reunion Arena as the home of the major sports franchises. Designed by architect David Schwarz in retro style, with Art Deco touches, it was built at a cost of $420 million on an old railway yard and opened, with a concert by the Eagles, in July 2001. New transport links all around have revitalised the area.

Another recent development in the area is the **Dallas World Aquarium & Zoological Garden ⓭** (1801 N. Griffin; open daily; entrance fee; tel: 214-720-2224). Two once-derelict warehouses now house this extremely popular attraction, which opened in 1992 and was expanded in 1996. It is home to the world's largest freshwater aquarium, containing manatees, turtles, giant catfish and more, plus a saltwater aquarium with rays and sea turtles among its inmates. The other major draw here is a South American rainforest, featuring exotic plants and wildlife, from toucans and sloths to monkeys and crocodiles, along its jungle walkway.

Culture District and Uptown

One block northeast of the distinctively shaped Fountain Place is the **Dallas Museum of Art (DMA) ⓮**, designed by Edward Larabee Barnes (1717 N. Harwood; closed Mon; entrance fee; tel: 214-922-1200). Its collection is impressive: there are American artifacts dating from the pre-Columbian and Spanish eras; Greek and Roman antiquities; a model of a boat from the Egyptian Middle Kingdom, *circa* 2000 BC; a magnificent Hindu shrine of silver and wood; plus 18th-century Gilbert Stuart and Copley portraits, 19th-century landscapes, and works by Toulouse-Lautrec, Léger, Picasso, Mary Cassatt, Georgia O'Keefe, Giacometti, Edward Hopper, Andrew Wyeth and the Modernists. One room

TIP

Note that it is not the custom to hail taxis in Dallas. Cabs should be requested by telephone.

BELOW: Dallas skyline at sunrise.

alone includes millions of dollars' worth of art by Courbet, Boudin, Pissarro, Degas, Cézanne, Monet, Rodin, Van Gogh and Vuillard. Contemporary artists represented include Pollock, Rothko, Stella and Warhol.

Between the DMA and the **Morton H. Meyerson Symphony Center** 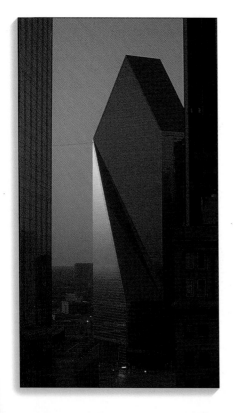 (financed by Meyerson's friend Ross Perot, the billionaire founder of Electronic Data Systems who garnered 19 percent of the vote when running for president in 1992) is the **Nasher Sculpture Center** ⑯ (entrance fee; tel: 214-891-8570). Scheduled to open in late 2003, the $50 million building designed by Renzo Piano will house more than 300 modern works. Adjacent stands the **Trammell Crow Building** surrounded by a score of valuable sculptures, including Rodin bronzes, and displays a collection of Asian art. Note the enormous Ellsworth Kelly painting in the building's east lobby and the 68-ton (62-metric ton) steel sculpture by Eduardo Chillada, which was requested by the building's architect, I.M. Pei. In front of the building, and flanked by the 1898 Cathedral Santuario de Nuestra Guadalupe, is **Artists' Square**, a venue for craft shows, with a stage for concerts and cultural events.

Uptown begins on the other side of the freeway. At Olive and Ross, **Belo Mansion** ⑰, a building now housing the Dallas Bar Association, was, in 1932, the funeral home where the body of Clyde Barrow once lay. The 25-year-old bank robber and his companion, 23-year-old Dallas-born Bonnie Parker, were both shot dead driving down a Louisiana country road. Their four-year crime spree had earned them headlines throughout the country. The gas station at 1620 Eagle Ford Road, built by Clyde's father, has been replaced with a new structure, but the Barrow house behind it still stands.

To head into northern Dallas, take one of the venerable 90-year-old streetcars (with velvet seats and stained-glass windows) that start from outside the DMA and run along bustling, brick-tiled **McKinney Avenue**, which is lined with restaurants, boutiques and galleries.

Northern Dallas

Visitors come from all over the US to shop in Dallas and, of course, thousands of locals spend countless hours in the malls that continue to spring up, largely in the northern part of the city. The very first was **Highland Park Village**, a pseudo-Colonial complex with outdoor cafés, an old-fashioned pharmacy and an old theater now converted into a cinema. It was designed by William David Cook, who also designed Beverly Hills, and it is America's oldest shopping center. It abuts the west side of I-75 north of downtown, and is easily accessible on the DART, which continues north to connect with a local trolley car in another shopping area, the prestigious **NorthPark Center**.

The **Biblical Arts Center** (7500 Park Lane at Boedeker; closed Mon; Sun pm only; free; tel: 214-691-4661), just north of University Park, was founded by the late Mattie Carruth Byrd. Its buildings resemble those of the early Christians and it houses a collection of art, ancient and modern. There is also an impressive 30-minute light and sound presentation (entrance fee) of the immense *Miracle at Pentecost* mural, which contains 200 Biblical characters.

The multi-million dollar Morton H. Meyerson Symphony Center is home to the Dallas Symphony Orchestra, rated one of the finest orchestras in the US.

BELOW: Fountain Place skyscraper.

The only theater ever built to a design by Frank Lloyd Wright, Dallas Theater Center's **Kalita Humphreys Theater** is on Turtle Creek Boulevard. In the same district is the most expensive institution of higher learning in Texas, **Southern Methodist University** (SMU). One of its benefactors was the late Algur H. Meadows, an oil magnate who in middle age began using his large fortune to build up a private art collection. He was aggrieved to discover that he was the owner of a number of Spanish School paintings wrongly attributed to masters, and that many of his supposed Braques, Picassos and Modiglianis were in fact counterfeits by the Hungarian master forger Elmyr de Hory. Meadows righted his collection with the help of an art historian and kindly donated it to the university. The hundred or so Spanish paintings now displayed at SMU's **Meadows Museum** (5900 Bishop Boulevard; closed Wed; Sun pm only; free; tel: 214-768-2516), by such masters as Murillo, Velasquez, Goya and Miró, are all of unquestioned authenticity.

Opulent hotels and homes

Dallas has some world-famous hotels, among which is the **Mansion on Turtle Creek** and the less well-known **Crescent Court** nearby. The latter, which is more "public", is so opulent that even the house cats live in their own designer "mini hotel" in the grounds. Turtle Creek has some of the classiest homes in the city, as does Mockingbird Lane which heads west from Highland Park to Love Field. Further north, but harder to reach without a car, is the upscale **Galleria** (LBJ Freeway and Dallas Parkway; tel: 972-702-7100), modeled after a prototype in Milan and housing a Westin hotel, 28 restaurants, 200 celebrated shops and an ice rink.

Between the small Love Field airport and Dallas/Fort Worth International

Map on page 120

TIP

A popular attraction in Las Colinas is the spectacular Flower Clock, at the junction of State Route 114 and O'Connor Road. The beds are refreshed no less than eight times a year.

BELOW: West End Historic District.

Neiman-Marcus

The Dallas-based Neiman-Marcus depart-ment store, world-renowned for its Christmas Book offering such "His and Her" gift suggestions as $1,600 mummy cases or pairs of matched camels ($16,000), prides itself on unstinting service. At the request of one customer, for example, the store discreetly investigated Queen Eliza-beth's stocking size so that she could be sent a pair of nylons.

Customers were made and kept, Stanley Marcus once explained, "by (the) ability to remember small details, such as anniversary dates... a promise to get a certain evening bag for a specific social occasion... a promise that the dress bought for a girlfriend would be billed to the Mr and not the Mrs account." This was not trivia: "... it's what specialty store retailing is all about."

Stanley, one of the sons of co-founder Carrie Marcus, has been probably the most responsible for the developing the store's

modern image, but Neiman-Marcus – now a chain with outlets in 32 US locations – was a success from the its start in 1907. Soon after that, Nebraska-born Al Neiman teamed up with (and married) Kentucky-born Carrie Marcus who, aged 21, had already proved herself to be the most suc-cessful saleswoman at the Dallas depart-ment store A. Harris & Co.

Together with Carrie's brother, Herbert, the trio set up a sales promotion business in Atlanta which was so successful that they sold the company from the Missouri franchise for a new bottled drink, Coca Cola. It became a family joke down through the years that Neiman-Marcus was founded on a bad busi-ness judgment.

They soon set up their Neiman-Marcus store in central Dallas. Neiman, the flam-boyant and egotistical buyer, traveled regu-larly between Dallas and New York City, acquiring clothes and constantly clashing with his partners over style and design. In the 1920s, Herbert bought him out for $250,000 and the Neiman marriage broke up at the same time.

At first, the store's wealthier clientele was, to a large extent, the state's cotton aristocracy but, just after the Great Depres-sion began (as the store was completing a major expansion), oil was discovered in East Texas. This produced a new group of mil-lionaires who soon became Neiman-Marcus customers.

In a history of American department stores, published in 1979, author Robert Hendrickson wrote that Neiman-Marcus oper-ated on the premise that "if we can please the 5 percent of our customers who are the most discriminating we will never have any difficulty in satisfying the other 95 percent who are less critical."

Certainly the 3 million recipients of the store's Christmas Book seem satisfied. Eight customers, for example, splashed out on the $11,200 Chinese junks offered one year. One page of the catalog is devoted to "How to Spend a Million Dollars at Neiman-Marcus," although other pages offer gifts for $25 and under. ❏

LEFT: the world-famous Neiman-Marcus department store.

Airport is the fast-growing area of **Las Colinas**. Here, gleaming corporate head-quarters are surrounded by acres of wide-open spaces and some upscale housing, set beside a winding, artifical lake called the Mandalay Canal. Part of the canal is lined wih a tree-dotted walkway of restaurants and boutiques. A Venetian-style water taxi cruises the water, facing part of which is Williams Square, on O'Connor Road, in which a group of nine oversized bronze mustangs, sculpted by Robert Glen, gallop across a stream. A short film about the work of Nairobi-born Glen is shown in the adjoining **Mustang Sculpture Exhibit** (Tue–Sat; free; tel: 972-869-9047).

Another Las Colinas attraction is the **Dallas Communications Complex** (6301 N. O'Connor Road), which, as well as a communications museum, houses a highly active movie studio where such films as *Silkwood*, *RoboCop* and *JFK* were filmed. Visitors taking a tour here (closed Sun; entrance fee; tel: 972-869-FILM) can inspect movie sets and props, watch a show explaining special effects and visit a museum that includes such artifacts as a Superman suit, Judy Garland's dress from the *The Wizard of Oz* and the costumes worn in *The Sound of Music*.

Las Colinas is but one section of the thriving town of **Irving** (pop. 191,000), irrevocably associated with the Dallas Cowboys football team, who play in the Texas Stadium (2401 E. Airport Freeway, just east of the University of Dallas). Irving Arts Center (3333 N. MacArthur Boulevard; tel: 972-252-7558) is an active cultural focus the year around and draws visitors from throughout the region for its symphony concerts, dance performances, puppet theater, plays and gospel events. Its sculpture garden features the work of Texan artists. Irving's downtown **Main Street**, lined with quaint shops and a drugstore complete with old-fashioned soda fountain, has been revitalized. In addition, its 1920s railroad station in **Heritage Park** has been restored, along with its primitive tele-type machine.

The big Ferris wheel at Dallas' Fair Park.

Midway between the two major cities, the Dallas/Forth Worth International Airport has been growing at a phenomenal rate and will soon be the world's busiest, according to a prediction by the Federal Aviation Administration. Covering 30 sq. miles (78 sq. km) – larger than Manhattan Island – with seven runways, it could contain the main airports of New York, Los Angeles and Chicago combined. American Airlines maintains its headquarters in Dallas and runs its own museum, named after its founder, **C.R. Smith** (near the airport at 4601 Highway 360; closed Mon; Sun pm only; free; tel: 817-967-1560).

BELOW: the Mustangs of Las Colinas.

Deep Ellum

Running almost parallel to the northbound loop of the DART, a few blocks east of Highland Park, is Greenville Avenue, whose lower end is jammed with hip bars, dance clubs and pool halls. It's the area to find ethnic restaurants of all kinds, although **Deep Ellum ⑱**, further to the south, offers a more concentrated experience (drive or take a taxi down Elm Street from midtown). Deep Ellum, which comes alive late at night, has been renowned for its blues and jazz clubs since the 1920s. It was here that famous Texan bluesmen like Blind Lemon Jefferson and Huddie "Leadbelly" Leadbetter began their careers, and today

it is also the home of artists, unusual shops and some of the city's best restaurants. The 12-block area, which housed a community of freed slaves after the Civil War, has always attracted the avant garde and owes its current revival to the "outlaw parties" in renovated warehouses that a group of musicians organized in the 1980s. Clubs began to open up, followed by art galleries, funky shops and eating spots. Stop by the **Main Street Brewery** (2656 Main Street) to watch beer being made.

Across I-30 from Deep Ellum is **Fair Park**, site of the 1936 Texas Centennial Exposition, which celebrated the battle at which Texans won their independence from Mexico. Every autumn here, the largest talking dummy in existence, Big Tex, greets visitors to the State Fair of Texas.

The park is also home to the largest collection of Art Deco buildings in the country. Included among the attractions are the **Texas Hall of State Ⓐ** (closed Mon; pm only Sun; free; tel: 214-421-4500), complete with mammoth murals and statues of heroes; the 68,000-seat **Cotton Bowl Stadium Ⓑ** (tel: 214-939-2222); the **Dallas Aquarium Ⓒ** (open daily; entrance fee; tel: 214-670-8443), with sharks, piranhas and 5,000 other water-loving creatures; an amusement park dominated by what is probably the country's biggest Ferris wheel, and several theaters. Next to the park's band shell, pleasant gardens and a conservatory make up the **Texas Discovery Gardens Ⓓ** (closed Mon; Sun pm only; entrance fee; tel: 214-428-7476), which includes a collection of plants indigenous to Texas.

Fair Park also has seven museums. **The Science Place Ⓔ** (open daily late Aug–late May; entrance fee; tel: 214-428-5555) features an IMAX Theater and has hands-on exhibits for the whole family, including an active cutaway beehive and a car that gets progressively drunker to demonstrate the dangers of drink dri-

Larry Hagman as sleazy oil executive J.R. Ewing in the TV series Dallas*, set at "Southfork Ranch" just outside the city.*

BELOW: West End Cattle Drive.

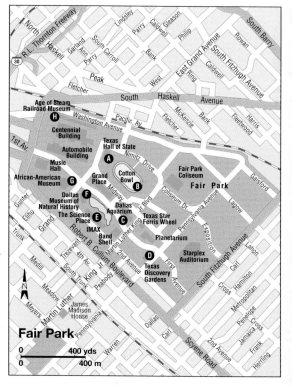

Fair Park

Maps:
City 120
Park 128

ving. Also worth visiting are the **Dallas Museum of Natural History** ❼ (open daily; entrance fee; tel: 214-421-3466), the **African-American Museum** ❽ (closed Mon; Tues–Fri and Sun pm only; free; tel: 214-565-9026), and the **Age of Steam Railroad Museum** ❾ (open Wed–Sun; entrance fee; tel: 214-285-8777).

East of Fair Park is the little community of **Mesquite**, which stages a rodeo every Friday and Saturday evening between April and September. Here, you can eat Texas barbecue and watch champion cowboys compete at roping, steer wrestling and bareback riding (for information tel: 972-222-2855).

Heading south

Interesting sites in the southern part of town include the **Dallas Zoo** (650 S.R.L. Thornton Freeway; open daily; entrance fee; tel: 214-670-5656), which offers a 20-minute narrated monorail safari through half a dozen African habitats. Also here is **Old City Park** ❿ (1717 Gano Street; closed Mon; pm only Sun; entrance fee; tel: 214-421-5141), which has a collection of century-old buildings and a Victorian bandstand on its village green. Nearby is the enormous **Farmers Market** ⓴ (1010 S. Pearl Street; open daily), one of the largest surviving fresh produce markets in the US.

Out of town

The television series *Dallas*, which first ran from 1978 to 1991, probably did more to spread the city's fame than anything else, even if the image of greedy oilmen and dysfunctional families was not exactly what the city fathers might have chosen. It made the **Southfork Ranch** (open daily; entrance fee; tel: 972-442-7800), half an hour's drive north of downtown via I-75 (take the Renner Road exit), where the Ewing clan supposedly lived, familiar to viewers in around 100 countries. Today, more than a decade after the series ended, Southfork remains the area's major tourist attraction. The family who lived there was forced to move out by the hordes of tourists, and the ranch has now become a popular location for events such as weddings and private rodeos. Tours start from J.R.'s Den.

McKinney, a historic county seat 20 miles (32 km) northeast of Dallas, is a fine example of a small town (pop. 54,000), with numerous Victorian houses, that has worked hard at retaining its old-time flavor. Victorian and Greek Revival houses around Chestnut Square, dating back to 1853, are furnished in period style and can be toured (Tue, Thur and Sat 11am; no tours August; entrance fee; tel: 972-562-8790).

In the sleepy center of town, many old buildings – with their tin ceilings preserved – have been refurbished as shops selling arts and crafts. On Kentucky Street, the Collin County Jail (1880), popular with moviemakers, once housed Frank James of the infamous James gang.

The **Heard Natural Science Museum** (open daily; pm only Sun; tel: 972-562-5566) pays tribute to its founder, Bessie Heard (1884–1988), scion of a venerable local family, meticulously documenting her life. The museum sits in a 287-acre (116-hectare) wildlife sanctuary with trails, a garden and a picnic area. ❑

BELOW: museum browsing in Dallas.

FORT WORTH

*From cowtown to cultural and commercial center:
Fort Worth has become a modern, sophisticated city but has
never forgotten its dusty, cattle-trading roots*

Map
on page
132

Fort Worth, which began life as a bastion against rampaging Comanche Indians, spent its first half century as a rough and tumble frontier town, dusty and lawless. The bad guys were quick to take advantage of the situation, and the area became a haven for bandits, outlaws and military deserters. One neighborhood famous for its notorious residents – including bank robbers Butch Cassidy (George Parker) and the Sundance Kid (Harry Longabaugh) – was known as Hell's Half Acre, until its destruction in the early 1900s.

What brought international fame and fortune to what had been just another dusty Western backwater, however, was the longhorn steer. By 1870, large numbers of cowboys had begun to take their rest and pleasure in Fort Worth as they drove great herds of longhorns along the Chisholm Trail from the South Texas ranches to railheads in Kansas. In Fort Worth, the trail's last major stop, they bathed, drank, gambled and whored to forget their arduous, lonely and monotonous trail-driving. After resting and having provisioned themselves, the cowboys went on their way with thousands of cattle, through dust or mud.

With the arrival of the Texas and Pacific Railroad in 1876, hundreds of miles were cut off the cattle drives, and eight lines eventually connected Fort Worth with northern markets. The cattle were, of course, the worse for wear – and thinner – for every mile they traveled, thus cattle freighted from Fort Worth were in much better condition than they would have been had they struggled all the way to Kansas. Acres of pens were built to receive the herds, which were fattened up before transportation.

Attendant industries such as meat-packing – the Armour and Swift companies became major players – developed here and remained Fort Worth's most important source of income through the 1920s. However, just as improvements in transportation had brought the cattle business to Fort Worth, further improvements took part of it away. Larger trucks and better highways made centralized marketing and fattening of cattle unnecessary. Cattlemen could fatten and auction herds locally, for truck delivery.

The Stockyards

Today, Fort Worth's **Stockyards National Historical District Ⓐ**, its streets cobbled and gaslit, looks much as it did a century ago. The cattle pens have been restored and Exchange Street is lined with the shops of artisans hand-crafting saddles, chaps and boots. Even today, in this sleek, modern city, one might still see a Stetson-wearing businessman, or a lawman on horseback.

At the famous **White Elephant Saloon** (tel: 817-624-1887), noted for its bullet-splintered floorboards,

LEFT: western festival, Fort Worth Stockyards.
BELOW: no-nonsense advertising.

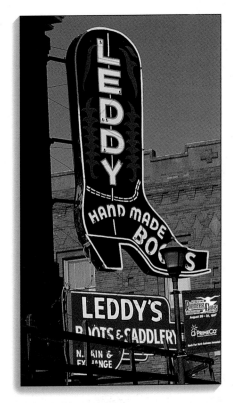

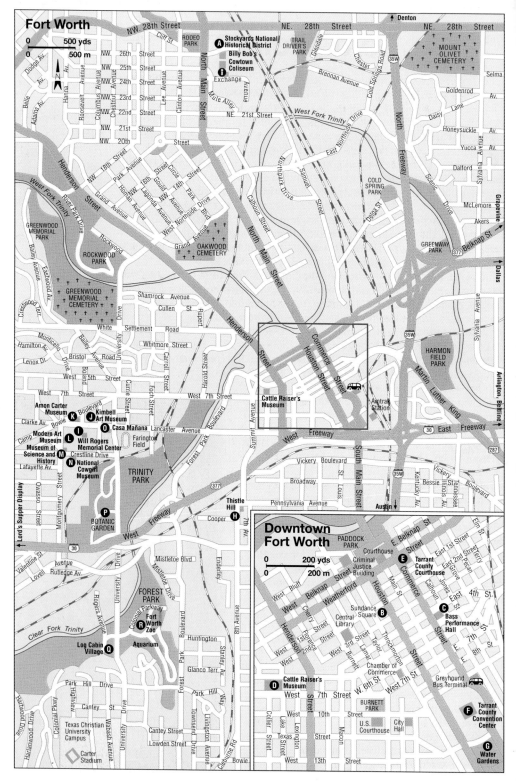

there's nightly country and western music, and the notorious 1887 gunfight between owner Luke Short and former marshall Jim Courtright is re-enacted on February 8 each year. The **Stockyards Hotel** (where Bonnie and Clyde once stayed) has been decorated in "cattle baron baroque," its saloon bar stools sporting saddles, while the mission-style **Cowtown Coliseum** (121 E. Exchange, tel: 817-625-1025), which since 1908 has featured performers as varied as Enrico Caruso and Elvis Presley, offers weekly rodeos. The world's first indoor rodeo was held here in 1918. Even the 6,000-capacity **Billy Bob's Texas** (tel: 817-624-7117), which describes itself as "the world's largest honky-tonk," has live bulls posturing in its indoor ring, inviting visitors to see how long they can stay aboard the pesky critters.

Next to the old hog and sheep pens (now housing art galleries, shops and eating places), the restored **Tarantula steam train** (tel: 817-625-RAIL), pulled by its 1896 engine, has resumed trips (Fri–Sun; diesel replacement Wed and Thur) to the little town of Grapevine (see page 139), 21 miles (34 km) northeast. Up on the hill, the old Swift meat-packing plant is decorated with early 20th-century antiques and houses an Italian restaurant.

This way for bronco bustin'!

Livestock auctions are still held weekly in Fort Worth and, in keeping with modern technology, entire herds of cattle are bought and sold via satellite communications. The city has also profited from the West Texas oil boom and serves as base for many oil companies.

Although the size of sprawling Fort Worth (pop. 504,000) makes it a bit of a problem to negotiate without a car, it has only two other major areas that draw most visitors – the historic downtown area, 2 miles (3 km) to the southeast of the Stockyards, and the Cultural District, a mile or two west of that. The three areas make up what is termed a "Western Triangle" and, sensibly, the city runs a shuttle between them.

BELOW: Fort Worth Live Stock Exchange, Fort Worth Stockyards.

Downtown

At the heart of downtown, **Sundance Square ❸**, between 2nd and 5th streets at Throckmorton, is especially lively at night, with crowded bars and clubs, and musicians entertaining the patrons of packed sidewalk cafés. In the old days, when rowdy cattlemen came here to celebrate, they were sometimes amused by a tightrope walker negotiating the wire between the Plaza Hotel and the Adelphi Theater across the street. Here at 309 Main Street, adjoining the 1908 hotel, long ago converted into offices, is the **Sid Richardson Collection of Western Art** (closed Mon; Sun pm only; free; tel: 817-332-6554), a permanent collection acquired by the late oilman. At one time, Richardson, who died in 1959 aged 67, owned 125 producing oil wells. His nephew, Perry Bass, and his sons acquired 38 square blocks of downtown after inheriting the Richardson fortune, and the Bass family – unsurprisingly among the nation's wealthiest individuals – have been major local philanthropists.

Surrounded by the collection's 56 paintings, primarily by Frederic Remington and Charles M. Russell, is a magnificent, silver-studded saddle by Ed Bohlin, given to Richardson by his close friend and

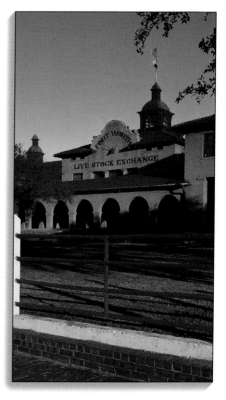

Cowboy's lariat.

fellow oilman Amon Carter. Almost everybody who's watched a Western movie has seen some of the art of Ed Bohlin, the Swedish-born farmer who migrated to the US with the dream of becoming a cowboy. He was commissioned by Buffalo Bill Cody to repair leather harnesses used in his traveling show, and then moved to Hollywood to create saddles, holsters and other leather tack for the studios. Among his customers were Roy Rogers, Tex Ritter, Gary Cooper, the Cisco Kid (Duncan Renaldo) and John Wayne, who habitually donned a Bohlin-made gunbelt and silver hatband.

The **Bass Performance Hall** ⦿ (4th and Calhoun streets, tel: 817-212-4325), home of the city's symphony orchestra, ballet and opera companies, is an awesome masterpiece designed by the Washington architect David M. Schwarz and completed in 1998. It is hoped that the 2,000-seat hall will last 300 years – as long as some of its European counterparts: "Great concert halls," Schwarz muses, "are symbols of an age. If they're done well they reflect a great moment in history." Surmounted by Hungarian sculptor Márton Váró's gigantic granite angels, blowing 6-ft (2-meter) trumpets, this hall is also noted for such extravagant decorative features as the cloud-filled, 80-ft (25-meter) wide Great Dome, which soars high above the auditorium. This, and the hall's other artwork, was the creation of Scott and Stuart Gentling.

Sundance Square is backdropped by the block-long (and very luxurious) Worthington Hotel, which is convenient to everything downtown, including Outlet Square, a vast indoor mall to which it is connected by a mezzanine passageway. This enables guests to bypass the scorching streets. A huge mural flanks the parking lot on 3rd Street: a three-story *trompe l'oeil* by Richard Haas of cowboys and longhorns on the Chisholm Trail.

BELOW: camaraderie in Fort Worth.

Map on page 132

Raising cattle and falling water

Famous branding irons and "a talking longhorn" can be inspected in the **Cattle Raiser's Museum ❶** (1301 W. 7th Street; open daily; entrance fee; tel: 817-332-8551). One exhibit here explains the importance of the brand inspector in the never-ending fight against rustlers.

At one end of what was once Hell's Half Acre, not far from the history exhibits in the newly refurbished Fire Station No. 1 (2nd and Commerce streets; open daily; free), is the **Tarrant County Courthouse ❺** (100 E. Weatherford), dating from the late 1900s. At the other end is the **Fort Worth/Tarrant County Convention Center ❻**, between Houston and Commerce. Opposite are the delightful **Water Gardens ❼** at Commerce and 15th streets, created by architect Philip Johnson and his associate, John Burgee, and imitated all over the country. Slabs are tipped at delicate angles to carry, direct, or stop water that is swirling, falling, sprinkling, or lying still. Adventurous souls negotiate the 38 steps to the pools at the bottom, while others watch from above. Most take photographs of their friends surrounded by pouring, pounding water. The effects sought are not intended to rival nature – rather, it brings to mind leaking dams, or streams of industrial coolant in flow to prevent meltdown.

One of the most remarkable features of the Kimbell Art Museum is the clever use of natural light, which allows exhibits to be seen to their best advantage.

Cultural District

The third region of the city's Western Triangle, the Cultural District, is 1½ miles (2 km) west of downtown. Roughly halfway between the two areas can be found **Thistle Hill ❽** (tours Mon–Fri and Sun pm; entrance fee; tel: 817-336-1212), an imposing example of a cattle baron's mansion dating from the turn of the 20th century. Cattleman W.T. Waggoner began building the house at 1509 Pennsylvania Avenue for his daughter in 1903, and another cattleman, Winfield Scott (one-time owner of the Plaza Hotel), completed it in 1910. The landscaped grounds are as interesting as the house restoration, which contains period furnishings and original pieces.

Dominant in the Cultural District is the **Will Rogers Memorial Center ❾** (3401 W. Lancaster Avenue, tel: 817-871-8150), but, apart from the staging of specific events (such as the annual Southwestern Exposition and Livestock Show in January), it requires less attention than other major museums here.

One of these, the **Kimbell Art Museum ❿** (3333 Camp Bowie Boulevard; closed Mon; Fri and Sun pm only; free; tel: 817-332-8451), designed by the late Louis Kahn, has long been regarded as one of the top two or three museums in America. Kahn, revered by many of his fellow architects, also designed La Jolla's Salk Institute, and his work, according to *Contemporary Architects* "had an absolutely monumental impact on the development and redirectioning of progressive design."

Combining concrete, marble, glass and vegetation with subtle modulations of natural light in a simple, exquisitely detailed whole, the Kimbell is human-sized with a wide collection that is constantly being expanded. There are objects which would, on their own, justify a visit: a Duccio, a Giovanni Bellini, Vuillards, a Cézanne, a Rubens, a Rembrandt and a

BELOW: Tarrant County Courthouse.

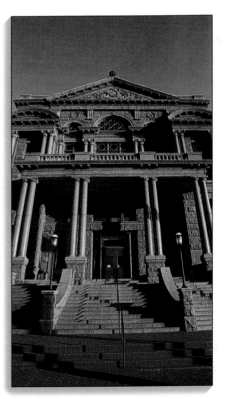

The National Cowgirl Museum is devoted not just to women who have worked the ranches. Entertainers like Dale Evans and Patsy Cline are also members of the Hall of Fame.

spectacular Oriental collection. The museum, founded with the art collection of oil tycoon Kay Kimbell on his death in 1964, explains its rationale: "that the individual work of outstanding merit and importance is more effective as an educational tool than a large number of representative examples."

Situated near the Kimbell is the **Amon Carter Museum** Ⓚ (closed Mon; Sun pm only; free; tel: 817-738-1933), the work of Philip Johnson, one of the many American architects who were influenced by the work of Louis Kahn. Founded by the Fort Worth publisher whose name it bears, the museum has just been given a $39 million extension (again by Philip Johnson) – the new building opened in October 2001. The museum is best known for collections of works by Frederic Remington and Charles M. Russell, who specialized in depicting life on the range and along the cattle trails.

In addition to the museum's collection of significant paintings by such revered American artists as Thomas Eakins and Winslow Homer, there are numerous intriguing paintings by anonymous 19th-century artists and some wonderful sepia prints. These feature gold mining scenes and were taken in an era when advances in photography had reduced the time needed for exposures to a mere 30 seconds. The pioneering "animal movement" photographer Eadweard Muybridge is also represented with an 1887 shot of a horse that shows all four of its feet off the ground.

The permanent collection of the **Modern Art Museum** Ⓛ (3200 Darnell Street; closed Mon; free; tel: 817-738-9215 – ironically the city's oldest – includes works by such 20th-century favorites as Frank Stella, Mark Rothko, Clyfford Still, Morris Louis, Joseph Cornell and even Pablo Picasso, with contemporary sculpture dotting the adjoining garden.

BELOW: dressed up for a Fort Worth art festival.

The Fort Worth Museum of Science and History (1501 Montgomery Street; open daily; Sun pm only; entrance fee; tel: 817-255-9300) employs every inch of space to entertain and educate its visitors, with even its toilet walls adorned with medical charts explaining aspects of the human body. Notes by the water fountains reveal that water covers three-quarters of the earth's surface, with only 3 percent of it fresh. The museum is exceptionally friendly to kids who can sit in a helicopter or dig for dinosaur bones. Additional attractions are an Omnimax theater, and astronomy programs and daily shows at the Noble Planetarium.

Everybody knows about cowboys, but information about their counterparts, the women who worked the ranches on horseback, has been hard to find. Now there's the **National Cowgirl Museum & Hall of Fame** (1720 Gendy Street; open daily; Sun pm only; free; tel: 817-336-4475), whose 153 inductees include Henrietta Chamberlain King, co-founder of the enormous King Ranch; sharpshooter Annie Oakley; world champion bull rider Lynn Jonckowski; and trick rider and calf roper Dixie Reger Moseley.

Casa Mañana (West Lancaster at University Drive; tel: 817-332-2272) is a theater-in-the-round whose roof is an early example of the geodesic dome invented by R. Buckminster Fuller. It was one of the city's tributes to the 1936 Texas Centennial Celebration. Based on the triangle, and requiring no internal support, the geodesic dome grows stronger as it grows larger, can withstand hurricanes and, unlike domes in general, has good acoustics. A later example forms the top of the Reunion Tower in Dallas.

One plot at Fort Worth's Botanic Garden has been planted particularly for the strength and variety of its scent, in anticipation of blind visitors.

Walks on the wild side

Several blocks to the south, near the intersection of I-30 and South University Drive, is the **Botanic Garden** (open daily; free; tel: 817-871-7686), a 114-acre (46-hectare) park watered by natural springs and containing more than 50 species of trees, all sorts of roses, and a Japanese Garden.

Further south still on Colonial Parkway, west of University Drive, is **Log Cabin Village** (closed Mon; Sun pm only; entrance fee; tel: 817-926-5881), featuring seven homes from the 1850s, with costumed pioneers, a grist mill and spinning wheels.

A short distance away is the **Fort Worth Zoo** (1989 Colonial Parkway; open daily; entrance fee; tel: 817-759-7555) in Forest Park. Set among natural habitats along winding paths are 5,000 animals, birds and reptiles. The zoo's unusual wildlife art gallery contains 28 enormous paintings by the German artist Wilhelm Kuhnert, who went into the East African bush to work from life. Several American buffalo live here on a 3,400-acre (1,375-hectare) range of their own. There is also a prairie dog "town," where small burrowing owls may be seen creeping in and out of the abandoned prairie dog holes. Trails of many descriptions divide the refuge.

The **Lord's Supper Display**, housed west of downtown Fort Worth at 2500 Ridgmar Plaza (open daily; Sun pm only; free; tel: 817-737-6251), displays a wax rendering of Leonardo da Vinci's famous painting of

BELOW: Cowtown Coliseum, with *The First Bulldogger* out front.

the Last Supper, as it might appear life-size and in three dimensions. Here, visitors can also view life-size Kennedy assassination tableaux.

Arlington

The Six Flags Over Texas amusement park specializes in white-knuckle rides, but there is plenty to entertain all ages, including mock shoot-outs, ice shows and appearances by popular "Looney Tunes" characters.

Though a separate town, **Arlington** (pop. 333,000) has become something of an eastern adjunct to Fort Worth. Its many residents are fans of the Texas Rangers and thus flock to the magnificent **Ballpark**, which costs as much as a Las Vegas hotel and offers almost as many attractions. The complex was designed by Washington architect David M. Schwarz, the man who designed the Bass Performance Hall and the new American Airlines Center in Dallas. An entire entertainment complex is rising around it, but already thousands come to enjoy the walking trails, admire the 19-ft (6-meter) architectural friezes depicting scenes from Texas history, see the huge murals of famous baseball heroes, visit the baseball museum, and even to test their angling skills at the cat fish-stocked lake. During games, no fan is ever further than about 75 ft (23 meters) from a bright television monitor – there are 2000 in the park. In the basement, enormous tanks pump soda to dozens of concession stands.

Visitors who take the 50-minute Ballpark tours (daily, game days am only; Sun pm only; entrance fee; tel: 817-273-5098) view the vast, open-air arena with its 49,000 seats, the dugouts, the luxurious player lounge displaying posters of every baseball movie, and the huge press balcony. Then many tourists spend hours in the **Legends of the Game Museum**, where all the heroes – Ty Cobb, Hank Aaron, Lou Gehrig and Babe Ruth among them – are represented through videos, trophies, jerseys and other memorabilia. One section is devoted to the little-known women's leagues. Upstairs in the Learning Center, baseball history is taught through interactive video quizzes, and there are various exhibits showing how bats and balls are made.

BELOW: riding the mechanical bull, Fort Worth Stockyards.

Fun and games

Heading away from the Ballpark, past Arlington's Convention Center, you reach **Six Flags Over Texas** (open daily; weekends only spring and fall; often closed winter; entrance fee; tel: 817-640-8900), at the junction of I-30 and Highway 360. This is the state's biggest tourist attraction and the original base of what is now a nationwide chain. The theme park devotes an area to each of the nations whose flag has flown over Texas – Spain, Mexico, France, Texas, the Confederacy and the US, and there are other attractions, too.

Next door, **Six Flags Hurricane Harbor** is the largest water park in the US, and offers a cool respite from the searingly hot temperatures that summer visitors to Texas can always expect (1800 E. Lamar Boulevard; open daily; limited opening spring and fall; closed winter; entrance fee; tel: 817-265-3356). Nearby, the **Air Combat School** (921 Six Flags Drive; open daily; entrance fee; tel: 817-640-1886) offers a chance to make a simulated jet fighter flight while strapped into an actual cockpit.

The Palace of Wax & Ripley's Believe It or Not! (open daily; entrance fee; tel: 972-263-2391) is to the east, along I-30 at Beltline, and there are attractions further afield: the **Johnson Plantation Cemetery** (open by appointment; entrance fee; tel: 817-460-4001), featuring an historic log cabin, lies at Center and Arkansas Lane, and, at the entrance to the River Legacy Parks near the lake at the west side of town is the **Living Science Center** (703 NW Green Oaks Boulevard; closed Mon; Sun pm only; closed Sun Nov–Mar; entrance fee; tel: 817-860-6752), housing environmental exhibits for all ages.

On the far side of Highway 360, which runs north to south on the eastern edge of Arlington, are shopping opportunities at Six Flags Mall (2911 E. Division), Forum 303 Mall (Highway 360 at Spur 303), and the enormous Traders Village Flea Market (2602 Mayfield Road), which displays the wares of 1,600 dealers at weekends.

Arlington's downtown attractions are clustered within walking distance of each other around Main Street. These include the perennial Johnny High's Country Music Revue at the Arlington Music Hall (224 N. Center; entrance fee; tel: 817-226-4400) and the 200-seat Theatre Arlington (305 W. Main Street; tel: 817-275-7661). The **Arlington Historical Society Museum** (1616 W. Abram; closed Mon and Tue; Sat and Sun pm only; donations accepted; tel: 817-460-4001) includes a veteran barber shop and general store. The **Arlington Museum of Art** (201 W. Main Street; open Wed–Sat; free; tel: 817-275-4600) concentrates on Texan artists.

Grapevine

More than 30 19th-century buildings have been preserved and restored in the little town of **Grapevine**, which sits at the other end of the Tarantula railroad line which begins at the Fort Worth Stockyards. Named for the wild

Map on page 132

TIP

Consider Arlington as a base for a visit to Dallas or Fort Worth. Not only is it halfway between the two centers, but it also has numerous attractions of its own, as well as plenty of restaurants and hotel rooms.

BELOW: inside the Kimbell Art Museum in Fort Worth.

In celebration of the local wine industry, Grapevine stages an annual "Grapefest" every September.

mustang grapes prevalent in the area, the town dates back to 1843 when General Sam Houston camped nearby before signing a peace treaty with Indian tribal leaders. There are numerous wineries in the area, the nearest being the château-style **Delaney Vineyards** (2000 Champagne Boulevard; tours Sat pm and weekdays by appointment; free; tel: 817-481-5668).

Grapevine is dotted with historical markers, and much of its Main Street is listed in the *National Register of Historical Places*. The tourist office (tel: 800-457-6338) is situated in the artfully reconstructed Wallis Hotel building, once filled with turn-of-the-20th-century traveling salesmen. *The Sidewalk Judge,* a lifelike sculpture by J. Seward Johnson, sitting on a bench outside, is an irresistible photo opportunity.

Across Main Street, at No. 308, the old **Palace Theater** (tel: 817-481-8733) has been restored as a home for the Grapevine Opry and, in the next block is the former **Grapevine Home Bank**, which was robbed by some of the Bonnie and Clyde gang back in 1932. Many of the buildings on Main Street now sell predominantly tacky souvenirs, but some display genuine arts and crafts. These include the Pueblo Connection (a range of Native American items), Beaux Arts Galleries and Off the Vine – a shop selling wine-related art such as hand-blown goblets.

What's known as the **Torian Log Cabin**, inhabited until the 1940s and still primitively furnished, sits near the gazebo in Liberty Park at the northern end of the street. The more interesting old homes are behind Main Street at the other end: a group of Victorian houses on College Street. One block west back on Main Street are the Heritage Center and the **Grapevine Depot**, the latter serving as the town's railroad station before being converted into an historical museum.

BELOW: Chisholm Trail round-up and ride into Fort Worth Stockyards.

The St Louis and Southwestern (Cotton Belt) Railroad depot once stood here and today, near the classic 1933 **Aeromotor Windmill**, which at one time pumped water for a nearby farm, is the terminal for the Tarantula steam train, plying daily between here and Fort Worth. At the blacksmith's shop, with its wild mustang grapevine, genial Jim White demonstrates forging brands while posing happily for visitors, and his neighbor, saddlemaker Aubrey Mauldin, presides over a leather shop filled with custom-made boots.

The cowboy boot is something special and the state produces more of them than any other place in the world. There were 600 Texas bootmakers at one time. Now only about one-tenth of that number still painstakingly cut and stitch every inch by hand, from pointed toe (to slip easily into the stirrup) to elevated arch and heel (to hold the foot firmly in place).

At the far end of the depot is **Grapevine Heritage Garden**, featuring such specimens as the swamp rose, the pink-flowered bouncing bet (once used as a soap substitute) and the crinum lily, all attracting butterflies and hummingbirds, and making the garden a visitors' delight.

North of town, 19-mile (30-km) long **Grapevine Lake** is a cool recreational oasis offering boating, swimming, fishing and all kinds of water activities. Beyond the lake, off Highway 26 at 3000 Grapevine Mills Parkway, near the airport, is the huge, brightly lit Grapevine Mills shopping mall, which is not a bad place to pass away a couple of hours between flights. A convenient shuttle bus runs to and from the airport.

A cowboy's best friend.

Denton

Thirty-five miles (56 km) northeast of Fort Worth, on US-35, is **Denton**. Its century-old limestone and granite courthouse dominates a square lined with renovated old buildings that now house restaurants and antiques and specialty stores. The **Courthouse-on-the-Square Museum** in the courthouse focuses on the history of the region (closed Sun; free; tel: 940-349 2850); bizarrely, the town's pioneer founder, Captain John B. Denton, is buried beneath the lawn.

Numerous movies (including the 1998 film, *Armageddon*) have been shot in Denton, especially among the old homes of the Oak-Hickory Historic District and at the Evers Hardware Store (109 W.Hickory; closed Sun), which has remained family owned ever since its founding in 1885.

To the south of town, the **Texas Motor Speedway** (I-35 and Highway 114) will be of interest to auto-racing enthusiasts, while the **Hangar 10 Airplane Museum** (open Mon–Sat; tel: 940-565-1945) at Denton Municipal Airport has vintage aircraft on display and will appeal to flying buffs.

Also in this area is the Texas Women's University (TWU), the largest of its kind in the nation, containing the **Daughters of the American Revolution Museum** (open by appointment; tel: 940-898-2000), which displays gowns worn by the First Ladies of Texas. In the vicinity is the **University of North Texas** (tel: 940-565-2000), which has a fashion collection of its own, as well as a famous library. ❑

BELOW: the Tarantula steam train at Stockyards Station.

WAXAHACHIE TO WACO

Map on page 146

It's easy to zoom by this stretch of Central Texas, but a detour from the Interstate is rewarded with a string of quirky towns, fine man-made lakes, distinctive architecture and absorbing museums

entral Texas is the backyard of Texas – not such a bad thing to be in a state with so many glamorous frontyards. Too often travelers, unless headed for the lakes or elderly relatives, race from Dallas to Austin without ever exiting the Interstate. Really to understand Texas, leave the causeway between Waxahachie and Waco and "come on around to the backyard."

Waxahachie

Waxahachie ❶ (pop. 22,000), located 35 miles (56 km) south of Dallas, is one of the latter's bedroom communities. Take the exit from I-35 East, the Dallas arm of the Fort Worth-Dallas "Y." The town's name derives from a Native American expression for buffalo creek; white settlers arrived here in the 1840s.

Much of the honey in Texas supermarkets comes from Waxahachie, a town that has become increasingly industrialized. Nevertheless, it still proudly preserves hundreds of other Victorian and early 20th-century houses, many of which can be toured along a "Gingerbread Trail" marked on a free map. This is available from the city's Visitors' Bureau (102 YMCA Drive; tel: 972-937-2390).

Photographs and pioneer artifacts in the **Ellis County Museum** (closed Mon; Sun pm only; free; tel: 972-937-0681), a former Masonic meeting-house on the **Courthouse Square**, are devoted to the history of Waxahachie. The red sandstone and granite 1895 Ellis County Courthouse (open Mon–Fri; free), a product of Texas courthouse architect James Reily Gordon, is one of the most-photographed buildings in the state. It cost $150,000 to construct – a substantial sum in the 1890s. According to legend, an Italian stonecutter who was working on the building is thought to have fallen in love with a Waxahachie telegraph operator, Mabel Frame, whose carved face is a recurring exterior motif.

The museum owns the red-brick Greek Revival **Mahoney-Thompson House** (604 W. Main; open during the Gingerbread Trail Days festival in early June; entrance fee; tel: 972-937-0681), packed with antique fans, furniture and Bohemian glass. It was built in 1904 at the height of Waxahachie's prosperity (based on cattle, grain and cotton), along with the **Chautauqua Auditorium**, still in use in Getzendaner Park. From the same era is the ornate Roman Revival **Nicholas P. Sims Library** (515 W. Main), with a richly decorated Carrara marble and gold interior.

Waxahachie, close to Dallas' already established film industry, and with its abundant period architecture, has become popular as a movie location. The 1985 *Peyton Place* remake was filmed here, as, more recently, were the movies *Tender Mercies* and *Places in the Heart*.

PRECEDING PAGES: Aquafest on Austin's Town Lake. **LEFT:** Baylor University, Waco. **BELOW:** Ellis County Museum/Old Masonic Lodge, Waxahachie.

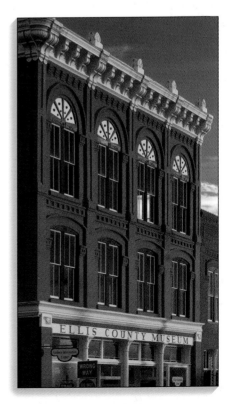

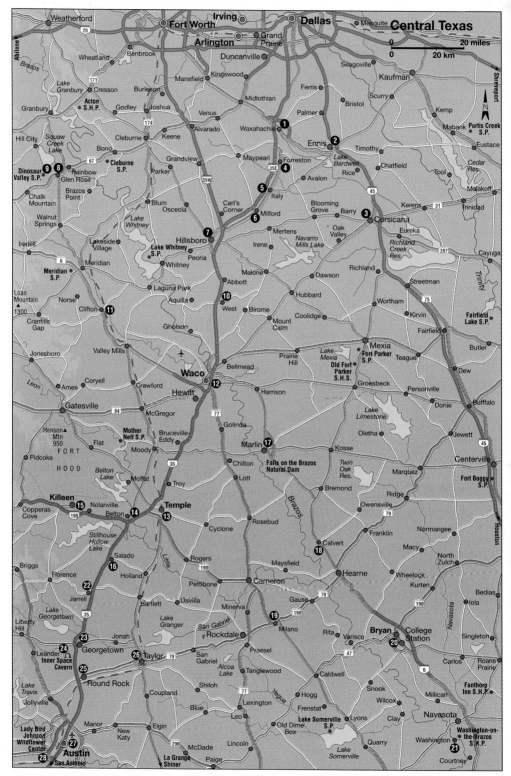

Central Texas

Polka Festival

Many of the state's Czech immigrants settled in this fertile, Central Texas cotton-growing belt, and almost all of them did well as cotton farmers here. Their descendants make up approximately half the population of **Ennis ❷**, on I-45 between Dallas and Houston. Since 1966, Ennis has sponsored the **National Polka Festival** in May, attracting crowds of 30,000. A parade of polka bands rolls down the main street, which may be the widest in Texas – divided into East and West Main by railroad tracks, it is 340 ft (104 meters) across. The town also has a **Railroad and Cultural Heritage Museum** (105 NE. Main Street; open daily; Sun pm only; entrance fee; tel: 972-875-1901), which showcases the Czech influence as well as railroad history.

On the water

Since 1900, more than 200 lakes have been created in Texas. **Lake Bardwell**, or the Bardwell Reservoir, on Waxahachie Creek, 4 miles (7 km) outside Ennis, was built by the US Corps of Engineers in the early 1960s. Like the other new lakes near Navarro Mills and Mexia, it is a popular recreation area, with pretty lakeside parks and camping. It also acts as the water supply for Ennis, Waxahachie and Corsicana. Visitors from out of state – especially New Englanders, whose reservoirs are fenced and carefully patrolled – are often surprised to find Texans fishing, water-skiing and sailing on theirs.

Faces carved into the columns of Ellis County Courthouse, Waxahachie.

Corsicana **❸**, the Navarro county seat, is 19 miles (30 km) south of Ennis on I-45. It is named for Corsica, home of the parents of the Texas hero José Antonio Navarro of San Antonio, who signed the Texas Declaration of Independence and helped write the first constitution. The first Texas gusher was not drilled at Corsicana as is commonly believed. However, a 12-year oil boom began in 1894 when the city dug an artesian well and struck oil instead of water. The strike made Corsicana the first oil boomtown in Texas. A current attraction, **Pioneer Village** (912 W. Park Avenue; open daily; Sun pm only; entrance fee; tel: 903-654-4846) is made up of reconstructed 19th-century log buildings, including an Indian trading post and slave quarters.

BELOW: dolls in Czech national costume at Ennis Railroad Museum.

Corsicana has achieved a minor sort of fame from a special local delicacy, the "Deluxe" fruitcake made by the **Collin Street Bakery** (401 W. 7th Avenue; open daily; tel: 800-504-1896), which has been exported all over the world – 1.6 million fruitcakes per year, to be exact. An essential ingredient is the inimitable Texas pecan, more than a million pounds (just under half a million kg) of which are used by the bakery annually.

Nameless place

Forreston ❹, 10 miles (16 km) south of Waxahachie on the Interstate, is the oldest town in the area. Another 5 miles (8 km) south, near **Italy ❺**, the Confederates operated a hat factory.

Italy was originally called "Houston Creek," because Sam Houston was reported to have camped nearby. Reputedly the post office would not issue a postmark unless the name of the town was changed

Map on page 146

Texas-born Audie Murphy (1924–71) was able to build on his honorable service record by becoming an actor, starring in a series of war and western films, most notably the Civil War movie The Red Badge of Courage *(1951).*

LEFT: Ellis County Courthouse depicted on the backdrop of the Chautauqua Auditorium.
RIGHT: the real thing.

and, after six different names had been rejected, settlers wrote back: "Let the post office be nameless, and be damned." The community was Nameless, Texas, from 1880 to 1890, and there is still a Nameless Schoolhouse and Nameless Road. Houston Creek eventually became Italy – a tribute, it is said, to the sunny Central Texas climate. The population of Italy has never exceeded 1,300, but it did receive the first fully endowed public library in Texas – the **Dunlap Library** – from businessman S.M. Dunlap.

Historical towns

Back on I-35, via State Route 22 from Corsicana, you arrives at **Milford ❻**, a town settled in the 1850s that once adopted the good-humored city motto: "The home of 700 friendly people and three or four old grouches." It is nothing more than human nature to leave the freeway in the hope of catching a glimpse of one of the grouches.

The town of **Hillsboro ❼**, just below the point where I-35 West joins I-35 East from Dallas, has been a crossroads since the 1850s, when there was a dirt-floor, elm-pole courthouse here. Today's hideous limestone Hill County Courthouse was built in 1889. Tradition has it that a Comanche chief called Hollow-Hole-in-the-Air died under a tree in the front yard of Harris House, the oldest house in Hillsboro. At Hill Junior College, the **Harold B. Simpson History Complex** (open Mon–Fri; entrance fee; tel: 254-582-2555, ext. 256) displays paintings, photographs and documents from the Civil War, around 200 guns and other weaponry from the Civil War to the present, and the uniform worn by Audie L. Murphy, the most decorated American soldier of World War II.

Northwest of Hillsboro on State Road 144 is **Glen Rose ❽**, where it is rumored

Map on page 146

John Wilkes Booth once lived – under the name John St Helen – after he assassinated President Lincoln. Glen Rose is sometimes known as the "Petrified City," because petrified wood is a popular building material here. Local history is explained in the **Somervell County Museum** (Mon–Fri; Sun pm only; weekends only in winter; free; tel: 254-898-0640) at Vernon and Elm streets.

Jurassic Park

Numerous dinosaur tracks can be found in Glen Rose and in the 1,270-acre (514-hectare) **Dinosaur Valley State Park ❾** (open daily; entrance fee; tel: 254-897-4588), 4 miles (6 km) west of the town. The tracks are easy to spot, but there is a steep trail to the river. Long before humans settled in the Bosque River Valley, Central Texas was coastal swampland and dinosaurs left their tracks – some of the best-preserved examples in the world – in the limestone river bed here. There are no "taildrag marks" in the dinosaurs trackway – the water here was deep enough for the dinosaurs' tails to float – but you can see where the mud oozed up between their toes. The park has facilities for camping, picnicking, hiking, biking and horse riding, and is one of the state parks in which part of the official State Longhorn Herd is kept.

Acrocanthosaurus footprint in Dinosaur Valley State Park.

West, Texas

The small town of **West ❿**, halfway between Hillsboro and Waco, has the misfortune from time to time of being confused with the region "West Texas," so it is called "West, Comma, Texas." Forty thousand people came here on September 15 1896 to view the ridiculous, staged spectacular of two locomotives of the Missouri, Kansas and Texas Railroad crash into each other. Their throt-

BELOW: house on Waxahachie's Gingerbread Trail.

The town of Waco was founded, and initially thrived, on the profits of five "C"s: cattle, cotton, corn, culture and collegians.

tles tied back to 50 mph (80 kmph), the trains exploded on impact, killing two spectators. The agent who dreamed up this reckless stunt was merely fired, and promptly rehired the next day.

The Bosque

Twenty miles (32 km) west of Hillsboro, across the Brazos river, is the region known as the **Bosque** (Spanish for woods, pronounced "boskay"). A number of Norwegians settled here as farmers between 1850 and 1875. They fiercely defended their log houses from attacks by the Kiowa and Comanche Indians and many relics and household items used by these early Scandinavian settlers have been collected for display in the **Bosque Memorial Museum** (open Tue–Sat; entrance fee; tel: 254-675-3845) on Avenue Q in **Clifton ⓫**. Clifton (pop. 3,200). Nordic heritage is also celebrated with a smorgasbord each November at **Norse**, near Clifton.

Waco

Until they were driven out, the Waco were a Wichita tribe occupying a site by the 840-mile (1,344-km) long Brazos river in Central Texas. When the whites first settled the area 160 years' ago, they took **Waco ⓬** as the name for their town. First came Fort Fisher, then and now a Texas Ranger outpost, but what really brought attention to the town was the construction, in 1870, of a massive suspension bridge across the river.

"That bridge was very important," explains local historian Roger Conger. "The Brazos was a veritable iron curtain across the center of Texas. After the Civil War many Southerners were going west. They had to come to Waco to

BELOW: Dr Pepper Museum, Waco.

cross the river." Six bridges span the river within the city today but the antique suspension bridge (now pedestrian-only) is still the most significant. When the 475-ft (145-meter) bridge supplanted the ferry, it was the longest single-span suspension bridge in America, and the second longest in the world. Supported by wire cables and 2,700,000 Waco bricks, it was built by New York engineer Thomas Griffith from the plans of New York's Thomas Roebling, designer of the Brooklyn Bridge. Longhorns and wagon trains bound for the Chisholm Trail traversed it in its earliest days and, until 1889, a toll was charged: "five cents for each loose animal of the cattle kind."

Earliest site

Some of the settlers who followed the Texas Rangers to this beautiful valley on the Brazos in the 1840s lived in log cabins on the site of what is now Cameron Park on Rotan Drive. Here are woods, hiking trails, the natural habitat **Cameron Park Zoo** (open daily; Sun pm only; entrance fee; tel: 254-750-8400) and Miss Nellie's Pretty Place, a wildflower preserve donated to the city by a former congressman's mother.

What the earliest settlement probably looked like can be seen adjoining the riverside Fort Fisher Campground, at **The Governor Bill and Vara Daniel Historic Village** (closed Sun; entrance fee; tel: 254-710-1160), on the campus of Baylor University. The largest Baptist university in the world, Baylor also houses the **Strecker Museum** (closed Sun; free; tel: 254-710-1110), devoted to natural history, and the fascinating marble-columned **Armstrong Browning Library** (closed Sun; Sat am only; free; tel: 254-710-3566) with portraits of, and 4,000 letters written by or to, the Victorian poets Robert and Elizabeth Barrett

Dr Pepper has a taste all of its own.

BELOW: the Texas Rangers Museum, Waco.

MAKE MINE A DR PEPPER

Probably the most unconventional cultural center in Waco is the Dr Pepper Museum, based at 300 S. 5th Street (open daily; Sun pm only; entrance fee; tel: 254-757-1025).

Dr Pepper was invented in 1885 in Waco's Old Corner Drug Store by pharmacist Charles Alderton. His boss, Dr Morrison named it Dr Pepper but why remains unclear. The museum, housed in a bottling plant opened in 1906, covers the history of Dr Pepper and the entire soft drink industry: "We're proud of our display on Waco's other soft drink, Big Red, invented about half a block from here," declares director Joe Cavanaugh. The site is now featured on the National Register of Historic Places but Dr Pepper has not been produced here since the 1920s.

If you want to visit the oldest working Dr Pepper plant (since 1891), make a trip to Dublin, 94 miles (150 km) west of Waco. Here you can sample Dr Pepper made to the original recipe, incorporating cane sugar rather than other sweeteners. Tours of the factory are offered and visitors on Tuesdays can see the bottling taking place.

The Waco site also includes an early soda fountain where you can sample traditional sodas and sundaes. There is no entrance fee if you just go in for a drink.

Map on page 146

Browning. The library's collection – assembled by Baylor's late Professor A.J. Armstrong – is supplemented by 50 lovely stained-glass windows depicting verses by the poetic pair.

Between the Baylor campus and US-81 is the Tourist Information Center (tel: 800-922-6386), adjoining the **First Street Cemetery**, which houses Confederate graves. Other attractions are the **Texas Sports Hall of Fame** (1108 University Parks Drive; open daily; Sun pm only; entrance fee; tel: 254-756-1633), where kids can try on helmets of the Houston Oilers or Dallas Cowboys, and the **Texas Ranger Hall of Fame & Museum** (open daily; entrance fee; tel: 254-750-8631). Jim Bowie's knife and the rifle he carried at the Alamo are here, as well as a jewel-studded saddle (which cost $5,800 in 1903), novelist James Michener's typewriter, the pistol Pat Garrett used to kill Billy the Kid and enough of the early Rangers' Colt revolvers to equip an army.

Six-shooter junction

In its prime, Waco was a rough cowtown. "Next stop, Waco," the train conductors would yell as the train approached, "Get out your six-shooters." The last legal hanging in Texas occurred here in 1923, witnessed by over 4,000 people, and, in 1955, a Waco television station was the first in the world to broadcast a murder trial.

A more genteel era is reflected by the city's group of 19th-century homes, operated from the gingerbread-style Hoffmann house by the Historic Waco Foundation (810 S. 4th Street; tel: 254-753-5166). The Foundation also hosts the annual Brazos River Festival in April. Two of these Victorian homes lie between I-35 and Waco Drive and can be toured on Saturday and Sunday afternoons (not Dec). They are the Greek Revival **Earle-Napier-Kinnard House** (814 S. 4th Street), completed in 1869, and **Fort House** (503 S. 4th Street), in which Alabama planter William Aldridge Fort lived with dozens of relatives and slaves in the 1870s. Across the river, at 100 Mill Street, is the Italianate **East Terrace**, shielded by elm and pecan trees, with walks down to the river. Home of industrialist John Wesley Mann, *circa* 1872, it contains original furniture.

At 1901 N. Fifth Street, the **Earle-Harrison House** (tel: 254-753-2032), sitting in 5-acre (2-hectare) gardens, is gloriously furnished. Portraits of General Robert E. Lee abound in some of these old homes, a reminder that Waco's men marched off to support Confederate armies in the Civil War. Six Confederate generals hailed from Waco, which has also been home to former Texas Governor Ann Richards and Madison Cooper Jr, whose 840,000-word novel, *Sironia, Texas* – on view in the public library – is said to be the longest ever written.

Another among Waco's dozen or more museums is the **Helen Marie Taylor Museum of Waco History** (Tues–Sat; entrance fee; tel: 254-752-4774), whose location at 701 Jefferson sits on the site of one of the Waco Indian tribe's main villages.

In 2001 a new downtown park was opened in front of City Hall (3rd and Austin). The walkways and fountains of **Heritage Square** were constructed on the site of an area devastated by a tornado in 1953. ❑

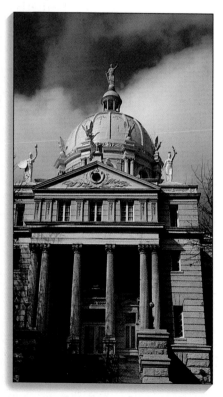

BELOW: McLennan County Courthouse, Waco.
RIGHT: the famous bridge over Waco's Brazos River.

WACO TO AUSTIN

Austin – college town, state capital and home of live music – dominates this part of Central Texas, but the many small towns around the city are worth a visit, too

Map on page 146

The impression is unavoidable: the young of Central Texas migrate to larger cities like Austin and Dallas as soon as possible. A disproportionately large percentage of the population remaining in rural areas appears to be old or very young. Past Waco, the pull of Austin, which is filled with students and ex-students, is unmistakable. Cars speed up, responding to the attraction of Texas' magnetic capital. Temple – with its fenced stretch of Interstate that does not look as if it is supposed to be exciting – Belton, Killeen and Salado (it rhymes with Laredo) zip by most I-35 drivers unnoticed, unless they are searching out the Dairy Queen or the Dixie Dog drive-in café. But this series of former railroad stops is more interesting than it looks, and repays a visit if examined with the eye of the novelist or sociologist.

Like most towns south of Waco, **Temple 🔞** and **Belton 🔞** were originally built around loading pens and general stores about a century ago. Today, the area is known primarily for the commanding presence of **Fort Hood**, the largest military base in the US, which is set on no fewer than 217,000 acres (87,800 hectares), near Lake Benton. The commandant, interviewed by a newspaper, admitted it had once been among the army's most dreaded assignments. Today, he says, the 37, 000 soldiers do not want to leave. The main drag of nearby Harker Heights is lined with car dealerships, eating places and fairly rowdy nightclubs.

Two historic army divisions maintain museums at Fort Hood: the **1st Cavalry Museum** on Headquarters Avenue and the **2nd Armored Division Museum** on Battalion Avenue (both open daily; Sat and Sun pm only; free). These and the many reconstructed frontier forts in Texas cannot really make the lives of soldiers seem real, but along with gun museums and collections of artifacts, they feed the imagination.

Life and death

There are a number of eateries in the Temple-Killeen area, and, in addition to plenty of hearty Texan specialties, they offer a good opportunity to observe small-town life. In fact, Texan-watching is at its best while sawing a batter-fried "corny dog" or a chicken-fried steak, a cheap cut of hammered beef breaded like fried chicken and served with potatoes and gravy.

The point of bars, clubs, honky-tonks, ice-houses and beer-joints in Texas is friendliness, not fighting. But making some new friends by fighting, particularly in hole-in-the-wall joints and motel rooms, is an ongoing frontier tradition. Invitations to do so should be firmly refused. Pistol-packing is not entirely unheard of, but is thankfully rare.

In backwater towns like Temple, Belton and **Killeen 🔞**, there is still much pleasure to be taken in

LEFT: the Governor's Mansion, Austin.
BELOW: hay bale Jack-o-Lantern in Central Texas.

TIP

Restaurants, hotels, museums, wildlife refuges and zoos are likely to change their names and hours, if not just disappear completely, in booming Texas. Where distances are great, telephone ahead or inquire at a Chamber of Commerce or other tourist agency.

day-to-day proceedings. There are as many original characters, language tricks and private jokes as anywhere else, possibly more, since the storytelling tradition remains strong in both rural and urban Texas. In this region, times are changing: Temple-Killeen's Standard Metropolitan Statistical Area (SMSA) is one of the 10 fastest-growing in the US.

Local history

I-35 follows the railroad – beside the Chisholm Trail, along which cattle were driven to rail-heads farther north – so busy Temple is a logical place to find the **Railroad and Pioneer Museum** (315 W. Avenue B; closed Sun and Mon; Sun pm only; entrance fee; 254-298-5172) in the Santa Fe depot at 31st Street and Avenue H. The **Czech Heritage Museum** (520 N. Main Street; closed Sat and Sun; free) exhibits an unusual collection related to Czech immigration at the Slovanska Podporujci Jednota Statu Texas (SPJST; Benevolent Order of the State of Texas) Insurance Building. There are SPJST halls in many Central Texas towns.

The **Bell County Museum** in Belton (201 N. Main Street; open Tue–Sat pm only; free; tel: 254-933-5243), is a local history museum occupying a 1905 Carnegie Library building.

Farms and plantations

The pretty little town of **Salado** ⑯, once a stage halt on Salado Creek, a few miles south of Killeen, is best known for its popular and picturesque Stagecoach Inn (1 Main Street), a restaurant with mid-19th century antecedents and modern motel additions. Across the street is the Central Texas Area Museum, where Sam Houston delivered an anti-secession speech from the balcony.

BELOW: Heep Ranch in Buda, near Austin.

Texas' first chapter of the Grange, an important organization of anti-corporate American farmers that flourished during the Progressive era, was founded at Salado in 1873. The related Farmers' Alliance, which had several million members throughout the country in its most successful days, originated at Lampasas, about 50 miles (80 km) west of Fort Hood, in 1875. Together they helped elect the famous Populist James Stephen Hogg, who was Governor of Texas 1891–95.

Near the I-35 access road at Salado, the antebellum **Robertson Plantation House** is unusually complete, with outbuildings, slave quarters and a family cemetery. It was built in 1854 by E.S.C. Robertson, son of Sterling Clack Robertson, who settled 600 families in the Brazos River Basin, northwest of Stephen F. Austin's colony.

The steady character, intelligence and diligence with which Austin won the respect of his fellow "Texans" were also displayed by Robertson. One of the directors of his "Nashville Company" was Sam Houston, who had already been the Governor of Tennessee and later became both President and Governor of the state of Texas.

The complex, ultimately unsuccessful attempt to turn the early settlers into Mexican citizens makes a long and stirring story. The patriarch Moses Austin, father of Stephen, who did not live to see the Anglo-Southerners enter the Promised Land, had wished to give his name to a great port, Austina, which would rival New Orleans. Instead, a new capital in the wilderness was named for the Father and Grandfather of Texas. The now-abandoned town of **Nashville**, one of the principal settlements of Robertson's colony, was also considered for the capital. If Nashville had been made capital of Texas instead of Austin, Robertson would be better-known today.

Map on page 146

The name "Salado" means "salty" in Spanish.

BELOW: Hamilton's Pool, a popular swimming place, west of Austin.

Once Buck-snort

There are a number of interesting cities to the east of I-35, where Central and East Texas merge. **Marlin** , 25 miles (40 km) east of Eddy, between Waco and Temple on State Route 7, was settled by Alabama and Tennessee farmers brought to Texas by Sterling Robertson. It was originally "Buck-snort." The Marlin for whom it is named was the first farmer to return after the "Runaway Scrape," when almost the whole population of the rebellious Republic fled before the invading Mexican army and the Indians from which their own army could not protect them. Local artifacts in the **Falls County Historical Museum** (145 Heritage Row; open Mon–Fri pm only; free; tel: 254-883-9101), include the gallows from the county jail.

The armadillo, the "State Mammal," is commonly found in rural Central Texas.

As the style of some of its architecture may suggest, Marlin has been one of the Central Texas spas since 1891, when hot water – not oil, as is often the case elsewhere – was struck in drilling an artesian well. The grand, château-like **Highlands Mansion** (1413 McClanahan Road; open daily; Sun pm only; entrance fee; tel: 254-803-2813), built in 1900, is a reminder of the prosperous times that arrived a considerable while after the Revolution. It now also sees duty as a luxurious bed and breakfast. Between Marlin and Lott, the land office for Robertson's colony of Sarahville de Viesca was located at Falls on the Brazos Natural Dam. Fort Milam, a Texas Ranger outpost, was founded nearby.

Reconstruction

Below: water skier on a central Texas lake.

Calvert 18, 41 miles (66 km) southeast of Marlin on State Route 6, is named for Robert Calvert, a descendant of Lord Baltimore and owner of one of the large cotton plantations in the area. The fields here were worked by slaves and, after the Civil War, by black convicts and Chinese and Italian immigrants. The theory was that Northern Europeans were incapable of laboring long in such a climate.

At Calvert, the reconstruction period was punitive and violent, in a manner reminiscent of the deep South. A cage for unreconstructed Confederate sympathizers, called a "sky parlor," was placed in a tree or atop a wooden pole where **Virginia Field Park** is now. But the cotton continued to grow: in the early 1870s, Calvert believed it possessed the world's largest cotton gin.

It is said that **Milano** 19, 15 miles (24 km) southwest of Hearne on State Route 79, owes its name to a post office blunder. At the time it applied for a postmark, it was called Milam, in honor of the Texas Revolutionary hero Ben Milam. Apparently there was some confusion in Washington, and authorization was ultimately given to use the misspelling.

A number of Italian immigrants, especially Sicilians, settled close by, in the flood-prone Brazos bottomland between Hearne and Bryan, and many Italian surnames are still found on country mailboxes.

College Town

Although Austin, home of the University of Texas (UT), is possibly the state's best-known college town, the huge campus of Texas Agricultural and Mechanical University (A&M) at **Bryan/College Station 20**, 18 miles (29 km) southeast of Hearne, is the largest in the United States. There are over 36,000 students studying here. A great rivalry exists between A&M and UT, if only because, whereas A&M receives a third of the oil revenue from public lands (endowed before the hidden oil was discovered on them), UT receives the remainder.

Many Texans have warmer feelings for Aggies – trusting, stalwart and stupid, as portrayed in the innumerable "Aggie jokes" – than UT "Longhorns," who tend to be more concerned with high style and fashion. In the budget wars between the Austin campus and the state government, politicians, including several colorful governors, have depicted UT to rural and poor voters as an arrogant, wasteful, rich man's school.

Tours of the A&M campus, including the **Sanders-Metzger Gun Collection** (free), displaying famous Colt pistols, can be arranged at the Information Center in the Rudder Tower. Also in College Station is the **George Bush Presidential Library and Museum** (1000 George Bush Drive West; open daily; Sun pm only; entrance fee; tel: 979-691-9552). Bush was an A&M student, and the museum houses a record of, and papers from, his presidency.

Independence site

Continuing its journey down to the Gulf of Mexico, the Brazos river reflects significant dates in Texas history at many points along its route. Eighty miles (128 km) southeast of Waco, at **Washington-on-the-Brazos 21** in 1836, Texas declared its independence from Mexico. Then the river was the lifeblood of the fledgling republic, as can be seen in the **Star of the Republic Museum** (open daily; entrance fee; tel: 936-878-2461).

Map on page 146

The settlement of Bryan/College Station is actually two towns, not one. Bryan, founded in 1859, was joined, in 1877, by College Station, developed as a railroad stop and new site for A&M University.

BELOW: country mailboxes in central Texas.

Expanding suburbs

At Salado, back on I-35 there are two possible routes to Austin, down the Interstate through **Jarrell ㉒**, an old Czech community which was a stage-coach stop, or across to Holland and south on State Route 95, a picturesque alternative with interesting small towns.

Austin's rapid growth zone would seem to promise that, within a few years, now-independent communities like **Georgetown ㉓** in Williamson County will be Austin metro stops. They are being rediscovered and enjoying a rebuilding period after many years of declining population, and, in uncovering their Victorian facades, they develop, just like Congress Avenue or 6th Street in downtown Austin, a solid sense of their history.

The north and south forks of the San Gabriel river flow together at Georgetown. **San Gabriel Park**, on the river east of the Interstate, and 1,200-acre (486-hectare) **Lake Georgetown** are splendid places to have a picnic. There are good-looking late 19th-century buildings in the **Courthouse Square**, a National Historic District.

Williamson County was originally to be called San Gabriel, but its state senator, "Three-Legged Willie" Williamson, is said to have protested that there were enough saints in Texas already. The upshot of his display of anti-Mexican sentiment was that the county was named for him.

East-west divide

Inner Space Cavern ㉔ (open daily; entrance fee; tel: 512-931-2283), on I-35 between Round Rock and Georgetown, is one of Texas' most accessible caves. Its large rooms are unusual in this part of the state, and the tour takes visitors into the most beautiful of them.

Lake Georgetown is a popular angling center, attracting fishermen with its stocks of smallmouth bass, channel cat and walleye.

BELOW:
tombstone at
D'Anis Cemetery,
Castroville, west of
San Antonio.
RIGHT:
central Texas
caves.

Such caves, the springs that one finds here, and the change in topography which at times is very noticeable, especially between Austin and San Antonio, are due to the activity of the **Balcones Fault Zone** that runs alongside I-35 from Mexico up to Oklahoma. To the west, the ground rose up producing what the Spanish called *Los Balcones* (balconies). The springs, around which early settlements grew, gush up through fissures in the rock. This important geological formation divides eastern and western Texas.

Stalactites and stalagmites in one of Texas' many natural caves.

Round Rock

In **Round Rock** ㉕, 10 miles (16 km) south of Georgetown on Brushy Creek, they celebrate the founding of the county with an Old Settlers Week. The eroded round rock, for which the city was named, was used to gauge the depth of the water of Bushy Creek, which was crossed by the old Chisholm Trail. Some of the buildings here alongside the stage route were built as early as the 1850s.

Sam Bass, the legendary train and stage-coach robber, who claimed never to have killed a man, was ambushed by Texas Rangers in the 100 block of East Main on July 19 1878. Businesses and condominium blocks are named after the outlaw, who became more famous after he was killed than he had ever been when alive. His grave is in the northwest corner of **Old Round Rock Cemetery** on Sam Bass Road, west of the intersection with Old Chisholm Trail. Covered with wildflowers in spring, the cemetery is easy to find and has an Anglo section, with crooked and cracked Victorian monuments, and a more colorful, smaller Mexican section, with paper and plastic flowers on the graves.

The **Palm House Museum** (212 E. Main; open Mon–Fri; free; tel: 512-255-5805) doubles as the Round Rock Chamber of Commerce office and adjoins a

BELOW: slave cemetery at Round Rock.

pharmacy that still has the pressed-tin ceiling once common in small-town stores. Another famous Round Rock son was Vander Clyde, a renowned aerialist, who had great success in Paris in the 1920s. Clyde made his entrance in an evening dress, completely convincing as a woman, and performed to the music of Wagner and Rimsky-Korsakov.

Snake sacking

US-79 East is the road to **Taylor** ㉖, famous for its barbecue and annual snake sacking contest. Snake sacking is highly controversial. Have the snakes been stunned or their mouths sewn up with monofilament? Animal lovers demonstrate outside, while the snake handlers, usually covered with bites, say all that preparation would be too much trouble.

State capital

Austin ㉗ (pop. 643,000) is the capital of Texas but is better known in many circles for its boast of being "the live music capital of the world." This reputation was bolstered for two decades by a popular, much-syndicated musical performance show, *Austin City Limits,* which featured many local and national artists from the various roots music genres, especially country and folk. Now a fading rose, the program was supplanted in the early 1990s by a wildly successful music conference and festival called South By Southwest (SXSW). Every March, Austin swarms with hundreds of acts and thousands of fans and industry types from all over the world, with dozens of music venues participating.

As the home of the University of Texas, the city melds an air of youthful exuberance with legislative seriousness, but it is primarily a college town with

Notorious bandit Sam Bass was high on the Texas Rangers' wanted list. They finally got their man in 1878, after a tip-off about a planned bank raid in Round Rock. They set an ambush, and Bass was badly injured in the gunfight. He died two days later.

BELOW: hiking and biking trail around Austin's Town Lake.

Maps:
Area 146
City 164

all that that implies. Only a few blocks from the Capitol complex – the heart of state government – renowned 6th Street reverberates with rock, jazz, blues, country and reggae until the early hours.

A growing city

Austin has, for years, been growing, partly because there was room for it to grow, though this period of over-development is coming to an end. Whole series of hilltops on which there were only trees and scrub a few years back were turned almost overnight into neighborhoods of slab-on-grade ranch houses, insensitive to the environment both esthetically and structurally. Compared with those elsewhere, costs and profits for developers here are good: Austin land prices are high, although not compared with the prices in bigger cities, while the cost of housing has recently caught up with the major metropolises. But nobody likes traffic, air, water or noise pollution, so city council members often run as development or environmentalist (or "neighborhood") candidates. Running against the developers is a good way to get elected.

Between the mid-1970s and mid-1980s, the strong anti-growth movement hoped to discourage development by refusing to provide roads and other utilities. But Austin has continued to grow anyway, and faster than other "Sunbelt" cities.

The SXSW music convention also includes a film festival – a sensible move in as much as the city of Austin is also a focal point for movie fanatics.

Walking downtown

Despite the city's sprawl, the downtown area is relatively easy to get around. It is dominated by government buildings, notably the pink granite **State Capitol Building** Ⓐ (12th Street and Congress Avenue; free guided tours; tel: 512-463-0063), which, in typically Texas style, is just a few feet higher than its model in

BELOW: the State Capitol, Austin.

Washington, DC. Construction began in 1882, but the building was not completed until 1888. A thorough renovation was completed in 1997 and includes a new underground extension, its roof landscaped to fit in with the historic wooded grounds around the Capitol.

The Texas State Capitol Building is the largest of all the state capitols in the United States and, on completion, was thought to have been the seventh biggest building in the world.

The State Capitol's tourist information office is in the Old Land Office building (11th and San Jacinto streets; tel: 512-305-8400). Informative 2-hour walking tours down historic Congress Avenue and along 6th Street leave the Capitol steps at 9am on Thursday, Friday and Saturday; also Sunday at 2pm (contact the Austin Visitor's Center, 201 E 2nd Street; tel: 800-926-2282). Across from the Capitol is the Greek Revival **Governor's Mansion** Ⓑ (1010 Colorado Street; free tours Mon–Thur; tel: 512-463-5516), built in 1856 by Abner Cook.

Bat Heaven

Surely one of the most unusual tourist attractions must be the colony of thousands of Mexican-freetail bats which congregate under **Congress Avenue Bridge** Ⓒ over Town Lake. At dusk, they set off in search of food. Between spring and fall, crowds gather every evening for a spectacle that can be thrilling.

The Austin-San Antonio area was called "bat heaven" by Dr Merlin Tuttle, the founder and president of Bat Conservation International. Most of the bats in this part of the country are Brazilian or Mexican free-tails. The largest known bat colony in the world is found in the "nursery cave," Bracken Cave near San Antonio, where experts say there are an estimated 200 baby bats per square foot.

Beside Town Lake (actually the Lower Colorado river), on the south side of the bridge, is Zilker Park, home of **Barton Springs Pool** (open daily; entrance fee; tel: 512-476-9044), generally regarded as the city's crown jewel. Thirty-two

BELOW: leader in the fight for Texas independence, Steven Austin.

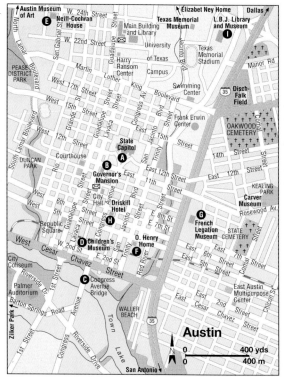

Austin

million gallons (121 million liters) of water a day flow from Barton Springs into this idyllic swimming hole, which was reinforced as a pool almost as long as a football field in 1930. The water temperature supposedly hovers around 68°F (20°C), but it feels much colder at first splash.

Bats also figure in the **Austin Children's Museum ⓓ** (201 Colorado Street; closed Mon; Sun pm only; entrance fee; tel: 512-472-2499), a fun, hands-on, educational facility that opened in 1997. Learning how these mammals fly is just one of the experiences available to all the family, alongside discovering how cities work, learning about health matters and more.

Homes now museums

Some especially interesting old buildings around town are now museums. The **Austin Museum of Art at Laguna Gloria** (closed Mon; Sun pm only; entrance fee; tel: 512-458-8191) is located at 3809 W. 35th Street, on the banks of Lake Austin, on a site chosen by Stephen F. Austin for his own home. A major renewal program is underway and certain sections may be closed until 2004. There is also a branch of the museum downtown.

Shiner beer, from the small town of the same name, southeast of Austin.

The 1855, Greek Revival-style **Neill-Cochran House ⓔ** (2310 San Gabriel Street; open Wed–Sun pm; entrance fee; tel: 512-478-2335) is now the Texas home of the grandly titled National Society of Colonial Dames of America and houses various historic documents.

The **O. Henry Home ⓕ** (409 E. 5th Street; open Wed–Sun pm only; free; tel: 512-472-1903) was the residence of short-story writer William Sydney Porter (who used "O. Henry" as a pen name) from 1893 to 1895. The home features a display of Porter's desk and writing materials, as well as some period furniture.

BELOW: evening flight of the Mexican free-tail bat.

Maps:
Area 146
City 164

The Lyndon B. Johnson Library and Museum in Austin contains a replica of the Oval Office in the White House, as it looked when LBJ was president in the 1960s.

BELOW: Lyndon B. Johnson library, Austin.

RIGHT: the Driskill Hotel, Austin.

Historic sites

The oldest building in the city is probably the **French Legation Museum ⑥** (802 San Marcos Street, east of I-35; open pm only; closed Mon; entrance fee; tel: 512-472-8180), a Creole-style mansion built in 1840 by Comte Alphonse Dubois de Saligny, French *chargé d'affaires*, who may never actually have lived in it. Saligny served under Maximilian I, the short-lived French-born emperor of Mexico who was executed in 1867, aged 35. It is a tradition in Normandy, where Saligny bought a château after making himself rich in America, for villagers to "dance on the old count's grave."

In the Maximilian Room of Austin's **Driskill Hotel ⑪** (604 Brazos Street; tel: 512-474-5911), you can see mirrors ordered by the tragic Maximilian for his mad Empress Carlotta. The Driskill, whose second owner is said to have won it in a poker game and swapped it five years later for a California vineyard, has stood at the western corner of the historic 6th Street block, also known as Old Pecan Street since 1886, among other Victorian buildings now doing time as trendy bars and restaurants.

Further to the north, at 304 E 44th Street, near the airport, is the former home of the German-born sculptress Elisabet Ney (closed Mon and Tue; Sun pm only; free; tel: 512-458-2255), who immigrated to the state in 1870 and whose marble busts and statues ordain many European palaces, as well as the Smithsonian in Washington, DC. The extensive collection in her studio here can be viewed.

Texan President

The most famous Texas-born president is memorialized in the grand **Lyndon B. Johnson Library and Museum ❶** (2313 Red River Street; open daily; free; tel: 512-721-0200) on the 357-acre (145-hectare) campus of the University of Texas. During his presidency (1963–69), Johnson was the recipient of hundreds of gifts from foreign heads of state and most of them seem to be here, along with his 1968 Lincoln limousine. There is also an interesting gift shop with authentic political memorabilia. Humanizing his life from boyhood onwards, the exhibitions include a 20-minute multimedia show, as well as a one-hour film of Lady Bird Johnson who is sometimes regarded with more affection than America's controversial 36th president.

For years Lady Bird has devoted herself to getting the **Lady Bird Johnson Wildflower Center ㉘** established on 60 acres (24 hectares) along the Colorado river. About 8 miles (13 km) southwest of Austin, at 4801 La Crosse Avenue (closed Mon; entrance fee; tel: 512-292-4100), it is a fine place for picnics among the flowers. There is also a visitor center, a library and "Ralph, the talking lawnmower."

Among the best places to see wildflowers, especially Texas bluebonnets blooming in the spring, is the region northeast of Austin where the Colorado river forms a series of lakes (one named for LBJ).

To the east and southeast of Austin the land is flat and fertile. Towns to look out for include **La Grange**, where the "Best Little Whorehouse in Texas" once stood, and **Shiner**, home of the Spoetzl Brewery, founded by German-Czech farmers in 1909. ❏

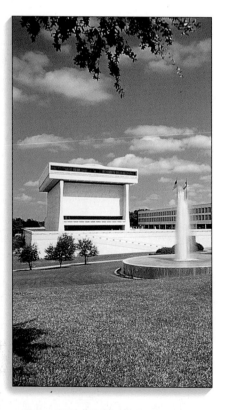

HILL COUNTRY

The Hill Country is a relatively undiscovered treasure, offering natural beauty, abundant wildlife, an intriguing slice of German culture and some of the friendliest towns in Texas

Map on page 172

The Hill Country of Central Texas, a gentle area of sheep and cattle raising, is centered around the pleasant town of **Bandera ❶** (the name is Spanish for "flag"), which describes itself as "the cowboy capital of the world." Bordered on three sides by the cypress-lined Medina river, its origins date to 1854 when a lumber mill was established. However, in the 1870s, it became a staging area for cattle drives through the Bandera Pass, where, in the 1840s, the Texas Rangers beat off a Comanche ambush.

Bandera is reputed to have once had a school operated by John Wilkes Booth under the name William J. Ryan. The old jail, one block north of the County Courthouse, is now the **Frontier Times Museum** (506 13th Street; open daily; Sun pm only; entrance fee; tel: 830-796-3864), which has 30,000 pieces from early Texas cultures and items of technology from the 19th and 20th centuries. Exhibits include a totem pole, a wooden idol from Easter Island and a 400-year-old pair of stirrups that once belonged to a conquistador. Bandera also has, on Main Street, two renowned honky tonk dance halls. Between May and Labor Day, there are rodeos twice a week, and in front of the Bandera Courthouse stands a bronze monument honoring the many national rodeo champions who live in the town.

Pretend cowboys

Before the close of the 19th century, Bandera was already a popular vacation area for families from Houston. They would be entertained by hard-riding ranch-hands from nearby spreads who would ride in on weekends to show off, and gradually the concept of the "dude," or vacation cowboy, developed. Today the Bandera area has dozens of dude ranches, with names like Silver Spur (tel: 830-796-3037); the Dixie (tel: 830-796-4481); Twin Elm Guest Ranch (tel: 830-796-3628); the Flying L (tel: 830-460-3001); the Running R (tel: 830-796-3984); and, on the Medina river, the Mayan (tel: 830-796-3312), nearly all offering comfortable accommodations, swimming pools, Western cuisine, cowboy-themed entertainment and horse-riding lessons. Some offer additional attractions such as golf and fishing.

Also of interest is a tour of the **LH7 Ranch** (entrance fee; tel: 830-796-4314), a 1,200-acre (485-hectare) ranch bought in 1982 by Maudeen Marks, whose family are dedicated to preserving the longhorn cattle. At **Mountain Home ❷**, near Kerrville, the **Y.O. Ranch** (tel: 830-640-3222) welcomes wildlife lovers, who can expect to see white tail deer, antelope and a majestic longhorn or two.

At **Kerrville ❸** itself, music plays a big part in life, with a folk festival in the spring, a wine and

PRECEDING PAGES: taking it easy in Luckenbach. **LEFT:** the Texas Bluebonnet – the State flower – in LBJ State Park. **BELOW:** the Admiral Nimitz Museum, Fredericksburg.

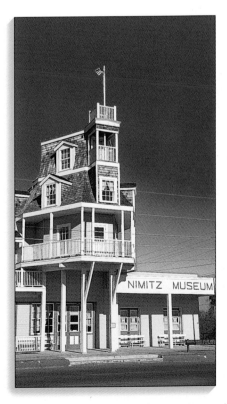

Roadside welcome.

music festival over the Labor Day weekend and a traditional festival of country music in the fall (for information, tel: 830-257-3600). The town's **Cowboy Artists of America Museum** (1550 Bandera Highway; open daily; Sun pm only; entrance fee; tel: 830-896-2553) is a treasure house of Western art, most of it executed by artists who have ridden the range, while the **Hill Country Museum** (226 Earl Garrett Street; closed Sun; entrance fee; tel: 830-896-8633), in a restored Victorian mansion, portrays the affluent life of the region's early days. In downtown Kerrville is Old Republic Square, with brick sidewalks, stone walls, fountains and cedar-finished buildings shaded by pecan trees. City slickers are invited to partake in "an authentic cowboy experience" on the five-day **Leon Harrel's Old West Adventure** (tel: 830-896-8802), where horsemanship lessons precede scenic trail rides and helpings of "cowboy cuisine."

Wildlife

Near the Guadalupe river is the **Riverside Nature Center** on Lemos Street (open daily; entrance fee; tel: 830-257-4837), incorporating a wildflower meadow and butterfly garden, surrounding a turn-of-the-20th-century house, which has exhibits and displays.

The Texas Hill Country is a bird-watcher's paradise, home to such rare species as the golden-cheek warbler, the green kingfisher, and the zone-tail hawk. Near Kerrville, at **Ingram**, is the Exotic Wildlife Association (tel: 830-367-7761), which has helped introduce to the region such animals as the llama, the greater kudu, the Siberian ibex, the sable antelope, the ostrich, the zebra, and many varieties of deer.

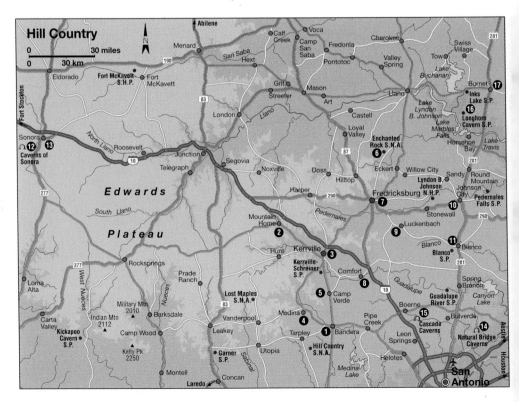

Apple capital

Fourteen miles (22 km) upriver from Bandera is tiny **Medina** ❹, surrounded by apple orchards, from which it derives the title of "the apple capital of Texas." The Texas International Apple Festival is held here annually, on the last Saturday of July, with displays by bagpipers, balloon blowers and apple bobbers. Medina Lake (back south of Bandera) offers good fishing; local wildlife includes deer, antelope, boar and wild turkey; and the Medina river is lined with cypress trees, which were harvested from 1853 in a mill staffed by early Polish immigrants.

Medina Lake is also the scene every September of the Cajun Festival (held at Lakehills Civic Center in Lakehills), home of the Great Gumbo Cookoff. Cajun music and history are also celebrated.

Camel country

Camp Verde ❺, 60 miles (96 km) northwest of San Antonio, is where Jefferson Davis conceived the idea of training a US Camel Corps to operate in rough desert terrain during the Mexican War. Initially, 33 camels were imported, along with experienced handlers from North Africa and, although the sight and scent of the unfamiliar beasts frightened horses and mules, they proved capable of transporting loads up to 500 lbs (227 kg) without any trouble. The project ultimately failed, however, and, after the Civil War, the camels were sold to individuals and zoos, although a handful continued to roam the hills for many years.

Enchanted Rock

South of Llano and north of Fredericksburg is the **Enchanted Rock State Natural Area** ❻, centered around a huge pink granite dome rising 425 ft

Map on page 172

TIP

For a flavor of old Hill Country, check out the online *Enchanted Rock Archives* (www.texfiles.com/ erarchives), which reprints the histories of people – settlers, adventurers and outlaws – who lived in the area in times past.

BELOW: Enchanted Rock.

TIP

Drive carefully when looking for Luckenbach. The little place is not easy to find. After the popularity of the song *Luckenbach, Texas*, so many road signs were stolen that the Texas Highway Department stopped erecting them.

(131 meters) above the ground. Tonkawa Indians believed ghost fires flickered at the top and heard weird creakings and groanings, which geologists explain as the noise of the hot rock contracting in the cool of the night. It's a good, stiff walk to the top.

Fredericksburg ❼ was founded in 1846 by German settlers and the town retains many traces of its ancestry in its architecture and in the German dialect heard on the streets. Large-scale German immigration continued right up until the Civil War. One notable characteristic is *Fachwerk* – a traditional German building technique consisting of heavy framing and diagonal bracing, with an infill of limestone. Early Germanic homes can be explored at the **Pioneer Museum Complex** (309 W. Main; open daily; Sun pm only; entrance fee; tel: 830-997-2835).

The town is popular with shoppers because of its antiques, gifts, ethnic foods and local wines, and its restaurants and bakeries offer a wide variety of cuisines. **Gish's Old West Museum** (502 N. Milam Street; call ahead, tel: 830-997-2794) is filled with saddles, lawmen's badges, guns and other relics. The **National Museum of the Pacific War** (340 E. Main Street; open daily; entrance fee; tel: 830-997-4379), formerly the Admiral Nimitz Museum, named for the naval officer born in the town, attracts visitors with an interest in World War II. It is housed in a "ship-shape" old hostelry and includes a Garden of Peace, donated by the people of Japan.

Nearby **Comfort** ❽, another town settled by German immigrants, has, in addition to numerous century-old stores in the business district, a distinctive 1892 German church. Tiny **Luckenbach** ❾, southeast of Fredericksburg, is world-famous because of the Waylon Jennings song of the same

BELOW: "Booteek" and gift shop, Luckenbach.

name. On the banks of the Grape Creek, it was never much more than a store, a post office and a saloon, but people came from miles around for the impromptu Sunday music gatherings, which were often attended by major country and western stars.

Map on page 172

LBJ Town

Johnson City ❿, at the intersection of US-290 and US-281, stages the Great Turkey Escape Festival at the end of October each year, when a hundred turkeys are driven through town, mimicking the turkey drives of the early 20th century. The town was named for the ancestors of 1960s President Lyndon Johnson, who was raised here. Tours of his restored **Boyhood Home** are given every half-hour (open daily; free; tel: 830-868-7128). Near Stonewall, between Fredericksburg and Johnson City, is the **Lyndon B. Johnson National Historical Park**, with buffalo, longhorns and white tail deer in enclosures and a restored 1908 house on the site of a working farm. From the park, tours can be taken of the LBJ Ranch (open daily; entrance fee; tel: 830-868-7128).

Another of the Hill Country's little towns that retains some of the quiet style of a bygone era is **Blanco** ⓫. Beside the river of the same name, it promotes its friendly atmosphere and, from Thanksgiving to New Year stages a "Christmas Homecoming" around an immense oak tree on the Courthouse Square.

Untouched by civilization

What was once a 5,400-acre (2,180-hectare) ranch was donated to Texas Parks and Wildlife in 1976, with the stipulation that it "be kept far removed and untouched by modern civilization, where everything is preserved intact, yet

Country singer Jerry Jeff Walker has recorded two live albums in the dance hall at Luckenbach.

BELOW: shoppers welcome here.

Map on page 172

One cave, to the southwest of the town of Bandera, took on increased importance during World War II. Ney Cave was used as the base for Project X-Ray, a secret plan to drop thousands of bats, carrying firebombs, on Japan.

BELOW:
Trinity Lutheran Church, Stonewall, attended by LBJ and his family.

put to a useful purpose." Today it is the **Hill Country State Natural Area**, 45 miles (72 km) northwest of San Antonio, a region of rocky limestone hills, flowing springs, oak groves, grasslands and canyons (for information, tel: 830-796-4413).

Five miles (8 km) north of Vanderpool, off State Route 187, is the **Lost Maples State Natural Area**, spectacularly colorful in November, but an attractive park the year round, offering camping and picnicking among rugged limestone canyons and bubbling springs (for information, tel: 830-966-3413).

Going underground

Over the centuries underground streams have carved out spectacular caverns all through this region. Among the best-known are the **Caverns of Sonora** ⑫ (open daily; entrance fee; tel: 915-387-3105), at exit 392 of I-10, 8 miles (13 km) south of the town of that name. With 8 miles (13 km) of passages lined with crystalline stalactites and stalagmites, it is one of Texas' longest caves. There is also a picnic area and a campground. From **Sonora** ⑬, between 1910 and 1921, a 250-ft (76-meter) wide, fenced track called Tillman's Lane ran 100 miles (160 km) northeast to Brady. Thousands of cattle were driven to the railroad on this track, which was equipped with holding pens, wells and windmills.

Natural Bridge Caverns ⑭ (I-35 exit 175; open daily; entrance fee; tel: 210-651-6101) offer exotic sights carved over thousands of years out of the area's natural limestone. The tourist brochure describes the colors as resembling "35 flavors of ice cream," with rocks "nearly as translucent as china and rooms nearly as large as football fields." Nearby is the **Natural Bridge Wildlife Ranch** (open daily; entrance fee; tel: 830-438-7400), home to everything from wallabies and camels to baboons and parrots. Similar to Natural Bridge Caverns are the **Cascade Caverns** ⑮ (on I-10 south of Boerne; open daily; entrance fee; tel: 830-755-8080), which include an interior, 100-ft (30-meter) waterfall.

One of the oldest commercial caves in Texas is Longhorn Cavern in the **Longhorn Cavern State Park** ⑯ (open daily; entrance fee; tel: 830-598-2283, near Burnet. This has seen a number of uses in the past 100 years but was opened as a tourist cave in 1938 by the Civilian Conservation Corporation. Camping is available in nearby Inks Lake State Park (tel: 512-793-2223).

Flying visit

For travelers seeking only a taste of Hill Country, a steam excursion train runs from Cedar Park City Hall, near US-183 and FM 1431, about 15 miles (24 km) northwest of Austin. The journey takes travelers through the Hill Country to **Burnet** ⑰, on US-281, once a frontier town from whose quarries marble for the State Capitol in Austin was mined. Running on weekends only, the 80-year-old Hill Country Flyer (tel: 512-477-8468) takes just over two hours each way, traveling through beautiful countryside and allowing a short stopover for shopping, museum browsing and refreshment. ❑

Texas Wines

Thanks to the Spanish, there was Texas wine at least 100 years before vineyards were planted in California. In the 19th century, Italian, German and Slavic immigrants to Texas also planted wine grapes and, when the root louse *phylloxera* destroyed millions of acres of European vineyards, it was Texas rootstock that saved the day. Thomas Volney Munson of Denison, whose rootstock was resistant to the *phylloxera*, sent over large amounts of it for grafting to French vines. In France there are at least three statues, and a *place* in Bordeaux, dedicated to Munson.

Since the 1960s, the revolution in wine making has swept into Texas, transforming the landscape, altering the agricultural economy and influencing Texans' choice of beverages to serve with barbecue or Tex-Mex dinners, as well as American or classic French cuisine.

Geology and geography in Texas are as complex as in any other wine-growing region of the world but the state's vineyards are generally concentrated in four basic areas: the limestone Hill Country to the west of Austin; the High Plains around Lubbock; the hilly plains west of Fort Worth; and the Davis Mountains in Far West Texas.

The rugged Davis Mountains are in the area of the state with the highest average elevation, a mile (1,600 meters) or more above sea level. The South Plains around Lubbock are around 3,000 ft (900 meters). Although daytime temperatures can go above 100°F (38°C) in summer, because of radiation cooling at these altitudes, temperatures at night fall to the 50s and 60s°F (10–20°C). In the Hill Country, which can also be very hot in summer, one of the vineyards is cooled by its proximity to a large lake.

On the whole, the climate is comparable to that of France and California, so that *vitis vinifera*, the grape variety that produces all their great wines, also thrives in Texas.

Soils in Texas are generally poor in organic matter. However, this is a condition wine grapes enjoy: the vines develop a widespread root system, with production of grapes limited – a necessity for fine wine.

Among red-wine grapes, Cabernet Sauvignon is a favorite with Texas wine makers. At least two wineries in the Lubbock region have produced fine Cabernets, as well as having considerable success with France's two greatest white-grape varieties, Chardonnay and Sauvignon Blanc. The Lubbock wineries also produce excellent Gewürztraminer, Johannisberg Riesling and Barbera.

World-class Sauvignon Blancs – complex, subtle and delicately herbaceous – are being produced near Austin, too, and halfway between Austin and San Antonio is the only sparkling wine producer in Texas, the Moyer Champagne Cellars, producing wine made from 100 percent Texas-grown *Chenin Blanc*. One of the most exciting developments in the Texas wine industry is the entry of the University of Texas, the owner of over 2 million acres (800,000 hectares), into partnership with the world-renowned, Bordeaux-based Cordier wine *négociant* Richter S.A. ❑

RIGHT: taking in the grape harvest at Bryan, Central Texas.

TEXAS CUSTOMS AND FESTIVALS

"Let the good times roll" is the motto of the Texas Cajun population, but it could easily apply to the rest of this fun-loving, party-throwing state

No matter when you arrive in Texas, there's always something going on – from the giant State Fair at Dallas, with Big Tex to greet the guests, right down to the small-town hoedown.

Texans are great party folk: they enjoy a celebration and they find plenty to celebrate. The pioneering past is a popular theme, seen in events like the Chisholm Trail Round-up in Fort Worth and Christmas at Old Fort Concho, which bring a taste of Old Texas back to life. The cowboy heritage is emphasized by the Texas Cowboy Reunion at Stamford and countless rodeos around the state, and historically important dates like Juneteenth (June 19), the day blacks were emancipated, are big occasions for fun and games. Regional specialties are highlighted in local happenings: the Tyler Rose Festival, the International Wine Classic at Lubbock – even the Great Texas Mosquito Festival, staged at Clute, on the Gulf.

All these events provide ample opportunity for good eating, but food fests, featuring anything from searingly hot chili and sizzling barbecue to Luckenbach's Big Picnic and Luling's Watermelon Thump, focus even more on the Texan appetite. And, like good food, good music is a Texan passion. Austin's South by SouthWest Music Conference and Fort Worth's Van Cliburn Piano Competition are huge draws, while the little town of Athens is home to the Old Fiddlers Reunion. In July, jazz takes over at Corpus Christi.

Texans are never shy about their heritage, achievements and individuality, but these festivals are the ultimate expression of that proud, strong Texan spirit.

▷ **ACTING IT OUT**
Dramatizing history keeps interest in Texas' past alive. The musical drama *Texas*, based around frontier settlers, is staged in the unrivaled setting of Palo Duro Canyon, with music in stereo echoing all around.

△ **TASTY COOK-OFFS**
Lubbock's Chuckwagon Cook-off complements events like Terlingua's chili contest, the Czech kolache bake-off in Caldwell and the Hill Country's *Wurstfest*.

△ **SCRAPING OUT A TUNE**
You're never far from a musical event in foot-tapping Texas, especially one featuring the fiddle, soul of much local music.

◁ **JUST FOR A LAUGH**
Most events are not meant to be taken too seriously. This clown entertains the crowds at the Funtier Days celebration, staged at Bandera in the Hill Country.

GOING BACK TO THEIR ROOTS

The ethnic diversity of the people of Texas expresses itself in numerous ways, but especially in the annual events that each racial group stages.

Fiesta Texas is San Antonio's celebration of its largely Hispanic past and takes the form of street parades, *mariachi* performances, fashion shows and general good, bustling fun. Mardi Gras is big in Galveston among the Cajun and Creole peoples, while Central Texas and the Hill Country commemorate their European roots: Little Ennis hosts the May Polka Festival, showcasing Czech food and entertainment, while Fredericksburg has its own German Oktoberfest and the colorful Easter Fires pageant.

In fall, Native Americans hold a major Pow-Wow, which features arts and crafts stalls as well as displays of dancing, at Grand Prairie, near Dallas.

For details of all these events, *see Travel Tips*.

▽ PLAYING DEAD

Wild West re-enactments provide the core of numerous local events. Cattle round-ups, trail rides and shoot-outs are enjoyed by ordinary folk dolled up in the authentic attire.

▷ RISING SUN/LONE STAR

Not all Texas festivals are introspective. The Sun & Star 1996 festival in Dallas was a three-month celebration of Japanese arts and crafts.

△ A CHRISTMAS CAROL

There's a distinctly British air to Galveston's Dickens on the Strand festival in December: plum puddings, roast chestnuts, bell ringers and Dickens' own works.

SAN ANTONIO

A cultural crossroads, San Antonio is where the United States and Mexico merge, with a splash of German tradition thrown in for good measure

Map on page 184

San Antonio (pop. 1.14 million), encompassing over 3,000 sq. miles (4,800 sq. km), is the ninth-largest city in the US and is sometimes called Mexico's northernmost city. Its majority Latino population is the largest of any city in the United States and the National Autonomous University of Mexico, the oldest institution of higher learning in this hemisphere, has maintained a campus in San Antonio since 1972.

Situated at the edge of the Mexican badlands – the mesquite and chapparal-covered flat "brush country" – and also at the edge of the pretty sheep and cattle-raising Hill Country, San Antonio has long been the principal city of both regions. To the east are the fertile South Central Texas plains, where the first Anglo-American colonists settled in the 1820s.

San Antonio hasn't always been slow-paced, but today that's exactly what attracts Texans and non-Texans alike to the city where tourism and the military are the major industries. The city's major delight is its 2½-mile (4-km) **River Walk Ⓐ** (open 24 hours and free). Here, 20 ft (6 meters) below street level, you will find a romantic sidewalk-lined river running through the heart of downtown, bordered by shops, restaurants, hotels, bars and museums.

For more than a century, the San Antonio river has been the scene of social clubs, carnivals, rodeos and circuses. There were private landings and wide lawns, children swam and the whole city picnicked on it, fished in it, and were baptized under it, sometimes en masse, as illustrated by photographs from earlier days.

PRECEDING PAGES: San Antonio's Riverwalk. **LEFT:** the Tower Life building, illuminated for Christmas. **BELOW:** local transport in San Antonio.

An early fan

The river was admired by one visitor as long ago as the 1850s. In his *A Journey Through Texas*, Frederick Law Olmsted noted: "Few cities have such a luxury… the streets are laid out in such a way that a great number of houses have a garden extending to the bank, and to a bathing-house, which is in constant use."

After the disastrous floods in 1921 and 1929, which left the business district under 8 ft (2.5 meters) of water, a three-block long river cut-off was created, joining the corners of the river where it bends around a 16-block area.

It is hard to believe today, but at one time there were plans to fill in the river, or run it underground so it would, in effect, be used as a sewer. Fortunately, the Conservation Society banded together to protect it and nearby landmarks, and, in 1938, aid was provided by the Works Progress Administration, a federal make-work scheme to cut unemployment. The river was dredged. Dams and rock retaining walls, the pleasant cobblestone and flagstone walks, and stairways from bridges were con-

structed. More than 11,000 trees were planted along the river's banks and, when it was complete, spotlights were deployed in the bushes. There are now 13 bridges crossing the River Walk.

During busy seasons, the sidewalks can become crowded with tourists, but the walk is still well worth the trouble. There is the choice of watching flat-bottomed *chalupa* boats drift by, or boarding the Yanaguana Cruises (daily tours; fee; tel: 210-244-5700) for a 45-minute round-trip boat ride. Tickets are available at the Rivercenter Mall. Private dinner cruises can also be arranged.

Central area

The main river, which runs roughly north to south, makes an almost circular loop between College and Villita streets, with the vast majority of the city's attractions housed within those perimeters.

The most convenient starting point for tours of the city is at the **Alamo** Ⓑ (open daily; free), originally known as the Mission San Antonio de Valero. Named after the viceroy at the time, it was built as the first of five missions in 1718, but its worldwide fame was established during 13 days of 1836, when "the Alamo" was besieged by 5,000 Mexican troops. Early in the century it had served as a garrison for (and earned its name from) a cavalry unit from Alamo de Parras, but, by the time General Santa Anna seized the Mexican presidency, the Anglo settlers in San Antonio were claiming the city for their own and it was in the Alamo they chose to make a stand when Santa Anna came to reclaim it. Barricading himself with his small force within the Alamo's thick stone walls, the commander of the Texians on February 24 1836 sent out an appeal for reinforcements.

Mural along the River Walk.

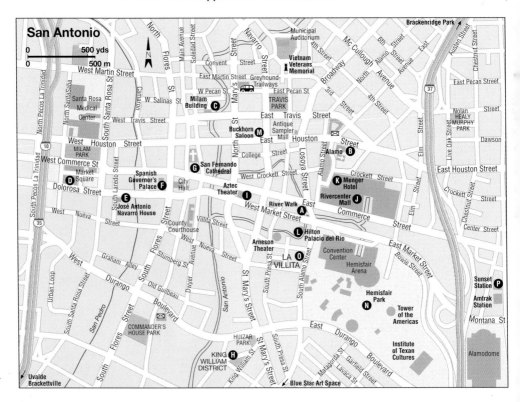

Map on page 184

The appeal read: "To the People of Texas and All Americans in the World – Fellow Citizens and Compatriots:

"I am besieged with a thousand or more of the Mexicans under Santa Anna. I have sustained a continual Bombardment and cannonade for 24 hours and have not lost a man. The enemy has demanded surrender at discretion, otherwise, the garrison is to be put to the sword, if the fort is taken. I have answered the demand with a cannon shot, and our flag still waves proudly from the walls. I shall never surrender or retreat. Then, I call upon you in the name of Liberty, of Patriotism, and everything dear to the American character, to come to our aid with all dispatch. The enemy is receiving reinforcements daily and will no doubt increase to three or four thousand in four or five days. If this call is neglected, I am determined to sustain myself as long as possible and die like a soldier who never forgets what is due his honor and that of his country. VICTORY or DEATH."

– William Barret Travis Lt. Col. Comdt.

The roll call of "Heroes of the Battle of the Alamo" does not only list citizens of American states. Among the countries represented are Ireland, Scotland, Wales, England, Denmark and Germany.

A few volunteers

Thirty-two Texans, or "Texians," from Gonzales, the Lexington of Texas where the first shot of the Revolution was fired, joined Travis after he wrote his stirring letter. They were supported in their defense by some notable Tennesseeans. These included Colonel James Bowie, who had disobeyed General Sam Houston's order to destroy the fortress, and the now-famous Davy Crockett. However, early on the morning of March 6, Santa Anna's men attacked the Alamo, overran the fortress and killed all 189 of its defenders. It turned out to be a Pyhrric victory. Forty-six days later, the cry

BELOW: Mission San Antonio de Valero (the Alamo).

Some historians complain about the presentation of the Alamo site today, that too much emphasis is placed on the famous battle, and not enough on the founding of the mission itself – effectively the founding of the city of San Antonio.

"Remember the Alamo" served as the inspiration for the Texans who surrounded and decisively beat Santa Anna's men at San Jacinto on April 21. (The date is still celebrated by the city of San Antonio with an annual fiesta.) Thus, the Republic of Texas was born.

The Alamo itself – preserved as a national monument, along with its library, gift shop and its grounds – in conjuction with Fort Sam Houston, 2 miles (3 km) north, has become a symbol of the state's stubbornly independent spirit.

Preserved forever

In 1883, the State of Texas bought the familiar chapel with its bullet-riddled walls, but the convent, the surrounding area around it where the beautiful Alamo Gardens are planted, belonged to a liquor dealer and it is said plans were being made to build a hotel. Sam Johnson, the father of President Johnson, has been called the "Savior of the Alamo" because, while a State Senator in 1905, he arranged for the state to buy the Alamo convent.

Clara Driscoll (owner of Laguna Gloria, the lakeside mansion in Austin which later became that city's art museum) is also known as the Savior of the Alamo, since she advanced Sam Johnson $25,000 to buy it until the state was able to do so. Today, the Alamo is managed by the Daughters of the Republic of Texas (DRT), whose members trace their lineage to the original citizens of the republic.

On **Alamo Plaza** you will find the Visitor's Center (tel: 210-207-6748), offering friendly advice and discount coupons for San Antonio attractions. A bus or Texas Trolley Car (tel: 210-228-9776) tour provides an excellent history of the city in the shortest amount of time. For around $10, a horse-drawn carriage

BELOW: San
Antonio skyline.

from the Yellow Rose Carriage Company (tel: 210-225-6490) can give you a 25-minute tour, with up to four children under 12 years riding free. Carriage stands are on either side of the Alamo.

Map on page 184

A walking tour

Visitors preferring to get away from the crowds, at least for a while, can begin their stroll on the quieter stretch of the River Walk – at 4th Street, for example, behind the Municipal Auditorium. The first major landmark on this route is at Travis Street, where the Art Deco **Milam Building** ◉ has been a landmark since the 1920s, when it housed the offices of early oil companies.

The next bridge – there are 35 within the city limits – is at Houston Street, from where a trolley can be taken to visit colorful **Market Square** ◉ (514 W Commerce), a few blocks to the west. A network of VIA streetcars continuously circle the most popular attractions and run until late evening for around 25¢ per ride. There's music in Market Square, as well as many souvenir shops, myriad restaurants, weekend celebrations and full-scale festivals in summer and fall. The huge Mi Tierra restaurant (218 Produce Row, tel: 210-225-1262) and bakery – open 24 hours – is a long-established landmark here and it's also where the *mariachi* bands gather. They will be happy to perform their music tableside, but this service is not free.

Mariachi *musician.*

Historic homes

Walking back to the river along Dolorosa Street, you'll pass the square, stuccoed limestone **José Antonio Navarro House** ◉ (Casa Navarro State Historical Park, 228 S. Laredo Street; open Wed–Sat; entrance fee; tel:

BELOW: on the River Walk.

210-226-4801), home of one of the two native-born Texans who signed the Texas Declaration of Independence. Also here is the 18th-century **Spanish Governor's Palace** ❼ (105 Plaza de Armas; open daily; entrance fee; tel: 210-224-0601), restored between 1929 and 1930. It was never, in fact, the house of any governor, but served the captain of the presidio.

Overlooking Main Plaza is the limestone Gothic Revival **San Fernando Cathedral** ❽ (open daily; tel: 210-227-1297), North America's oldest sanctuary, founded in 1731 and rebuilt in 1873. A plaque stating that the remains of the Alamo dead are located here may be inaccurate, as Santa Anna probably burned the bodies. Here, Graham Greene was reminded of Victorian albums and valentines by the *mantillas* worn by the Hispanic women. He wondered if the San Antonio river wound itself into a heart shape and, in fact, it very nearly does.

In 1938, the pecan "shelleries," as Greene called them, still flourished on the West Side, where impoverished pecan shellers worked for a few cents a day. Greene attended a rally sponsored by Catholic Action, at which "pale and weak and self-conscious" Anglo girls mixed with the "dark sensual confident... half casters – who knew instinctively, you felt, all the beauty and the horror of the flesh."

The plaza fronting the cathedral is the earliest permanently settled spot (by European immigrants) in the state. After the Revolution, it became the liveliest place in town, featuring market stalls and feisty, flirtatious "chili queens," who were ordered to remove their chili stands when San Antonio's new City Hall and the red sandstone and granite Bexar County Courthouse, by James R. Gordon, were completed in the 1890s.

San Fernando Cathedral was founded by settlers from the Canary Islands.

BELOW: Market Square.

The German quarter

Soon after the Republic of Texas was established, a sizeable influx of German immigrants established themselves in the historic **King William District ⊕** – named after the Prussian king – between the river and S. St Mary's Street. Here, in this 25-block area, many refurbished Victorian homes can be admired on a walking tour conducted by the San Antonio Conservation Society (107 King William Street), which can supply a map of the neighborhood. At 509 King William Street is **The Steves Homestead** (open daily; entrance fee; tel: 210-2225-5924), an impressive 1876 mansion filled with period antiques and surrounded by an exceptional garden and fountain.

Across the river, at 1420 S Alamo, is the **Blue Star Art Space** (tel: 210-227-6960), a restored old warehouse district now rife with shops, contemporary art galleries and studios, as well as a brew pub, restaurant and theater.

The San Antonio Conservation Society, organized in 1924, primarily to preserve and restore many of the Alamo buildings, later turned its attention to saving a trio of the city's Art Deco movie theaters. The facade is all that remains of the Texas (1926), while the Majestic (1929) is now a performing arts center. The third is the **Aztec Theater ❶** (1926), whose architect gained his inspiration from studying Mexico's Mayan and Aztec ruins.

The colonnade at Mitla was the model for the foyer, and each column is decorated with a plaster mask of the Aztec moon goddess. A 2-ton (1.8-metric ton) chandelier is a replica of a sacrificial stone. On the fire curtain, the meeting of Cortez and Montezuma is depicted, and over the proscenium Quetzalcoatl, the plumed serpent god of the Aztecs, appears. The theater is now being renovated as a major movie-world tourist experience.

The Blue Star Art Space is run by a non-profit making artists' collective and has a strong community-involvement ethic.

BELOW: more color on Market Square.

TIP

Save a visit to the Rivercenter Mall for a rainy day. As well as plenty of name shops, and the familiar food court, it has the benefit of an IMAX theater, where *The Alamo* movie is just one of a series of daily features.

BELOW: the "Blessing of the Animals" on 17 January.
RIGHT: enjoying coffee on the River Walk.

Hotels old and new

Behind the Alamo, another loop of the river is flanked by two Marriott Hotels (one of the many points you can board a boat for a sightseeing cruise). Here, too, is the **Rivercenter Mall ❶** (849 E. Commerce; open daily), with 130 shops, and the city's huge Convention Center. The story of the hallowed Alamo is told in appropriately spectacular fashion on the six-story screen of the IMAX theater (tel: 210-247-4629) in the Rivercenter Mall, between the 1909 Crockett Hotel and the limestone and stucco **Menger Hotel ❿**, the city's first deluxe hostelry.

In the 1850s, William Menger opened a brewery on the grounds of the Battle of the Alamo and, soon afterwards, he and his wife offered rooms to German farmers from Fredericksburg, Seguin, Comfort and New Braunfels, who rode into San Antonio every so often in ox carts.

Old German farmers gave way at the Menger to presidents, generals and writers, including Oscar Wilde and O. Henry, Jenny Lind, Sarah Bernhardt, and consumptive poet Sidney Lanier, who came to San Antonio for his health. At the Menger, people still use the old lobby (the "rotunda") and patio.

A few good men

There is a theory that, just as the Menger had to send all the way to Boston for ice in those days, so Boston sent to Spanish Texas for horses. Accordingly, the horse Paul Revere chose for his famous midnight ride was obtained from a ranch 20 miles (32 km) southeast of San Antonio, where the Polish town of Cestohowa is now located. In a similar vein, in 1898, during the Spanish-American War, Teddy Roosevelt recruited members of the U.S. Volunteer Cavalry ("Rough Riders") in the Menger Bar (now located at the other side of the hotel). "I need

a few good men," he is reputed to have said, "who can ride a horse, shoot a gun, and want to serve their country." This elite corps of cowboys and millionaires from the East generated a great deal of attention before they went on to Cuba.

In contrast, the 21-story **Hilton Palacio del Rio** Ⓛ, which overlooks the river a few blocks to the south, was built in record time in 1968. It was claimed to have been the world's first hotel put together from pre-constructed rooms produced on an "assembly line." As its honeycomb facade suggests, the rooms, completely furnished and ready to assign to guests, were lifted into place by a crane, and then nudged and straightened with the help of a helicopter.

Fun and thrills

For some fun, next to the Visitor Information Center on Alamo Plaza you will find such attractions as **The Texas Adventure** (open daily; entrance fee; tel: 210-227-8224), a film history that, inevitably, includes yet another Alamo re-enactment, and the **Plaza Wax Theater** (open daily; entrance fee; tel: 210-224-9299), which includes Ripley's Believe It or Not!

Another unusual attraction is the historic (1881) **Buckhorn Saloon and Museum** Ⓜ (318 E. Houston; open daily; free), which contains the world's largest collection of horns.

Panoramic view

Further down Alamo, past the Convention Center, is **Hemisfair Park** Ⓝ – site of the 1968 World's Fair – dominated by the 750-ft (231-meter) Tower of the Americas (open daily; entrance fee), which has glass elevators to take you to an observation deck for a panoramic view of the city. Above the observation deck

Map on page 184

BELOW: the famous Menger Hotel.

is a restaurant that rotates once each hour. Here also are the Institute of Texan Cultures (closed Mon; entrance fee; tel: 210-458-2300) and the Mexican Cultural Institute (open daily; free; tel: 210-227-0123), both displaying interesting historical and contemporary exhibits.

Little Village

Opposite Hemisfair Park is **La Villita** ("Little Village"), the old town of Béjar, now spelled "Bexar," from which Santa Anna's troops set up their cannon line for the Alamo siege in 1836. The previous year, Santa Anna's brother-in-law, General Martin Perfecto de Cos, had stayed in a house here while in command of the Mexican forces sent to calm the Texans.

Despite its name, La Villita is not an exclusively Spanish neighborhood, for Germans and others moved here during the Republic. When it was restored, the intention was to honor San Antonio's Spanish, German, Mexican, French, American and Texan heritage, evidence of which is found in La Villita's architectural styles.

Today, the tiny limestone and adobe buildings contain craft shops, art galleries, restaurants and boutiques. Walk towards the river and you will find the grassy steps of the open-air **Arneson Theater** (tel: 210-207-0527), which often puts on dance and musical performances in summer and during Fiesta. Bring a blanket or a lawn chair.

To the east of I-37, close to the Alamodome sports and convention hall, is **Sunset Station** (1174 E. Commerce), a strikingly distinctive 1902 railroad station that was refurbished in 1998 into an entertainment center. Where once the hoots and whistles of steam trains could be heard, today the noise and bustle

---

The Tower of the Americas is open until 10pm (11pm on Friday and Saturday) and is worth a visit for a night-time view over the city.

LEFT: Tower of the Americas.
RIGHT: the Polish settlement of Panna Maria, near San Antonio.

and bustle come from live music events and the clientele of the depot's restaurants, bars and nightclubs.

Annual Fiesta

San Antonio is invariably associated by most people with the mid-April Fiesta, but it looks festive most of the time. Fiesta is a 10-day, non-stop celebration revealing the heart and history of San Antonio. There are far too many parades, festivals and events to list here (over 100 of them), but check the Convention and Visitor's Bureau website for a schedule (www.sanantoniocvb.com).

San Antonio is the most Roman Catholic, and perhaps one of the most cosmopolitan, cities in America. European visitors feel at home here right away, especially if they are from Mediterranean countries, in a way they rarely do in the rest of the United States.

"Of distinctive Spanish cast," was the 1893 description in *Baedeker's Guide to the United States*, when, with its population of 40–50,000 "Americans, Mexicans, and Germans, with a few Coloured People," it was Texas' largest and best-known city.

Once less than law-abiding

Yet, in some ways, San Antonio is an attypical Texas city. There is not as much aggressive friendliness here as there is in other parts of the state where tourism is not a mainstay. And, in the past, San Antonio was often somewhat less than law-abiding.

"Hardly a day passes," wrote Frederick Law Olmsted in 1857, "without some noise… the street affrays are numerous and characteristic… More often than otherwise, the parties meet upon the plaza by chance, and each, on catching sight of his enemy, draws a revolver, and fires away. As the actors are under more or less excitement, their aim is not apt to be of the most careful and sure, consequently it is not seldom the passers-by who suffer. Sometimes it is a young man at a quiet dinner in a restaurant, who receives a ball in the head; sometimes an old Negro woman, returning from market, who gets winged.

After disposing of all their lead, the parties close, to try their steel, but as this species of metallic amusement is less popular, they generally contrive to be separated by friends before the wounds are mortal. If neither is seriously injured, they are brought to drink together on the following day, and the town waits for the next excitement."

As long as San Antonio lay at the beginning of the Chisholm Trail, there were murders, lynchings and gunfights by cowboys, according to the memoirs of Mary Maverick, the wife of Sam Maverick who lived by the Alamo, where so many of his friends died. And more than once it occurred to someone to call the city a frontier Venice.

When President Roosevelt toured San Antonio's red light district on East Commerce Street in 1936, with LBJ and the New Deal mayor Maury Maverick in tow, he exclaimed he had never seen so many taverns in one block. In fact, the taverns of San Antonio

Map on page 184

TIP

Pick up a copy of the city's own free weekly magazine, *San Antonio Current*, which lists all the local and nearby festivals, as well as music, theater, arts and nightlife.

BELOW: San Antonio's Visitor Information Center.

The Chisholm Trail

From 1867 to 1884, the major route north for cattle was the Chisholm Trail, named for Jesse Chisholm who had established regular trade with northern Indian camps.

At first the trail went by such names as the Kansas, or Abilene, Trail but "Chisholm" soon became the common term for its entire length, from the Rio Grande to Central Kansas. It became the most favored route after fears about Texas tick fever led six states to close off other trails. (The Texan longhorns had built up an immunity to the fever, but it had caused huge losses of cattle in other regions.)

Running from San Antonio through Austin, following what is, roughly speaking, today's I-35, and splitting up at Waco, the Chisholm Trail headed up to Fort Worth and turned eastward at Decatur, to the crossing at Red River Station, which marked the beginning of Indian Territory.

Author Wayne Gard, President of the Texas Historical Association, who wrote the definitive book on the Chisholm Trail, observed that it was like a tree, with the roots being the feeder trails from South Texas, the trunk the main route from San Antonio across Indian Territory, and the branches extending to the various railheads in Kansas.

In many places, such as Salado, the trail headed right up a town's main street. Only here, and at river crossings, were the cattle squeezed down to a group 50–60 ft (15–18 meters) across and confined to a specific trail: they were normally spread out across possibly half a mile (nearly 1 km) of prairie, grazing as they continued on their guided drift north.

Individual cattle tended to keep roughly the same position each day, but there was always an ambitious steer or two to take the lead, and usually a trail boss could rely on a favorite steer to give the herd a lead and be the first into the water at a river crossing.

Wayne Gard once told of a stampeding herd of 1,200 on a northbound trek, in the then small town of Dallas. The two steers that had led the drive stayed in place, remaining perfectly still, and eventually the frightened cattle returned to gather peacefully around them.

The writer J Frank Dobie also stressed the importance of one's companions. Two sayings on the range, he wrote, best expressed the utmost in trustworthiness: "He will do to tie to" and "He will do to ride the river with."

When the railroads eventually penetrated the state and made the Chisholm Trail an anachronism, Texas had more cattle than there had been at the beginning and, although drives continued until the mid-1880s, they were on a reduced basis. In the quarter-century of its existence, the Chisholm Trail saw the passage of more than five million cattle, plus a million mustangs.

Jesse Chisholm himself died in 1838. "No one ever left his home cold or hungry," said the epitaph over his grave. Today's Highway 81 follows the route of the old Chisholm Trail from Fort Worth right through to Newton, Kansas. ❑

LEFT: giant mural commemorating the historic Chisholm Trail, Fort Worth.

never closed, for the city totally ignored Prohibition. Later on, Governor W. Lee (Pappy) O'Daniel sent Texas Rangers here to enforce the state laws by smashing bars and gambling halls.

Hispanics and Native Americans

The first Hispanic mayor of any major US city, San Antonio's Henry Cisneros, elected in 1981 and re-elected in 1985, was good for the self-esteem of young *Chicanos* – one of the many labels Hispanics have to choose from. (Texas Hispanics are called Mexican, Mejicano, Mexican American or Mexican-American, brown, Tejano, Tex-Mex, Hispanic, Hispano, Indio, Indio-Hispanic and La Raza. Each of these terms has a slightly different meaning: for example, Chicano and Indio acknowledge one's Native American heritage.)

Some of this early Native American history, as well as natural science exhibits and local flora and fauna, is documented in the Art Deco **Witte Museum** (open daily; Sun pm only; Tue till 9pm; entrance fee; tel: 210-357-1900) in Brackenridge Park. Behind the museum is a complex of historic houses, including one owned by Francisco Ruiz, who was uncle of José Antonio Navarro and the second of the two native-born Texans who signed the Texas Declaration of Independence. A new addition is the four-story Science Treehouse for kids of all ages.

Park life

Brackenridge Park, which adjoins Fort Sam Houston, lies between US-281 and the Austin Highway, northeast of the city. In its 340 acres (138 hectares) can be found the well-stocked San Antonio Zoo (open daily; entrance fee; tel: 210-734-7184), the Japanese Tea Gardens, the Sunken Gardens Amphitheater,

TIP

The Witte Museum is a good place to take children. It depicts the ecology and wildlife of Texas through plenty of hands-on exhibits.

BELOW: acting out the Wild West at Alamo Village, Brackettville.

Map on page 184

Alamo Village was built between the years 1957 and 1959, specifically for the film The Alamo. *Other movies and TV dramas shot here include the classic* Lonesome Dove. *The set is housed on a working ranch.*

BELOW: stained-glass image of St Anthony in San Fernando Cathedral. **RIGHT:** San Fernando Cathedral at Christmas.

Brackenridge Golf Course, riding stables, a sky ride and a carousel, as well as a miniature train ride.

To the west, in a redesigned old brewery on Jones Avenue, is the **San Antonio Museum of Art** (closed Mon; Sun pm only; Tue till 9pm; entrance fee; tel: 210-978-8100). Further north, before the airport, at 6000 N. New Braunfels, is the **McNay Art Museum** (closed Mon; Sun pm only; free; tel: 210-824-5368), housing the collection of an oil heiress, Marion Koogler McNay, who donated it to the state. Artists showcased include Gaugin, Picasso, Matisse and Cézanne.

On the trail of the Missions

The Witte now stands where, at the headwaters of the San Antonio river – named by the Spaniards for St Anthony of Padua – Spaniards and Native Americans may have encountered one another for the first time. It was here that Don Martin de Alcaron and Fra Antonio de San Buenaventura Olivares arrived with settlers, soldiers and Franciscans in 1718. After the Mission San Antonio de Valero (now the Alamo) and the Villa de Béjar (now Bexar) were established, four more missions were founded. Today, these are part of the **San Antonio Missions National Historical Park** (open daily; free; tel: 210-932-1001), stretching over a 6-mile (10-km) route to the south, beside or close to the river (*see pages 198–9*).

"Ol' San Antone"

San Antonio used to be the "Tin Pan Alley" of Texas. Like Austin today, the city attracted a variety of musicians, and many of them wrote songs about their new home. In many cases, the first time people outside of Texas heard about the city was through the music, and you still find tourists today who are expecting to find the "ol' San Antone" made famous in song.

Out of town

Several thousand German settlers in the mid-1800s formed farming communities – **Gruene**, **Comfort** and **New Braunfels** – just northwest of San Antonio, where the German heritage survives in the form of *fachwerk* houses replete with gingerbread trimmings. Gruene is the most interesting historically and is home to the oldest dance hall in Texas, Gruene Hall (1878).

Heading out of San Antonio along US-90 will bring you to the border at Del Rio, 150 miles (240 km) to the west. Along the way, sightseeing stops might include the **Garner Memorial Museum** at Uvalde (333 N. Park Street; closed Sat and Sun; tel: 830-278-5018), and the **Alamo Village Movie Location** (on Ranch Road 674, north of Brackettville; open daily; entrance fee; tel: 830-563-2580). Uvalde was the home of John Nance Garner, or "Cactus Jack," controversial two-term vice-president to Franklin Roosevelt. Alamo Village was the first movie location built in Texas and has been the base for hundreds of television shows, commercials and films. Its reconstruction of an early Western village, adjoining the Alamo set, includes an Indian store, a saloon and a museum dedicated to John Wayne. ❑

THE CRUCIAL ROLE OF THE SPANISH MISSIONS

Some of North America's oldest buildings survive in Texas, built by Spanish missionaries who sought to educate and "civilize" the local natives

▷ **MISSION UNDER SIEGE**
The most famous mission of them all, though not universally known as such, is the bullet-riddled Alamo – or Mission San Antonio de Valero – founded in 1718 and now surrounded by city-center structures.

△ **ATTENTION TO DETAIL**
The craftsmanship of the builders working on the missions is demonstrated by the Rose Window at San José Mission, San Antonio.

Across Southern Texas lies a chain of early Spanish outposts. Established in the 18th century, these "missions" are evidence of the early efforts made by Spain to colonize the region, but the missions soon found a role in developing the Catholic faith among the local natives, bringing Indian communities under the Christian banner.

Many of the missions in the East became threatened by French incursions from Louisiana, and their communities relocated to San Antonio. The city is the mission heartland of Texas today, housing four separate complexes (five if you include the Alamo) within its boundaries. The four lie to the south, at 2-mile (3-km) intervals along the San Antonio river. The most beautiful is San José, dubbed "Queen of the Missions." Mission Concepción *(above)* is noted for its handsome twin towers, while Missions San Juan and Espada have distinctive three-bell towers. All can be explored using the San Antonio Missions Trail, with literature from the tourist office.

Each complex presents a different theme about mission life for the visitor. Concepción deals with the religious role of the mission; San José handles the defense and social functions; San Juan focuses on the economic importance; and Espada looks after the educational angle.

▷ **ENLIGHTENMENT**
Inside, the mission churches are calm and mysterious, lit mostly by feeble window light and the glow of votive candles, such as these at Mission San José.

◁ **QUIET SIMPLICITY**
Mission church decor is simple: bare walls and beams, the occasional fresco and a dotting of religious icons.

NATIVE AMERICAN INFLUENCES

In addition to the one in and around San Antonio, Texas has another mission trail beginning in El Paso. Stretching some 8 miles (13 km) out to the east of the city, it covers three historic sites: Ysleta Mission, Socorro Mission and San Elizario Presidio.

These centers differ from the San Antonio missions in that they were established by the Spanish together with the local Indian communities. The Native American influence is apparent. The oldest is Ysleta *(above)*, which stands next to the Tigua Indian Cultural Center; it was rebuilt in 1908. Socorro, like Ysleta, dates originally from the late 1600s, though the current structure was completed in 1840. Its foundation by Piro Indians is reflected in the Indian traits in the architecture. San Elizario is the chapel of a former fort and was rebuilt in 1877. All three sites can be visited independently or as part of a trolley-bus tour, departing 10.30am daily from El Paso's Civic Center.

◁ **THE TRAIL OUT WEST**
Socorro Mission, one of the three missions on the El Paso Trail. The original building was destroyed by flooding in 1829.

▷ **COMMUNITY CENTER**
The mission was more than a church: it was the base for a community, its grounds housing animals, gardens, workshops, granaries, kilns and sleeping quarters.

◁ **OUR DAILY BREAD**
Links between the old El Paso missions and the local Native Americans remain strong. This traditional Indian *(horno)* oven forms part of the Ysleta Mission.

▷ **RECONSTRUCTION**
The wooden Mission of San Francisco de los Tejas, the first mission in East Texas, was founded in 1690. It has now been fully rebuilt.

Map on page 204

HOUSTON

Bustling port, financial hub and the gateway to the stars, Houston is an eccentric boomtown: an enjoyable, fast-changing metropolis, with a wealth of attractions

Houston is without a doubt the weirdest, most entertaining city in Texas, a combination of subtropical funk, life in the fast lane, cowboys, a layer of oil, and spacemen: "Houston" was the first word spoken from the moon when the astronauts made contact with home base. Virtually a small town as recently as the late 1950s, Houston's population of over 4 million now makes it the largest city in Texas and the fourth-largest in the US, most of it recently built. One must really search in Houston to find buildings erected before 1960.

Houston is a success in spite of itself. The freeway traffic is as thick as Tokyo's, and the hot humid summers as bad as Calcutta's, once inspiring President George Bush, now the city's most famous retiree, to install air conditioners on outdoor sidewalks to cool G-7 delegates. The lack of initial planning has created a sprawl: an unchecked, wide open city overlaid with intersecting highways, creating a score of separate and distinct neighborhoods.

Surreal scale and proportion result from the lack of zoning: a small boutique may stand next to a 60-story office building, adjoining a house next to a heliport. Houston, more than anywhere else in Texas, operates according to the wildcatter's philosophy: "Dig a little deeper where others have given up, and maybe you'll bring something in."

PRECEDING PAGES: Houston skyline. **LEFT:** the Galleria shopping center. **BELOW:** Houston skyscraper.

Risk-taking wildcatters

Its economy is based on black gold, on an oil and gas industry notorious for the eccentrics and risk-takers it spawns. Because of the oil-price fluctuation in the 1970s, Houston's fortunes rose more quickly than those of any other Texas city. After the drop in world oil prices and demand for energy supplies, its growth slowed to merely brisk. However, the boom that had shaped the city for three decades faltered following Enron's spectacular plunge into bankruptcy in 2001. The collapse of the Houston-based energy company left thousands unemployed, accelerating the city's dip into recession.

But Houston's listless economy has picked up, and there is still plenty of room here for personal and professional growth. Another legacy of the 1970s is the rich ethnic mix – Hispanics, Blacks, Native Americans, Indians, Iranians, Chinese, Thai and Vietnamese – many of whom came to work in the energy industry. The ethnic mix contributes to Houston's resilience, and is undoubtedly part of the reason that it is so tolerant of individuality – and eccentricity.

Near this utterly flat city are low hills and pine forests, salt marshes, swamps and steamy "bayous" (marshy inlets), some of which are infested with alligators. Far to the west, but no more than a day's drive, are real hills, then cactus and the desert. And it is only an hour's drive to the Gulf of Mexico beaches.

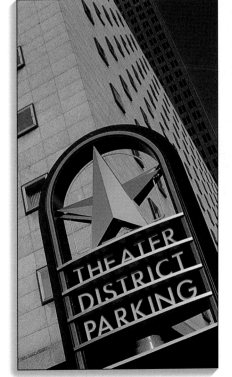

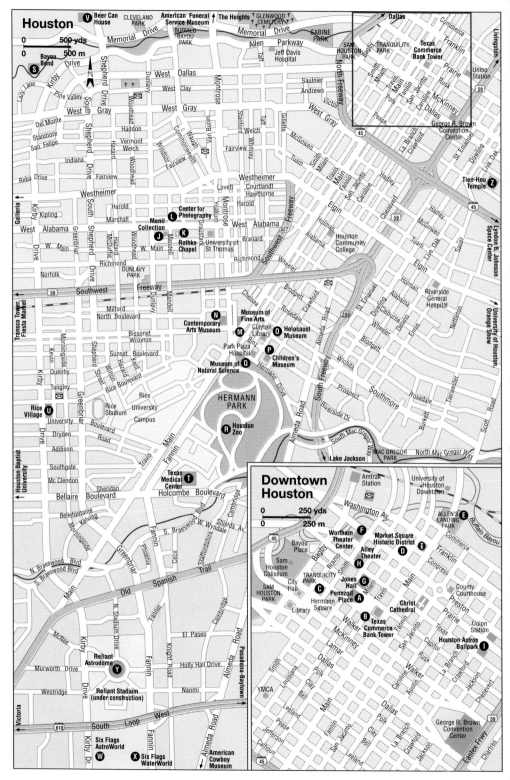

Houston

0 ___ 500 yds
0 ___ 500 m

Beer Can House · CLEVELAND PARK · American Funeral Service Museum · The Heights · GLENWOOD CEMETERY · Dallas · Commerce · Livingston

Memorial Drive · BUFFALO BAYOU PARK · Memorial Drive · Allen Parkway · SABINE PARK · SAM HOUSTON PARK · TRANQUILITY PARK · Texas Commerce Bank Tower · Franklin

Bayou Bend Drive · Jeff Davis Hospital · North Freeway · Bagby · Smith · Milam · Travis · Main · Fannin · San Jacinto · Caroline · McKinney · Dallas · Union Station

Kirby · Lazy Lane · Pine Valley · Shepherd Drive · Dunlavy · West Dallas · Woodhead · West Clay · Montrose · Saulnier · Andrews · Polk · Pease · George R. Brown Convention Center · St. Emanuel · 59

West Gray · West Gray · Haddon · Welch · Gillette · McGowen · Victor · Hadley · Live Oak · Tien-Hou Temple · Z

Del Monte · Stanmore · San Felipe · Indiana · Reba Drive · Fairview · Hazard · Vermont · Welch · Windsor · Fairview · Whitney · Tuam · Smith · Milam · Travis · Main · Fannin · Caroline · Hadley · McGowen · Dowling · Live Oak · Sauer · 45

Westheimer · Lovett · Courtlandt · Hawthorne · Elgin · Holman · Alabama · Houston Community College · Tuam · Live Oak · Elgin · Lyndon B. Johnson Space Center

West Alabama · Center for Photography · Menil Collection · Rothko Chapel · University of St Thomas · West Alabama · 527 · Richmond · Wheeler · Holman · Alabama · Wheeler · Delano · Ennis · Riverside General Hospital · University of Houston, Orange Show

Kirby · Kipling · Greenbriar · Shepherd · Harold · Marshall · W. Main · Branard · Dunlavy ·

West Alabama · W. Main · McDuffie · Hazard · Woodhead · Mandell · Grauston

Norfolk · Drive · DUNLAVY PARK · Chelsea · Blodgett · Crawford · 288 · Dowling · Cleburne · Wheeler · Blodgett · Birket · Rosedale · Tierwester · Scott Road

Transco Tower, Fiesta Market · 59 · Southwest Freeway · Milford · North Boulevard · Rosedale ·

Bissonet · Wroxton · Contemporary Arts Museum · N · Museum of Fine Arts · Clayton Library · Holocaust Museum · O · Wichita · Prospect · Southmore · Rosedale ·

Morningside · Kevin · Quenby · Sunset Boulevard · Kent · Binz · M · Park Plaza Hospital · P · Children's Museum · Museum of Natural Science · Q · Hermann Drive · Riverside Dr ·

Kirby · Tangley · Rice · Rice Boulevard · Rice · University · Campus · HERMANN PARK · Almeda Road · South Freeway · Riverside Dr · MAC GREGOR PARK · North Mac Gregor Way

Rice Village · U · University · Boulevard · Rice Stadium · Houston Zoo · R · South Mac Gregor Way · MAC GREGOR Way · Lake Jackson

Houston Baptist University · Dryden · Addison · Southgate · Mc Clendon · Bellaire · Texas Medical Center · T · Holcombe Boulevard ·

Bellefontaine · Kelving · Travis · Fannin · Main · Sheridan · Boulevard · Shields Av. · S. Braeswood Blvd · W. Wyndale · Cambridge ·

Phoenix · Cecil · Staffordshire · Morningside · N. Braeswood Blvd · S. Braeswood Blvd · Old · Spanish · Trail · Greenbriar · El Paseo ·

Victoria · Main · N. Stadium Drive · McNee · Reliant Astrodome · Y · Murworth Drive · Westridge · Reliant Stadium (under construction) · Fannin · Knight Road · Holly Hall Drive · Naomi · Pasadena-Baytown ·

610 · SOUTH LOOP WEST ·

Kirby Dr. · Six Flags AstroWorld · W · Six Flags WaterWorld · X · Almeda Road · American Cowboy Museum · 45

Galleria ←

Downtown Houston

0 ___ 250 yds
0 ___ 250 m

Amtrak Station · University of Houston Downtown · ALLEN'S LANDING PARK · E · Buffalo Bayou

Washington Av. · Commerce

45 · Bayou Place · Wortham Theater Center · F · Market Square Historic District · i · Congress · Franklin ·

Sam Houston Coliseum · SAM HOUSTON PARK · City Hall · TRANQUILITY PARK · Alley Theater · H · Jones Hall · G · D · Main · County Courthouse

Hermann Square · Library · Pennzoil Place · A · C · Christ Cathedral · B · Texas Commerce Bank Tower · Preston · Prairie · Union Station ·

Walker · McKinney · Lamar · Dallas · Polk · Clay · Bell · Leeland · Pease · Clay · Jefferson · Cahoun · Smith · Louisiana · Main · Fannin · San Jacinto · Caroline · Austin · Capitol · Rusk · Walker · Crawford · Jackson · Houston Astros Ballpark · I · George R. Brown Convention Center · 59

YMCA · La Branch · Chenevert · Eastex Frwy · Charles · 45

Freeway life

Because of its size, the only logical way to tour Houston is by car, in which many Houstonians spend more time than at home, just as they spend more on car payments than on rent. The downtown area is enclosed by I-45 on the west and, some way to the east, US-59, with two other much-visited areas – the Museum District and the Texas Medical Center – to the southwest. The city sprawls between a vast network of busy highways, as a result of which buildings are consciously designed as "freeway architecture." Since there are no changes in elevation, tall buildings function as the only landmarks for the driver.

The I-610 loop that garlands the city also divides it as surely as the Wall once separated Berlin. Snobbery on the part of those who live inside the Loop, where all the desirable neighborhoods and almost all of the tourist attractions are located, is an accepted feature of local life. Perhaps the best-known downtown structure is Philip Johnson's **Pennzoil Place** Ⓐ, with its two towers that appear to separate and then come together as one drives around the city. One block from Pennzoil Place is I.M. Pei's distinctive **Texas Commerce Bank Tower** Ⓑ, a cool, gray slab nicknamed "the Texas Tombstone."

Statue of General Sam Houston, the Texan hero who gave his name to the city.

Tranquility Park Ⓒ, near Sam Houston Park and its restored century-old structures, including an 1878 general store, is named for the moon base Tranquility. Five gold towers in the park resemble space rockets.

The oldest part of the original city is **Market Square** Ⓓ, opposite the Visitor Information Center (801 Congress Street, tel: 800-365-7575), but more significant is **Allen's Landing Park** Ⓔ, a few blocks north, beside the bayou. Here is where Houston's founders, Augustus and John Allen, first came ashore in 1836.

BELOW: much of Houston's city architecture is very modern.

A 6-mile (10-km) system of **underground tunnels** connects 55 buildings with three hotels in Houston's downtown area, making it possible to visit more than 100 shops and restaurants without surfacing into the heat. This subterranean city is open from 7am to 6pm weekdays and maps are available at banks along the route.

Entertainment areas

Downtown Houston is also the upscale entertainment district, home of the **Wortham Theater Center** Ⓕ, (510 Preston Street, tel: 713-237-1439), hosting both the city's Grand Opera and Ballet companies. The Houston Symphony bunks down in **Jones Hall** Ⓖ (615 Louisiana Street, tel: 713-227-3974), and drama has its main home at the acclaimed **Alley Theater** Ⓗ (615 Texas Avenue, tel: 713-228-9341).

A new ballpark has been constructed downtown for the Houston Astros baseball team. **Houston Astros Ballpark** Ⓘ opened in 2000 at Union Station and features a full-size vintage locomotive along one side. The stadium has a retractable roof to cater for all aspects of the Texan climate. Tours are available daily (closed Sun; entrance fee; call in advance 713-259-8687).

Heading south on Montrose Boulevard, west of downtown, brings you to the **Montrose** district, a major entertainment area whose center is the intersection of Westheimer and Montrose. Driving from downtown along Gray Street takes you through the old Fourth Ward, a tough neighborhood of single-

TIP

To get a feel for the diversity of lifestyles in the Montrose area, grab a drink at one of the sidewalk cafés and watch a colorful parade of punks, college kids, trendy singles and transvestites cruise by on foot and in cars.

corridor houses. Montrose is the home of the largest gay community in Texas, as well as artists, designers, museum personnel and trendy young singles. In its back streets, gay bars cater to every taste; on the main drag, Westheimer, entertainment is directed to a broader spectrum and boutiques display vintage clothing, erotic birthday cakes, neon hair ornaments and punk garb. In the 5000–6000 blocks are elegant shops such as Fendi and Barney's New York. East of the intersection is a string of restaurants and bars, characterized by Tex-Mex cuisine, lasers, videos and neon.

Art and interfaith

As Montrose Boulevard heads south, it becomes more elegant prior to crossing US-59 and heading into the grassy purlieus of the Museum District. A few blocks west, at 1515 Sul Ross, in a specially designed building, is the vast **Menil Collection** ❶ (open Wed–Sun; free; tel: 713-525-9400), a legacy of the de Menil family, with exhibits ranging from medieval and Byzantine art to contemporary works, including the world's largest private collection of surrealist art.

Across the street is a Greek Orthodox church offering a collection of icons for public viewing, and facing it, at the corner of Yupon, is the **Rothko Chapel** ❶, commissioned by John and Dominique de Menil to house 14 paintings by the abstract expressionist Mark Rothko. This interfaith chapel, its entrance flanked by the Broken Obelisk – a memorial to Dr Martin Luther King – is open every day (free; tel: 713-524-9839). Near here can be found the **Houston Center for Photography** ❶ (1441 W. Alabama; closed Mon and Tue; Sat and Sun pm only; free; tel: 713-529-4755), a worthwhile visit for those with an interest in the subject.

BELOW: the Cockrell Butterfly Center.

Where Montrose Boulevard crosses Bissonnet Street, heavy culture sets in: the **Museum of Fine Arts (MFA)** (1001 Bissonnet; closed Mon; Sun pm only; free Thur; tel: 713-639-7300) and the **Contemporary Arts Museum (CAM)** Ⓝ (5216 Montrose; closed Mon; Sun pm only; free; tel: 713-284-8250) sit across the street from each other. The MFA, whose modern addition was the work of the renowned architect Ludwig Mies Van der Rohe, houses a large permanent collection from all periods, with strong holdings of French Impressionists and 20th-century Americans. Across the street, the museum's Cullen Sculpture Garden is open until 10pm. The CAM does not have a permanent collection, but is a stainless steel *kunsthalle* staging nine exhibitions each year, featuring the latest wrinkles in new art. The circle with a huge fountain in the center, just past the MFA on Montrose, was reportedly Frank Sinatra's favorite place in the US. A more sombre experience is offered at the **Holocaust Museum** Ⓞ (5401 Caroline Street; open daily; Sat and Sun pm only; free; tel: 713-942-8000), an educational facility aimed at eliminating prejudice and hatred through poignant permanent and visiting exhibitions.

Science and nature

Four blocks down Binz Street is the **Children's Museum** Ⓟ (closed Mon; Sun pm only; entrance fee; tel: 713-522-1138), with hands-on exhibits. In nearby Hermann Park there is the **Museum of Natural Science** Ⓠ, home to a Space Age Museum and a planetarium (both open daily; entrance fee; tel: 713-639-4629). Part of the complex houses the **Lillie and Roy Cullen Gallery of Earth Science**, containing more minerals and gemstone varieties than you knew existed, and the **Wortham IMAX Theater**, which projects movies hourly onto a six-story screen (tel: 713-639-4629 for schedule). As you enter the park you might want to take a few moments to smell the roses at the Garden Center (open daily; free).

There are other attractions in the park. A six-story glass cone houses the **Cockrell Butterfly Center** (open daily; entrance fee; tel: 713-639-4600), in which thousands of brightly colored lepidoptera flutter around a waterfall in a tropical garden, while the **Houston Zoo** Ⓡ (open daily; entrance fee; tel: 713-529-2632) have a Tropical Bird House, which takes the form of an Asian jungle.

More museums

There are more museums and art galleries in Houston than in any other Texas city. The Museum of Fine Arts, for example, also owns **Bayou Bend** Ⓢ (1 Westcott Street; open Tue–Fri pm, plus Sat am; entrance fee; tel: 713-639-7750), just before Memorial Park. This stunning 24-room mansion, designed by Houston architect John F. Staub, is filled with renowned American art from Colonial times to the early part of the 20th century. The collection was left to the museum by the philanthropist Ima Hogg (it was her real name), daughter of the state's first Texas-born Governor, James Stephen Hogg. The 14 acres (6 hectares) of landscaped grounds are open to the public every day except Sunday and Monday (entrance fee).

Map on page 204

Hermann Park covers some 455 acres (185 hectares) of wooded land and, as well as museums and gardens, includes facilities for sports such as golf, tennis, cycling and hiking.

BELOW: Jean DeBuffet sculpture.

Also not to be overlooked is the **Blaffer Gallery** (closed Mon; Sat and Sun pm only; free; tel: 713-743-9530) – described as a "laboratory for the visual arts and contemporary culture" – at the University of Houston. Echoes of the old West are preserved in the **American Cowboy Museum** (11822 Almeda; open by appointment; (tel: 713-433-4441), and the **American Funeral Service Museum** (415 Barren Springs Drive; open daily; Sat and Sun pm only; entrance fee; tel: 281-876-3063), with a collection of hearses, sarcophagi and coffins, always evokes curiosity from macabre-minded visitors.

Exhibit at Houston's Museum of Medical Science, another attraction in the Museum District.

Oak-shaded campus

The gentle Victorian Romanesque campus of **Rice University**, surrounded by giant live oaks, abuts Hermann Park to the west. **Rice University Art Gallery**, displaying contemporary art, is open to the public (closed Mon; Sun pm only; free; tel: 713-348-6069). Beyond Rice is the immense and highly regarded **Texas Medical Center** ❶, whose 700-acre (283-hectare) complex is home to celebrity surgeons like Denton Cooley and Michael Debakey. Rice, a pleasant retreat from the sterile towers of the Medical Center, has set up a monumental sculpture by Michael Heizer – three 70-ton (63.5-metric ton) blocks of pink Texas granite.

Eccentric architecture

The area around Rice is the most beautiful in Houston. **Rice Village** ❶, at Kirby and University, was Houston's first upscale shopping center and its 325 stores are still a major attraction today. Two stately streets, North and South Boulevard, set the local standard for majestic oak tree canopies, and, behind Georgian Revival facades live the old moneyed classes of Houston eccentricity, as seen in a totally pink house at the corner of Hazard and Sunset streets. Everything, including the fence and garage, is painted tropical flamingo pink.

BELOW:
glistening Houston skyscraper.

A comprehensive tour of Houston architecture would also have to include the unbelievable **Beer Can House** ❶ (222 Malone Street, off Memorial Drive), constructed from 50,000 cans, near the extensive and lovely Memorial Park. Equally unbelievable is the **Orange Show** (2402 Munger Street; open Sat and Sun pm and Wed–Fri am in summer; entrance fee; tel: 713-926-6368), a labyrinth of passages, murals, antiques and a tiny museum, otherwise impossible to describe. The life's work of retired postal worker Jeff McKissack, who built it over 26 years out of junkyard scraps, it promotes the life-giving qualities of the orange. "Be smart; eat oranges" is spelled out in mosaic tiles.

Art Deco tower

Heading out from the city center, US-59, also called the Southwest Freeway, carries a river of commuters every day, with rush hours lasting 6–9am and 2–8pm. At the point where it intersects with Loop 610 stands the ultimate in freeway architecture, the **Transco Tower**, designed by Philip Johnson and John Burgee. The facade, inspired in part by the San Jacinto Monument, is the same on all four sides, in order to be admired from any direction, and its Art Deco lines can easily be taken in while driving at 55 mph (88 kmph). A beautiful nearby fountain rewards those who see it on foot.

Map on page 204

Upscale shopping

A byproduct of Houston's geographical fragmentation has been the emergence of a galaxy of shopping malls. The best-known is the **Galleria** area, centered around Post Oak Road and Westheimer Road near the West Loop (I-610), not far from the Transco Tower. Here can be found a *Who's Who* of retailing – Neiman-Marcus, Saks Fifth Avenue, Gucci, Tiffany, Cartier, and Versace, to name but a few. The area is marked by glamorous buildings designed by Cesar Pelli and Johnson and Burgee, and the enclosed Galleria itself is modeled on Milan's Galleria, but blown up to immense size. Every luxury store under the sun is represented, as well as an ice-skating rink and a jogging track around the roof.

Who shops at the famous Houston Galleria? Well, everyone does now, but in its early years it was supported by the well-heeled from sections like **River Oaks**, west of downtown. Kirby Drive and River Oaks Boulevard are the main streets of River Oaks, Houston's Monument Valley of money and conspicuous consumption. The mansions along streets like River Oaks Boulevard, Lazy Lane and Inwood belong to captains of industry, oil and cattle barons, their descendants and a few Arab sheiks. First-run foreign and independent movies can be seen at the 1939 vintage **River Oaks Theater** (W Gray Street, near Shepherd; tel: 713-524-2175).

The Galleria is home to around 250 stores, in three sections and on three levels. Deluxe department stores like Neiman-Marcus grab the headlines but even the cheapest goods can be bought in the center.

Restaurant row

Further west, the stretch of Richmond Avenue between Chimney Rock and Hillcroft emulates a Parisian-style boulevard, lined with art galleries and side-

BELOW: Rice University.

walk cafés. Many of the city's best restaurants are found around here, some offering entertainment nightly – blues at **Magnolia Bar and Grill** (tel: 713-781-6207), and bowling and electronic games at **Dave & Buster's** (tel: 713-952-2233), both on Richmond near Fountainview. Houstonians are said to eat out more than residents of any other US community and there are over 6,000 restaurants in the Houston area from which to choose.

With its increased Asian population, Houston is no longer just known for its Cajun or Tex-Mex cooking. Here you can eat Chinese, Vietnamese, Thai, Japanese, Indian and many other exotic cuisines.

Fiesta Market

If you exit the Southwest Freeway at Hillcroft and head south toward the Bellaire intersection, you will come to the **Fiesta Market**, the ultimate ethnic grocery store. Advertising is in Spanish, Vietnamese, Chinese, Hindi and English. Fiesta sells everything from cowboy boots to goat's milk. It is always jammed with shoppers, and the interior is ablaze with huge neon signs. It is an astonishing and hilarious store, now replicated at several other locations. Farther along are the famous giant neon cockroach at 5617 Southwest Freeway and the giant neon grand piano at 3133 Southwest Freeway.

Lots of young working people live out in this direction, usually in huge apartment complexes, and there is a plethora of bars, restaurants, discos and movie theaters in Southwest Houston ("Sin Alley").

Heading north

Just north of the center of the city, and slightly west, is a mixed residential and industrial neighborhood called **The Heights**. The houses are older and more graceful, but one of the highlights of The Heights is the grave of Texas billionaire Howard Hughes in **Glenwood Cemetery**, off Washington Boule-

BELOW: Hermann Park.

Map on page 204

vard. Hughes' grave is as simply marked as those of his parents nearby. All three are completely overshadowed by the dramatic figure of a weeping angel embellishing an adjacent grave. This flamboyant monument was prepared by a local interior designer in advance for himself.

Down south

In the southern part of the city are **Six Flags AstroWorld** 🆆 (610 Loop at Kirby Drive; open daily; limited opening spring and autumn; closed winter; entrance fee; tel: 713-799-1234), with rollercoasters and other rides, and **Six Flags WaterWorld** 🆇 (open daily May–Sept; other details as for AstroWorld).

Nearby is the **Reliant Astrodome** 🆈 (tel: 713-667-1400), which has to be seen to be believed. It is vast – large enough to fit an 18-story building inside – and everything that takes place there is a Texas-sized spectacle: especially the not-to-be-missed annual Livestock Show and Rodeo, which fills the stadium with fans of bronco-busting and chuck-wagon racing over 17 days every February.

Almost every kind of sporting event takes place under the roof of the Astrodome. The complex can be toured (entrance fee) every day at 11am and 1pm. The Astrodome now forms part of **Reliant Park**, along with the adjacent Astrohall and Astroarena, plus the new **Reliant Stadium** (home of NFL team the Houston Texans) and an exhibition center. The stadium has a retractable roof, seats nearly 70,000 spectators and is due to take over the hosting of the Rodeo. The future of the Astrodome itself is unclear, especially as the Astros baseball team has moved downtown.

The Harris County Domed Stadium, or Reliant Astrodome, is 218 ft (67 meters) tall at its highest point and can seat up to 65,000 spectators.

BELOW: the Astrodome.

Map on page 204

At the base of the San Jacinto Monument is a free museum dedicated to the history of the region, covering events from the Native American period through to the Civil War and beyond.

BELOW: Texas Commerce Bank.
RIGHT: San Jacinto Monument.

Houston's Orient

Many of Houston's attractions are to the east of town, beginning, on the other side of US-59, with **Old Chinatown**, whose major landmark is the **Tien-Hou Taoist Temple ❷** (1507 Delano Street, tel: 713-236-1015). Here visitors can determine their fortune by shaking out numbered reeds. Be sure to visit the nearby **Kim Son** (2001 Jefferson Street, tel: 713-222-2461), a Vietnamese landmark and the largest Oriental restaurant in the state. Across town there's a burgeoning Vietnamese community operating other restaurants on Milam Street, just south of downtown, while Chinese immigrants and their descendants shop and eat in **New Chinatown**, located in Southwest Houston along Bellaire Boulevard, between Gessner and Wilcrest. New Chinatown is sometimes referred to as the Bellaire Corridor, or the Diho Area, after the **Diho Supermarket**, a large, Chinese food mart.

Ships and spaceships

The wealth Houston enjoys today derives not only from oil discovered elsewhere but the 50-mile (80-km) **Ship Channel** that turned it into an inland port. Houston businessmen persuaded the government to pay for the Channel, which developed their city into one of the three busiest ports in the US, stealing the glory (and the trade) from coastal Galveston, after an apocalyptic storm wrecked the latter city's harbor in 1900. The Channel's turning basin, off US-90A near Navigation Boulevard, is site of free harbor tours, but a more rewarding trip is to visit the other end of the Channel, where it enters Burnett Bay and ends its journey to the sea.

The way there, however, takes one through the **Pasadena–Baytown Industrial Corridor**, a district filled with every kind of petrochemical processing plant. The air, smells like floor cleaner and plays havoc with the sinuses, although at night the industrial landscape assumes a beautiful, otherworldly quality. Pasadena also has a landmark: the vast **Armand Bayou Nature Center** (8500 Bay Area Blvd; closed Mon; Sun pm only; entrance fee; tel: 281-474-2551).

There are two attractions at this end of the Channel: the World War I dreadnought **Battleship *Texas*** (open daily; entrance fee; tel: 281-479-2431), which served as General Eisenhower's flagship during the 1944 D-Day invasion, and the **San Jacinto Monument**. The latter commemorates the Battle of San Jacinto on April 21 1836, making it arguably the most significant monument in the state, as it marks the date on which Texas won its freedom from Mexico with General Sam Houston's defeat of Mexico's Santa Anna. Only weeks after the ignominy of the Alamo, revenge must have been sweet. The Art Deco monument (3523 Highway 134; open daily; entrance fee; tel: 281-479-2421), offers an elevator ride 570 ft (174 meters) to the top for a view of downtown Houston on one side and a spaghetti bowl of pipelines on the other.

Notwithstanding its varied other attractions, what has brought Houston to worldwide attention in recent decades has been the **Lyndon B. Johnson Space Center** (*see pages 214–215*), 25 miles (40 km) southeast of downtown (take I-45, then NASA Road 1; open daily; entrance fee; tel: 281-244-2100). Thanks to this facility, the name "Houston" has now taken on universal significance. ❑

HOUSTON: THE EARTH'S SPACE CAPITAL

Houston, as home base for NASA's Apollo lunar missions, can claim to be the Earth's most important city in these early days of space travel

In the future, should aliens look back on man's first tentative steps beyond his home planet, the name Houston will be on the tips of their tongues, tentacles or whatever it is they use for speaking. Texas' biggest city has never actually launched a man into orbit, but US-manned space flights have relied upon ground staff here to guide them on their way. Houston is the home of Mission Control, the focus of all earthly activity when an astronaut is up there in the deep blue yonder. But, as well as guiding space craft during their missions, Houston is also the selection and training base for NASA astronauts. It is here that they go through their paces, physically and mentally, before being allowed into orbit.

The Manned Space Center, later re-named the Johnson Space Center, was opened by NASA (National Aeronautics and Space Administration) in 1962, part of a plan to fulfil President Kennedy's declared intention for America to land a man on the moon and return him safely to earth before the decade was out. The Center played its part to perfection, and "Houston" was the first word spoken from the surface of the moon, by Apollo XI commander Neil Armstrong.

In 1981, NASA launched the Space Shuttle, the first re-usable space exploration vehicle, and Houston was again central to its success. Plans are already in hand for further developments, like the International Space Station, a co-operative venture between the US and Russia.

▷ **GIANT LEAP**
The men who made history – the crew of Apollo XI, the first mission to land on the moon: Neil Armstrong, Michael Collins and Edwin "Buzz" Aldrin.

△ **SPACE SHUTTLE**
The Space Shuttle, like earlier rockets, blasts off from Florida but is guided by Houston.

▷ **ASTRONAUT'S VIEW**
From the air, the enormity of the Space Center's 1,625-acre (660-hectare) site is immediately apparent.

◁ ROCKET POWER

One of the Center's biggest attractions is the 363-ft (110-meter) long Saturn V rocket. The most powerful rocket of its day, it lifted the Apollo craft into space.

△ GALACTIC HONOR

Originally known as the Manned Space Center, NASA's Houston site was later renamed to honor Texan-born President Lyndon B. Johnson.

▽ MISSION CONTROL

In 1995, NASA opened a new Mission Control Center at the site. Costing around $250 million, it replaced the old Mission Control, which had monitored the Apollo and Space Shuttle crews.

SPACE-AGE FUN FOR ALL

NASA was established in 1958 as a US Government agency for research into aeronautics and space flight. Throughout the 1960s, it enjoyed substantial funding and plenty of glory, but times have become harder since, with both politicians and the public losing interest in the agency's work. NASA now needs to publicly justify every mission. Part of the PR exercise has been the opening up to the general public of bases like Kennedy Space Center in Florida and the Johnson Space Center in Houston.

Following the tourism success of the Florida center, the Houston base, which already allowed limited guided tours, opened a new visitor center of its own in 1992. With the help of the Walt Disney Corporation's creative genius, NASA has developed a fascinating entertainment and educational exhibit. Now $1\frac{1}{2}$ million visitors a year drop by to see IMAX films, moon rocks, spacecraft and other memorabilia, and to take tram tours of previously off-limits areas. Interactive exhibits allow them to land a Space Shuttle or retrieve a satellite.

NATIONAL AERONAUTICS & SPACE ADMINISTRATION
LYNDON B. JOHNSON SPACE CENTER

EAST TEXAS

Unparalleled woodland, stunning lakes and historic towns make this often ignored part of Texas a discovery; even the oil-producing cities of the "Cajun Triangle" have much to interest the traveler

Map on page 220

There's a whole section of the state larger than New England – and containing more trees – that is certain to confuse most newcomers with its "unTexan" topography. It's the **Piney Woods**, the timber country between Louisiana and Central Texas, the region which was the state's economic launching pad. It was here that industrial interests first wrestled with Mother Nature, raking timber off the land and squeezing oil from below it. A lot of scars remain, but it is known as much for its natural beauty as for its oil and timber industries.

The economic significance of the Gulf and the salt dome geological formations along the relatively unsettled coast mean that the region's largest metropolitan area is found at its southeastern corner, specifically around Beaumont, Port Arthur and Orange. Practically located in Louisiana, the trio of cities – often called the "Cajun Triangle" – flanking I-10, together have a metropolitan population approaching 200,000.

Good guess

Founded in 1835, **Beaumont ❶**, the state's first oil boomtown, sits 21 miles (32 km) up from the Gulf on a deep-water ship channel dredged from the Neches river. Geologists of the late-19th century had scoffed at the theory that oil reservoirs might be tucked inside the salt domes but a local real estate developer, Patillo Higgins, suspected the gaseous vapors and sulfurous water at nearby Spindletop Hill indicated a pool of the valuable liquid. Along with an Austrian immigrant, Anthony F. Lucas, he drilled several unsuccessful wells in 1900 before hitting the Lucas Gusher. After the Spindletop oil discovery on January 10 1901, Texas was transformed from an agriculturally dominated economy into one that could tap very fast-flowing pockets of wealth.

In the space of two years, Beaumont's population swelled from 9,000 to 50,000 as East Texas became the kind of get-rich-quick magnet the nation had seen a half-century before in the California gold rush of 1849. Oil derricks sprouted here as thick as the pines, and their furious pumping of the salt domes took their toll. At the appropriately named **Sour Lake ❷**, about 20 miles (32 km) west of Beaumont on State Route 105, visitors can still survey the damage in the form of a 10-acre (4-hectare) sinkhole created in 1929 by three decades of drilling.

Among the many museums devoted to the industry's fascinating history are Beaumont's reconstructed **Gladys City Boomtown** (open pm only; closed Mon; entrance fee; tel: 409-835-0823) on the Lamar University campus, and the **Texas Energy Museum**, situated on Main Street (closed Mon; Sun pm only; entrance fee; tel: 409-833-5100).

PRECEDING PAGES: East Texas farming. **LEFT:** Kilgore Rangerette. **BELOW:** East Texas pines.

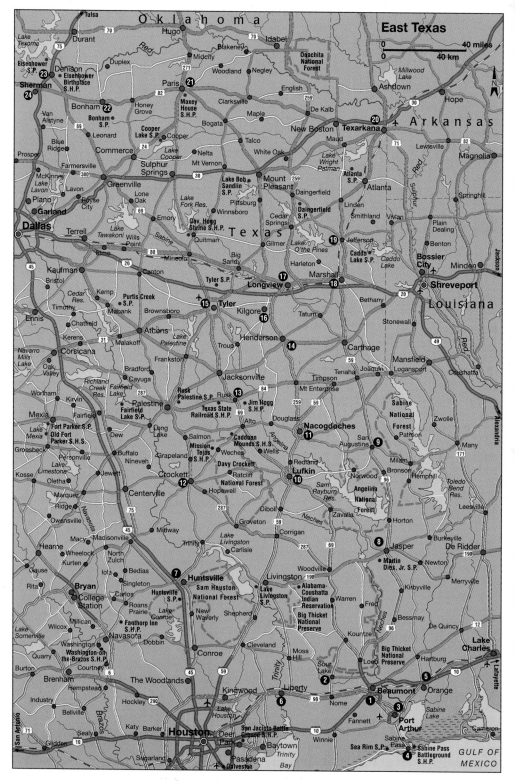

East Texas

The city's oldest home, the **John Jay French Historic House Museum** (2985 French Road; closed Mon; Sun pm only; entrance fee; tel: 409-898-3267), depicts the life of the Connecticut-born trader who settled here in 1845, while the elegant **McFaddin-Ward House** (1906 McFaddin Avenue; closed Mon; Sun pm only; entrance fee; tel: 409-832-1906) is a 17-room mansion owned by an early 20th-century oilman. Among the city's other sights are the **Edison Plaza Museum** (350 Pine Street; open Tues–Fri pm; free; tel: 409-839-3089), housed, appropriately, in a converted power station and devoted to the life of the great inventor; the **Fire Museum of Texas** (400 Walnut Street; closed Sat and Sun; free; tel: 409-880-3927), and a memorial (open daily; free; tel: 409-833-4622) on I-10 to the state's most famous athlete, Babe Didrickson Zaharias, the Beaumont-born triple winner of track and field events at the 1932 Los Angeles Olympics.

The marshy areas of East Texas are alligator country – beware!

Lively Cajuns

Beaumont's sister city to the southeast is **Port Arthur ❸**. Home of the world's largest petrochemical complex, it is noted for its fleet of shrimp boats, its superlative seafood and its Cajun nightclubs with their fiddle music and rowdy atmosphere. "*Les le Bon Ton Roule!*" – Let the good times roll! – is a much-quoted Cajun saying, which the tourist board never tires of pointing out.

Port Arthur was the home of the late rock singer Janis Joplin, whose birthday is celebrated every January 19, and is the kind of place where tourists can attend a genuine, music-filled Cajun wedding – of two alligators.

The city was founded in 1895 as the seaport terminus of his Gulf Coast Railroad by Arthur Stilwell, who ran out of money and lost ownership to a famous speculator, John "Bet-a-Million" Gates. But the glamorous mansions of what was once "Stilwells' Dream City" still remain along the white sandy shores of **Lake Sabine**, some 9 miles (14 km) long and 7½ miles (12 km) across, and joined to the ocean by the Sabine–Neches Ship Channel, which flows right through the city.

The little town of **Sabine Pass ❹**, laid out by Sam Houston himself in 1836, was the site of a famous 1863 Civil War battle. About 40 Confederates, led by a barkeeper named Dick Dowling, deployed half a dozen cannons to drive off a Federal force at least a hundred times as large. Today, Sabine Pass, long ago annexed by its larger neighbor, is famous for fishing and a seafood restaurant, the Channel Inn (5157 S. Gulfway; tel: 409-971-2400), which boasts "if it were any fresher, it would be swimming."

The most famous house in Port Arthur is **Pompeiian Villa** (1953 Lakeshore Drive; closed Sat and Sun; entrance fee; tel: 409-983-5977), an historical site built in 1900 for the barbed-wire inventor Isaac Ellwood. He sold it to a fellow tycoon, Diamond Match Company president James Hopkins. When Hopkins' wife arrived to discover Port Arthur's oppressive heat, mosquitoes and muddy streets she turned right round and returned to St Louis, so Hopkins traded the mansion to banker George Craig for 10 percent of the stock in the newly formed Texas

BELOW: East Texas lakes.

Oil Company (which became Texaco). When chivvied later about why he'd given up his stock for what became known as "the billion dollar house," Craig replied: "Oil companies were a dime a dozen then. How did I know the Texas Oil Company would survive?"

Two other old Lakeshore mansions are worth visiting: **Rose Hill Manor** (100 Woodworth Street; tel: 409-985-7292) and **White Haven** (2545 Lakeshore Drive; tel: 409-982-3068) – both of which are open for guided tours (Mon, Wed and Fri am; entrance fee) – and Port Arthur's heritage is further displayed in its **Museum of the Gulf Coast** (700 Procter Street; open daily; Sun pm only; entrance fee; tel: 409-982-7000), where such celebrated locals as Janis Joplin, the Big Bopper, Harry James, Babe Didrickson Zaharias and artist Robert Rauschenberg are honored. One-hour hard-hat tours can also be made of the oil refineries (tel: 800-235-7822 for appointments).

Over the Rainbow

Rainbow Bridge, a 1½-mile (2.5-km) graceful arc over the Neches river, at a clearance height of 177 ft (56 meters), is the tallest on the coast and joins Port Arthur with the city of **Orange ❺**. Here Farmer's Mercantile on Division Street, a funky store that opened in 1928, is not only still in business but carries some of the same items as when it began.

On Green Avenue, the **Stark Museum of Art** (closed Sun and Mon; free; tel: 409-883-6661) and nearby **W.H. Stark House** (guided tours Tue–Sat; entrance fee; reservations requested; tel: 409-883-0871) are eye-popping structures whose exteriors are almost as interesting as the furniture and artworks that they contain. From Orange, fascinating airboat tours can be taken (tel: 409-883-7725) of the alligator-infested swamps, salt marshes and bayous that surround the area. The rice fields and marshlands, with their moss-laden trees and tropical palms, are a refuge for hundreds of thousands of migrating waterfowl, attractive alike to the birdwatcher and, alas, the hunter.

Further north

Liberty ❻, on US-90 near the Trinity River, between Beaumont and Houston, traces its history back to the Spanish mission erected nearby and its downtown area created by the Mexican government in 1831.

Huntsville ❼, 70 miles (113 km) north of Houston, on US-75 and I-45 – which marks the western boundary of the East Texas pioneer region – was founded in 1830 by settlers from Huntsville, Alabama. It has the state prison and Sam Houston State University, and claims added significance as the town where Sam Houston lived his later life. The site of Houston's grave is also here.

Jasper ❽, 100 miles (160 km) to the east, where US-190 meets US-96 (which runs part of the way alongside Sabine National Forest), offers visitors another chance to view historic sites. Founded in 1824 beside the Angelina river, Jasper was the home of the **Tavern Oak**, a 250-year-old giant pine oak (connected to a tavern there in 1839 but unfortunately destroyed by a tornado in 1996). Several old historic

BELOW: the late Janis Joplin grew up in East Texas.

houses, from around the middle of the 19th century, do, however, exist.

Almost in Louisiana, **San Augustine** ❾ is a town where, at one time or another, nearly every famous Texan in those early days walked the streets, including Davy Crockett who was given a feast here on the way to the Alamo. Historic places include the 1839 house of the famous Texas judge Ezekiel W. Cullen (Congress and Market streets; open Mon–Sat pm); the site of the 18th-century Mission Señora de los Dolores de los Ais; and the Old Town Well, dug to a depth of 27 ft (8 meters) by slaves in 1860 to serve travelers.

Wood wealth

After the political turmoil of the early 1800s had been quelled, a new wave of boomtowns grew up in East Texas, built on another economic base: timber. **Lufkin** ❿, on US-69, southeast of San Augustine, was founded in 1882 and was the home of the South's first paper mill. It remains the center of the state's timber industry.

One main attraction in this city of 38,000 people is the newly expanded **Texas Forestry Museum** (1905 Atkinson Drive; open daily; Sun pm only; free; tel: 936-632-9535), built in a grove of Texas pines, with large glass windows bringing the forest right inside. A moonshiner's still and a blacksmith's forge are among the exhibits. Lufkin also stages an annual Forest Festival every September.

Nacogdoches ⓫, 20 miles (32 km) further north on US-259, was originally settled by Native Americans several thousand years ago and claims to be the first incorporated town in Texas. Now a modern city of 34,000, with a solid economic base of manufacturing, agriculture, retail trade and tourism, Nacogdoches,

Map on page 220

The Mission Señora de los Ais (also known as the Dolores Mission) was founded in 1716 and abandoned in 1773. Nothing remains of the historic structure but its site is marked.

BELOW:
Rainbow Bridge.

almost midway between Houston and Texarkana, makes a fine base for exploring the rest of East Texas.

Nacogdoches has numerous historic sites, of which the most interesting, just north of town, is possibly **Millard's Crossing** (6020 North Street; open daily; Sun pm only; entrance fee; tel: 936-564-6631). It comprises a dozen or more structures, including a church and schoolhouse, some dating back as far as 1820 and many stocked with original artifacts. **La Calle del Norte** (presently North Street) once linked the original Native American settlement to villages in the north, and is said to be the oldest public thoroughfare in the United States.

At Pilar and Lanana streets is the **Sterne-Hoya Home** (closed Sun; free; tel: 936-560-5426), built in 1828 by a pioneer merchant who helped found the state, and now occupied by a library. Here too, is the **Old Stone Fort Museum** (closed Mon; Sun pm only; free; tel: 936-468-2408), a 1779 Spanish trading post reconstructed on the campus of Stephen F. Austin State University. The fort marks the site of four unsuccessful rebellions, and the museum features tribal artifacts alongside memorabilia from the eras of the eight flags that have flown above the fort – Spain, Magee-Gutierrez Expedition, Long Republic, Fredonian Republic, Mexico, Republic of Texas, Confederacy and US.

El Camino Real

Nacogdoches is on one of the most historic routes in America: **El Camino Real**, blazed by the Spanish as "The King's Highway," or the Old San Antonio Road. Travelers can follow that path today by taking US-21 out of Nacogdoches in either direction. El Camino Real linked colonial Mexico with Spanish settlements in Texas and Louisiana by following Native American trails,

The town of Nacogdoches has one further claim to fame: it was here that Texas' first newspaper, the Gaceta de Tejas, was published.

BELOW: Texas State Railroad, Rusk Station.

Map on page 220

shallow fords or rivers. Incorporated into the state highway system in 1929 as Highway 21, El Camino Real connects innumerable other historical sites. Not far to the west, for example, is **Crockett** ⓬, founded in 1837 on the spot where Davy Crockett camped en route to his martyrdom at the Alamo. Historical markers note the location of Davy Crockett Memorial Park, 35 wooded acres (15 hectares) that are ideal for picnics and relaxing.

Trains and Confederate guns

Rusk ⓭, at the intersection of US-84 and US-69, between Lufkin and Tyler, was founded in 1846 and is home of the **Texas State Railroad Historical Park** (trains depart 11am Sat and Sun mid-Mar–mid-Nov plus Thur and Fri in summer; fee; tel: 903-683-2561), a train track which forms the nation's longest and narrowest state park. Visitors can climb aboard for an enjoyable 50-mile (80-km) round-trip journey through the Piney Woods and across 30 bridges, one a 1,000-ft (300-meter) crossing of the Neches river.

Tyler roses.

Historic Fifth Street features old homes and what is claimed to be the nation's longest footbridge, a 547-ft (168-meter) span built in 1861, separating the business district from the old residential area. As an important Confederate Army conscription center, Rusk figured prominently in the Civil War. Look for the historical marker that denotes the Confederate Gun Factory. Two miles (3 km) west of town is the Jim Hogg State Historical Park, 178 acres (72 hectares) dedicated as the birthplace of Texas' first native-born governor (1891–95).

Henderson ⓮, on US-259 in the center of Rusk County, is another find for visitors in search of old houses, with 44 historic properties on the National Register. Founded in 1843 on land owned by the Cherokee Indians, Henderson's attractions include The Depot (514 N. High Street; closed Sun; Sat am only; entrance fee; tel: 903-657-4303), an old railroad depot restored as a museum and children's learning center.

BELOW: Sam Rayburn Library, Bonham.

Metropolitan centres

Three other metropolitan centers – Tyler, Longview and Marshall – are located well within East Texas and are the most representative of purely East Texan urban life, with their oil and timber economic foundations.

Tyler ⓯ (pop. 80,000), the largest, is located about 100 miles (160 km) east of Dallas on I-20 and is a petroleum production center. Also known as the "Rose Capital of America," the town markets more than 50 percent of the nation's rose bushes, maintaining a 14-acre (6-hectare) Municipal Rose Garden (W Front Street; open daily; free; tel: 903-531-1212), containing over 30,000 bushes and more than 400 varieties. The garden is at its best from May through October.

The oil boom of 1900 at Beaumont proved a harbinger of things to come for the entire region, as wildcatters scattered throughout the Piney Woods prospecting for oil. The frenzy peaked in 1930 with the discovery of the biggest well of all, in Rusk County. This well, known as the Great East Texas Oil Field, was a discovery that held the state's economic spotlight until the fields of West Texas surfaced after World War II.

TIP

Auto travel remains the best way to explore the scattered East Texas cities and towns, and the Longview Visitors Bureau can suggest several routes.

The boom town associated more than any other with the 1930 strike is **Kilgore** , just off US-259, 25 miles (40 km) east of Tyler. It lies in the center of the field, with more than 1,000 oil-producing wells. The "world's richest acre" was the description for a downtown block of Kilgore, where 24 oil wells once produced simultaneously. The town's **East Texas Oil Museum** (US-259 and Ross Street; closed Mon; Sun pm only; entrance fee; tel: 903-983-8295) tells the story. Another attraction is the **Rangerette Showcase** (closed Sun; Sat pm only; free; tel: 903-983-8265) at Kilgore College, which pays tribute to the College's high-kicking precision dance team, formed in 1940 to provide half-time entertainment at football games.

On I-20 is **Longview** ⑰ (pop. 72,000), 10 miles (16 km) northeast of Kilgore, which enjoyed explosive growth in the oil-crazed 1930s. Thanks to a dynamic industrialization program begun after World War II, Longview considers its location – among the tall pines, near several well-stocked bass lakes – a magnet for industry as well as recreation. The town's **R.G. Le Tourneau Museum** (2100 S. Mobberly Avenue; open Mon–Fri; free; tel: 903-233-3675, ext. 314), on the university campus, displays patents and objects related to the man who became the world's foremost inventor of heavy earth-moving equipment.

Confederate base

Continuing east on I-20, next comes **Marshall** ⑱ (pop. 26,000), a once-wealthy city that supplied gunpowder and ammunition to the Confederacy, for which it became an administrative center. Originally a stagecoach stop, it achieved its prosperity after the arrival of the Texas and Pacific Railroad. A reminder

BELOW: French trading post.

of those early days is provided by the venerable **Ginocchio Hotel** (1896), which anchors the town's three-block historic district.

Historic homes

When experts on East Texas gather to swap yarns, there's always debate about which town reigns as the best place to see old homes. San Augustine usually wins great praise, but **Jefferson** (pop. 2,200) on US-59, just 58 miles (93 km) south of Texarkana, must be considered a required stop. It is a living museum of antebellum houses.

Laid out in 1842 as a river landing on Big Cypress Bayou, Jefferson boomed into early Texas' primary river port, as steamboats from New Orleans brought settlers westward. With them came the plantation culture and architecture of the Old South. But decline began when the city refused a rail depot.

Many of the city's fine old homes are open during the Annual Historical Pilgrimage on the first weekend in May. Highlights include **The Freeman Plantation** (State Route 49; tours pm daily, except Wed; entrance fee; tel: 903-665-1665), built in 1850 in Greek Revival style and embodying the grandeur of Louisiana plantation life.

Famous patrons

Jefferson's **Excelsior House Hotel** (211 W. Austin; tours daily at 1pm and 2pm; entrance fee; tel: 903-665-2513), dating from 1858, is the second-oldest hotel in Texas, a place patronized by Presidents Rutherford B. Hayes and Ulysses S. Grant, as well as Oscar Wilde and the famous 19th-century industrialist Jay Gould. Still in operation today, it offers guests a chance to relax

Map on page 220

For an easy insight into Jefferson's past, board one of the City Trolley Tours (tel: 903-665-1665). The trolleys run three times a day from Historic Jefferson Tour HQ (222 E. Austin) and take in all the town's historic buildings.

BELOW: Caddo Lake cypress trees, draped with Spanish moss.

amid period furnishings, many of them acquired when the hotel first opened more than a century ago. Nearby is Jay Gould's well-preserved luxury railroad car, named the *Atalanta* (open daily; entrance fee). From **Jefferson Landing**, across the bridge from downtown Jefferson, visitors have the chance to take a 45-minute river tour along the old steamboat channel in 20-ft (6-meter) handcrafted river boats.

Sign on the state border.

Twice as nice

In the northeastern corner of the region is **Texarkana** ❷⓿ (pop. 33,000), perched on the Texas-Arkansas state line and thus half in each state. Texarkana is an agribusiness center for farming, livestock and timber interests in Arkansas, Louisiana and Texas. It's slogan is "Twice as Nice," a phrase to describe the city's unique status, which is best illustrated by one of its most unusual landmarks – the Post Office Building, which straddles the state line.

In addition to the town's **Museum of Regional History** (219 State Line Avenue; closed Sun and Mon; entrance fee; tel: 903-793-4831), depicting 19th-century life in the region, there is the multi-faceted **Ace of Clubs House** (420 Pine Street; closed Sun and Mon; entrance fee; tel: 903-793-4831), built over a century ago by the winner of a poker game and still containing the original furnishings.

Pioneer towns

Another notable pioneer town is **Paris** ❷❶ (pop. 25,000), on US-82 near the Oklahoma border. Founded in 1839, Paris became home to a notorious list of frontiersmen, including retired outlaw Frank James (brother of Jesse James) and bandit queen Belle Starr. Here (by appointment) visitors can tour the

BELOW: jet skiing on Lake Texoma.

Map on page 220

Maxey House State Historical Park (812 S. Church Street; closed Mon–Thur; Fri and Sun pm only; entrance fee; tel: 903-785-5716), an exquisite Victorian home built in 1868 by a Confederate general.

A lesser-known victim of the Alamo siege in 1836, James B. Bonham, had a town named after him the following year. It can be found on US-82 in the northern part of the state. **Bonham ㉒** (pop. 9,000) was the home of Sam Rayburn, the Texas politician who served as Speaker of the US House of Representatives for longer than anyone else. The **Sam Rayburn House Museum** (US-82; closed Mon; Sun pm only free; tel: 903-583-5558), with the nearby Library, contains papers of the farmer's son from Fannin County who was Speaker from 1940 until his death in 1961, apart from two brief interludes.

The **Fannin County Museum of History** (1 Main Street; open Tue–Sat; pm only in winter; free; tel: 903-583-8042), in a restored railroad depot, is an absorbing collection of pioneer artifacts, ranging from ancient costumes to railroad tools. **Fort Inglish Park** (W. Sam Rayburn Drive; closed Mon and Sept–Apr; free; tel: 903-583-3441) displays replicas of the blockhouse and stockade built by Bailey Inglish in 1837.

TIP

When visiting any of the East Texas natural areas, don't forget your insect repellent. The mosquitoes can be ferocious!

Eisenhower country

Denison ㉓ and **Sherman ㉔** on the Oklahoma border near Lake Texoma – an impoundment of the Red River – are rich from farming and livestock industries. While it is well known that Texas produced President Lyndon Johnson, another president also came from the Lone Star State, and Denison takes pride in honoring that favorite son, Dwight D. Eisenhower. The **Eisenhower Birthplace** (208 East Day Street; closed Mon; Sun pm only; entrance fee; tel: 903-465-8908), a two-story frame house, has been restored to its appearance in 1890, the year Ike was born. The adjoining visitor center depicts life during the years when he was president.

BELOW: Native American at the Alabama-Coushatta Reservation.

Green preserves

Despite the development of East Texas – and the disregard of its ecological system – there have been some attempts at conservation. The four national forests offer visitors the opportunity to sample the Piney Woods in their most primitive form, while the **Alabama-Coushatta Indian Reservation** has existed since 1854. Sam Houston established it as a reward to this tribe for their courageous neutrality during the war for Texan independence.

The **Big Thicket National Preserve**, with an information station 7 miles (11 km) north of Kountze (open daily; tel: 420-246-2337), is a dense and mysterious forest that blankets much of the southeast. It was established during the Depression, when the Federal government bought the area from hard-pressed timber companies. A botanist's and ornithologist's delight, the Big Thicket withstood challenges from the oil and timber industries for decades, until environmentalists, in 1974, finally persuaded the US government to establish the Preserve. Its 97,000 acres (39,260 hectares) attract tourists with hiking trails, seminars and guided walks conducted by Park Rangers. ❏

THE GULF COAST

The sea border of Texas runs from Louisiana in the east to Mexico in the south. Its sweeping arc encompasses countless unspoiled beaches, several wildlife sanctuaries and two historic cities

Map on page 234

It's been called a lot of different things – "funky," "scruffy," oddly even "Byzantine" – but one label has rarely been pinned on the Texas Gulf Coast: "chic" just does not fit. It's not the Riviera, and it isn't Rio. Even Daytona and Malibu are very distant American cousins. But, from South Padre Island north to the Bolivar Peninsula, the Gulf Coast ranks as one of Texas' most powerful magnets for travelers. It exudes history.

When the European explorers arrived, its shores were home to beachcombing Native Americans, some of them with a reputation for cannibalism. In keeping with its faded, once rather barbaric image, the coast actually sheltered early 19th-century pirates, seeking refuge from the young United States Navy, which established strongholds on the Gulf. From such a heritage sprang a prosperous trading culture in the late 19th century. The inheritors of that legacy are the present-day developers who have ventured cautiously on to its shores in order to build condominiums and professional buildings. They tread lightly with good reason because, within that legacy, lies a pattern of destruction which visits with clockwork regularity.

Nature's fury

Here on the Texas coast, nature has demonstrated its powers as it has nowhere else. Galveston is the site of the most celebrated catastrophe in US history – the 1900 hurricane, which destroyed the city and killed thousands of people.

Whether or not the wind and rain are pounding from above, the Gulf of Mexico is always pulling from below, eating at the shoreline and claiming the land. Engineers have predicted the eventual reclamation of beach homes at many points during the 21st century.

The great escape

Still, developers take their risks and beach visitors continue to seek that special relationship with the sea. Between storms, and in spite of their fears, coastal Texans have created an enchanting domain. The Gulf of Mexico in summertime is as warm as bath water, and the hour's drive from the urban monster, Houston, to nearby tranquil Galveston provides a contrast that can literally be felt as well as seen.

Less cluttered by neon and glitz than most modern coastlines, Texas' Gulf shore is a welcome escape hatch for city refugees. Visitors won't find the world's best surf, but they will find isolated beaches and sleepy villages with a lifestyle that is as surprising as it is charming.

The Texas coastline runs 367 miles (590 km) in a great arc that forms the southeastern corner of the

PRECEDING PAGES: beach chairs, Padre Island. **LEFT:** king mackerel catch on the Gulf Coast. **BELOW:** Gulf Coast seafood restaurant.

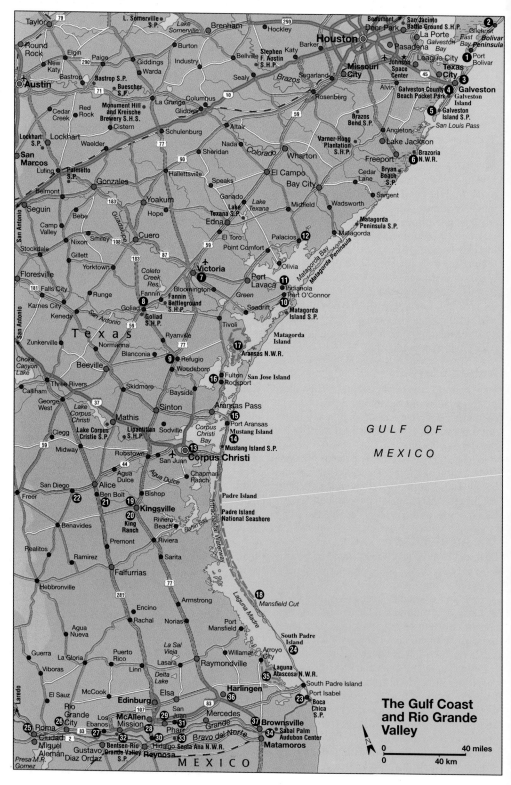

The Gulf Coast and Rio Grande Valley

state. The land here does not end in the abrupt cliffs and rocky shores to be found in other parts of America. In Texas, the land surrenders gradually to the water, drifting from the region of rolling hills and pine forests known as the Coastal Plains into a grassy marshland called the Coastal Prairie. The Coastal Plains includes East Texas and the Rio Grande Valley; the Coastal Prairie is, more precisely, the Texas coast.

Starting at Bolivar Peninsula, just north of Galveston, the Texas shore forms the world's longest chain of barrier islands as it slips towards Mexico: 624 miles (1,000 km) of tidewater coast, when you add the bays, lagoons, and swamps between the bayou marshland in the north and coastal brush in the south. The region includes two cities – Galveston to the north and Corpus Christi to the south.

Diamond in the rough

Unspoiled South Padre Island, to the south, is generally considered the tourist's best chance for a Caribbean resort-style vacation in this state. Compared with South Padre, **Bolivar ❶**, to the far north, is a diamond in the rough. But it can be a true gem for those who appreciate a holiday uncluttered with glitz.

Extending like a long finger down the Texas Coast from Louisiana, the peninsula was named in 1815 to honor the Latin American revolutionary Simon Bolivar, during an era when the Gulf Coast and the Caribbean were aflame with anti-Spanish sentiment. A free ferry carries cars and their passengers from Galveston's east end to State Route 87 on the peninsula, and provides the only convenient access to Bolivar's beaches, unless visitors relish a 70-mile (110-km) drive from Port Arthur. But this very remoteness has guaranteed splendid isolation for Bolivar's beach-goers.

The **Bolivar Point Lighthouse** poses for pictures at Port Bolivar. Constructed in 1852, it was dismantled by Confederates in the "War Between the States" and rebuilt in 1872. Ramshackle beach houses can be rented, but reservations should be made in advance through one of Galveston's real estate companies.

Gilchrist ❷ is a small town about 20 miles (32 km) north on State Route 87 and its main attraction is **Rollover Pass**, a channel that slices through the center of town, serving up some of the best bankside fishing in the state. Elsewhere along the peninsula, visitors will find a montage of honky-tonk taverns, hamburger joints and convenience stores.

Galveston

This island city of 65,000 residents has been described as the only part of the coast you'd want to visit on a rainy day. Visitors who head directly for the beach will miss plenty, because, in addition to the sea, recreational attractions and good shopping, **Galveston ❸** offers a unique historical perspective.

But for that 1900 hurricane, Galveston might have been today *the* industrial heavyweight, instead of its neighbor, Houston. After a roguish beginning as a seaport haven for the pirate clan of Jean Lafitte, Galveston was one of the South's most significant cities by the end of the 19th century.

Map on page 234

Anyone looking for something fancy will be disappointed with Bolivar Peninsula. But it is its simplicity that many find most appealing, and it still stands as one of the best reasons to venture anywhere on the Texas Gulf Coast.

BELOW: the historic Strand district, Galveston.

The French-born Jean Lafitte and his brother, Pierre, were already legendary smugglers in nearby New Orleans, when, in 1817, they founded a town called Campeachy on Galveston Island. Their fort, Maison Rouge, attracted a "navy" of over 1,000 men, who continually disrupted Spanish shipping in the Gulf of Mexico. Lafitte's pirate "den," as it has been called, was a wicked place: slaving, gaming, drunkenness and whoring abounded. He sold all the blacks of Galveston, including freed slaves, in New Orleans. To some a romantic figure, Lafitte was the last of the pirates on the Gulf – until the US Navy forced him out of the area in the early 1820s. He sailed away to Mugeres Island off Yucatan.

Juneteenth, or Emancipation Day, is celebrated in cities all over Texas, with marching bands, music (especially gospel) and dance.

Galveston was then developed as a seaport during the Republic, and soon became the state's largest city. Blockaded during the Civil War, the city remained in Confederate hands, except for a few months in 1862. The Union Navy entered the harbor in October, landed on Christmas morning and was expelled on New Year's Day 1863. They were back on June 19, 1865, to take over the city and proclaim the freedom of the slaves. "Juneteenth" has been celebrated by blacks in Texas ever since.

Sulfurous harbor

Galveston continued to grow, but its population was eventually surpassed by San Antonio and Houston. Much of Texas' cotton was exported through the city – ancient cotton warehouses and grain elevators survive today – and the water of the bay is still yellow from the shipping of sulfur. A hub of commercial activity between the 1870s and 1900, Galveston had Texas' first telegraph, electric lights, brewery and medical college. Splendid mansions were erected, paid for with the profits from all the city's commerce.

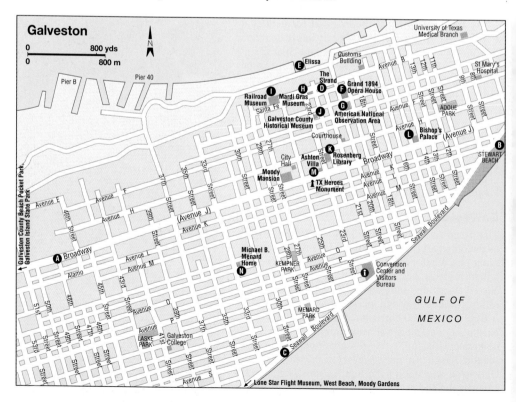

Like the flipping of a switch, the 1900 hurricane on September 8 and 9, dimmed Galveston's glow in a matter of hours. Winds sometimes in excess of 100 mph (160 km/h) swept tides of 4–6 ft (1–2 meters) across the island to produce one of the nation's worst natural disasters. There was nothing to break the hurricane's force: Galveston's highest elevation was a mere 8 ft (2.5 meters). It is said that at one point the water rose 4 ft (just over a meter) in four seconds: 1,500 acres (600 hectares) of houses were completely destroyed. Death estimates have ranged from 5,000 to 8,000.

So complete was the devastation that many wanted to abandon the place, but, stubbornly, Galveston refused to surrender. The people resurrected their demolished homes and constructed a 17-ft (5-meter) seawall, protection against future ravaging by the waters of the Gulf. The present seawall is 10 miles (16 km) long, 16 ft (5 meters) wide at its base and 5 ft (1.5 meters) wide at the top.

Meanwhile, its big rival, Houston, with more people and better rail connections, seized its opportunity and, with Federal money, began dredging a ship channel in the Buffalo Bayou to the San Jacinto river and, from there, into the Gulf. So, Houston – 50 miles inland – became a port city while Galveston, although remaining a port, became less important and was frequently referred to as "that island city south of Houston."

Onto the island

Primary access to the island city is via I-45, a freeway which stretches from Dallas, through Houston, and over a bridge into Galveston. Once on the island, it becomes **Broadway Ⓐ**, Galveston's main street, which carries you through the oldest part of the city to **Stewart Beach Ⓑ**. A right turn on to 61st Street,

Maps:
Area 234
City 236

"Galveston" is an anglicized version of "Galvez," the original Spanish name for the island settlement. It was named for Bernardo de Galvez, the Spanish Governor of Louisiana.

BELOW: Galveston shrimp fleet.

before I-45 becomes Broadway, bypasses the central city and takes you to the island's most popular beach district, **West Beach**, on the south shore. In Galveston, all other roads seem to lead eventually to **Seawall Boulevard** , a broad avenue along the waterline above the city's dramatic seawall, with an array of shops, restaurants, motels, bicycle rentals, arcades and other amusements lining one side, and the Gulf of Mexico pleasantly filling the horizon on the other. The tourist office is at No. 2428 (tel: 888-425-4753).

Popular seafood restaurants on Seawall include Gaido's, founded in 1911, and the adjoining Casey's. The Flagship Hotel is built on a pier out over the Gulf. The Boulevard has several fishing piers where visitors can rent equipment and try their luck at catching redfish, trout and other Gulf game fish, depending on the season.

Buildings restored

Visitors should start with a walk in the **The Strand** , a 12-block area that parallels Broadway between 20th and 25th streets, which was once part of the city's warehouse district. The solid, iron-fronted Victorian structures have been refurbished with more than 90 shops and restaurants. An old-style trolley (tel: 409-763-4311 for schedule) operates around here.

Some highlights in the area include Colonel Bubbie's Surplus Store, possibly the world's best army-navy surplus center, stocking more than 10,000 items from 100 different countries; La King's Confectionery, home of old-fashioned ice-cream; Hendley Market (Victorian clothing, antique postcards); and the 400-ton (363-metric ton) *Elissa*  (open daily; entrance fee), a restored square-rigged tall ship built in Scotland in 1877. The *Elissa* is docked at Pier 21 and,

The Elissa *at sea.*

BELOW: fun in the sun at Galveston Pier.

Map on page 236

in the theater here (open daily; entrance fee), visitors can enjoy a 17-minute documentary about the ship's restoration. Three blocks away are the art galleries and shops of Gallery Row.

Another historic structure is the spectacular **Grand 1894 Opera House** ➍ (2020 Postoffice; open daily; entrance fee; tel: 409-763-7173) where contemporary Broadway musicals are performed. The best overall view of the city is also from this area, at Galveston's only skyscraper, the **American National Observation Area** ➐ (20th and Market streets; entrance fee).

Mardi Gras

The Strand's ambiance is reminiscent of New Orleans' Bourbon Street and, like that colorful Louisiana city, Galveston makes a big thing of the Mardi Gras. The entire city turns out for the parade that marks Fat Tuesday. Beads and token coins fill the air as the Strand celebrates and rejoices. The **Mardi Gras Museum** ➑ is devoted to the subject (The Strand at 23rd Street; open daily; Sun pm only; tel: 409-765-5930), displaying costumes and other historic memorabilia.

The **Railroad Museum** ➒ (25th Street and The Strand; open daily; entrance fee; tel: 409-765-5700), with audiovisual displays and a collection of 35 old rail cars, is situated in the wonderfully restored Santa Fe Railroad Depot on Shearn Moody Plaza. Sculptured life-like figures sit optimistically in the waiting room.

The **Galveston County Historical Museum** ➓ (2219 Market Street; open daily; Sun pm only; donations accepted; tel: 409-766-2340) contains exhibits about Jean Lafitte, the 1900 hurricane and other important local events and characters. More history is exhibited at the **Rosenberg Library** ⓚ (23rd and Sealy streets; closed Sun), opened in 1902 as the first library in the state.

The stage of the Grand 1894 Opera House has, in its time, played host to the likes of actress Sarah Bernhardt, singer Al Jolson and the Marx Brothers.

BELOW: mural along Galveston sea wall.

Historic homes

The city is rich in old mansions and these include the pink granite **Bishop's Palace** ❶ (1402 Broadway; open daily; Sun pm only; entrance fee), the only building in Texas on the American Institute of Architecture's list of 100 outstanding structures. Owned since 1923 by the Galveston-Houston diocese of the Roman Catholic Church, it serves as the bishop's official residence. The 138-year-old **Ashton Villa** ⓜ (Broadway at 24th Street; open daily; Sun pm only; entrance fee), with its wide wrought-iron balcony, is now a museum containing 19th-century treasures, as is the **Moody Mansion** (2618 Broadway; open daily; Sun pm only; Jan–Mar: closed Mon; entrance fee). The oldest mansion is the **Michael B. Menard Home** ⓝ (1605 33rd Street; open Fri–Sun pm; entrance fee; tel: 409-762-3933), built in 1838. Michael B. Menard was the founder of Galveston in the time of the Republic of Texas. His mansion has now been restored and houses remarkable period furnishings and other antiques.

Coastal mix

Between Galveston and Houston is the Kemah-Seabrook area, a region where visitors are certain to find a real mixture of Texas coastal dwellers, ranging from space scientists on their day off from NASA to old seadogs and fishermen swapping yarns at popular hangouts like Jimmy Walker's and Maribelle's.

In the west, **Galveston County Beach Pocket Park** ❹ and **Galveston Island State Park** ❺ provide beach access with parking, for picnics, swimming, sunbathing, or just relaxing by the water. Out here, just south of I-45, you will also find the **Moody Gardens** (open daily; various entrance fees; tel: 800-582-4673), Galveston's major tourist attraction. Among their highlights is a 10-story

BELOW: Corpus Christi sand armadillos.

glass Rainforest Pyramid packed with exotic flora and fauna, which thrive among waterfalls, cliffs, caverns and forests. There's also a Bat Cave, an IMAX 3D Theater, an authentic reproduction of an 1800s paddlewheel, which offers cruises along the bayou, and an aquarium. Newer attractions are the Discovery Pyramid and an IMAX Ride Film Theater, developed in conjunction with NASA's Johnson Space Center. A 300-room convention hotel has also been added.

Not far from Moody Gardens, at Galveston International Airport, is the **Lone Star Flight Museum** (2002 Terminal Drive; open daily; entrance fee; tel: 409-740-7722), a magnet for fans of vintage aircraft, with more than 40 restored planes on display.

Down the coast

Just down the coast, at the point where the Brazos river empties into the Gulf, is the **Brazoria National Wildlife Refuge 6**. It was near here that Stephen F. Austin and his colonists first landed and also where the new government of the Republic of Texas held its first session.

Between the cities of Galveston and Corpus Christi, on US-59, the **Texas Zoo** (Riverside Park; open daily; entrance fee) at **Victoria 7** is the only zoo featuring animals solely found within the state (200 species).

Another place of interest is historic **Goliad 8**, at the crossroads of Highways 59 and 77. Here, not far from the Fannin Battlefield, are the graves of Col. James Fannin and the 342 men who, in 1836, were massacred after surrendering to Mexican general Santa Anna. "Remember Goliad!" became a battlecry of the Texas Revolution. At **Refugio 9**, visitors can take haywagon rides and watch cowboys at work at the Dos Vaqueros ranch (tel: 361-543-4905).

Maps:
Area 234
City 236

TIP

Make a point of visiting Goliad State Historical Park, 1 mile (1.5 km) south off US-183. The huge park includes the reconstructed Mission Espiritu Santo, which was established in 1749. You can also camp, picnic and fish.

BELOW: Gulf Coast beach homes on stilts.

Seashore towns

There are a number of relatively unspoiled little seashore towns close to State Route 35, among them **Port O'Connor ⑩**, a focal point for serious fishermen and duck hunters. **Indianola ⑪**, now reduced to just a few fishing families living among stone foundations at the water's edge, rivaled Galveston as the top Texas port until September 17 1875, when a hurricane literally blew the place away. Further up the coast, **Palacios ⑫**, with its ancient, family-style Luther Hotel, is worthy of note, as are Freeport and Surfside.

Corpus Christi

For fans of sparkling seaside development, **Corpus Christi ⑬** has the flavour of a young Miami Beach. With a population of 278,000, it is the state's eighth-largest city, yet its semitropical climate and reputation as a recreation capital have created the image of tranquility. "The isles of Texas" is the tourist department's description, and those visitors who experience the offshore beaches, deep-sea fishing, catamaran trips and the sailboarding and jetskiing might well remember it that way.

Corpus Christi's 2-mile (3-km) **Seawall Ⓐ**, 14 ft (4 meters) high and 20 ft (6 meters) wide, is an attraction in itself, having been designed by the famous sculptor Gutzon Borglum, who went on to carve the presidential heads on Mount Rushmore. Steps from the seawall down to the beach provide a popular resting place, while joggers, strollers and cyclists populate the top.

Driving in Corpus Christi requires a good map. Because it follows the curve of the bay, few of its streets run straight. The focal point for activity is the **Bayfront Arts and Sciences Park Ⓑ**, at the north end of Shoreline Drive. In

The "Wind in the Sails" statue, on Corpus Christi's Shoreline Drive.

BELOW: taking a rest on a Gulf Coast beach.

addition to a convention center and auditorium, the complex contains the **Art Museum of South Texas** (1902 N Shoreline; closed Mon; Sun pm only; entrance fee; tel: 361-825-3500), designed by Philip Johnson; the Marina; and the Harbor Playhouse – all built right beside the water. Near here is the **Corpus Christi Museum of Science and History** (1900 N. Chaparral; closed Mon; Sun pm only; entrance fee; tel: 361-883-2862), which includes a fascinating display of shipwreck artifacts.

Another site worth viewing is the surprising **Asian Cultures Museum** ❶ (1809 N Chaparral; closed Mon; entrance fee; tel: 361-882-2641), home of a prize collection of treasures from Japan acquired by a Corpus native, Billie Trimble Chandler, during her 17 years as a teacher there.

North Beach

Corpus Christi first came to life as a tent city and shipping point for the US Army, when the annexation of Texas sparked a war with Mexico. In the 1920s, the US government sent in the dredgers to create what became the deepest port on the coast and one that has retained its military ties, with half of the US Navy's air training bases located in the area.

Just across the 620-ft (191-meter) **Harbor Bridge** ❶ – at 250 ft (77 meters) above the water, the state's second highest – is **Corpus Christi Beach** ❶. This area was famous for its casinos and amusement parks in the 1930s, but fell out of favor until a revival in the 1970s. Natives call it "North Beach," and it offers the city's most challenging surf. Also here are the **Texas State Aquarium** ❶ (2710 N. Shoreline Boulevard; open daily; entrance fee; tel: 361-881-1200), and the WWII aircraft carrier USS *Lexington* ❶ (open daily; entrance fee; tel:

The USS Lexington was the longest-serving carrier in the US Navy. It saw action in the waters around Japan during World War II. Self-guided tours take in most areas of the ship, including the massive flight deck. There is also a new MEGA-Screen film theater.

BELOW:
Municipal Marina, Corpus Christi.

361-888-4873). About a mile (1.5 km) to the south is the much shorter **Magee Beach** , a popular attraction for families with small children, on account of its calm and shallow bay waters.

Wild horses

From the crook of Corpus Christi Bay, the city allows excellent access northeast to Mustang Island, Port Aransas and Aransas Pass, known as the "Shrimp Capital of Texas." **Mustang Island** ⑭, earning its name from the wild mustang ponies left behind by the Spaniards several hundred years ago, is a barrier between the bay and the Gulf of Mexico. It protects the city to some extent from hurricanes. Visitors will find one of the state's finest beaches located at Mustang Island State Park, and, at the northern end of the island, they'll find one of the state's best fishing ports.

A (free) 24-hour ferry runs across from where Highway 361 ends to **Port Aransas** ⑮, home for hundreds of shrimp boats moored in Conn Brown Harbor. Among numerous places offering accommodation is the landmark Tarpon Inn (200 E Cotter) – an old hotel once favored by President Franklin Roosevelt. Its lobby walls are covered with tarpon scales autographed by successful fishermen.

Whooping cranes

This whole seashore is a big draw to bird-watchers. The **Rockport-Fulton** ⑯ area attracts thousands of hummingbirds, which rest over to gain weight for their 500-mile (800-km) flight across the Gulf of Mexico. Nearby, famous for the November migration of whooping cranes, is the **Aransas National Wildlife**

TIP

Stock up before you visit Aransas National Wildlife Refuge: the site has no facilities for food or fuel.

BELOW: surf shop, South Padre Island.

Refuge (open daily; entrance fee, tel: 361-286-3559). These protected birds arrive from Canada for the winter and evoke admiration in thousands of tourists with their 7-ft (2-meter) wingspans, long black legs and voracious appetites. The rescue of the whooping cranes from near extinction is a real success story: in 1941 there were only 16 known whoopers; now as many as 170 birds turn up at Aransas. They can be viewed through binoculars from an observation tower, or seen closer up on one of the frequent boat tours, many of which feature talks by professional ornithologists.

Padre Island

Further south, **Padre Island National Seashore**, divided from South Padre Island by **Mansfield Cut** , and preserved from developers, is the finest stretch of natural beach in America. It was named for Padre Nicolas Balli, who bought it from the Spanish Crown for 400 pesos. In 1844, the last of the Balli family moved away and three years later John Singer and his family were shipwrecked on the island. They chose to build a home and stay here. Singer became rich from his shares in his brother's sewing machine company and reputedly buried treasure on the island before leaving. It has never been found and, after a century of storms disrupting the island's landscape, it is doubtful if it ever will be.

Ranch country

Inland, the closest you can get to the coast is along US-77 through ranch country and **Kingsville** ⑲. From here, a diversion should be made westwards along Highway 141 to the headquarters of the famous **King Ranch** ⑳ (open daily; Sun pm only; entrance fee; tel: 361-592-8055). Visitors can watch a video and

Maps:
Area 234
City 242

TIP

The first 9 miles (14 km) of Padre Island have a paved roadway and another 5 miles (8 km) can be driven by car. But the 55 rugged miles (90 km) to Mansfield Cut demand four-wheeling. For beachcombers and shell collectors, however, this trip is mandatory.

BELOW: South Padre condos.

Map on page 234

Whooping crane at Aransas N.W.R.

BELOW: Port Isabel lighthouse.
RIGHT: South Padre Island.

then take a guided tour along a 12-mile (19-km) loop of the immense ranch known for its wealth – worldwide holdings include almost 10 million acres (over 4 million hectares) in seven countries. It also has a stable of Kentucky Derby winners and its own breed of Santa Gertrudis cattle.

Nearby, on State Route 281, is **Ben Bolt** ㉑ (a tiny place with about 100 inhabitants), where a legendary Headless Horseman is buried. This phantom-like figure, who terrorized the region in the mid-1800s with a head dangling from his saddlehorn, was actually a rustler who had been killed by a Texas Ranger, his head tied to a wild mustang as a warning to others.

Northwest of Kingsville, the town of **San Diego** ㉒, on State Route 44, was an important cattle shipping center that grew to be so rowdy that a special detachment of Texas Rangers was stationed there. Their task was to deal with the bands of rustlers which infested the back country.

South to the border

Between the coast and Padre Island, the Intracoastal Waterway continues all the way down to **Port Isabel** ㉓. The Port Isabel Lighthouse (open daily; entrance fee), irresistible to photographers, was built in 1852 on a site used by General Zachary Taylor's army in the Mexican War.

The most unusual wildlife refuge around here is the home of Ila Loetscher, who has made a bayside haven for the endangered Ridley turtle. Loetscher is the founder of **Sea Turtle Inc.**, a non-profit organization that works to find suitable nesting places for the turtle, a species once hunted almost to extinction (6617 Padre Boulevard, South Padre Island; open Tue–Sun; "Meet the Turtles" Tue and Sat 10am; entrance fee; tel: 956-761-1720). Mexican harvests of eggs and

turtles, and the popularity of places like Port Isabel (Boca Chica Beach makes it well worth a trip), threaten their existence.

South Padre Island ㉔, a 34-mile (54-km) section of what is really just a 100-mile (160-km) sandbar, is nowhere more than half a mile (0.8 km) wide, yet it has become the state's premier beach resort, thanks to its windswept dunes, gorgeous beaches and balmy tropical temperatures. Discovered by Spanish explorers in 1519, it was first named *Isla Blanca* for its white sands, whose purity has been preserved despite extensive development.

Only one paved road, Padre Boulevard, running up the center of the island, carries on beyond the city limits, but it peters out after a few miles amidst sand dunes, marshes and birdlife.

Even after the island was joined to the mainland by a causeway in 1974, development barely took off, but, later, a real estate boom began when the causeway was widened and the Texas legislature passed laws forcing the insurance industry to provide coverage to coastal areas.

The island's **Visitor Center** (tel: 800-767-2373), located just north of the causeway from the mainland, offers brochures and information about local accommodation and such attractions as shopping, fishing, water sports and windsurfing. The nearest airports are at the border town of Brownsville. ❑

RIO GRANDE VALLEY

*Drab and downbeat to some, a warm winter haven for others,
the Rio Grande Valley looks set to diversify from its
citrus-growing past and may well become the new Florida*

Along the river, from the dusty Tex-Mex town of Roma to the sultry fishing village of Port Isabel, lies the Rio Grande Valley, a region packed with the history of border wars, steamboat navigation and nomadic Indians who have long since disappeared. There are 38 communities scattered along 110 miles (177 km) of alluvial plain, but most of the towns situated between Falcon Lake and the lower Rio Grande Valley are nothing but caution lights and an extra lane along the highway.

Roma ㉕, founded in 1765, might be considered the beginning of the Valley. Marlon Brando came to Roma in the early 1950s to film several scenes for *Viva Zapata*, a movie about the most romantic hero of the Mexican Revolution, Emiliano Zapata. (Much of the film was also shot in the sleepy (and more picturesque) village of **San Ygnacio** further up the river. The 1830 Jose Trevino house here was chosen because of its typical Mexican design.)

Roma is a border town in economic and architectural decline. There is some interesting old architecture, but the place is so dreary that one South Texas newspaperman declared sarcastically after Falcon Dam was built that a real opportunity had been passed up when Roma wasn't relocated to its middle. The 5-mile (8-km) long dam, constructed in 1953 to control irrigation, was built jointly by the US and Mexico and bears the seals of both countries at the international border line.

Joined by a suspension bridge across the river from Roma is **Ciudad Miguel Alemán** *(ciudad* means city), a clean, modern and uninteresting Mexican town named after a former president. Eleven miles (18 km) northwest of Ciudad Alemán is the forgettable Mexican town of **Mier**. Mier was the site of the capture, in 1842, of the renegade Republic of Texas soldiers involved in the "black bean incident." After capturing Mier, the Texans had to surrender to the Mexican army. They were marched farther into Mexico to Saltillo where 17 of the 176 were executed. A lottery determined who was to die; those who drew one of the black beans from a pot were shot by a firing squad.

LEFT: a *resaca* (oxbow lake) in Rio Grande Valley.
BELOW: Rio Grande Valley wild turkeys.

Roman hills

Along this stretch of the Rio Grande there are some tenuous connections with continental culture. Until the 1830s, Roma was called Garcia's Ranch. A visiting priest convinced himself, and the locals, that the hills here were like those of Rome. It still looks like Garcia's Ranch. In **Rio Grande City** ㉖, a Catholic priest built a replica of the Grotto at Lourdes in France, while, in the same town, a nostalgic François La Borde, in 1899, commissioned a Paris architect to design the family residence. Now the **La Borde Hotel** (601 E. Main Street), it has been restored.

Until the arrival of the railroads, the river was the Valley's principal avenue of commerce, and Rio Grande City, complete with Victorian-era buildings, was an important riverboat terminal. The buildings are still there but the river has retreated to the south, leaving the town high and dry.

The Magic Valley

Americans fleeing the bitter winters of the North are known familiarly here as "snowbirds." But their economic contribution to the Valley is never underestimated.

The "Magic Valley," as it is described by local developers, is where thousands of winter Texans live in their campers. They are fugitives from the mid-continental weather of Minnesota, Michigan, Wisconsin and Lubbock, who finance huge trailers with what they save on heating bills back home. The population here swells in winter months, and it's not uncommon to see citrus orchards doubling as seasonal trailer parks.

Winter Texans provide important extra income for small orchard owners. Citrus emperors like US senator Lloyd Bentsen and his family, McAllen mayor Othal Brand, and the family of late Texas governor Allan Shivers have managed to weather recent changes in the natural and economic climate, as have the region's other agribusiness giants.

Rich soils

BELOW: winter Texans live in campers.

Centuries of flooding have deposited layers of rich alluvial soil along the Rio Grande's banks, helping to make Hidalgo County one of the state's richest agricultural regions, with sugar cane, cotton and vegetables – especially onions – grown the year-round. The land produces 56 varieties of fruit and vegetables and 99 percent of the aloe vera grown in the US. But a series of unprecedented cold snaps has occasionally frozen not only the winter citrus crops but many of the

trees themselves. Some of the growers of the famous Texas Ruby Red grapefruit have sold out rather than replant.

Since the 1970s, when the peso began its protracted decline, most of the economic news here has been bad: unemployment is higher than in any other part of the state, and a drop in price and demand for oil has further crippled the once booming Mexican economy on which the Valley depended. Some argue that the only steady and respectable source of income remaining is smuggling.

If there is anything for the steady and respectable to market, it is the Valley's balmy subtropical climate. Some here are describing the Rio Grande Valley as the Florida of the future, and they are predicting an economic rebirth – good news for a region where one out of every four of the permanent residents lives below the poverty level. Conditions may be right for its growth. Land prices are depressed, retirees are looking for more than water and electricity hook-ups for their trailers, and the state's condominium and mall developers are displaying interest. All of this within a short drive of the best beaches on the Texas coast at South Padre Island. Meanwhile, like the three-car, hand-drawn ferry at **Los Ebanos** ☼ – the last of its kind, running since 1954 – things move slowly.

Bigger and better

Many consider **McAllen** ☼ one of the better places in the Valley to live. It is bigger (pop. 106,000), tidier and a little more upbeat than most surrounding cities. There are adequate hotels and restaurants, though these are usually full during the September white-wing dove hunting season. The city also has a good deal of large shopping centers and chain restaurants. The ancient **Oblate Mission** is where the fathers planted the region's first citrus orchards, but the

Map on page 234

White prickly poppy in the Bentsen-Rio Grande Valley State Park.

LEFT: hand-drawn ferry at Los Ebanos.
RIGHT: Ruby Red grapefruits.

TIP

For detailed advice about crossing the border into Mexico – even just for a few hours – and all the formalities involved, see *Travel Tips* at the back of this book.

valley's vast citrus industry began with the McAllen estate of John Shary. Although his estate is still privately owned, the lush orchards, their trees heavy with fruit in winter, can be observed from the road, and, in spring, the air is heavy with the fragrance of orange and grapefruit blossoms.

East of McAllen, the little town of **Pharr** ㉙ boasts Ye Olde Clock Museum (929 E. Preston Street; open daily; free; tel: 956-787-1923), some of whose 2,000 exhibits are more than 200 years old. The museum may soon be relocated to the town's Texas Theater. Used clothing shops *(ropa usada)* are plentiful in Pharr and it's easy to find a bargain.

Hot spot

The Mexican border is a political hot spot. Farm workers and growers here will continue to square off across picket lines. Mexicans and Central Americans will continue to slip across the river to work in a country where the streets may not be paved with gold, but are at least paved.

The river is 8 miles (13 km) to the south and here the International Bridge connects the American "town" of **Hidalgo** ㉚ – a cluster of freight-forwarding houses – with **Reynosa**, a rapidly expanding Mexican city of 750,000. Parking is available on the American side of the bridge.

Within walking distance of the bridge is Reynosa's Plaza Hidalgo and an open shopping mall in the town's *zona rosa* ("pink zone"). In addition to housing tourist-oriented stalls, shops and restaurants, the zone features bars, discos and hotels. Most of the men in khaki uniforms are not policemen, but *cuidadores*, public parking attendants who, for a reasonable fee, will watch your car and attend to the parking meter while you roam.

BELOW: Rio Grande City from the Mexican side.

Border trouble

This muddy stretch of the Rio Grande, called the Rio Bravo by Mexicans, is shallow enough that undocumented immigrants can tie their shoes and belongings around their necks and hazard an illegal entry into the US. Sometimes they hire a "mule," who will carry passengers on his back. When the river is high, inner tubes or small boats shuttle the illegal immigrants – usually young men, hoping to find work – to the American side.

US Immigration and Naturalization Service officers – *la Migra* – each year apprehend nearly half a million undocumented aliens in Texas, most of whom crossed here. What discourages illegals from crossing further north is the brutal, unforgiving desert, but, from here, Corpus Christi, San Antonio or Austin can be reached within days. And once within a large American community, Mexicans easily disappear into the largely Hispanic population.

Miraculous medicine

East of McAllen at **San Juan** ㉛, on I-83, the reconstructed Shrine of La Virgen de San Juan, built by a Barcelona-based religious organization, houses a replica of a Mexican statue of the *Virgen de Los Lagos*. This local statue won an identity of its own in 1970 when it survived a plane crash that destroyed the original. *Curanderas*, or religious faith-healers, often invoke the *Virgen* to work healings and offer some competition to the more legitimate medical practitioners here.

On the Mexican side of the river, Mexican doctors have established clinics that offer treatments the Food and Drug Administration refuses to approve. Some alternative services are available through long-established clinics; others through doctors trying to compete with a glut of other doctors in Mexico's cities.

Map on page 234

The Rio Grande is the 21st longest river in the world, traveling 1,885 miles (3,030 km) from its source in Colorado to its estuary on the Gulf of Mexico.

BELOW: San Ygnacio, between Laredo and Roma.

Map on page 234

Green jay in the Santa Ana Wildlife Refuge.

BELOW: Boca Chica Beach.
RIGHT: barbecue Texas-style.

Wildlife

The Rio Grande Valley is a bird-lover's paradise. The Texas Parks and Wildlife Department publishes a list of some 274 species sighted in the **Bentsen-Rio Grande Valley State Park** ❷. The subtropical woodland near Mission has been preserved as a wildlife habitat. Other wildlife can be observed at **Santa Ana National Wildlife Refuge** ❸, south of Alamo, which includes over 380 bird species, plus bobcats, coyotes, ocelots and jaguarundi cats. Most of the animals are more commonly seen in Mexico. Nature trails run through the preserve and a tram takes visitors on tours with a skilled guide (daily Thanksgiving–April; fee.)

On FM 1419, south of Brownsville, is the **Sabal Palm Audubon Center and Wildlife Sanctuary** ❹ (open daily; entrance fee; 956-541-8034), an attractive preserve with self-guided trails. Also open to the public is the **Laguna Atascosa National Wildlife Refuge** ❺ (open daily; entrance fee; 956-748-3607). The refuge of open water, marshes, coastal prairie, cropland and brushland is a sanctuary for deer, bobcat and migrating birds, located on the coast south of Port Mansfield.

Half an hour's drive west of the refuge is **Harlingen** ❻, noted for its original working model of the famous Iwo Jima War Memorial (320 Iwo Jima Boulevard; open daily; Sun pm only; free) at Arlington National Cemetery. It depicts the raising of the flag in World War II and was sculpted by Dr Felix W. de Weldon.

Brownsville

To the south, **Brownsville** ❼, connected to the Gulf of Mexico by a 17-mile (27-km) ship canal, is the largest American city on the lower border. A twice-daily Historic Trolley Tour (tel: 956-546-3721) takes visitors around the sites of the town, but, if there is one attraction, other than the nearby beach, that draws visitors to this city, it is the **Gladys Porter Zoo** (500 Ringgold Street; open daily; entrance fee; tel: 956-546-2177). This cageless habitat allows endangered and other species to reside on mini-islands, separated by moats and streams. Visitors can wander along ingenious water-fringed walkways.

North of Brownsville, near the intersection of FM 1847 and 511, is where an artillery duel opened the Mexican War on May 8, 1846. At the Palmito Ranch, south of the city, on May 12–13, 1865, the last battle of the American Civil War took place. Confederate troops (who won) changed places with their prisoners when they learned that Lee had surrendered at Appomatox a month earlier. Photographs of such ancient battles can be inspected in the **Historic Brownsville Museum** (641 E. Madison Street; closed Mon; Sun pm only; entrance fee; tel: 956-548-1313) in the old Southern Pacific Railroad Depot.

Crossing the border

Thousands of people cross every day over the border between Brownsville and Matamoros on the Mexican side. Because of the need for Mexican automobile insurance, many visitors choose to park their cars near the Brownsville Civic Center on International Boulevard, or across from the Chamber of Commerce on Elizabeth Street, both of which are close to the Gateway International Bridge. ❏

DEL RIO TO LAREDO

This well-watered stretch of the Rio Grande Valley has long been a magnet for colorful characters, attracted by the ease of crossing into Mexico and the trade the border region encourages

Map on page 260

Water has been the moving force in Del Rio's history, as in the history of all the Texas border towns. Around 1870, there was considerable development of San Felipe Springs, whose 90 million gallons (over 340 million liters) of water a day attracted farmers and ranchers, and provided agricultural and drinking water for the region. In more recent times, the damming of the Rio Grande and the Devils and Pecos rivers has created a massive lake with huge recreational potential.

Friendship Lake

Lake Amistad ❶ ("Friendship" in Spanish), a reservoir with more than 1,000 miles (1,600 km) of shoreline, was created in 1969. Boat rentals and scuba diving are available here in what is reputedly the state's best lake for bass fishing and the second-best for underwater visibility. Hunting licenses for deer, turkey, dove, quail and the more exotic game found in this National Recreational Area are available on a daily or seasonal basis.

Native American cave paintings, some dating back 8,000 years, are also found along the shores of Lake Amistad and, although many are inaccessible, others such as Panther Cave can be reached by boat if lake levels are high enough. Sadly, hundreds of caves were inundated when the Amistad Dam was built, and many of the more accessible ones today have been defaced by vandals. However, some of the better paintings are now protected by the State of Texas at **Seminole Canyon State Park ❷** (open daily; entrance fee), on the northern extension of the lake. All 400 or so archeological sites on the lakeshore are owned jointly by the United States and Mexico.

PRECEDING PAGES: Lake Amistad. **LEFT:** Rio Grande River, Big Bend National Park. **BELOW:** barber shop in Del Rio.

Wool capital

Del Rio ❸ (pop. 35,000), south of the lake, regards itself as the wool and mohair capital of the world. The area remains free of the hearts of tourists that frequent the towns of the Lower Rio Grande valley. There is also wine in this desert. San Felipe Springs has kept the Qualia family prospering at the **Val Verde Winery**, along Qualia Drive, for more than 100 years. Val Verde, Texas' oldest vintner, offers free tours every day (tel: 830-775-9714).

Del Rio's downtown area has a fine variety of 19th-century architecture, and it is a city devoted to tourism. There is lively quarterhorse racing on the weekends, at which pari-mutuel gambling has been introduced after much effort (and not a little controversy) from some lawmakers.

Across the river from Del Rio is the city named after the romantic, but ultimately suicidal, Manuel Acuña (1849–73), one of Mexico's most widely read

poets. In order to reach **Ciudad Acuña** (pop. 85,000), drive out of Hudson or Las Vacas to the International Bridge. There is ample parking on the American side and most of the shops offering typical souvenirs are clustered together on Hidalgo Street near the bridge.

Radio healing

Driving at night, you may hear – even as far away as the Canadian border – the religious programming broadcast from **XER**, one of the Mexican border-blaster radio stations. In the 1950s, Wolfman Jack worked at a border-blaster and introduced a generation of Americans to rock 'n' roll. Nowadays, the standard fare is patent medicine commercials and cassette-tape Christianity. These airwave evangelists suggest that to be saved and healed (via the US Postal Service and 200,000 watts of Christianity), just put your hand on the radio and a check in the mail.

The American Medical Association had its reservations about the authenticity of the "goat gland pills and elixir" marketed by one early Del Rio citizen. The proximity of the Mexican border probably made Del Rio seem a favorable business climate to Dr Johnny Brinkley of Kansas, who made a career of peddling exotic cures. In 1933, Brinkley used his own border radio station – on which he cranked the power up to 1 million watts – to sell goat-gland transplants and extended virility to thousands of Americans. He became wealthy, spent some time in jail, and built **The Dr John R. Brinkley Mansion**, which still stands at 512 Qualia Drive, a tribute to his entrepreneurial spirit.

The city's **Whitehead Memorial Museum** (1308 S. Main Street; closed Mon; Sun pm only; entrance fee; tel: 830-774-7568) houses a collection of reconstructed pioneer buildings put together by a local ranching family. Exhibits

Actress Lily Langtry, for whom Judge Roy Bean named the town of Langtry.

RIGHT: Judge Roy Bean.

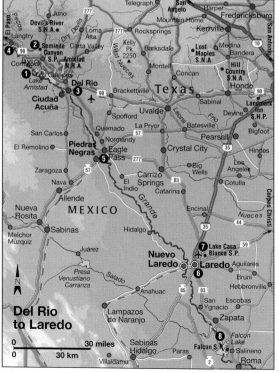

Del Rio to Laredo

include a replica of the famous saloon and courtroom of the notorious Judge Roy Bean who, along with his son, is buried in the grounds.

Map on page 260

Langtry

Bean's original Jersey Lilly Saloon, named after Lily Langtry, the English actress whom he admired from a distance, still stands in tiny **Langtry ④** (pop. 30), northwest on US-90, near the Pecos river. Proclaiming himself "Law West of the Pecos," the illiterate Judge Bean doffed his bar apron in favor of a waistcoat whenever court was in session, drafting a jury from drinkers at the bar. One example of his unconventional justice came during an inquest, when $40 and a pistol was found on the corpse. Fining the corpse $40 for having a concealed weapon, Bean pocketed the money.

Strangers from the east would drop off the train to drink beer at the saloon and buy a round for the judge's pet bear, Bruno. In 1904, the year after the 78-year-old Bean died after a drunken outing, Lily Langtry made her first visit to the town, admired her portrait (which still hangs in the saloon) and was given one of Bean's six-shooters. Today, 85,000 visitors a year call in the Judge Roy Bean Visitor Center in the tiny hamlet to watch a video about the old judge.

Further downstream is the small town of **Comstock**, before the river runs into Lake Amistad and joins the Rio Grande.

A humble storekeeper by profession, Roy Bean was created a Justice of the Peace by the Texas Rangers when the new town, which Bean named Langtry, was founded in 1880. His novel law-keeping methods have been described as "creative," but suitable for the times.

Closed twice

Fifty-six miles (90 km) south of Del Rio is **Eagle Pass ⑤** (pop. 27,000) and its Mexican neighbor, Piedras Negras (pop. 122,000). Other than Mexican political unrest that closed the International Bridge on several occasions in 1985,

BELOW: Judge Roy Bean's Jersey Lilly saloon in Langtry.

The town of Piedras Negras (or "Black Rocks") was named for a seam of coal which had been made visible by the effect of erosion.

not much has happened here since **Fort Duncan** was closed for the second and last time after World War I. It had been established by the US Army in 1849, and a detachment of mixed-race Native American scouts, descended from runaway black slaves, served there after the Civil War. Many of the original buildings, now restored, comprise the **Fort Duncan Museum** (Bliss Street; open Mon–Sat pm only; entrance fee; tel: 830-773-3224), featuring military memorabilia and relics of mid-19th-century Texas.

Military history buffs may also want to hazard a guess as to the precise spot along the Rio Grande from which Confederate General Joseph O. Shelby, on July 4, 1865, ordered his Confederate flag weighted and lowered into the river. Shelby, in the romantic tradition of the South, also tore the plume from his hat and cast it into the water.

Black Rocks and nachos

Eagle Pass is the seat of Maverick County, named after early rancher and signer of the Texas Declaration of Independence Samuel Maverick *(see page 42).* Piedras Negras ("Black Rocks") and Eagle Pass (*Paso de Aguila*) are regular stops for Kickapoo Indians who, under a US-Mexican agreement, are free to reside in either country. Kickapoos sell handcrafted goods at the border, and at their settlement across the border in Coahuila, Yacamiento.

Piedras Negras remains a stop-and-shop Mexican town with a few good restaurants. Indeed, the most famous building in the area is probably the **Restaurant Bar Moderno** (Allende 407 Oriente; 878-782-0684), which, in its former guise of the Victory Club, claims to have invented nachos. In October each year, the town organizes a nacho cookoff, attracting over 3,000 hungry visitors.

BELOW: prickly pear cacti.

Twin Laredos

Laredo and its Mexican neighbor, Nuevo Laredo, together form a city of some 480,000, with 90 percent of the residents on the Texas side Hispanic. The cities were outposts in what was once the backwater of Spain's American colony, and retain little of what colonial charm they may once have had. Most of the culture here is commercial. Residents from each side of the border line up on the other for bargains. Downtown Laredo caters to Mexican shoppers buying inexpensive clothing, various electrical items – often made in Asia – and some processed foods. This seedy area has been abandoned by many American shoppers, but competition for the Mexican buyer has lowered prices on portable TVs, stereos, tape players and a variety of other appliances and clothing unavailable in Mexico. Away from the bridge, the downtown area improves. River-drive Mall, on Water Street, includes outlets of national chains.

San Agustín Plaza, where the Texas city began as a Spanish settlement in the 1750s, is flanked by the 130-year-old church, La Posada Hotel and the former Capitol of the Republic of the Rio Grande, now a museum (closed Mon; Sun pm only; entrance fee). The Republic was a short-lived revolt led by disenchanted Mexican federalists who met in convention in what was still a Mexican city in 1840. Somewhere between the rapidly expanding Manifest Destiny of the United States and the rapidly receding border of Mexico, the Republic of the Rio Grande was lost. The museum's exhibits explain some of this history.

Two blocks north, at San Bernardo and Washington streets, is Bruni Plaza, named for Antonio Mateo Bruni, an Italian immigrant who died a politician and wealthy rancher in 1931. Engraved on a plaque here is part of his philosophy: "God has given us political power to be used for the welfare of the people."

Laredo was often seen as a "no man's land," abandoned between Texas and Mexico. Only when the Rio Grande was formally recognized as the international frontier in 1848 did Laredo finally settle north of the border.

BELOW: campers at Seminole Canyon State Historical Park.

Map on page 260

About two-thirds of the US trade with Mexico crosses the border here, a volume that has only increased since the passage of the NAFTA agreements. Customs and Immigration offices are open 24 hours daily. On the US side, customs agents collect hundreds of millions of dollars in duties each year. *Casas de cambio,* or currency exchange houses, on both sides of the bridge, usually offer a fair exchange rate for pesos and dollars, and they are convenient. Check the banks (Mexican banks are generally open weekdays 9am–1.30pm) before changing large amounts.

Across the border

Nuevo Laredo, a short walk across the old International Bridge, is something of a Texas Tijuana, with the usual plethora of tacky tourist souvenir shops. Nuevo (New) Laredo is old, but not attractive. There are quite a few good restaurants, many of which observe the common Mexican practice of posting menus at the entrance. The local specialty is *cabrito,* charbroiled kid goat, which can be seen cooking spread-eagled on spits in restaurant windows.

Nuevo Laredo has some interesting nightspots, and there are tourists' treasures in local shops. Mexican and colonial-style handcrafted furniture is a regional product. At shops along Guerrero, near the old bridge, there is always a vast array of clothing, jewelry and other collectibles from Mexico and Central and South America. There is also a traditional *mercado central,* where tourists and locals can haggle over the price of produce, inexpensive jewelry, clothing and a variety of *curiosidades.* As in the other Mexican border towns, liquor prices are low compared with the US. The bullring in Nuevo Laredo, just beyond the airport, provides a small and slow *Death in the Afternoon* on Sundays during the season, which runs from February to October.

BELOW: ocotillo plant.

Surrounding Laredo are miles of the Texas one sees in movies. Ranches are enormous, since making a living on arid scrubland requires a "Ponderosa"-sized spread. When oil and gas were discovered, most of the region's wealth, although greatly increased, remained concentrated in the hands of a few people. Poverty is still the norm here and many of the streets of Laredo remain unpaved.

Lake Casa Blanca State Park ❼ (off Highway 59, at the eastern edge of Laredo; entrance fee) offers swimming, boating, fishing and camping (tel: 956-725-3826 for reservations), and 78 miles (125 km) south of Laredo is **Falcon Lake** ❽, a jointly owned American-Mexican impoundment (State Park open daily; entrance fee; tel: 956-848-5327). Falcon, a massive reservoir covering 87,210 acres (35,293 hectares), has an international reputation for black bass and catfish, as well as deer and dove hunting in the surrounding countryside. Downriver from here, the landscape gradually changes from semi-arid, scrubby hills to the lush delta of the Lower Rio Grande Valley.

Summer can be blisteringly hot in these parts and the ideal month to visit Laredo is February when many festivals, including a 10-day celebration of George Washington's birthday, take place. ❑

Tex-Mex Food

Visitors to Texas are guaranteed to encounter Mexican food – and plenty of it. But it's not exactly Mexican. What you will find is a Texan version of it called "Tex-Mex." These dishes are quite a bit hotter than California-Mex or Arizona-Mex, so keep plenty of yoghurt or rice handy.

Visitors to Texas will discover that discussing what precisely constitutes Tex-Mex is a state pastime – so don't expect to discover any definitive answers. Most Texans would probably agree that, in its most elemental form, Tex-Mex food consists of some preparation of flat cornmeal tortilla breads, beans, and tomatoes, onions and chili peppers, frequently chopped together in a picante (hot) sauce. They'd possibly also accept in the definition cheese and chili meat sauce, but beyond that they're likely to disagree.

Texans are more unified in their definition of what Tex-Mex isn't. Any part of the States with a Mexican heritage will have its own related version of "Mex" cooking, but the cuisine of Mexico is not Tex-Mex. Neither is New Mexico-Mex, with its refined green *tomatillo* sauces and blue cornmeal; neither is California-Mex, rich with sour cream and lavish produce. Tex-Mex food is not fancy. What little meat it includes is usually inexpensive and tough, chopped or marinated into submission. Tex-Mex food is home fare, the food of the common people. But, most importantly, it is the supreme expression of the noble chili pepper, and as such it must be as hot as the hinges of Hell's Front Door.

Where to find the best Tex-Mex is a bigger debate than what it contains. Serious devotees contend that real Tex-Mex food can't be found north of Waco (mid-state) but all Texans agree it doesn't exist outside Texas.

Most Tex-Mex is eaten as Mexican restaurant fare. The menu traditionally consists of the following: baskets of fried *tortilla* chips and bowls of *picante* sauce, accompanied by beer or iced tea, are offered while the order is prepared. Shortly afterwards, a hot plate of several different specialties arrives.

These might include *enchiladas* – *tortillas* wrapped around cheese and onions and covered with meat or a spicy tomato sauce; *tacos* – *tortillas* folded, fried and stuffed with ground meat, beans, cheese and the above-mentioned vegetables; a *guacamole* salad of mashed avocados; and *fajitas* – marinated and grilled bits of steak. The meal is served with rice and beans, hot *tortillas*, and, of course, several more bowls of *picante* sauce to spoon over everything. Dessert may be a token scoop of sherbet, or a praline candy purchased at the cash register counter.

Tex-Mex cooking has recently absorbed some refinements – in the preparation of better cuts of meat than its beloved *cabrito* (roast kid) and *menudo* (tripe stew) for example; and the "Tex-Mex cuisine" gaining popularity in the eastern US and Europe is a considerably cooled down version of it. The more accessible it becomes, the less it resembles real Tex-Mex. To a certain extent this is necessary: every ethnic food has ingredients that appeal only to those who have been raised on them. ❑

RIGHT: colorful, spicy, authentic Tex-Mex dishes can only be truly savored in Texas itself.

Maps:
Area 278
City 270

EL PASO

Thanks to its Indian roots, its proximity to Mexico and its distance from other major towns, El Paso – the former haunt of Wild West outlaws – is quite unlike any other Texas city

For some 1,200 miles (1,930 km), the Rio Grande twists and turns, widens, then roars through tight places, all the while uniting Texas with the Mexican states of Chihuahua, Coahuila, Nuevo Leon and Tamaulipas. In Spanish it is described best, as a region, as *la frontera* – the border. La Frontera is a place apart, where you will find neither the best of Texas nor Mexico, being, in a sense, one of the few places where the First World meets the Third World. On the Mexican side, *maquiladoras* – American-owned assembly plants – enjoy proximity to the border, combined with Third World operating costs. American retail businesses, despite continuing devaluations, sell Mexicans what their country can't or won't manufacture: TVs, stereos, medical instruments and designer jeans. They capitalize on a widely held Mexican belief: *Lo gringo es lo mejor* – American-made is best.

The differences in lifestyle and economic status are striking. Outside a Zenith assembly plant in Reynosa, a 40-year-old man scratches out an existence selling salted pumpkin seeds. *"Semillas, semillas, semillas,"* he sings to passing workers. Mostly, he is ignored. A University of Texas professor in El Paso writes poetry describing the "trenchant sadness" of the Mexico framed in the window of his office. In the lower Rio Grande Valley, a Border Patrol officer quietly delivers three Salvadoran refugees, who were apprehended an hour earlier, to a church-sponsored sanctuary house.

PRECEDING PAGES: cacti grows wild all over Texas. **LEFT:** Tigua Indian baking bread. **BELOW:** Eagle Dancer statue outside the Speaking Rock Casino.

The final barrier

For the Central Americans, the Rio Grande river represents the last geographical obstacle in their struggle toward a better life, here in *el Norte*. Most are only a few weeks away from a country ravaged by war and poverty. And most of them enter the US illegally. For the fortunate few who find their way to the sanctuary houses, the chances of remaining in the country usually improve. Nevertheless, many will spend their first, and last, night in *América* in one of the border detention facilities operated by the US Immigration and Naturalization Service.

Despite the Rio Grande's length, fewer than 10 international cities straddle the river. In and around them has gathered a unique mixture of Texans and Mexicans, including a motley crew of international hucksters of low culture and high commerce. If you're looking for the cosmopolitan culture of Mexico City, or the quiet charm of San Antonio, it's unlikely that you'll find it here. But this place is worth a closer look: *la frontera*, if nothing else, is unique.

Much of what this border is about is people queueing up on one side to cross over for something on the other. Border regulars start lining up before dawn:

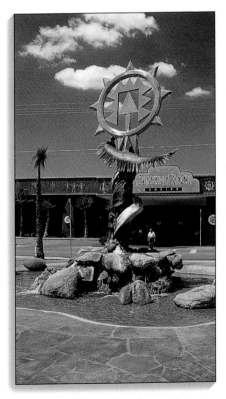

green carders, Mexican agricultural laborers, waiting for the contractor's bus to take them to their day's work. By seven it's too late; they've missed their ride. By 11, the lines are on the other side. The American day trippers are here – stereotypical tourists, out for an afternoon in the market, and dinner. Almost all will be home before dark, with a bottle of José Cuervo tequila, crepe flowers and something for the kids. And so it goes. Dollars to pesos, pesos to dollars. You can usually spend both on either side. Money is the motor that moves this place.

Cash flow

Much of the recent history of this border can be read in the rate of exchange of two currencies. For some 30 years, the peso was tied to the dollar at an exchange rate of 12.5 to one. Most border towns seemed to be slouching toward prosperity. But since the first devaluation in 1976, and then another devaluation in the early 1990s, the value of the peso has fallen precipitously and the economic climate on both sides of the river has been, at best, cloudy.

Virgin Mary icon at Socorro Mission.

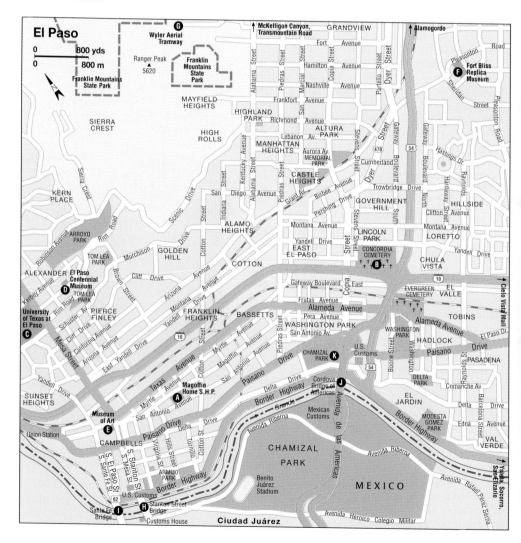

Part of what the diminished peso means is longer lines on both sides. Mexican workers, with or without papers, find the lure of the dollar irresistible. And why shouldn't they? The federally fixed *daily* wage on the Mexican side is usually about the same as the *hourly* rate on the American side. For the American tourist, the lure is undervalued Mexican goods and accommodations.

Consider **El Paso ❶**. To get there from most Texas cities requires driving from dawn to sundown. Politicians and cartographers claim that El Paso is part of Texas. Most Texans know better. About halfway between Houston and San Diego, California, El Paso's heart belongs to New Mexico.

Maps:
Area 278
City 270

The pictographs at Hueco Tanks are sacred to the Tigua Indians. One of the most revered sites is Speaking Rock – hence the name of the tribe's gambling center at Ysleta.

Indian foundations

Sprawling across the Valley of El Paso del Norte, **El Paso-Juárez** is an international city of 2 million people, regarded by some as the best city on the border and, with its mix of three cultures, certainly one of the most interesting. The Tigua (or Tiwa) Indians were here first, followed by Norteño Mexicans and Southwestern Americans. Related to the Pueblo Indians of New Mexico, the Tiguas moved to the Spanish mission of San Antonio (later San Augustín) de la Isleta del Sur in the 1680s, when the Pueblos went to war with the Spanish. They claim to be the oldest continuously occupied Native American community in the country.

Today, the Tiguas still reside about 12 miles (19 km) from downtown at **Ysleta ❷** (an archaic Spanish spelling of "little island"), although most work in El Paso. This is a large agricultural community, and there is a tourist-oriented reservation – fine breads but near-lethally hot chili. The Tiguas operate the 850-seat Speaking Rock Casino (tel: 915-860-7777), just behind the mission.

BELOW: Tigua Indians.

There are a few other Native American communities around the city but the major legacy of early Native Americans can be found in **Hueco Tanks State Historical Park ❸** (open daily; entrance fee; tel: 915-857-1135), 32 miles (51 km) to the northeast, with its thousands of colorful and engaging pictographs of human, animal and mythological figures.

Early missions

The mission at Ysleta is still in use, as is the Socorro Mission in **Socorro ❹** (tel: 915-859-7718), which was built in the same decade, the 1680s, and is the oldest continuously active parish in the US. Across the border in Juárez, the even older (1668) Guadalupe Mission is famous for the legend that its shadows point to the Lost Padre Mine – in the nearby Franklin Mountains, a 24,000-acre (9,700-hectare) park within city limits – where Spanish gold is said to be hidden. The famous El Camino Real, once a royal highway but today a quiet farm road, connects the Ysleta and Socorro missions with the San Elizario Presidio Church in **San Elizario ❺**, built in 1789 in a mixture of Spanish colonial and native architectural styles, as a fortified base for the army and reconstructed in 1877.

Ever since the Spanish explorer Juan de Oñate laid claim to El Paso del Rio Grande del Norte – a self-explanatory name – this city has been Hispanic,

TIP

John Wesley Hardin is
buried in the "Boot
Hill" section of
Concordia Cemetery
near the west
entrance to the walled
Chinese section.

as are most of its residents. Far removed from the events of the Texas Revolution, El Paso for a long time shared a common religion, language and history with Juárez, becoming a part of Texas a full five years after Texas itself became a state.

There are few other historic buildings in the city, the main one being the **Magoffin Home State Historical Park** Ⓐ (1120 Magoffin Avenue; open daily; entrance fee; tel: 915-533-5147), an 1875 adobe mansion containing many of the original family furnishings and paintings.

El Paso, whose 800,000 population makes it Texas' fourth-largest city, nevertheless retains something of the ambiance of the slap-leather town that it was in 1896, when gunman John Wesley Hardin was shot dead in the Acme Saloon. Hardin had been pardoned, reformed, and was practising law in El Paso when a local constable ended his life. Along with other notorious gunslingers, he is buried in **Concordia Cemetery** Ⓑ, east of downtown. Years after his death, the city remained a convenient place for outlaws to cross the river.

El Paso also has a small Chinese community, descendants of the "Chinamen" who laid the tracks for the railroad that reached here in 1881. It grew with Mexican revolutionary Pancho Villa's 1910 attacks on the Chinese living in the neighboring Mexican states of Chihuahua and Coahuila.

Tibetan revival

An unrelated Oriental feature is the Tibetan architecture on the **University of Texas at El Paso (UTEP)** Ⓒ campus. Katherine Worrell, the wife of the Dean when UTEP was known as the Texas State School of Mines and Metallurgy, lifted the design from *National Geographic* after a 1916 fire destroyed almost

BELOW: the historic Socorro Mission in El Paso.

half of the campus. The three oldest buildings are pure "Bhutanese eclectic," copied from a Tibetan monastery and fortress at Grag-Gye-Jong, in the Himalayas. Most later buildings are variations on this style. Also on the campus is the **El Paso Centennial Museum** (closed Sun and Mon; free; tel: 915-747-5565), where displays include ancient pottery, dinosaur bones and relics from the Ice Age.

Texas-El Paso, in the foothills of the Franklin Mountains, is a large state university that began life in 1914. Its stadium hosts college football on weekends during the season and is the site of the **Sun Bowl**, an annual football classic, second only in age to Pasadena's Rose Bowl. The game is usually played in late December, but the weather is invariably fine: El Paso has more sunny days than almost every other city in the country. Occasional music events are also staged at the stadium. North of UTEP, **McKelligon Canyon**, popular with hikers, is the site of the summer-long outdoor dance extravaganza ¡*Viva El Paso!* (for information tel: 915-565-6900).

A unique feature of El Paso is "The Star on the Mountain" – a 460 by 280-ft (140 by 85-meter) star erected by the local electrical utility in 1940. Illuminated by 459 white light bulbs, it can be dedicated by anybody to a friend or relative by the night, week or month. The El Paso Times publishes the dedications daily, and sponsors get a star-shaped pin and certificate.

Downtown

San Jacinto Plaza marks the original city square and is the starting point for bus routes. Around here is what remains of the El Paso that has been documented, along with downtown Juárez, by Elroy Bode, the city's master of

Maps:
Area 278
City 270

TIP

If you can't acquire tickets for the Sun Bowl, pack your binoculars and drag a blanket up the side of the mountain along with the locals and students.

BELOW: El Paso from the hills.

the *bosquejo*, or literary sketch. Until the 1960s, alligators were kept in the plaza.

The El Paso Chamber of Commerce on Civic Center Plaza publishes a free guidebook that includes walking and driving tours, and focuses on points of interest and border crossings. Also on the plaza is the Visitors' Bureau. Nearby is the **Museum of Art** Ⓔ (closed Mon; Sun pm only; free; tel: 915-532-1707), which, in addition to its European collection and contemporary American works, possesses an unusually impressive collection of Mexican Colonial art.

Also interesting, northeast of the city, off US-54, are **Fort Bliss Replica Museum** Ⓕ (open daily; free; tel: 915-568-4518), where history buffs can wander through the adobe pre-Civil War army outpost. It is a re-creation of what a frontier fort of the late 1800s would have looked like. The **Wilderness Park Museum** (4301 Woodrow Bean Transmountain Road; closed Mon; free; 915-755-4332), highlights lifestyles of the local Native Americans, and the **Border Patrol Museum** (4315 Woodrow Bean Transmountain Road; closed Mon; free), chronicles the ways and means of the Border Patrol unit since its inception in 1924.

All of El Paso can be seen from the **Wyler Aerial Tramway** Ⓖ, which can be caught at the intersection of McKinley and Piedras streets. Northwest of the city, scenic drives across the Franklin Mountains, and especially along **Transmountain Road** (exit off I-10 West), provide spectacular views.

Across the border

Back in 1911, El Pasoans were able to gather on the flat roofs of their houses for "battle teas" and watch the Mexican Revolution unfold in **Ciudad Juárez** across the Rio Grande. For a while, Pancho Villa took refuge north of the

Trans-Pecos cactus.

BELOW: Bridge over Rio Grande.

border, acquiring a taste for ice cream and learning to ride a motorcycle here.

Political geography, as well as climate, shaped the character of this Mexican city. It was named for Benito Juárez, who fled here in the 1860s when Napoleon III made the Austrian Archduke Maximilian the Emperor of Mexico. Juárez, a Zapotecan Indian, fought as President to make Mexico a secular state.

Maps:
Area 278
City 270

Mexican bargains

Like most border towns, Juárez offers something for almost everyone. The **Museo de Arte e Historia**, on Avenida Lincoln, exhibits Mexican art by period, from pre-Hispanic to the present. The building's design is modern, unique and certainly worth a look. The museum is situated in a tourist-oriented commercial center that includes the government-sponsored FONART artisans' market. This is not as fecund as the *mercado central*, and there is no haggling with vendors, but it is interesting nonetheless. Along Lincoln, between FONART and the intersection of Avenida de las Americas, are a number of artisans' and curio shops, providing a good walking tour for shoppers.

Shopping is a popular pastime on both sides of the border. In El Paso, the fly-and-buy tourist will find the boutiques of La Placita conveniently located near the airport, and, at I-10 and Hawkins is the Cielo Vista Mall.

Around El Paso, great bargains can be found at factory outlets for cowboy boots and Western wear. On the other side of the river, in the central *mercado*, Avenida 16 de Septiembre, you'll discover a variety of regionally manufactured goods – generally leather and textiles – and local produce.

Pedestrians can enter Mexico over the downtown **Stanton Street Bridge** ⬤, which is the closest approach to the Mexican Tourist Center, and walk back across the river by the **Santa Fe Bridge** ⬤. Most automobile traffic crosses via the **Cordova Bridge of Americas** ⬤, off I-10, the largest bridge – and best avoided at rush hours. Close to the bridge terminals, on both sides, are parks named **Chamizal** ⬤, which memorialize the victims of the border war of a century ago and mark its peaceful settlement. Here the **Chamizal Museum** (800 South San Marcial; open daily; free; tel: 915-532-7273) records how the border has been surveyed over the centuries. Park entertainments – which take place in an art gallery, an indoor theater and an al fresco amphitheater – vary from displays of local artworks and musical performances to films and temporary exhibitions. A fourth bridge, the **Zaragosa Bridge**, can be found on the far eastern side of El Paso.

Much of Juárez can be seen on foot and most cab drivers speak English (but you should agree on a price before closing the door). Spanish and English are spoken in both towns.

The atmosphere in Juárez is a little more *picante* – spicy – than in El Paso. There are lots of good and bad bars, and equally good and bad restaurants. Women are discouraged from visiting – and in some cases turned away from – *cantinas*, the traditional "men's bars." In fact, several working-class *cantinas* in downtown Juárez are best avoided by all tourists: size things up before you decide to hang around. ❑

BELOW: Benito Juárez.

THE TRANS-PECOS

This arid region is as tough as it gets, a land dominated by unforgiving desert and a lack of drinkable water, but a land rich in minerals and natural beauty, with the highest peaks in the state

Map on page 278

West of the Pecos was the title of Zane Grey's classic novel, which described an area as "desolate, gray and lonely, an utter solitude uninhabited even by beasts of the hills or fowls of the air." The Spanish conquistadors who discovered it in the 16th century named the region *el despoblado*, the uninhabited place, and 300 years later a pioneer cattleman, Charles Goodnight, cursed it as "the graveyard of the cowman's hopes." General Sheridan summed up his impressions by saying that, if he owned Texas, he would "rent it out and live in hell."

The Pecos river

Beginning as a clear stream in the Sangre del Cristo mountains north of Santa Fe, the Pecos flows 900 miles (1,440 km) southwards to the Rio Grande, entering "a flat, hellish desert of mesquite and greasewood" even before it reaches Texas. "Buzzards soar above the flat, torrid land," wrote Bryan Wooley in the *Dallas Morning News* about the Pecos region, "Dust devils dance across the plain like small brown tornadoes. Oil well pump jacks dot the landscape, many of them leaking. Quicksand forms below the river's banks and its water turns too salty for man or beast to drink." It was a major hazard to all who had to cross it, from the Indian fighters marching to their West Texas forts to the early 1850s immigrants on their way to search for gold in California.

The mythical Pecos Bill, legendarily reared by coyotes and who fed his horse barbed wire, stems from this region of tall tales and great accomplishments. Such an accomplishment was featured in Larry McMurtry's *Lonesome Dove*, which was inspired by the way that Goodnight and Oliver Loving expanded the range of the longhorn hundreds of miles north, driving a quarter of a million cattle across the Pecos. In that era – the 1860s – the river was 50–100 ft (15–30 meters) wide, spreading to a mile (1.5 km) after floods and leaving deadly lakes of poisonous alkaline water behind when the floods receded.

Spanish gold is said to be buried in the desert, though it would take unimaginable endurance to search for it. In the 1930s, Hollywood struck a rich vein of its own with a raft of titles such as *The Pecos Kid*, *The Stranger from Pecos*, *King of the Pecos* (starring John Wayne) and *Robin Hood of the Pecos* (Roy Rogers). "The Pecos river holds a fascination for people," Paul Patterson, a 90-year-old cowboy who has lived along the river most of his life, told the *Dallas Morning News,* "unless they have to stop and camp and drink the water." A local joke maintains that when a coyote drinks the water he immediately licks his behind to get the bad taste out of his mouth.

LEFT: McDonald Observatory.
BELOW: Sul Ross State University, Alpine.

The fossil clock

Perhaps nowhere else in the United States can the history of the earth be read so clearly as in dry Far West Texas, where vegetation has not scrawled its graffiti of decay. Nature's first attempts at complex creatures can still be seen in the 600-million-year-old remains of algal colonies in pre-Cambrian limestone, 2½ miles (4 km) north of Allamoore, which is 10 miles (16 km) northwest of **Van Horn ❻** (pop. 3,000). Van Horn is an historic crossroads of the old Bankhead Highway and the Old Spanish Trail, 150 miles (240 km) southeast of El Paso. US-90 and I-10 cross here today. Petroglyph tours are conducted from the town, most of whose income comes from tourism.

Heading west, I-10 crosses the foothills of the Sierra Diablo Mountains before passing through **Sierra Blanca ❼**, with dramatic views of 6,950-ft (2,120-meter) Sierra Blanca mountain and "forests" of Spanish dagger yucca plants. This is where Chinese railroad workers from the west met Irish laborers from the east to complete the second transcontinental railroad.

James Dean, star of Giant, *which was filmed at Marfa.*

Marfa

Beginning life in 1883 as a water stop and freight headquarters for the Galveston, Harrisburg and San Antonio Railway, **Marfa ❽** (pop. 2,100), 75 miles (120 km) south of Van Horn, was named for a character in Feodor Dostoevski's *The Brothers Karamazov*. The book was being read at the time by the wife of the chief railroad engineer. By 1885, when the impressive courthouse was built, poker bets in the saloons were being made with town lots. At 4,688 ft (1,428 meters), in a semi-arid region, Marfa boasts a superb climate and, in summer, is one of the coolest places in Texas. It has the highest golf course in

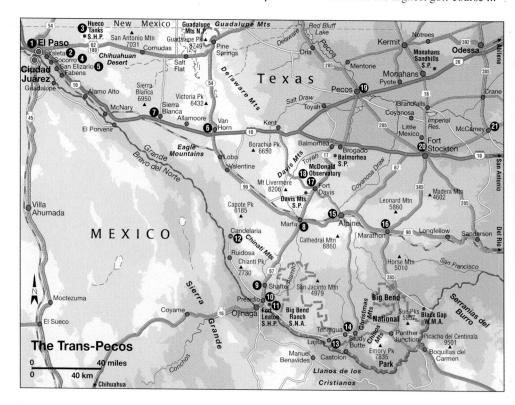

The Trans-Pecos

Map on page 278

the state and holds the championships for sailplane soaring. Mike's Place on N Highland Street advertises "Seven days without a Mike's Burger makes one weak." Among movies shot in the town are *Giant* (1956), starring Rock Hudson, Elizabeth Taylor and James Dean, and *The Andromeda Strain* (1971). A major tourist attraction are the mysterious lights *(see page 287)* that, for more than a century, have been observed to the southwest in the Chinati Mountains. Here, fluorite is found in the igneous rocks of **Chinati Peak**. Its phosphorescent glow and its fluorescence in ultra-violet light make it particularly worth looking for.

Presidio's fame today is largely meteorological: on many days it is the hottest spot in the nation. In summer, temperatures range from 100 to 110°F (37 to 43°C). And it very rarely rains.

Fort Russell

Spain had practically abandoned Far West Texas by the time it became a part of independent Mexico in 1821. As the Anglo frontier moved westward, the fierce mounted Comanche war parties began to prey on wagon trains and Mexican and Anglo settlements along the Comanche War Trail, especially during the late summer and early fall harvest season. To counter these depredations, a line of cavalry forts was established soon after the Republic of Texas joined the United States in 1846. Near Marfa, **Fort Russell**, the army's last horse-mounted cavalry post, has now been transformed into a monumental space for the permanent installation of modern sculpture (tours Thur–Sat pm; free).

The New York sculptor Don Judd fathered the $4 million project, with Houston oil heiress Philippa de Menil Pelizzi Friedrich as reluctant mother. Judd needed isolation for himself and open spaces for his work, both of which Marfa offers in abundance. His variously permutated groups of large rectangular concrete structures are rhythmically arranged in an endless progression toward the far horizon; some 100 aluminum pieces are housed in a glass-walled gun shed. There are also works by other prominent contemporary artists on display in the fort, such as the crushed auto-body sculptures of John Chamberlain and the fluorescent sculptures of Dan Flavin.

BELOW: urban 'scapes in Marfa.

Down to the border

From Marfa, US-67 heads southwest through the mountains to **Shafter ❾**, a ghost town in the Chinati Mountains, where millions of dollars of silver were mined and where stories persist about treasure buried in caves. Further south, on the banks of the Rio Grande, is **Presidio ❿** (pop. 4,100), described in the WPA guidebook to Texas in 1940 as "an old town of sunbaked adobe houses, squatting like an ancient *hombre* in the shade of giant cottonwoods." The town, which was founded by Franciscan missionaries in 1683, hosts an annual onion festival (May). **Fort Leaton ⓫** (open daily; entrance fee; tel: 915-229-4651), an interesting example of native adobe construction, southeast of town, was not a military outpost but a trading post operated in the mid-19th century by a certain Ben Leaton. Leaton had been among the first "Anglo" settlers to arrive in Presidio. In their fortified trading post, he and his wife outfitted and accommodated travelers who were somehow drawn to this backwater of civilization. The Texas Rangers had

The Big Bend Ranch State Natural Area should not be confused with Big Bend National Park, although it is equally stunning in many ways. The land was acquired by Texas Parks and Wildlife Department in 1988.

a base here when Pancho Villa was rampaging south of the border, but the post was abandoned in 1926. Most of the old outpost has now been restored by the State of Texas.

Across the river from Presidio is **Ojinaga** ("o-hee-NAH-ga"). Since Presidio gets few visitors, Ojinaga lacks the touristy feel of most border towns. There are a few good restaurants, and at least one good hotel.

The highest waterfall in Texas is located on a private ranch near the tiny settlement of **Candelaria** ⓬, northwest of Presidio. Capote Falls crashes 175 ft (54 meters) on to the rocks below. Inquire locally about making a visit.

El Camino del Rio (Farm Road 170) follows the Rio Grande southeast from Presidio down to the tiny village of **Lajitas** ⓭, a spectacular drive with sharp curves, steep grades and occasional wandering livestock. The village owes its origins to the 1915 US Army base established to protect settlers against Pancho Villa's border raids, and is a useful base from which to explore the area. The Cavalry Post, one of three motels in town, is built on the site of the trading post established by General Jack Pershing before he mounted his "punitive expedition" against Villa.

This unsuccessful foray demonstrated the army's lack of experience in fighting on foreign terrain. A young lieutenant by the name of George Patton saw his first action here, as a member of Pershing's expedition, and killed two men and a horse. The hotels in Lajitas are part of a large conference center which has a variety of recreational activities including a nine hole golf course, a pool and a saloon/dance hall.

Several companies licensed by the National Park Service offer raft trips of one to nine days' duration on the Rio Grande river, through narrow 1,500-ft (460-meter) deep canyons, or farther down in challenging rapids. Among them is

BELOW: the world's largest roadrunner, Fort Stockton.

Farflung Adventures (tel: 800-359-4138). Just east of Lajitas, on FM 170, is the Barton Warnock Environmental Educational Center (open daily; entrance fee), named after a local botanist and acting as a gateway to the Big Bend Ranch State Natural Area.

Gem hunting

FM 170 continues onwards to **Terlingua** (pop. 25), now a collection of mostly abandoned stone and adobe ruins, but, at the turn of the 20th century, a prosperous mining town of 2,000 inhabitants. Here red cinnabar ore was mined and cooked to yield millions of dollars' worth of mercury. The 27 miles (43 km) of tunnels and shafts – some as much as 900 ft (275 meters) deep – of the abandoned mercury mines have yielded a treasure trove of rocks, fossils and mineral specimens cast aside by miners, as well as abundant specimens of cinnabar. This looks much like lipstick smears on the fissured surfaces of igneous rocks.

Views of the nearby Chisos Mountains in Big Bend National Park *(see pages 289–292)*, and multicolored badlands on every side, form a surreal backdrop for rock hounds and cactus collectors, who can run amok here. Amber, the hard golden resin of prehistoric plants, is occasionally collected from cretaceous coal outcrops along **Terlingua Creek**, just west of Big Bend.

On the banks of Terlingua Creek, mysterious lights of uncertain source illuminate the walls of La Kiva Restaurant and Bar. Here, furniture is made from redwood stumps and cowhide. The mountains in this region were once the hideout of outlaws, renegades and the like – especially the little settlement of **Valentine** (pop. 260) on US-90, northwest of Marfa. They now attract rock hunters, on account of the numerous minerals and gems they yield. An outstanding

Map on page 278

TIP

If you're a fan of hot food, Terlingua is the place to make for on the first Saturday in November. Since 1967, the desolate town has been the venue for the International Chili Cookoff. Expect the few hotels to be full.

BELOW: Terlingua ghost town and cemetery.

THE LAW WEST OF THE PECOS – RULES FOR SURVIVAL

The Trans Pecos region is a tough country. It has bred the toughest of men who have had to fight for everything they have gained. The region has not traditionally taken kindly to strangers. Since, it is claimed, there is still damned little "law west of the Pecos," the celebrated Judge Roy Bean's legacy notwithstanding, here in writing is the unwritten code of conduct for these parts:

1. Never go on a man's land without his permission.
2. Don't ask a man how much land he has.
3. Never step over a man sleeping on the floor.
4. Don't mess with a man's hat.
5. Never throw a hat on a bed.
6. Never rope another man's cow that wanders onto your land.
7. Never take a man's last chaw of tobacco.

Adherence to these rules allows a man to leave Texas with as many enemies as he came with.

Desert Plantlife

The flowering plants of the Chihuahuan Desert perform a spectacular, although brief, extravaganza after the spring rains; but most of the rest of the year they are occupied with vegetative survival rather than reproductive exhibitionism. If you see a *lechuguilla* plant, you'll know where you are, since the habitat of this member of the amarillis family coincides perfectly with the boundaries of the Chihuahuan Desert. *Lechuguilla*, which means "little lettuce" in Spanish, is easily recognized by its rosette of succulent bluish-green, spine-tipped leaves about 2 ft (0.67 meters) long and 1½ inches (4 cm) wide. In true desert plant fashion, it can inflict a painful wound on the unwary.

The yucca species are somewhat similar to agave but are actually members of the lily family. They have narrower, more flexible and less succulent leaves, and flower annually. The torrey yucca grows almost to the height of a tree north and west of Van Horn, forming the only "forest" in the desert lowlands.

The cactus family, that classic form of desert life, originated in the southwestern US and Mexico and has attained its greatest diversity there. Over 100 species of cacti are Texas residents.

Ocotillo is a cactus prevalent in the Far West. It looks like a naked spider on its back and its long 6–20-ft (2–6-meter) legs, protected by stiff spines, are used as living fences by goat raisers. This cautious species puts out leaves only after rainfall and discards them as soon as drought returns.

Greasewood, or the creosote bush, is, along with cactus, almost ubiquitous in North American deserts, taking its name from the thick resin on its small yellowish-green paired leaflets. Usually only around a meter in height, it has been used as fuel by the desert cultures for thousands of years. Its wide, even spacing and the general absence of competing species are the result of special adaptation to the limited availability of water, for greasewood secretes a poison that kills even its own seedlings.

Another plant particularly common on mesas and hillsides is sotol, called "bear grass" for its 4-ft (1.25-meter) long, arching, narrow leaves with small claw-like spines along the margins. Its slender, 4–15-ft (1.25–4.5-meter) brush-like, flowering stalk may persist for several seasons.

All of these large plants were important to the Native Americans who inhabited the area. Their leaves provided fiber for clothing and utensils, as well as soap, and the thick basal stems were baked in stone-lined fireplaces, of which the scattered remains can be seen.

The pea family is also well represented by thorny shrubs like the infamous cat claw acacia, or "wait-a-minute bush," from the automatic cry of "Wait a minute!" as hikers try to extricate themselves from this vegetable's clutches.

Devil's head cactus is an interesting plant about a foot (31cm) in diameter which lurks partially buried, ready to snare a hoof, paw or tennis shoe with its four-pronged spines. On the whole desert plants are best admired from a safe distance. ❏

LEFT: flowering eagles claw cactus, in Big Bend National Park.

example is the famous Texas plumed agate, in which red flames and black feather shapes are captured in a translucent white matrix. It is most easily found near Marfa and Alpine.

Map on page 278

Alpine

Alpine ⑮ (pop. 5,800) is the main center of activity in this mountain region of Texas, and it must be noted that, to someone arriving from the broiling flatlands, the town's 4,500-ft (1,370-meter) altitude can seem alpine. In the heart of cattle country, Alpine is a stop on AMTRAK's Sunset Limited, between Chicago and Los Angeles. Many people choose the town for their vacation headquarters and enjoy summer theater productions and museums at **Sul Ross State University**, which stages the annual Cowboy Poetry Gathering every February or March.

Marathon

Less than one hour to the south of Alpine, at the junction of US-385 and US-90, **Marathon** ⑯ (pop. 800) is centrally isolated in a desolate area of interest only to naturalists. Geologists are delighted by the diversity of rocks and minerals in the vicinity, while rugged nature photographers use Marathon as a jumping-off point for trips to **Black Gap Wildlife Management Area**, 58 miles (93 km) away. Though 80 miles (129 km) distant, Big Bend National Park is the next sign of civilization toward the south.

Trans-Pecos region prairie dog.

The town's 1920s Gage Hotel has been well renovated and furnished with antiques, Native American artifacts and Mexican furniture, in keeping with its role as a desert way-station. The restaurant is an oasis in a culinary wasteland.

BELOW: claret-cup cactus in bloom.

TIP

Travelers interested in astronomy should try one of the McDonald Observatory's Star Parties, held after sunset Tuesday, Friday and Saturday.

Fort Davis

To the north of Alpine, at the intersection of highways 17 and 118, is **Fort Davis** ⑰, named after the much-honored Jefferson Davis, who was President of the Confederate States of America but is remembered locally as the man who, as Secretary of War, introduced camels to West Texas. The fort stands dramatically with its back to a wall of volcanic rock named Sleeping Lion Mountain. At 5,000 ft (1,540 meters), the community is the highest in Texas and boasts of not possessing a single shopping mall.

In the **Fort Davis National Historic Site** (open daily; entrance fee; tel: 432-426-3224), the life of the late 19th-century frontier soldier has been recreated. Actual buildings survive from the days when such soldiers mounted up to escort wagon trains on the Chihuahuan Trail, or stage coaches on the Butterfield Overland Mail Route.

The **Chihuahuan Desert Research Institute** (open daily April–Aug; Mon–Fri only early Sept–Mar); free; tel: 915-364-2499), on Highway 118 a few miles south of Fort Davis, is a popular port of call for those fascinated by native desert plants. Among its attractions is a cactus greenhouse.

Visitors can also, in two hours, drive a scenic loop on highways 166 and 118 through the Davis Mountains, whose gentle, weathered slopes belie their violent volcanic origins. From Wild Rose Pass on, one has the same view of Limpia Brook, as it runs between high cliffs, that the Apache and Comanche raiding parties had as they lay in ambush.

In this area, the **McDonald Observatory** ⑱, perched atop Mount Lock, houses the third-largest astronomical telescope in the United States, a giant 107-inch (274-cm) reflector (tours 11.30am and 2pm daily; entrance fee; tel: 432-426-3641).

BELOW: tumblin' tumbleweeds.

The mountains

Interstate roads I-10 (which runs through Fort Stockton) and I-20 (through Pecos) meet to the west, on the edge of the Davis Mountains. This vast range (under different names) runs from the New Mexico border – apart from a gap between Fort Davis and Alpine – all the way south to the Big Bend National Park on the Rio Grande. Islands of green – the forests and meadows of the high mountains – rise in the sea of brown.

Six of them soar to over 8,000 ft (2,400 meters), including **Mount Livermore** at 8,206 ft (2,525 meters). In these enclaves of pine, fir, maple and oak, there are small populations of elk, black bear, bighorn sheep and mountain lions, the reminders of better, wetter grazing times. There has been a drying trend over the past 100 years and livestock has been allowed to overgraze the land. The grass has not returned, so the steppe has become a desert hell.

The youngest ranges are the Franklin Mountains at El Paso and the Delaware Mountains north of Kent, which are part of the Rocky Mountain system and still rise at an average rate of more than ¼ inch (0.65 cm) per year. Many of the ranges in the mountain and basin area of Texas were formed during the tumultuous Tertiary period about 60 million years ago. Massive uplifting and faulting led to intrusions of molten rock, like those in the Chisos Mountains of Big Bend National Park, and extensive lava flows which created the Davis Mountains. These volcanic formations cover mountains from earlier periods, as well as marine sediments and coral reefs. Folding and overthrust faulting have left young rock strata covered by a layer 150 million years older in places – a picture puzzle complex enough to delight the most jaded structural geologist.

Map on page 278

The Davis Mountains State Park attracts more than 150,000 visitors each year. Facilities include camping sites, hiking trails and fishing.

BELOW: roadside shrine in Reeves County.

Map on page 278

Cantaloupes are a popular fruit in Pecos

BELOW: white sand dunes near Guadalupe Mountains National Park.

Texas' highest and most majestic mountains, the Guadalupes, at the New Mexico border, began as a massive coral reef, some 250 million years ago. Two periods of uplifting have raised these marine remains to an altitude of over 8,000 ft (2,440 meters). The dominant feature here is the 8,749-ft (2,667-meter) **Guadalupe Peak**, the highest point in Texas. Approached from the west on US-62/180, this giant wedge of limestone resembles an enormous ship moving over the desert. The cliffs of El Capitan Peak form the prow, towering above a white sea of salt.

Cantaloupes and rodeos

Pecos ⓳ (pop. 9,500) is the biggest town along the river of the same name. Gourmets take note: Pecos is to cantaloupe what Smithfield, Virginia, is to ham. Here, in 1883, the world's first rodeo took place. The boys from the Hashknife outfit challenged boys from other ranches to horse-racing, bronc busting, and calf-roping contests. The tradition is carried on by holding a major rodeo here around July 4 each year. The **West-of-the-Pecos Museum and Park** (120 E. First Street; Apr–early Sept: open daily, Sun pm only; mid-Sept–Mar: open Tues–Sat; entrance fee; tel: 915-445-5076) displays a century-old saloon in one of its 50 rooms.

North of Pecos, bordering New Mexico, is **Loving**, the most sparsely populated county in the US – 67 people with an average 10 sq. miles (26 sq. km) each. So despite the name and with such a sparsely spread population, not a whole lot of loving goes on. Four hundred oil leases have been registered here, but there is no water – it has to be trucked in.

The only reservoir in Texas along the Pecos river is Red Bluff in Loving County, but it has only once been full in the past 60 years. New Mexico defended itself in court for 16 years against Texan charges that it was taking too much water out of the river. Finally, in 1988, the US Supreme Court ruled in Texas' favor and its neighbor was forced to pay $14 million in damages.

The first place of any size along the river south of Pecos is **Fort Stockton** ⓴ (pop. 7,800). By the mid-1880s, with no enemies left to fight, the fort was abandoned but it has been restored to its earlier appearance. Four of the original fort's buildings, built in 1867, can be visited and a museum (closed Sun; entrance fee; tel: 915-336-2400) has been established in the old barracks. Also worth seeing is the Atkins Antique Car Museum and Art Gallery (closed Sun; tel: 915-336-8421), a combination of art gallery, craft shop and vintage car collection. Most of the other interesting local sites are included on daily Roadrunner Bus Tours (tel: (915) 336-8052).

Forty miles (64 km) east of Fort Stockton, at the junction of US-67 and US-385, is **McCamey** ㉑, an "instant town" on November 16 1925, when the No. 1 Baker oil well blew in. Within months, there were 10,000 people in town and the solitary Texas Ranger – lacking a jail – was obliged to chain prisoners to a post. One group of tethered roughnecks uprooted the pole and took it to the nearest saloon. In 1936, McCamey was the scene of the world's first Rattlesnake Derby, with a $200 purse for the winner. ❏

The Marfa Lights

Robert Reed Ellison, a young cowhand, was the first to report the Marfa Lights. Looking across to the Chinati Mountains in West Texas he saw them twinkling in the night and figured they must have been the campfires of Apache Indians. But when he went searching the next day he found no Indians – nor even the ashes of any fires. This was 114 years ago and people have been watching the lights ever since, but still without being able to explain what they are and where they're coming from. As elusive as rainbows, they disappear as soon as you think you're getting up close.

According to one guidebook the lights "move about, split apart, melt together, disappear and reappear." In recent years they have become such a tourist attraction that the Texas State Highways Department has built a special parking area from which to view them along US- 90, about 10 miles (16 km) east of town. And at the Apache Trading Post, just west of Alpine, there's now a Screening Room where visitors can view films and videotape of the lights.

During World War II, pilots training at the nearby army base conducted an aerial search but were no more successful than previous investigators: the lights remained a mystery. Superstitious locals tend to reflect the views of a Mrs W.T. Giddings who claims they are a friendly source that once saved her father from a blizzard by leading him to a cave. Other explanations have included: electrostatic discharge; St Elmo's Fire, swamp gas, or other natural gases, igniting; moonlight reflecting on veins of mica; and even the ghosts of conquistadors in search of gold.

A New Handbook of Texas says the most likely explanation is that the lights are a mirage caused by atmospheric conditions, produced by the interaction of cold and warm layers of air that bend light so that it can be seen from a distance but not up close.

The Desert Candle, the local newspaper, has run numerous reports of sightings, some of which were compiled in a book by editor Judith M. Brueske, who suggests that the spaciousness of the Big Bend region and "the relatively low light contaminant," compared to more heavily populated areas, might make such lights easier to see. In *The Marfa Lights*, she offers several explanations, ranging from the phenomenon known as *ignis fatuus* (the spontaneous combustion of natural gases) or static electricity to the combination of moisture with bat guano phosphates (there are many bat caves in the mountains). And she, too, brings up the possibility that many of the sightings could be mirages, pointing out that, especially at sea, people have conjured up the vision of islands or villages.

What argues against this theory is the sheer ubiquity of the sightings. Usually they are small and seen at a distance but occasionally lights as big as footballs have come close to people's cars. Nobody has ever reported being harmed.

Marfa Lights are visible every clear night between Marfa and Paisano Pass as one faces Chinati Mountains. ❑

RIGHT: the historic El Paisano Hotel, Marfa, named for the nearby Paisano Mountain Pass.

BIG BEND NATIONAL PARK

*Beautiful Big Bend, where the Rio Grande lurches to the northeast,
has canyons, waterfalls and hiking trails galore, but with far fewer
visitors than you'll find at Yosemite or the Grand Canyon*

The state's largest park, Big Bend National Park, is most challenging to backpackers and nature lovers. The Chisos Mountains, the wide desert, the Rio Grande river and the magnificent canyons combine to form a true wilderness, sections of which are still relatively unexplored.

Big Bend (open daily; entrance fee) is one of those places you have to be going to in order to get there. The closest town is Alpine, about 65 miles (105 km) to the northwest of the northernmost tip. The park encompasses a vast area of 801,163 acres (324,230 hectares) and varies in altitude from 1,850 ft (570 meters) all the way up to 7,835 ft (2,410 meters). There are hundreds of trails, 100 miles (160 km) of paved roads and 170 miles (272 km) of dirt roads. There is a trailer park, a post office and a gas station. **Panther Junction ❶** is the park headquarters and home of the visitors' center, while, open year-round, the Chisos Mountains Lodge (tel: 915-447-2291), at **Chisos Basin ❷**, provides camping and motel accommodations. Trailer and tent camping areas are also available at **Rio Grande Village ❸**, near Boquillas, and at Cottonwood, near Castolon. Permits (free) are required for back-country camping.

LEFT: Boot Canyon in the Chisos Mountains.
BELOW: exploring Big Bend.

Wild country

"In 1902, the Big Bend was pretty wild country. The stage brought mail and passengers once a week from Marfa and that was the only connection there was… the area at the time was a favorite hangout for cattle rustlers," wrote topographical surveyor Stuart T. Penick. "It was easy to run cattle from one side of the Rio Grande to the other. Texas Rangers were scarce and didn't get to that part of the country very often." Big Bend's first cattleman, Don Milton Faver, had a herd of longhorns and burro-riding cowboys. Many were unbranded and were stolen. His cattle drives were the subject of TV's *Rawhide* series.

King of the air around here is the endangered peregrine falcon, whose concentration of eyries is the largest in the contiguous 48 states. Golden eagles are frequently seen in winter, near the mountains and over the high grasslands, but, as the clouds move across this desolate land, you may be reminded of the gargantuan pterosaur whose 51-ft (15.5-meter) reptilian wings cast terrifying shadows on the lesser dinosaurs below. The remains of these cretaceous creatures, the largest animals ever to fly, were found in the Big Bend area in the early 1970s.

The great outdoors

The real Big Bend is best seen from its hiking trails, or from a canoe expedition on the Rio Grande river. Extensive information about getting the best out of

TIP

Water can be a real problem on both long and short hikes. Dehydration comes on quickly in the Big Bend's dry air, and springs and streams are not reliable for drinking. Make sure you always take your own water and drink some frequently.

your visit through hiking, camping, canoeing, scenic hikes and river trips is available from the National Park Service. But Big Bend is wild country, and should be respected as such.

Hit the trail

Some of the 36 marked hiking trails are strenuous and treacherous; others are easy. Many are interpreted by self-guiding leaflets and trail signs. A number of trails take off from near Chisos Basin.

During the summer, a hike down the easy, 1½-mile (2.5-km) **Chisos Basin Trail** is guided by a park naturalist. At the overlook about halfway along the trail, the major features of the Chisos Basin stand out against the sky: towering Emory Peak, at 7,825 ft (2,400 meters) the highest in the park; Ward Mountain; Carter Peak and The Window; Vernon Bailey Peak and Pulliam Ridge; Casa Grande and Toll Mountain. This trail provides a good introduction to the major features of the Big Bend park.

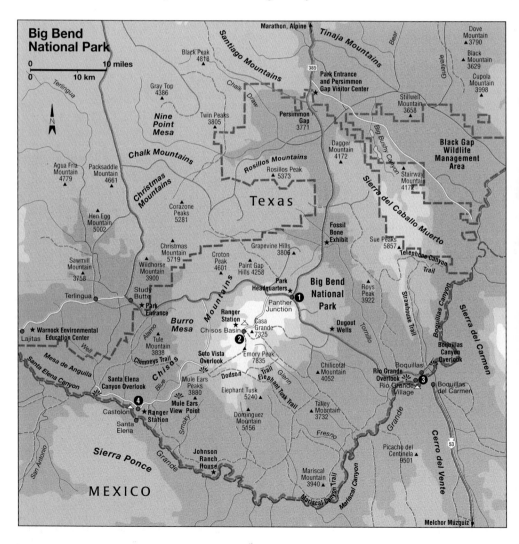

Map on page 290

Halfway between The Basin and Panther Junction, the **Pine Canyon Trail** explores a wooded canyon for 4 miles (6.5 km). At trail's end, a waterfall pours down the 200-ft (60-meter) cliff after a heavy rain.

Just north of The Basin, the moderately difficult 5-mile (8-km) **Lost Mine Trail** follows the north slope of Casa Grande and leads to a point high on the west side of Lost Mine Peak. It affords beautiful views of the surrounding mountains and canyons. A very difficult trek up the 7,500-ft (2,300-meter) Casa Grande Peak takes off from the Juniper Canyon Overlook along the Lost Mine Trail.

The 5-mile (8-km) **Chimneys Trail** lies southwest of The Basin and leads to a group of high rock outcroppings, or "chimneys," the southernmost of which contains ancient Native American pictographs.

Two groups of trails into the Chisos lie south of The Basin: the High Chisos Complex trails and the Outer Mountain Loop trails. The High Chisos trails are some of the most beautiful, but they require serious hiking and climbing. The panorama from the **South Rim Trail** includes Santa Elena Canyon 20 miles (30 km) to the west, Emory Peak to the north, and the mountains in Mexico to the south. Various trails branch off from this one and, for instance, lead up Emory Peak into Boot Canyon – the summer home of the Colima Warbler, found nowhere else in the United States.

While the High Chisos trails are strenuous, they are, at least, well-marked. The **Outer Mountain Loop** trails, on the other hand, are not so well-marked and hardly flat at all. Among these, **Blue Creek Trail** is known for its colorful balanced rocks and pinnacles. However, these two series of trails can be combined for a lengthier expedition into the Big Bend wilderness.

White-tailed deer roam in Big Bend National Park.

BELOW: Grapevine Hills, Big Bend.

Map
on page
290

TIP

If you're planning to drive out and explore Big Bend for yourself, check the condition of all roads within the park beforehand with the Park Rangers.

RIGHT: the Alto Relex escarpment, seen from Big Bend.
BELOW: sotol flower.

Spectacular canyons

Another popular trailhead is the Rio Grande Village area, near the river in the eastern part of the park. The very easy **Rio Grande Village Nature Trail**, ¾ mile (1 km) long, interprets several plant habitats, including the lush river plain-flood and the arid desert. An overlook at trail's end gives breathtaking views of Mexico, the river, the Chisos Mountains and Boquillas Canyon.

Boquillas, the longest canyon in the park, is also accessible along the 1½-mile (2.5-km) **Boquillas Canyon Trail**. For the more adventurous, a three-day trip covering 17 miles (27 km) in the canyon and 8 miles (13 km) on the Rio Grande can be a wonderful experience, with all the side canyons there are to explore on both banks, in Texas and Mexico.

Santa Elena Canyon

The most spectacular of the Big Bend canyons, **Santa Elena**, can be seen on an easy 1½-mile (2.5-km) trail that crosses Terlingua Creek and wanders through the magnificent 17-mile (27-km) canyon to the river.

If you decide to run the waters of this most spectacular of canyons, bear in mind that the river is very tricky, especially in high or low water. Eleven miles (18 km) of scenic river precede the canyon entrance, but watch for strong currents over hidden rocks. The most dangerous part of the canyon is the rockslide about a mile (1.5 km) beyond the entrance. Running the slide is always difficult, and downright dangerous at high and low water levels. Portaging it is socially acceptable and no blemish whatsoever on anyone's manhood. After the slide, navigation is more tranquil and boaters can enjoy colorful canyon walls and also explore the jewel-like Fern Canyon.

Mariscal Canyon, the most isolated of the three major canyons, is accessible on a strenuous, unshaded 6½-mile (10-km) hike. The rim affords a wide view of the canyon 1,500 ft (460 meters) below, to reward the persevering hiker.

By car

Even from a car the Big Bend visitor can see the wild country. The River Road traverses the 51 miles (82 km) between the Boquillas-Rio Grande Village road and Castolon. The road can be traveled by most high-clearance vehicles, but its side roads usually require four-wheel-drive. Old ranches and fishing camps occasionally appear along the road, and it passes the ruins of Mariscal Mine, an old mercury working at the foot of Mariscal Mountain. The ruins are fun to explore, but beware of open, unmarked mine shafts. Further west lie the remains of the Johnson Ranch House, probably the largest adobe ruin in the park. The road ends at **Castolon ❹**, a 19th-century farming settlement and early 20th-century US Cavalry and Texas Ranger post.

Big Bend has facilities and adventures to offer everyone – from automobile tours to rugged mountain trails and river running, in moderate mountain temperatures or hot-as-Texas sun. But the visitor does well to remember that it's still wild country and must be enjoyed on its own terms. ❑

THE WONDERFUL WILDLIFE OF TEXAS

You don't need to venture deep into the Texas countryside to discover the state's weird and wonderful wildlife. But, if you do, take care

They're big; they're small. They run, they fly and they crawl. They enchant you with their beauty; they make you reel with horror. *They* are the wild animals of Texas.

IT'S A JUNGLE OUT THERE

As you wander the civilized streets of Dallas or Houston, catching your reflection in a glass skyscraper, it's easy to forget that this is still the Wild West. "Wild" in the sense that the animals that call Texas their home remain as unfazed by progress as they were in the days of the frontier pioneers. The scurrying armadillo is a familiar sight in many parts of the state. Other creatures are more regionalized, preferring the marshy wetness of the East, or the unrelenting dryness and heat of the Far West. Some Texas wildlife is continually on the move, winging, crawling or grubbing its way into new corners of the state.

However, the comical antics of the prairie dog, the elegance of deer grazing in the Hill Country or the smiling dolphins off the Gulf Coast should not lead visitors into a false sense of security. Like the prickly desert plants, native Texan beasts must be met on their own terms, if met at all. They can bite, they can sting. They can annoy, they can maim. The key rule is: Don't mess. If you leave the animals to themselves, the chances are they'll keep well away from you. Be sensible. Follow all warning signs and don't tempt danger. But, for all the cougars, black bears, rattlesnakes, alligators and coyotes, there are also stunning birds, majestic buffalo, thriving longhorns, languid sea turtles and exotic fish you won't find anywhere else.

And with scores of natural refuges for "safe" viewing, the beautiful creatures of Texas can still charm and enthrall.

△ **SNAP SHOT**
In the marshy bayous of East Texas lurk some 200,000 alligators, the state's largest reptile. They feed on fish and other small animals, and seldom attack humans – but don't push it!

▷ **BATTY BEHAVIOR**
The caves of Central Texas are the breeding grounds for a variety of bat species. The adults here are all female, the males being left in South America.

◁ **PRAIRIE DOG**
This burrowing member of the squirrel family lives in colonies of thousands. Its name is derived from its cry, or "bark."

SNAKES IN THE GRASS

The statistics tell the truth: there is more chance of being killed by a lightning strike in Texas than from a snake bite. Nevertheless, the thought of a venomous rattler is enough to panic many Texas visitors.

The state is home to more than 100 species of snake, but less than 10 percent are a danger to humans. The rattlesnake (actually 11 varieties) is the most feared. It can be found in most parts of Texas, but is prevalent in the Trans-Pecos region. The coral snake *(above)* is also a nasty little wriggler and may be encountered in areas from Central Texas south. The same territory is inhabited by the copperhead, equally dangerous if provoked, while the cottonmouth is semi-aquatic and lives mostly around rivers in Central and East Texas.

▷ **JAVELINA**
Despite being armed with tusks and musk, the nearsighted javelina, a cousin of the South American tapir, is not dangerous.

▽ **BLOODSHOT EYES**
The prickly looking horned lizard, often mistakenly referred to as the "horny toad," can shoot a stream of blood from its eyes.

▷ **THE LION'S SHARE**
Cougars are found in the mountains of the Trans-Pecos. As this warning notice confirms, they should not be approached. Smaller cats live elsewhere in the state: lynx-like bobcats in East Texas and jaguarundi in South Texas. Look out for wild dogs, too, particularly coyotes and wolves.

LION WARNING

YOUNG LIONS ARE CURRENTLY IN THE AREA, AND MAY DISPLAY AGGRESSION TOWARD HUMANS.

AVOID
- TAKING SMALL CHILDREN INTO AREA-THEY ARE MOST AT RISK. IF YOU MUST TAKE THEM KEEP THEM ALONE
- HIKING ALONE
- HIKING IN EVENING, EARLY MORNING, OR NIGHT HOURS.

IF YOU SEE A LION
- DO NOT SHOW FEAR
- DO NOT RUN AWAY
- DO NOT SQUAT DOWN

DO
- PICK UP SMALL CHILDREN
- GATHER YOURSELVES TOGETHER - APPEAR AS LARGE AS POSSIBLE
- WAVE ARMS AND SHOUT AGGRESSIVELY
- THROW STONES OR STICKS
- SCARE CAT AWAY
- REPORT INCIDENT TO A RANGER AS SOON AS POSSIBLE

THE WEST

West Texas, a hard land to colonize, has changed its complexion with every industrial advance – from coal mining to oil extraction – yet it buzzes with the spirit of self-reliance imprinted on its citizens

Map on page 298

The people of southern North Central Texas call themselves "West" Texans, not out of geographical ignorance, but out of a sense of history and place. After the Civil War, their ancestors from Arkansas, Tennessee and other Southern states, knowing no place else to go to begin a new life, headed west, where they encountered a foe more relentless than General Sherman: the slow-yielding, tightfisted land itself, ruled by distance, drought and the most ferocious aboriginal army ever to ride horseback. Thus, mile after uncertain mile was conquered by people who were not searching for wealth, but for a place to survive. They did survive, and left their descendants with the knowledge that anything is possible if one is self-reliant and looks toward the horizon.

Travel in this relatively featureless landscape can become an agonizingly slow unfolding of geography, if you expect to be constantly entertained by the fluff and fanfare of tourist extravaganzas. However, if you adopt the easy-going friendliness of its people, and attune yourself to the voices of its heroic past, West Texas will be an unforgettable experience.

LEFT: a Texas icon: the oil pump. **BELOW:** Wild West cowboy on the range.

Fort Worth to El Paso

West of Fort Worth, where I-20 drops down from rough-cut juniper and oak-covered hills on to the fitful beginning of the plains, are the ruins of **Thurber ❶**, a coal-mining town better suited to northeastern Pennsylvania or the Ruhr Valley than post-frontier Texas. Where 10,000 people from 17 counties lived between 1880 and 1922 there now exist only a tall brick smoke stack, a restaurant-museum, the remains of a great brick factory and a service station. The rest of the town has been sold brick by brick, down to the last utility pole. As one looks across the now empty valley to the conical piles of black coal spoil and "red dog" cinders, it is difficult to imagine the wealthy, cosmopolitan city that stood here on the near side of frontier times. Thurber is where the Metropolitan Opera of New York performed, where Miss Wallis "Wildcat" Warfield, later the Duchess of Windsor, grew up in one of the mansions along Silk Stocking Road on New York Hill, and where a World War I clothing drive netted no fewer than four dozen mink coats.

In 1895, Thurber was one of the first completely electrified cities in the world. After a long, bitter strike presided over by Texas Rangers, Thurber became the first and perhaps the only 100 percent unionized town in America. The 100 million tons (90 million metric tons) of coal mined here powered the belching, billowing locomotives of Jay Gould's Texas & Pacific (T&P) Railway as they trundled across the prairie. In 1881, the last 595 miles (958 km) of the T&P main

line, parallel to I-20, were completed between Fort Worth and Sierra Blanca in a phenomenal 11 months, by a crew of 300 hard-drinking Irishmen.

The railroad's role in the rapid demise of the frontier is dramatically demonstrated by the almost simultaneous founding of Abilene, Big Spring, Midland, Odessa and the other major cities of the region. They were shipping points for cattle, eliminating the long trail drives to Dodge City and Abilene in Kansas. The change from coal- to oil-powered locomotives led to the dismantling of Thurber and helped set the stage for the meteoric emergence of **Ranger ❷**, 13 miles (21 km) to the west and the most rip-snorting boomtown of all.

Oil boom doom

Derricks and pump jacks are still in evidence, but the quiet streets of modern Ranger fail to suggest the frenzy of the weeks in 1917, after oil rig McClesky No. 1 blew in with 1,700 barrels a day. At World War I prices, a good well yielded $250,000 a week. The 10 trains that rolled into Ranger every day were

Decorated pump jacks brighten fields.

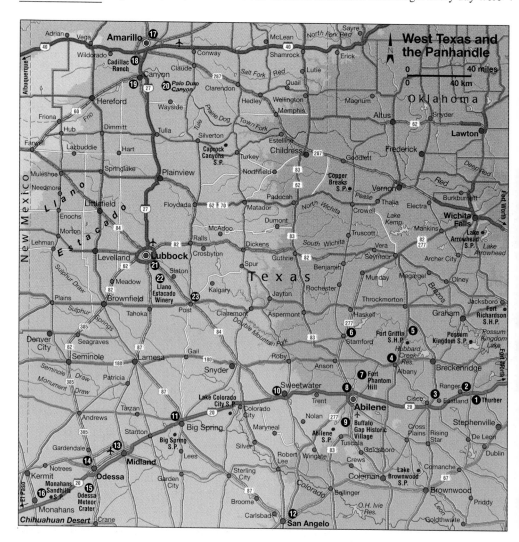

filled with speculators, jacklegs, riffraff and ruffians, ambitious men and loose women. The town exploded from a village of 1,000 to a seething city of 40,000 in a matter of months. Streets turned into a sea of mud, traversed on sleds or the backs of men in hip boots. Guests in those days paid luxury hotel rates to sleep in armchairs. The evangelist Billy Sunday went in search of souls to saloons called the Grizzly Bear, the Blue Moose and Oklahoma, where as many as five people a day met their oil boom doom.

Small wonder there was violence when, for example, one lease changed hands three times on a Friday, increasing in value from $150 to $15,000. Everyone in the trade but the middle man must have felt taken. Talk to some of the old-timers, or ask the local historian at Ranger Junior College for more details of the years when Ranger's oil produced more wealth than the California gold rush at its peak.

Rest In Peace

A few miles west lies **Eastland ❸**, another boomtown gone bust. Today its principal claims to fame are the Post Office Mural, a montage of 11,217 stamps, which depicts the history of the communications service; the **Kendrick Religious Museum** displaying biblical dioramas (west of town on State Route 6; open daily; entrance fee); and a horned toad named Rip (Rest in Peace), which was sealed into the cornerstone of the old courthouse in 1897 and found to be alive when the new courthouse was built some 28 years later. The creature died a year later, after achieving national fame. His stuffed body was then placed in a glass case in the new building. In his miniature coffin, he resembles a rather flat and very prickly pin-cushion, about the size of a child's hand.

Today, one approaches **Albany ❹**, northwest of Cisco, over the same rolling

Map on page 298

Horny toads like Rip, an Eastland celebrity, are not actually amphibians, but lizards. Although the little critters are unable to cause warts, they do shoot a thin stream of blood out of the corners of their eyes, to a distance of up to 4 ft (1.2 meters).

BELOW: barbed wire and tumbleweed in West Texas.

red plains the cowboys covered on the trail to Dodge City in the 1870s. Due to overgrazing, however, the lush prairie grasses they found here are gone. There is only the eroded soil and lacy-leaved mesquite trees. Although mesquite steals precious moisture from the soil, it puts back nitrogen, since it is a leguminous plant. Its beans were ground into a flour by the nomadic Plains Indians and are still eaten by cattle in times of drought. Its wood is considered by many Texans to be without parallel for cooking barbecue.

In spite of all its agricultural and culinary benefits, Texas ranchers hate mesquite and hire "wetbacks," illegal immigrants from Mexico, to remove it from time to time.

Only in Albany

At first sight, Albany is as unimposing as the mesquite "forests" that surround it, but this prairie town of 2,000 possesses an exceptional collection of 20th-century art, displayed in **The Old Jail Art Center** (201 S. Second Street; closed Mon; Sun pm only; free; tel: 325-762-2269), a place where drunken cowboys and assorted desperados were once detained. The limestone building itself (*circa* 1878) is a good example of frontier architecture, with its decoratively routed and scored casements and cistern out front. Alongside pre-Columbian displays, among the many artists represented in the large permanent collection are Matisse, Rouault, Picasso, Modigliani, Miró, Henry Moore and Giacometti.

Albany's Fort Griffin "Fandangle" is an outdoor historical pageant staged during the last two weeks in June. The roles of Native Americans, cowboys, buffalo hunters, soldiers, bandits and settlers are sung and acted, as they have been since 1938, by the descendants of those who originally occupied the Texas frontier (tel: 915-762-3838). Before leaving Albany, head for the **Ledbetter Picket House Museum** (24 S. Main Street; hours vary; free), a

BELOW: roadside cowboy.

Map on page 298

restored frontier ranch house with many authentic furnishings. A similar ranch house served as the commandant's headquarters in the early days of what is now **Fort Griffin State Historical Park ❺** (open daily; entrance fee 915-762-3592), 15 miles (24 km) north of Albany on US-283. Established in 1867, Fort Griffin belonged to the outer line of frontier defense. The first line, which swung in a wide arc southwest from Fort Worth to San Antonio, was established in the late 1840s on the edge of Comanche territory. Its line of forts was a buffer between the Plains Indians and white colonies.

The roughest town in Texas

From its hilltop, the stone ruins and partially reconstructed wooden remains of the fort look down on what was possibly the roughest, most brawling and iniquitous town in the history of Texas: "The Flats." Never has a lustier mixture of manhood been stirred in one pot. Imagine them bellied up to the same bar: bitter, defeated Southern veterans of the Civil War alongside the blue-jacketed conquerors and the "buffalo soldiers," as the Native Americans called freed slaves who were part of the army. As if they were not enough, add buffalo hunters flush from selling hides, plus the professional gamblers and bandits who preyed on them, and the bounty hunters who preyed in turn on them. Ironically, one of the few original buildings remaining in "The Flats" was far more respectable: it served as the church, school and Masonic lodge.

Herds of the once-threatened longhorn cattle are found in increasing numbers again across the state, but they are particularly accessible to the public at Fort Griffin State Park. Cowboys still exist, too, and you can find them at the Texas Cowboy Reunion at **Stamford ❻**, around July 4. This is no slick, professional

The Texas longhorn, protected at Fort Griffin State Park.

BELOW: the Sierra del Carmen.

Fort Phantom Hill is housed on private land. You can visit the site for no charge, but bear in mind that there are no special visitor facilities.

production in an air-conditioned coliseum. This is where "good ol' boys" risk their necks, not for love of money, but for love of their favorite roping horses or even the love of their girls who perch on the top rail of the arena fence.

Further west, 14 miles (22 km) north of Abilene, is **Fort Phantom Hill ❼**. The very name has the chill of desolation to it. Loneliness still lingers about the tall, solitary chimneys, the empty commissary, guardhouse and powder magazine, especially in the dim red light of dusk. From its founding in 1850, to protect the region from hostile Indians, there were frequent desertions from this post, where boredom alternated with Comanche raids. After its abandonment in 1854, the hated fort was burned by one of the withdrawing soldiers. Later it became an overnight stop for mail coaches on the Butterfield Trail.

In making your way through the scrub oak and mesquite to Abilene, you will probably see the silver and salmon flash of the scissor-tailed flycatcher. In excited flight, the graceful tails, which are twice as long as the bodies, almost seem to flitter like a carnival bird on a stick.

God's glorious city

Abilene ❽ (pop. 116,000) likes to promote its slogan "A Whole Lotta Texas Goin On," but might more aptly be described as the "Glorious City of God," being the home of three religiously affiliated institutions of learning – McMurry University, Abilene Christian University and the Southern Baptists' Hardin-Simmons. Round-the-clock prayer meetings for rain didn't bring an end to the drought of the early 1950s, but they must have made an impression: the region has been blessed with oil discoveries ever since. A rig was set up on the **Taylor County Exposition Center** (Highway 36 at 11th Street) grounds here for demon-

BELOW: West Texas on the right track.

stration and, of course, it struck oil. Rodeos are held here each spring and fall.

Abilene's **Historical Museum** (part of the Grace Museum; 102 Cypress Street; open Tue–Sat; entrance fee; free on Thur eve; tel: 915-673-4587) has exhibits relating to Camp Barkeley, the World War II army base and prison camp, whose ruins can still be seen on US-277, south of town. There are other museums in this complex devoted to children and fine arts.

Buffalo Gap

An authentic taste of the Old West is to be had 10 miles (16 km) southwest of town, where the low, dark juniper-covered hills of the Calahan Divide are broken abruptly at **Buffalo Gap Historic Village** ❾ (mid-Mar–mid-Nov: open daily; mid-Nov–mid-Mar: open Fri–Sun; Sun pm only; entrance fee; tel: 915-572-3365). A mix of authentic frontier buildings and new tourist attractions are found here. An old courthouse, jail and log cabins are among the old buildings. A doctor's office, a barber shop and a print shop are modern reconstructions. Twice a year, in the 19th century, buffalo passed through the mountain gap here, indelibly etching a permanent trail. When this brown, woolly group flowed between these ancient hills, Tonkawa and Comanche Indians still camped in the cool shade of the native pecan groves and made arrowheads, traces of which can still be found. Charles Goodnight, one of the most celebrated of early longhorn ranchers out west, described the main buffalo herd as being 125 miles (200 km) long and 25 miles (40 km) wide. The trail they blazed was later the one he used to drive his own cattle to the Kansas railheads. When the area was settled by whites in the 1870s, this natural funnel through the hills continued to be a focus for the region. Today, 19 of the original buildings have been restored,

Map on page 298

The Texan town of Abilene, founded by cattlemen in 1881, was named for Abilene in Kansas, which was the final stop on the Chisholm Trail.

BELOW: crop dusting in West Texas.

including the limestone courthouse and jail. Gravestones, of Civil War veterans and others, in the Buffalo Gap Cemetery, tell the history of the settling of West Texas in a few poignant words. Nearby Lake Abilene and **Abilene State Park** (open daily; entrance fee; tel: 915-572-3204), with their hiking and picnicking possibilities, complete the tourist picture.

Gypsum deposits

It was the sheer abundance of rattlesnakes, which were troubling local ranchers and farmers, that led the town of Sweetwater to organize the first rattlesnake roundup.

The town of **Sweetwater** , 40 miles (64 km) west of Abilene on I-20, was well-named in this area where many of the streams are tainted with gypsum. Gypsum, otherwise known as Epsom salts, is fine for soaking tired feet but, as a drink, keeps one on the run. The rich local gypsum deposits have been put to constructive use in the manufacture of wallboard by two large factories.

One of the few towns in West Texas to predate the coming of the railroad, Sweetwater began in 1877 as a general store for buffalo hunters, dug into the banks of Sweetwater Creek. The world's largest rattlesnake roundup is held here during the second weekend in March, at the Nolan County Coliseum (for information, tel: 915-235-3484). It is a bring-em-back-alive affair in which the snakes are milked for their venom and prizes are given for the longest, shortest and heaviest (by the pound). A record 14,000 lbs (6,350 kg) were delivered in 1985. If you have ever had a hankering to eat a fried 6-ft (2-meter) long western diamondback, or buy a transparent toilet seat with a rattler coiled in it, here is such an opportunity.

A few moments on the weed-broken tarmac of the Old Sweetwater Army Airfield will resurrect memories of the 1940s, when the Women's Airforce Service Pilots (WASPs) received their flight training here. Further west, past Colorado City (locally pronounced *Cahla Rayda Cidy*), is the town of **Big**

BELOW: Lake Colorado City State Park.

![Lake Colorado City State Park at sunset with three people fishing in silhouette](N)

Spring **⑪**, a site important in another war. This natural oasis was occupied by Native Americans as long as 10,000 years ago and served as a major rest stop for the tribes on the Comanche War Trail, halfway between their home on the High Plains to the north and the white settlements in Texas and Mexico to the south. The Native Americans shared its precious water with antelope, buffalo and wild mustang horses. The appeal of this ancient oasis is still felt in the cool late afternoon among the trees of Comanche Trail Park, while the **Big Spring State Park** (open daily; entrance fee) provides a view of the entire area from a 200-ft (60-meter) mesa within the city limits.

Southbound travelers along US-87 from Big Spring will pass through **San Angelo ⑫**, a modern city of lakes and rivers on the edge of the Texas Hill Country. Like San Antonio, it has a River Walk, winding its way past landscaped gardens, parks and beautiful homes by the Concho river. **Fort Concho**, the best-preserved of the Indian War stockades, is filled with exhibits from frontier times (630 S. Oakes Street; closed Mon; Sun pm only; entrance fee; tel: 325-481-2646).

The Permian Basin oil field

At the midway point of the 600-mile (965-km) drive from Fort Worth to El Paso, a mirage of civilization rises out of the endless illusion of water over the highway ahead. The small city of **Midland ⑬** (pop. 95,000), the hometown of President George W. Bush, is dominated by glass and steel towers, containing the offices of more than 650 firms dedicated to coaxing crude oil from the bottom of a 250-million-year-old sea, now buried tens of thousands of feet below the desert sand. The city is a vibrant, modern haven with an active cultural scene. It has weathered the roughest historic and economic storms. The city was in the thick of battles between Commanches and settlers. When the oil boom arrived, prosperity flooded the region. Consequently, when Texas oil went bad, the city faced rough times.

The **Permian Basin Oil Field** is the second-largest in the world, and the price of a barrel of Texas Permian Intermediate Weight Crude is the standard against which the prices of all other US oils are determined. The nodding, hobbyhorse-like pump jacks seem to repeat as they suck at the earth: "Fiftydollars, fiftydollars, fiftydollars…" Not only have their rhythms enriched many a slouch-hatted rancher, but the University of Texas as well. In the 19th century, having virtually no funds to offer the fledgling institution, the state legislature apologetically proffered 2.2 million acres (890,000 hectares) of sand and desert scrubland. That these holdings coincide with the outlines of the Permian Basin is a happy coincidence that has bequeathed the University around $2.5 billion.

The science and technology of oil are brilliantly explained in the **Petroleum Museum** (1500 I-20 West, exit 136; open daily; Sun pm only; entrance fee; tel: 432-683-4403), where visitors can stroll along the bottom of the sea. Another educational site is the **American Airpower Heritage Museum of the Confederate Air Force**, near the airport (9600 Wright Drive; open daily; Sun pm only; entrance fee; 915-567-3009) with a collection of World War II aircraft and a new Aviation Art Gallery.

Map on page 298

TIP

For a taste of old fort life, visit Fort Concho on the first weekend in December, when an 1880s-style celebration is held, re-enacting a Christmas holiday from that era.

BELOW: prairie dog.

Map on page 298

Midland's other claim to fame is that it is the "Tumbleweed Capital of the World." In the scorching 100+°F (38+°C) days of summer, when all else turns brown, legions of prickly green tumbleweeds crowd the roadside and abandoned fields. These tumbleweeds resist the heat as they grow up to 8 ft (2.5 meters) tall, awaiting the moment in the fall when they break free of the earth to rush pell-mell down the road. Since Bob Nolan and the Sons of the Pioneers immortalized this common nuisance in the song *Tumbling Tumbleweed*, the plant has become a symbol for the spirit of movement that led to the development of the West Texas frontier, especially in the person of the drifting cowboy.

Odessa

The Presidential Museum recalls past election campaigns.

BELOW:
historic oil derrick and pump jack in Reagan County.
RIGHT: Highway 54 in West Texas.

Traveling on to **Odessa ⓮**, one finds the authentic West Texas "redneck." Midland is the business center of the Permian Basin, and Odessa is the home of the oil field worker or "roughneck." "Oil field trash and proud of it," say bumper stickers often seen on pickup trucks with loaded rifles hung in the back window. No need to search further for the modern counterpart of the frontier cowboy.

Odessa does hold a few surprises though. For example, the Globe of the Great Southwest Theater, a replica of Shakespeare's Globe Theatre in London, plus a replica of the Anne Hathaway Cottage, complete with Shakespeare library, can be found on the local college campus (tours available, call in advance; tel: 915-332-1586). A professional repertory company produces the classics plus an annual Shakespeare Festival. There is also a Permian Playhouse Theater and a symphony orchestra. At 622 N Lee Street is the **Presidential Museum** (closed Sun and Mon; entrance fee; tel: 915-332-7123), an intriguing exhibit dedicated to the US Presidency, including campaigning memorabilia and First Lady dolls.

For a natural wonder, inspect the **Odessa Meteor Crater ⓯**, just west of town, off Farm Road 1936. The nation's second largest, it has a diameter of 500 ft (152 meters). The crater was formed when some 2 million lbs (907,200 kg) of extraterrestrial iron crashed into the earth during the last Ice Age.

West of Odessa, at the western edge of "West Texas," the great Chihuahuan Desert begins and continues across the Trans-Pecos region into Mexico. The best vantage point for an eyeful of sandy "desert-scape" is **Monahans Sandhills State Park ⓰**, 24 miles (38 km) west of Odessa on I-20, exit Park Road 41 (open daily; entrance fee; four-wheel drive tours available; tel: 915-943-2092), where naked dunes tower up to 70 ft (21 meters) high and stretch north and south for 200 miles (320 km).

America's most bizarre forest grows along the margin of this desolation. The Havard oak forms a dense, at times almost impenetrable, growth which is easily overlooked, because the mature trees stand only about 3 ft (1 meter) tall. West Texans call the trees shin oak and the forest the "shinnery." These plants are marvelously well-adapted to drought, with roots that can reach a depth of 90 ft (27 meters). But, even when transplanted to moist conditions, the Havard oak remains dwarfed – obviously as suspicious of easy times as the hardy humans who settled in the region. ❑

AMARILLO TO LUBBOCK

Arid high plains give way to the dramatic natural beauty of Palo Duro Canyon, while the cattle city of Amarillo and Buddy Holly's home town of Lubbock have more to offer than at first glance

Map on page 298

The Panhandle of Texas is referred to as "West Texas" by the people who live here. The landscape stretches in an unbroken line, with perhaps an occasional pump jack or farmhouse on the horizon. The sunsets can be breathtaking: with nothing to obscure the view, the sky blazes with oranges, yellows and reds, and fades to soft pinks and purples. Driving at night, you can see the lights of many small towns in all directions. Because of the high altitude, the air is very clear and dry. And, after the sun sets in the summer, the evening brings cool breezes.

Amarillo

In the northern Panhandle is **Amarillo** ⓱ (pop. 174,000), which means "yellow" in Spanish. In 1887, there was a shipping point here for hauling cattle to market by rail. It is still a major center for cattle distribution; Amarillo claims to have the world's largest private cattle auction. The Amarillo Livestock Auction (100 Manhattan Street; tours daily; auctions Tue; free; tel: 806-373-7464), sells over 300,000 head a year.

Equine fans will appreciate the American Quarter Horse Heritage Center and Museum, (2601 E. I-40; open daily; Sun pm only; entrance fee; tel: 806-376-5181), where visitors learn why this particular breed was the cowboy's favorite mount. Amarillo is headquarters for the Working Ranch Cowboys Association, which organizes the World Championship Ranch Rodeo every November.

Visitors to the Don Harrington Discovery Center (1200 Streit Drive; closed Mon; Sun pm only; entrance fee; tel: 806-355-9548) can enjoy the experience of an interactive science and technology attraction, as well as laser and planetarium shows (open daily; entrance fee).

Suburban **Old San Jacinto**, with antique and gift stores along a section of historic Route 66, calls itself "the heart of Amarillo."

Cadillac Ranch

West of Amarillo on I-40 is one of the area's most celebrated sights: 10 cadillacs, nose down in an orderly row. This **Cadillac Ranch** ⓲ was conceived by Stanley Marsh, an Amarillo rancher and artist on whose land they are buried.

Further south is the town of **Canyon** ⓳, home of West Texas A&M University, founded in 1909, and the sprawling Panhandle-Plains Historical Museum (2503 4th Avenue; open daily; Sun pm only; entrance fee; tel: 806-656-2244). This is the largest Texas state museum and contains an art collection, geological exhibits and a reconstructed pioneer town of a cen-

LEFT: the Big Texan Steak Ranch, Amarillo, home of the "free" 72-oz steak. **BELOW:** Cadillac Ranch.

tury ago. One wing of the museum is devoted to the oil boom years of the Texas Panhandle during the 1920s and 1930s, displaying equipment from that period and showing a short feature film. A new exhibit, People of the Plains, relates 14,000 years of man's occupation of the Southern Great Plains.

Search for Gold

Rusty Spur Outpost, Palo Duro Canyon.

Here at Canyon, 20 miles (32 km) south of Amarillo, the flat plains come to a dead halt. What lies ahead is a vast chasm – the **Palo Duro Canyon** ㉟. The multicolored canyon – second-largest in the US – is 120 miles (193 km) long, up to 20 miles (32 km) wide, and has 800-ft (245-meter) walls. In summertime, there are nightly (except Sundays) performances of the spectacular, rousing musical drama *Texas* (reservations tel: 806-655-2181). With a canyon wall as a backdrop, a cast of 80 brings to life, in song and dance, Paul Green's Pulitzer Prize-winning play about the settling of West Texas.

Geologists say over 90 million years of erosion by creeks and streams, abetted by incessant wind, formed this majestic canyon. *Palo Duro* is Spanish, meaning "hard wood", and refers to the juniper trees found in the area. A Spanish explorer, Francisco Vasquez de Coronado, is believed to have come upon Palo Duro in 1541 while searching for Quivira, the richest of the mythical Cities of Gold. In the 19th century, the canyon became a stronghold of the Comanche Indians led by Chief Quanah Parker, who suffered their final defeat in 1874. They were surprised by a cavalry force commanded by General Ranald Mackenzie, who drove 1,500 horses and mules out of Palo Duro and slaughtered them. Without their horses, the Native Americans were helpless. The Comanches were removed to reservations in Oklahoma.

BELOW: Amarillo.

Today, **Palo Duro State Park** (open daily; entrance fee) comprises more than 16,400 acres (6,600 hectares). Hiking and camping are possible, along with horseback riding in season.

The great ranches

The legendary figure of Charles Goodnight, the first rancher to move into the Panhandle in the 1870s, is closely associated with Palo Duro Canyon and with the beginning of the cattle drives. Goodnight designed the first chuckwagon. Backed by the British financier John Adair (their cattle were branded with "JA"), Goodnight built up his herd to as many as 100,000 head. For a while in the 1880s, theirs was the largest ranch in Texas – more than 700,000 acres (over 283,000 hectares). Then in 1885, the XIT Ranch was established in the far northern Panhandle on over 3 million acres (1.25 million hectares), which the State of Texas had traded for the new State Capitol building in Austin.

In order to stock the XIT Ranch, British investors were again brought in. An XIT Reunion is held at **Dalhart**, about 80 miles (130 km) north of Amarillo every year, in the first full week of August. The amateur rodeo and enormous barbecue attract thousands.

Cowboy Morning (open Apr–Oct; entrance fee; tel: 800-658-2613) on the Figure 3 Ranch always draws plenty of guests. It begins with a chuckwagon breakfast on the rim of Palo Duro, to which visitors are carried in a horse-drawn wagon from Tom Christian's ranch near Claude, off US-287 east of Amarillo. Before returning, time is set aside for exploring the path leading to the canyon floor, for short horseback rides and for visiting with the cowboys, who demonstrate particular skills such as lariat tricks and cattle branding. Another popular

Map on page 298

TIP

Take advantage of the fact that Palo Duro is one of America's more accessible canyons. A spectacular 10-mile (16-km) drive by car can be made year-round across the canyon floor.

BELOW: statue of Will Rogers at Texas Tech University, Lubbock.

Buddy Holly

Charles Hardin Holley, better known as *Buddy Holly* (his name was misspelled on his first recording contract), was born at Lubbock, Texas, on September 7, 1936, into a loving, musical family. As a child he played piano, then accompanied himself with guitar on favorite country songs, particularly those of Hank Williams who, along with Bill Monroe and the Bluegrass Boys, was to influence his singing style.

By the time Buddy reached his late teens, rock 'n' roll was being played on radio station KSEL, but the music was mostly rhythm and blues by black performers. Little Richard, Fats Domino, the Clovers and the Drifters were making personal appearances locally and, early in 1955, KDAV booked Elvis Presley into the Cotton Club, Lubbock's leading country dance hall. Hearing Elvis changed Buddy's style forever, prompting him to distill a blend of pop, blues and country. They became close friends.

In 1955 a Decca recording agent saw Buddy and his group and, the following year, invited him to Nashville, where he recorded *Blue Days, Black Nights,* his first single release. With a country melody, but a blues inflection, the track was difficult for some reviewers to categorize.

In February 1957, Buddy, Jerry Allison, Niki Sullivan and Larry Welborn, as the Crickets, recorded *That'll Be the Day* at Norman Petty's studios in Clovis, New Mexico. This was the beginning of the Crickets, a name chosen by flipping through an encyclopedia. *That'll Be the Day* topped the charts in September 1957 and was followed by *Peggy Sue.* Its innovative "Holly sound" included steady guitar strumming, rapid, accented drumming and his famous vocal "hiccup." With *Words of Love* (also 1957) Buddy introduced another innovation – overdubbing.

The following year, Buddy and the Crickets toured widely and appeared twice on the top-rated *Ed Sullivan Show.* They also toured Britain – where their records were even more successful than in the US – and visited Australia. While in New York in 1958, Buddy met and married Maria Elena Santiago. The same year, the Crickets released *Rave On* (many believing it was the most exciting record the Crickets ever made), *Heartbeat, Not Fade Away, Oh Boy!, Maybe Baby* and *It's So Easy.*

On February 3, 1959, a few weeks into a tour with singers Ritchie Valens and J.P. Richardson (the "Big Bopper"), Buddy was killed when their plane crashed in a snowstorm near Clear Lake, Iowa.

Although his dream was cut short, Buddy Holly left a stylistic legacy to generations of musicians. His statue now stands outside Lubbock's Civic Center and visitors from all over the world pay homage at his grave in the Lubbock Cemetery on East 34th Street, near Quirt. The city also has a museum in his honor. Holly is the most famous Lubbockite, but he is only one of the many West Texans who have made their mark in contemporary music, some of whom – Waylon Jennings, Roy Orbison, Jimmy Dean and Mac Davis among them – are honored in the city's Walk of Fame. ❏

LEFT: Not Fade Away: the Buddy Holly statue and Walk of Fame Memorial, Lubbock.

attraction is the nightly **Old West Show** at the **Creekwood Ranch** (tel: 806-356-9256), which begins with a wagon ride to the campsite, where supper is cooked over an open campfire.

Lubbock

Even though the singer Mac Davis claims "happiness is Lubbock, Texas, in my rear-view mirror," most residents of **Lubbock** ㉑ (pop. 200,000) would live nowhere else. Even Mac concedes at the end of his song that now "happiness is Lubbock, Texas, getting nearer and dearer." Lubbock, a center for cotton growing in the region, and which also ships grain and livestock, is situated at one of the southernmost tips of the Llano Estacado, or "Staked Plains." This is the name for the immense Great Plains that sweep for 1,600 miles (2,560 km) through America's center, all the way up to Canada, and produce a substantial proportion of the country's grain, meat and fiber. A plaque marking the Llano Estacado's eastern boundary sits on US-84 southeast of town.

Texas Tech University, at 4th Street and Indiana Avenue, is one of Lubbock's main attractions. Its full sports agenda entices enthusiastic crowds. The University's teams are known as Red Raiders and are members of the Southwest Conference.

The University has established the Texas Tech Museum (closed Mon; Sun pm only; free; tel: 806-742-2490) and the Ranching Heritage Center (3121 4th Street; open daily; Sun pm only; free; tel: 806-742-0498), a 12-acre (4.8-hectare) area through which winds a trail past more than 30 buildings (schoolhouse, blacksmith's shop, homes, barns, windmills), representing ranching's early days. The museum offers a mixed bag of paintings of the American

Map on page 298

TIP

For somewhere to eat in Lubbock, check out the Historic Depot District. This collection of restaurants and clubs is housed in the old Fort Worth to Denver Railroad Depot in the downtown area. It is also the home of the Buddy Holly Center.

BELOW: working cowboys at Goodnight Stables, Palo Duro Canyon.

Map
on page
298

*Cask at the Llano
Estacado Winery.*

BELOW: ranch gate
ornamentation.
RIGHT: a wooden
eclipse windmill.

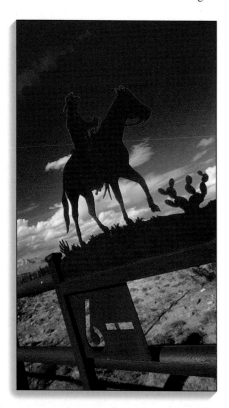

West, along with European art, sculpture, ceramics and Currier and Ives lithographs. Changing exhibitions narrate the story of the region from prehistoric times through the Spanish explorations and the settling of the region by ranchers and farmers.

The museum also contains the **Moody Planetarium** (entrance fee), and operates an archeological site beside Lubbock Lake (northwest of the city, near US-84 and Loop 289; closed Mon; Sun pm only; free; tel: 806-742-1116). This has yielded artifacts and tools from all known cultural groups who once lived in the Southwest, from the elephant-hunters 20,000 years ago to the Comanches of the 19th century. No other New World site houses such a complete chronological record (guided tours Sat 10am and 1pm, and Sun 2pm; tel: 806-742-2456).

A new museum dedicated to Lubbock's most celebrated musical son is housed in the Historic Depot District. The **Buddy Holly Center** (1801 Avenue G; open Tue–Sat; entrance fee; tel: 806-767-2686) honors the rock 'n' roll pioneer.

Off University Avenue, 3 miles (5 km) south of town, is **Science Spectrum** (2579 S. Loop 289; open daily; Sun pm only; closed Mon in winter; entrance fee; tel: 806-745-2525), a hands-on science, nature and technology museum, along with **OMNIMAX**, a cinema with a giant domed screen, 58 ft (18 meters) in diameter (shows daily; entrance fee; tel: 806-745-6299).

The Canyon Lakes Project is a string of five lakes in Lubbock's **Yellowhouse Canyon**, where man-made waterfalls, boat-loading ramps, fishing piers, camping and picnicking areas, and hike and bike trails, attract fans of the outdoors. Part of the canyon is devoted to **Mackenzie State Park**, where one of the few remaining colonies of prairie dogs resides. These amusing, squirrel-like creatures provide much entertainment for visitors today, but proved such a pest at one time that farmers did their best to exterminate them. Living in giant underground colonies, their "towns" covered thousands of square miles under the prairie grass before civilization overtook them.

One might not expect the farmland surrounding Lubbock to include prize-winning vineyards, but the region's soil and climatic conditions have proved to be excellent for most of the California-type wines. There are several vineyards, among them the **Llano Estacado Winery ㉒**, 3 miles (5 km) east of US-87, on FM 1585. Here, free daily tours and wine tastings are offered (tel: 806-745-2258).

Post

Fifteen miles (24 km) southeast of Lubbock, on US-84, is **Post ㉓** (pop. 3,700), a town named for cereal magnate Charles W. Post. He founded it in 1907, after an extended stay in the Kellogg brothers' Battle Creek Sanitarium for his health. Noting that the Kelloggs had devised for their patients food substitutes made from grain, Post blended wheat, bran and molasses to create a coffee substitute called Postum. In the decade beginning in 1902, he spent $60 million to advertise Postum and such other products as Grape Nuts and Post Toasties. Long after his death in 1914, the Postum cereal company became General Foods Corporation. ❑

TEXAS PARKS

Camping, fishing and watersports are major attractions in the state's many parks, but these well-tended sites also provide fascinating lessons in geography, history and natural science

Map on pages 320–21

Parks in Texas are as varied as the people and the landscape. There are very large areas, like the massive Big Bend National Park *(see pages 289–292)*, while, at the opposite extreme, the most intimate one is probably the grave of Davy Crockett's wife in **Acton State Historical Park ❶**, near Granbury, in the heart of the Cross Timbers region. Parks planned around lakes and rivers are especially plentiful, testifying to the Texans' love affair with water, historically a rare and even a mystical commodity in much of the state.

Tent and trailer camping, hiking, picnicking, birdwatching, horse-riding, golf and all manner of zoos are found in parks throughout the state. Best of all, Texas parks showcase the natural features of their region, whether they are the moss-laden cypresses of Caddo Lake in East Texas, the cliffs of Palo Duro Canyon in the Panhandle or the lonely shell-strewn beaches of Padre Island.

Ten parks are operated by the National Park Service, 131 are state-owned, and there are countless roadside parks. At least one park is found in every Texas town or county and beside every lake. Facilities and standards of maintenance vary, but all these parks exist because of Texans' strong attachment to the outdoors. Many were developed by the Civilian Conservation Corps (CCC), established as part of Roosevelt's New Deal program.

Many Texas parks are built around water. Large lakes are found in various parts of the state. Although mainly for power generation and flood and drought control, they are the basis of some of the best park fun in the Lone Star State, and especially sports such as skiing, boating and fishing. While most lakes are man-made, the parks on Texas rivers are notable for their natural scenery and features. And the many miles of Texas beaches are just plain fun-in-the-sun.

PRECEDING PAGES: Guadalupe Mountains National Park. **LEFT:** Indian pictograph, Hueco Tanks State Historical Park. **BELOW:** grave of Davy Crockett's wife in Acton.

National Forests

Angelina National Forest, one of the four national forests in Texas, lies on both sides of the Sam Rayburn Reservoir, a 115,000-acre (47,000-hectare) lake east of Lufkin, 160 miles (256 km) northeast of Houston. This is Texas' largest reservoir and its surrounding recreation areas provide a wide variety of boating, hiking and camping activities in the towering pine forest and along the lake branches. Backpacking and primitive camping are permitted throughout the 153,000-acre (62,000-hectare) forest, unless otherwise posted.

West of Angelina, the **Davy Crockett National Forest** covers more than 160,000 acres (65,000 hectares) along the Neches river. A second-growth forest, it has made a remarkable comeback since logging stopped in the 1920s. The 4-C Trail, a scenic 20-mile (32-km) trek, connects Ratcliff Lake Recreation Area with the Neches Bluff Recreation Area. It

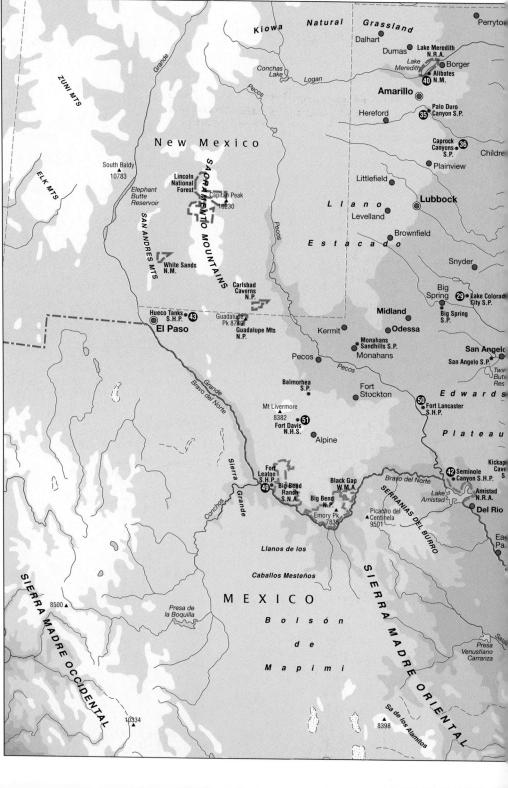

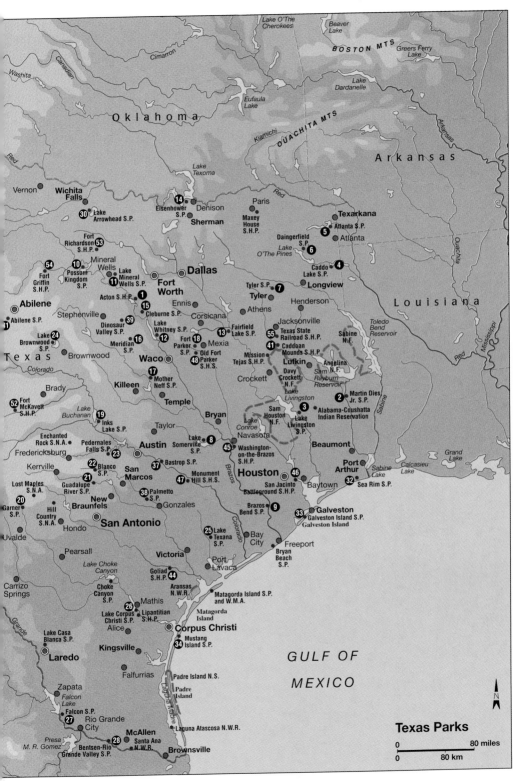

Texas Parks

0   80 miles

0   80 km

TIP

Spring and fall are the prettiest times of the year to visit parks in East Texas; summertime, as in the deep South, is hot, humid and bug-ridden. Remember to bring a good insect repellent.

BELOW: Fort Concho, National Historic Site, San Angelo.

is best to travel along it in the fall, winter or spring, when the climate is more hospitable and the bugs are less numerous. Basic camping is allowed along the 4-C Trail, but be suspicious of the water. Carry your own or use water purifiers.

Sabine National Forest, the state's largest with 160,000 acres (65,000 hectares), stretches along the Texas side of the Toledo Bend Reservoir on the Louisiana border. It includes an historic battleground where a 47-strong band of Confederates prevented a Union invasion of Texas. There are facilities for hikers, campers, boaters and anglers. Catfish, bass and crappie are the major fish to be found in the smaller lakes, but be sure to have a current fishing license and observe all bag limits.

Hiking in the east

In East Texas, the **Sam Houston National Forest** offers excellent hiking and camping between Huntsville and Lake Livingston. Its highlight is the **Lone Star Trail**, the longest developed hiking route in the state, at 128 miles (205 km). The forest's Double Lake and Stubblefield Recreation areas have extensive camping and picnicking, and serve well as trailheads. Camping is also permitted along the trail and in designated areas. Hikers are advised to tote their own water in and garbage out. But beware: from mid-November until January 1, hiking can be dangerous, because the hunting season is open.

On the water

Martin Dies, Jr. State Park ❷, on Steinhagen Reservoir, lies 15 miles (24 km) east of the town of Woodville. The trees are gorgeous in the fall and, in addition to water sports, there is a wide variety of birdlife along its trail.

Map on pages 320–21

Lake Livingston State Park ❸, 75 miles (120 km) northeast of Houston, occupies the east shore of the 85,000-acre (34,000-hectare) lake. Ninety-eight species of birds have been spotted along its 4 miles (6 km) of trails.

Just 15 miles (24 km) east is the **Alabama-Coushatta Indian Reservation**, established in 1854, when the state legislature gave 1,280 acres (520 hectares) to the Alabama Indians, who had settled in East Texas 40 years before. Additional land has since been added. In summer, the Indian Village is open daily, selling handicrafts and featuring dances. A drama presentation illustrates the history of Native American tribes.

Mossy cypresses

Further north, **Caddo Lake State Park ❹**, near Marshall, is the largest natural lake in the state. Spanish moss drapes its ancient cypress trees. Waterskiing is possible on sections of the lake, but drifting along in a canoe is better suited to its peaceful nature.

In the northeast corner of Texas, **Atlanta State Park ❺** sits on the banks of Lake Wright Patman, in a forest of oak, pine and dogwood. Near the town of Daingerfield, 30 miles (50 km) to the southeast, **Daingerfield State Park ❻** surrounds a small lake often filled with blooming water lilies. Its trails reward hikers with glimpses of wildlife, including deer and raccoons.

Tyler State Park ❼, just north of the city of Tyler, is a large park where swimming areas and a good fishing lake can be found. When the dogwood blooms in spring, Tyler Park is at its best.

Lake Somerville State Parks and Trailway ❽, on the western edge of East Texas near Brenham, 85 miles (135 km) northwest of Houston, consists of two

About 550 Native Americans still live on the Alabama-Coushatta Reservation. Their homes are now made of brick, or are wood-framed, they only wear traditional dress for ceremonies, and many work in the timber industry.

BELOW: fishing in an East Texas park.

TIP

If you plan to visit
several Texas State
Parks, invest $50 in
an annual Gold Texas
Conservation Passport,
which allows unlimited
admission to the parks
and to some areas
closed to the general
public, for all the
passengers in your
vehicle. Contact Texas
Parks and Wildlife
Department on
(800) 792-1112.

BELOW: Highway
Department rest
area on the Rio
Grande river road.

units on either side of the lake. They are connected by a 13-mile (21-km) trail, along which some of the campgrounds are especially for equestrians. There is also a wildlife management area in the park.

On the Brazos river less than 70 miles (110 km) south of Houston, **Brazos Bend State Park ❾** has 3¼ miles (5 km) of river frontage. The alligator and hundreds of bird species are stars here, and migrating waterfowl lure so many visitors in the fall that reservations are necessary for its overnight facilities.

New lakes

Drought and flood control projects of the 1950s and 1960s created a multitude of new lakes in the central and western parts of Texas. There are no pine forests surrounding these lakes, but they often have their own special appeal.

About 100 miles (160 km) west of Fort Worth is **Possum Kingdom State Park ❿**, its 10 miles (16 km) of shoreline shaded by deciduous oaks and the juniper trees which many Texans call "cedar." Waterskiing and scuba diving are popular here. About 55 miles (89 km) southeast, **Lake Mineral Wells State Park ⓫** sits in a pretty valley with an equestrian trail and small boats for rent.

Down the road, **Lake Whitney State Park ⓬**, 75 miles (120 km) south of Fort Worth, is excellent for waterskiing and bass fishing. Its numerous facilities include an airfield for campers who fly in with the herons and geese.

Anglers in search of a good fishing lake with a lot of variety will enjoy **Fairfield Lake State Park ⓭**, 90 miles (145 km) southeast of Dallas, noted for redfish, large-mouth bass, crappie, catfish, bluegill and drum.

On the Red River border separating Texas and Oklahoma, Lake Texoma is popular with sail-and ski-boaters. Anglers go after the native Red river white bass,

and the black and striped bass. **Eisenhower State Park**  lies on the cliffs above Lake Texoma, offering plenty of room for campers, fishermen and boaters, and even a protected cove for swimmers. There are campgrounds along the lake's 15-mile (24-km) Cross Timbers Trail but water is not available, except in the developed areas, and the presence of snakes requires caution. Five miles (8 km) southeast in Denison is the restored two-story birthplace of President Dwight D. Eisenhower.

Less crowded

Four parks in North Central Texas, more or less along the Fort Worth–Waco corridor, are very pleasant, have good facilities and are not often crowded. **Cleburne State Park** ⓖ, near the town of the same name, was built around a small lake, while **Meridian State Park** ⓖ, 70 miles (110 km) southwest of Fort Worth, also has a small lake with a hiking trail around.

Mother Neff State Park ⓗ, 128 miles (206 km) south of Fort Worth, was the first Texas state park, the first 6 acres (2.5 hectares) being donated by Governor Pat Neff's mother. The governor gave an additional 250 acres (100 hectares) in 1933. Developed by the CCC in the 1930s, it is a fitting tribute to early park pioneers. **Fort Parker State Park** ⓘ on Fort Parker Lake, near Mexia, provides waterskiing and fishing; the grounds incorporate the now-dead town of Springfield – only its cemetery remains.

Hill Country

Large lakes and cypress-shaded rivers in the Texas Hill Country host a wide array of water activities. There are six large lakes on the lower Colorado river alone, all dotted with informal camping and fishing areas, and with private

Denison's most famous son, Dwight D. Eisenhower, who has a State Park named after him.

BELOW: space wins in Texas State Parks.

TIP

On the Guadalupe and other rivers in the state, the water levels are unpredictable and are subject to rapid rises and falls. Be forewarned.

marinas and resorts, while the Guadalupe river feeds Canyon Lake, about 40 miles (65 km) southwest of Austin, and six smaller lakes. The most popular lake park is probably **Inks Lake State Park** , near Burnet, offering water-skiing, scuba diving and fishing, as well as a nine-hole golf course and a 7-mile (11-km) hiking trail. Reservations are essential.

Garner State Park, on the Frio river, 30 miles (50 km) north of Uvalde, although now enlarged, still tends to be crowded, with reservations necessary year-round for the picturesque cabins. *Frio* means cold in Spanish, and this river usually is. The scenery is at its best when the spring wild flowers make their show. One of the best ways to see the beautiful river canyon is from a rented pedal boat or inner tube.

Guadalupe River State Park is a favorite spot for canoeing, which is a growing sport in Texas. Thirty miles (50 km) north of San Antonio, the park's four rapids have excited enthusiasts of all skill levels. Deer, coyotes, raccoons and gray foxes can often be spied directly from the hiking trails, and bird watching enthusiasts will find golden-cheeked warblers nesting in a stand of Ashe juniper from March to late summer.

Within an hour's drive north of San Antonio, **Blanco State Park** straddles 1½ miles (2.5 km) of the Blanco river, near its namesake town. Its small size seems to discourage crowds. The park's main activities are swimming, fishing and watching the river go by.

The diversity of the Hill Country is especially evident at **Pedernales Falls State Park**, about 45 miles (70 km) west of Austin. Along parts of the Pedernales river, one finds lush vegetation and armadillos among the scrub cedar. The Pedernales, like a lot of Texas rivers, floods when it rains, but is otherwise

BELOW: end of the day in one of the parks.

a peaceful stream running over a rock bed into calm pools. Watch out for flash floods and an occasional treacherous waterfall or whirlpool, especially when the river is rising. The 7-mile (11-km) Wolf Mountain Trail is rewarding to skilled backpackers and hardy novices alike.

Lake Brownwood State Park is 22 miles (35 km) west of Brownwood, where the Texas Hill Country segues into West Texas. Its many facilities include picturesquely situated stone cabins. The 7,300-acre (3,000-hectare) lake imposes no limit on boat size.

Keeping cool

Perhaps nowhere in the state are watersports more appreciated than in South Texas, often a pretty dry place which can get very hot in the summer. Spring and fall are the most enjoyable seasons for both locals and visitors. **Lake Texana State Park** is well-stocked with catfish, large-mouth bass and striped bass, with early spring being the best time for fishing. Additional campsites are available at the nearby Lavaca-Navidad River Authority's Brackenridge Campground.

Although **Lake Corpus Christi State Park** was developed by the CCC in the 1930s, most of its facilities are more modern. Fishing, especially for catfish, is good. Because of its mild climate and proximity to Corpus Christi, 35 miles (55 km) to the south, the park is popular all year round and can be crowded.

Up the Rio Grande, near Del Rio, **Amistad National Recreation Area** provides facilities all along the American side of Lake Amistad for watersports. Scuba diving is especially good because the water is so clear. Deer (with bow and arrow only) and bird hunting are allowed in certain areas during the season.

One of the largest lakes in Texas, Falcon Lake, is also on the US-Mexican border. **Falcon State Park ㉗**, 15 miles (24 km) north of the historic border town of Roma, has comfortable accommodations. Birders here are rewarded with a variety of rare species, including the green kingfisher.

Bentsen-Rio Grande Valley State Park ㉘, on the river near Mission, is most popular in the winter, when its subtropical climate attracts many wintering tourists. Its nature trail interprets the hundreds of rare birds, animals and plants in the area.

Hunting and boating

As in South Texas, where large lakes make summer more acceptable, way up in the Panhandle, 35 miles (56 km) east of Amarillo, **Lake Meredith National Recreation Area** cools the arid Llano Estacado. Deer and bird hunting is permitted in certain parts of this park during the season. There is usually a good wind for sailing, but storms are unpredictable and boaters of all types should always be very cautious on this stretch of water.

Not as heavily developed as Lake Meredith, other West Texas lakes still give welcome recreational relief to many Texans and tourists. **Lake Colorado City State Park ㉙**, between Big Spring and Abilene, and **Lake Arrowhead State Park ㉚**, near Wichita Falls, are both on good-sized lakes and are popular with motor boaters and waterskiers.

Map on pages 320–21

TIP

Nature lovers should make plans to stay overnight at Bentsen-Rio Grande Valley State Park, in order to observe the park's nocturnal inhabitants, as well as those normally seen in the daytime.

BELOW: whooping crane at Aransas National Wildlife Refuge.

TIP

Remember that hiking is taxing on soft beaches, and even the most experienced trekkers should be thoroughly prepared before setting out on any extended hike along the seashore.

Abilene State Park ⬢, about 20 miles (30 km) southwest of town, is just across the road from Lake Abilene, and not far from an area once rife with wild buffalo. The park's campgrounds and swimming pool are set in an historic pecan tree grove.

At the beach

The beaches of the Gulf of Mexico are the site of some of the state's best-developed and most popular parks. **Sea Rim State Park ⬢**, on the coast near the Louisiana border, is one of the more tranquil. The greater part of the large park is an extensive marsh inhabited by a multitude of alligators, nutria, mink, raccoons and wintering waterfowl.

Galveston Island State Park ⬢, on the west end of the island, has well-situated beach campgrounds and picnicking areas. Occupying 5½ miles (9 km) of Gulf beach, down the coast, is **Mustang Island State Park ⬢**, with hundreds of campsites and picnic sites. About half of the beach front is undeveloped. At both parks, reservations are advisable, especially in the summer.

Fourteen miles (23 km) further south is **Padre Island National Seashore**, America's largest designated national seashore whose camping facilities stretch along a 66-mile (106-km) white sand beach – probably the prettiest white sand beach in Texas.

The most remote beach park has to be **Matagorda Island State Park and Wildlife Management Area**. Accessible only by ferry across Aransas Bay, the park has no drinking water, no electricity and no telephones. Public hunts are occasionally held in the area. Make sure you contact the park headquarters in Port O'Connor prior to a visit.

BELOW: Padre Island beach.

To the mountains

Guadalupe Mountains National Park straddles the New Mexico-Texas border, about 100 miles (160 km) due east of El Paso. These mountains, which range in both states, are probably the largest fossil reef in the world and contain the Carlsbad Caverns, as well as the highest point in Texas, Guadalupe Peak, at 8,749 ft (2,667 meters). The landscapes of the park are the most varied in the whole state. Here, the Chihuahuan Desert rises to spectacular evergreen forests, likelier to be located in the Colorado mountains than in Texas. The sheer cliffs of El Capitán tower 2,000 ft (610 meters). Greasewood and lechuguilla give way to lush ferns in the protected canyons, and more than 170 species of birds and over 50 different reptiles and amphibians live in the Guadalupe Park, as well as elk, mule deer, coyotes and a mountain lion and black bear or two.

McKittrick Canyon is one of the highlights. Open only during the day, the canyon displays a rare and varied collection of vegetation. High sheltering walls and year-round streams ensure the right conditions for ferns, big-tooth maples and little-leaf walnuts to grow. The marked trail into it is not difficult, but stay on the trail to avoid disturbing the fragile ecological system.

Rugged landscapes also characterize **Palo Duro Canyon State Park ⓭**, in the Panhandle, spectacular from every angle. Smaller canyons can be found at **Caprock Canyons State Park ⓰**, 60 miles (100 km) southeast of Palo Duro.

Central Texas

Central Texas has its share of natural and scenic attractions, too, although the scale is less awesome. **Enchanted Rock State Natural Area**, 18 miles (30 km) north of Fredericksburg, centers around a billion-year-old granite mountain.

Map on pages 320–21

Lifeguard station, Galveston Island.

BELOW: El Capitán.

TIP

The most popular time to visit Lost Maples is late October/early November, when the leaves turn stunning colors. If you want to visit at this time, make it a weekday, when the crowds aren't so pervasive.

BELOW: Padre Island National Seashore.

Its prominence in the landscape made it a source of Native American ghost tales and a traveler's landmark. While most trails around the rock are taxing, one trail to the top is manageable by most healthy hikers.

A large stand of big-tooth maples, 35 miles (55 km) southwest of Kerrville, is the focus of **Lost Maples State Natural Area**. One of the few remnants of the large maple forests of a less arid time in Texas, these trees provide glorious color in October. Most of the trails here are challenging, but a short one along the Sabinal river is easy. The park is pleasant at all times and is particularly popular with birders. Golden and bald eagles can often be seen in winter.

In a relic pine forest less than 30 miles (45 km) southeast of Austin, rustic **Bastrop State Park** ❸ gives another glimpse of an earlier Texas. Its picturesque cabins were built by the CCC. Reservations are necessary for these and for the park's campgrounds.

Palmetto State Park ❸, 60 miles (95 km) east of San Antonio, near Gonzales, has hiking trails that show off the plant and animal life and the extensive bird population. Its Ottine Swamp contains a tropical forest of palmettos (low-growing palms native to Texas) and other exotic flora. Spring and fall are the best times to visit: summer can be humid and stifling.

Wildlife refuges

Aransas National Wildlife Refuge, on San Antonio Bay near Rockport, has a visitors' center and miles of trails for viewing the refuge wildlife, including the rare and endangered whooping cranes who winter here. Sixteen miles (26 km) of roads give glimpses of the many deer, alligators and javelinas, as well as the multitude of other birds who live here year-round. Probably the

LOCAL HERITAGE

Like much of the rest of the United States, Texas has gradually become more aware of its cultural heritage over the past 30 years.

Almost every city and town has at least one historic house museum that local folks point to with pride. Some are large groupings of houses with a paid staff and long opening hours, like **Sam Houston Park** in Huntsville, which has gathered together buildings associated with the Texas hero, including two homes, a gazebo and a blacksmith's shop.

Others are smaller, often the work of dedicated volunteers, like **French's Trading Post**, now the **John Jay French Museum**, in Beaumont, the city's first two-story house. In the same vein are the **Annie Riggs Hotel**, a museum in Fort Stockton which once accommodated passengers on the Butterfield Overland Mail coaches, the **Bishop's Palace** in Galveston (his official, not actual residence), and the **Charles Stillman House** in Brownsville, built in 1851 by Charles Stillman, founder of the city, himself.

The majority of these fine historic sites and structures date from the 19th century. Individually and collectively, they skillfully illustrate life during that colorful era.

surest way to see the whoopers is to take the boat that goes out from the Sea Gun Inn, near Fulton from October to early April. Campgrounds are handy at nearby **Goose Island State Park**.

The **Laguna Atascosa National Wildlife Refuge** is just north of Port Isabel on the Laguna Madre. When ducks and geese fly south for the winter, this is where many of them come. Camping is not allowed, but there are auto and walking trails.

Santa Ana National Wildlife Refuge, on the Rio Grande near McAllen, has 12 miles (19 km) of hiking trails through its 2,000-acre (800-hectare) sub-tropical forest. It is the northern limit of many Mexican birds' migration. Furthermore, one of the forest's ebony trees may be the oldest and largest in the United States.

Cultural past

A large and growing class of parks protect and display the cultural heritage of the state. The historical and recreational are often combined in these parks, providing fun flavored with a little education.

Dinosaur Valley State Park ③ exhibits the tracks made by the Pleurocoelus and Acrocanthosaurus dinosaurs, prehistoric reptiles who walked around this swamp millions of years ago. The interpretive center explains the tracks, and a trail leads right to them. Camping, hiking and picnicking are also provided in this park, which is centered 60 miles (95 km) southwest of Fort Worth, near Glen Rose.

Remnants of other prehistoric Texas cultures are preserved in several parks. **Alibates National Monument ④**, in the Panhandle, was the source of a particular flint. **Caddoan Mounds State Historical Park ④**, clear across the state in East Texas, 30 miles (50 km) west of Nacogdoches, was the home of a group

Map on pages 320–21

The Alibates flint, found in the quarries of Alibates National Monument, was named for Ali Bates, a one-time local cowboy.

BELOW: Dinosaur Valley State Park, Glen Rose.

of agricultural Texans from the 8th to the 14th centuries. A sedentary people who may have had some association with the pyramid builders in Mexico, they left behind three large earthen mounds, filled with religious and other artifacts. Interpretive exhibits and a self-guided tour explain as much as is known about these ancient people. During summer, archeological digs sometimes take place, and visitors are invited to watch.

Recreational and camping facilities are convenient at **Mission Tejas State Historical Park**, 8 miles (13 km) down the road.

Pictographs

Indian pictograph at Hueco Tanks State Park.

Close to Del Rio, on the border, is another site with striking evidence of inhabitants 2,000–8,000 years ago. These ancient nomadic people painted the walls and ceilings of their cave dwellings, in what is today **Seminole Canyon State Historical Park ⓫**, with fanciful animals and other images whose meaning is now lost. One pictograph-covered shelter is open to visitors on a guided tour. The trail leading to it takes stamina, particularly in the summer heat. An award-winning exhibit at the Visitors' Center interprets the prehistory and history of the park. Campsites with water are available.

Rock art is also found at **Hueco Tanks State Historical Park ⓭**, 32 miles (51 km) northeast of El Paso. Tribes may have come through the area as long as 10,000 years ago. Water held in the depressions of the rocks made it a popular place for travelers in the surrounding desert. There is Pueblo rock art dating from AD 1000 and Mescalero Apache images from the 18th century. The artworks can be seen on a self-guiding tour. Bird- and animal-watching is also fruitful here, and campsites and picnic areas are both available.

BELOW: Goliad State Historical Park.

Spanish colonial

The first colonizers of Texas, the Spanish, have left substantial reminders of their presence. The **San Antonio Missions National Historical Park** *(see pages 198–9)* includes four 18th-century mission churches, a dam and an aqueduct. The Spanish mission of Nuestra Señora Espiritu Santo de Zuniga is the centerpiece of **Goliad State Historic Park ㊹**, just south of the historic town of Goliad. The mission was reconstructed by the CCC on the ruins of the 1749 church. The park has a scenic campground on the river and exhibits in the church and granary. The nearby Presidio La Bahia gained notoriety in 1836 when it was the site of Santa Anna's execution of Fannin's men during the Texas Revolution – hence "Remember Goliad!" The old *presidio* has been reconstructed and is open to the public.

Independent Texas

Washington-on-the-Brazos State Historical Park ㊺ is the site of the proclamation of the Texas Declaration of Independence on March 2, 1836. Nothing much remains of the bustling 1850s town, but a replica of Texas' Independence Hall and the home of the Republic's last president have been reconstructed. Re-enactors bring 19th-century life to present-day visitors. The Star of the Republic Museum, operated by Brenham's Blinn College, sits in the park grounds and has a number of good exhibits about life in early Texas. The park's riverside picnic area is on a bluff above the Brazos.

Six weeks after the declaration of Texas' Independence, Sam Houston's small band of Texans routed Santa Anna in the marshes of Buffalo Bayou, now commemorated by the **San Jacinto Battleground State Historical Park ㊻**. In La Porte, just east of Houston, the San Jacinto Monument rises in the midst of the battleground and houses a museum. The park provides picnic areas, but no campgrounds.

Although the Texas Republic was established by the April 1836 battle at San Jacinto, it struggled against continued Mexican incursions for the next 10 years. **Monument Hill State Historic Site ㊼**, in La Grange, 70 miles (115 km) east of Austin, honors the Texans who died in two responses to such attacks, the Dawson and Mier expeditions. The **Kreische Brewery State Historic Site** is contiguous and contains the ruins of a mid-19th-century brewery, at one time the third-largest in the state. The sites share a well-developed picnic area and grand views of the Colorado river. No camping is available.

Frontier forts

Fortifications of many types are scattered around the state and represent battles of various sorts fought on Texas soil. The most famous of all, of course, is the Alamo in San Antonio. **Old Fort Parker State Historic Site ㊽**, about 35 miles (55 km) east of Waco, commemorates another famous battle of 1836, the Native American attack on Parker's Fort and the capture of little Cynthia Ann Parker. The "Fall of Fort Ceremony" each May vividly recounts the story of this family fort and the lives and deaths of its inhabitants.

The Texas frontier, after annexation by the United States in 1845, stretched long and wide, and was

It's hard to believe that the little village of Washington-on-the-Brazos was once capital of the independent Republic of Texas. Today, it has only around 250 inhabitants.

BELOW: Washington-on-the-Brazos State Historical Park.

Map on pages 320–21

almost unprotected. Settlers in the most remote areas had to create their own defense systems against hostile Native Americans and outlaws. **Fort Leaton State Historical Park ㊾**, on the Rio Grande near present-day Presidio, was built by a border trader (some called him a smuggler), Ben Leaton.

The Federal government also built forts to cope with Native American threats to the advancing settlers, and a group of fort parks represents the 40-year struggle. **Fort Lancaster State Historical Park ㊿**, **Fort Davis National Historic Site (51)** and **Fort McKavett State Historical Park (52)** were all forts built before the Civil War.

Fort Lancaster's adobe ruins lie about 70 miles (115 km) east of Fort Stockton, and are interpreted in the visitors' center and via a self-guided tour of the old parade field. At Fort McKavett, about 40 miles (65 km) northwest of Junction, and Fort Davis, in the Davis Mountains 25 miles (40 km) north of Alpine, little is left of their earliest incarnations, but they have been restored to their post-Civil War state. More forts were built after the war, when Native American hostilities reached their height. **Fort Richardson State Historical Park (53)** in Jacksboro, 100 miles (160 km) northwest of Fort Worth, and **Fort Griffin State Historical Park (54)**, 50 miles (80 km) north of Abilene, have been developed with pleasant camping and picnicking adjuncts. Highlights of visits to all the forts are occasional military re-enactments: check individual parks for details.

Steaming along the Texas State Railroad State Historical Park.

BELOW: McKittrick Canyon, Guadalupe Mountains National Park. **RIGHT:** Monahans Sandhills State Park.

Parks of another kind

Some parks defy the usual categories. **Texas State Railroad State Historical Park (55)** runs for 25 miles (40 km) between Rusk and Palestine, and is one of the most popular parks in East Texas. The turn-of-the-20th-century rolling stock gives an authentic flavor to the scenic ride along the historic route. The round trip takes three hours. There are picnic sites at both ends to round off the journey.

The **Battleship Texas State Historic Site**, a memorial to Texans who fought in World War II, is moored at San Jacinto Battleground State Historical Park in La Porte. Commissioned in 1914, it is the only surviving Navy ship that served in both wars, notably in D-Day operations off the coast of Normandy in 1944 and in the Pacific at Iwo Jima and Okinawa in 1945. Open to the public seven days a week, the ship features a self-guided tour and interesting displays about ship life.

It is not the only warship to be named after Texas. More recently a nuclear submarine was named after the city of Corpus Christi, which is the home of a naval air station. The name had to be changed when complaints about the implications of its Latin meaning (Body of Christ) were voiced.

Beyond words and pictures

There are, of course, many excellent parks in the state that have not been mentioned here, through lack of space. But the list is also incomplete in that no words or pictures can ever fully capture the beauty and spirit of the Texas landscape like a campout in the East Texas Piney Woods, a hike through a dusty, rugged canyon, or a quiet afternoon's sailing on a placid lake on a late fall afternoon. ❑

INSIGHT GUIDES
Travel Tips

✺ INSIGHT GUIDES Phonecard

One global card to keep travellers in touch. Easy. Convenient. Saves you time and money.

It's a global phonecard

Save up to 70%* on international calls from over 55 countries

Free 24 hour global customer service

Recharge your card at any time via customer service or online

It's a message service

Family and friends can send you voice messages for free.

Listen to these messages using the phone* or online

Free email service - you can even listen to your email over the phone*

It's a travel assistance service

24 hour emergency travel assistance – if and when you need it.

Store important travel documents online in your own secure vault

For more information, call rates, and all Access Numbers in over 55 countries, (check your destination is covered) go to **www.insightguides.ekit.com** or call Customer Service.

JOIN now and receive US$ 5 bonus when you join for US$ 20 or more.

Join today at

www.insightguides.ekit.com

When requested use ref code: **INSAD0103**

OR SIMPLY FREE CALL
24 HOUR CUSTOMER SERVICE

UK	0800 376 1705
USA	1800 706 1333
Canada	1800 808 5773
Australia	1800 11 44 78
South Africa	0800 997 285

THEN PRESS ⓪

For all other countries please go to "Access Numbers" at **www.insightguides.ekit.com**

* Retrieval rates apply for listening to messages. Savings based on using a hotel or payphone and calling to a landline. Correct at time of printing 01.03

(INS001)

powered by ✺ekit

"The easiest way to make calls and receive messages around the world"

CONTENTS

Getting Acquainted

The Place

Area: 267,000 sq. miles (692,000 sq. km).
Capital: Austin.
Highest mountain: Guadalupe Peak, 8,749 ft (2,692 metres).
Coastline: 367 miles (591 km).
Population: 20.85 million.
Largest City: Houston (pop. 1.95 million).
Language: English; Spanish minority language.
Time Zones: Most of Texas is in the Central Standard Time Zone (CST), which is 6 hours behind Greenwich Mean Time (GMT); the western region of the state, west of Van Horn and including El Paso, is in the Mountain Time Zone, 7 hours behind GMT.
Currency: US dollars/cents.
Weights & Measures: Imperial.
Electricity: 110 volts.
State flower: Bluebonnet.
State fish: Guadalupe bass.
International dialing code: (1)

Economy

An unusually wide range of soil varieties enables farmers to grow almost anything, beef, cattle and cotton are the agricultural mainstays of Texas. Chemicals, food products, electrical equipment, petroleum products, machinery and transportation equipment are the principal manufactured goods.

Originally heavily dependent on oil and natural gas (Texas produces one-fourth of US oil), the state has now increased its production of aircraft, electronics and chemicals. Manufacturing accounts for 13 percent of gross state production. The rapidly expanding service sector

10 Fascinating Facts About Texas

1. The best-known "Texans" who defended the Alamo were actually Tennesseeans: Davy Crockett and Jim Bowie.
2. In 1904, responding to the Post Office's suggested names for one community, the town leaders replied: "Pick your choice" – and Choice (pop. 71) has been its name ever since.
3. The suggestion by John Nance Garner (US vice-president 1933–41) that the cactus become Texas' state flower was rejected by the legislature in favour of the bluebonnet.
4. The international border between Texas and Mexico holds the dubious distinction of marking the world's greatest income disparity between adjoining countries.
5. When a community sprang up around a slaughter house and hog-rendering plant near Goliad in

1898, its residents defiantly named it Cologne.
6. Three out of America's 10 largest cities are in Texas: Dallas, Houston and San Antonio.
7. Every Thanksgiving, Johnson City has the Great Turkey Escape, when 100 turkeys too small for the oven are driven through the streets before being fattened up for Christmas.
8. The short tie rope connecting the newborn calf to its mother along the trail was called a "dogie". Hence: "Get along little dogie."
9. Oddly named Texas communities include Art, Anchor, Bacontown, Black Ankle, Cash, Divot, Sand and Uncertain.
10. The most visited of all presidential libraries is the one devoted to Texas native Lyndon Baines Johnson on the University of Texas campus in Austin.

accounts for a further 19 percent. The Dallas/Fort Worth area houses the corporate headquarters of many national companies.

Generally, prices in Texas are a bit lower than the US average, largely because of the overall deflationary state economy. Gasoline, hotels and food are noticeably cheaper than many other parts of the US

Government

The state's most recent constitution – its fifth – was adopted in 1876. The governor (an office that is held for a four-year term) appoints the secretary of state and the adjutant general, with all other state offices being elective. Both the Texas House of Representatives (150 members, two-year terms) and the Senate (31 members, four-year terms) meet in the State Capitol in Austin. Texas has 254 counties, more than any other state, each governed by a County Commis-sioners Court, which sets the county budget and taxes.

Climate

A uniform description of either winter or summer weather in Texas is impossible: while it's snowing in the Panhandle, people wintering on the Gulf Coast may be getting a tan at the beach; Central Texas may be baking in the late-summer heat while the maples and aspens turn to fiery shades of red in the Guadalupe Mountains.

Although average temperatures of 30–50˚F (around 0–10˚C) in winter, 70–90˚F (20–30˚C) in summer do not vary greatly around the state, the humidity factor and elevation affect the comfort level considerably. Central Texas, East Texas, the Coastal Prairie and Rio Grande Valley are humid and close to sea level, so it is usually very hot and sticky in the summer, often climbing into the hundreds 100˚F (38˚C) between May and October.

Although it doesn't usually snow or freeze in these areas, occasionally it does so in a big way. Fairly recently, San Antonio and Austin have been blanketed with snow and ice, with businesses and roads completely closed down for the duration. In the Panhandle and the higher elevations of the Davis Mountains, Guadalupe Mountains and Big Bend area, where fall comes earlier than in the southern part of the state, there is little humidity except snow, which is common in the winters, sometimes causing roads and mountain areas to be closed to the public.

"Tornado Alley" runs through the state and peak twister season lasts from late spring to early summer.

Annual rainfall ranges from 8–16 inches (20–40 cm) in the dry Trans-Pecos region to over 48 inches (122 cm) in the wettest parts of the state, such as Houston and far East Texas. The best time for statewide travel is late October–November, March and April, and late May/early June. This will avoid, for the most part, Texas' hottest and coldest temperatures and the heaviest rainfall.

Planning the Trip

Passports and Visas

Most foreign visitors need a passport (which should be valid for at least six months longer than their intended stay) and a visa to enter the United States. You should also be able to provide evidence that you intend to leave the United States after your visit is over (usually in the form of a return or onward ticket), and visitors from some countries need an international vaccination certificate.

Certain foreign nationals are exempt from the normal visa requirements. Canadian citizens with a valid Canadian passport need no visa. Nor do Mexican citizens provided they have a Mexican passport and a US Border Crossing Card (Form I-186 or I-586), and as long as they are residents of Mexico.

A special "visa-waiver" program means that citizens of some countries do not require a visa if they are entering the US for less than 90 days and have a round-trip or onward ticket and (from October 1 2003) a machine-readable passport. The issuing authority will be able to tell you if your passport is machine-readable. These countries include New Zealand, Japan, the UK and about 18 other European nations.

Regulations at city gateways vary regarding transit stops, and a visa may be required for re-entry after a visit outside the US.

Anyone requiring a visa or visa information can apply by mail or by personal application to the US Embassy or Consulate nearest their home.

Money Matters

Foreign visitors are advised to take US dollar travelers' checks to Texas, since exchanging foreign currency – whether as cash or checks – can prove problematic. An increasing number of banks offer foreign exchange facilities, but this practice is not universal. Some department store chains offer foreign currency exchange.

Most shops, restaurants, and other establishments accept travelers' checks in US dollars and will give change in cash. Alternatively, checks can be converted into cash at the bank.

Credit Cards are very much part of daily life in Texas, as in other parts of the US. They can be used to pay for pretty much anything, and it is also common for car rental firms and hotels to take an imprint of your card as a deposit. Rental companies may oblige you to pay a large deposit in cash if you do not have a card.

You can also use your credit card

Public Holidays

Banks, federal, state, county and city offices and private businesses often close during public holidays. Many stores remain open during weekends and holidays.

● **New Year's Day** 1 January
● **Martin Luther King Jr.'s Birthday** 15 January, although observed the third Monday in January
● **Presidents' Day** Third Monday in February
● **Easter Sunday** Late March/early April
● **Memorial Day** Last Monday in May
● **Independence Day** 4 July
● **Labor Day** First Monday in September
● **Columbus Day** Second Monday in October
● **Veteran's Day** 11 November
● **Thanksgiving Day** Fourth Thursday in November
● **Christmas Day** 25 December

to withdraw cash from ATMS (Automatic Teller Machines). Before you leave home, make sure you know your PIN and find out which ATM system will accept your card. The most widely accepted cards are Visa, American Express, MasterCard, Diners Club, Japanese Credit Bureau and Discovery.

What to Bring

For clothing, natural fabrics such as cotton, linen and wool provide the best comfort in the Texas climate. Go particularly light in summer, but because of varying altitude and cool breezes, a sweater may be needed in the evening. The midwinters of Central and East Texas, the Coastal Prairie and the Rio Grande Valley usually require only a lightweight coat. In the mountains, High Plains and Panhandle, winters can be so severe that you need layers of warm clothes.

And don't forget your jeans! Texans are very casual dressers and away from the office blue jeans are the norm. They are worn almost anywhere, anytime of the day, dressed up or down by changing a shirt, sweater, jacket or accessories. People in Dallas and Houston dress formally for some evening events, but casual pants and dresses for women and shirt-sleeves or tieless shirts and jackets for men are acceptable almost anywhere you go.

Health

Depending upon the country from which you are traveling or through which you have just come, you may need an international vaccination certificate. Many types of over-the-counter medications are readily available, but if you're using prescription medication, it's best to bring extra along with a spare pair of prescription glasses if you use them. Tap water is fine to drink, but if you're out camping in the more remote parts of some of the state's National Parks or National Forests, it is best to bring your own or use purifiers. *(See page 344 for Emergency Services and Pests.)*

Information on Texas

The *Texas State Travel Guide*, published by the Department of Transportation, lists Texas cities with their attractions and is available free from P.O. Box 149249, Austin, TX 78714-9249, or by calling 800-452-9242. Information on road conditions and routes is also available from the same number.

To request information on standard Texas travel, call or write the Tourism Division, Texas Department of Commerce, P.O. Box 12728, Austin, TX 78711, tel: 512-462-9191, or check www.traveltex.com

Travel Insurance

Sunburn and mosquito bites in summer are the main nuisance for the majority of visitors to Texas. Even so, you should never leave home without travel insurance to cover both yourself and your belongings. Your own insurance company or travel agent can advise you on policies, but shop around since rates vary. Make sure you are covered for accidental death, emergency medical care, trip cancelation and baggage or document loss.

Getting There

BY AIR

Air passengers to Texas usually arrive at Dallas–Fort Worth Airport or George Bush Intercontinental Airport in Houston, although many touch down in El Paso to change planes or take on additional passengers.

A network of smaller airports serves the state with scheduled flights to over 30 cities. Connections are easy to arrange, even between different carriers, and there are frequent shuttles between major cities all day.

Dallas–Fort Worth Airport

The airport is 18 miles (29 km) northwest of Dallas and within four hours of most cities in the US. It handles 2,300 flights a day. Tel: 972-574-8083;

Love Field Airport

The airport is 7 miles (11 km) northwest of downtown Dallas, and within the city limits. Tel: 214-670-6073.

George Bush Intercontinental

Located 18 miles (29 km) north of downtown Houston, this airport has daily services to 114 US cities and 33 international destinations, and is a hub for Continental Airlines. Tel: 281-230-3000.

Taxis taking you downtown cost about $35 and the shuttle service $19. Houston's city transit system operates between downtown and the Intercontinental Airport every 25 minutes from 6–10am and 2–7pm, Mon–Fri. The fare is $1.50.

Hobby Airport

Serving as a hub for Southwest Airlines the airport is 8 miles (13 km) southeast of downtown Houston – about $18 by taxi and $14 by shuttle. Airport Express, tel: 713-523-8888, transports passengers to all parts by van or minibus. Tel: 713-643-4597.

Airline Companies

The services of the major airlines such as American, Continental, and Delta, are conveniently supplemented by smaller ones such as Southwest, Chaparral, Texas and Muse. Air fares change frequently, as do schedules and special bargain rates. It is wise to arrange your trip through a travel consultant, who has the most current information. However, all airlines can be contacted directly by telephone for information and reservations. Local or toll-free central numbers can be obtained either from directory assistance (in Texas, dial 1-411) or the *Yellow Pages* of the local telephone directory. Here are the phone numbers for international airlines:

● **American** 800-433-7300
● **British Airways** 800-247-9297

- **Continental** 800-231-0856
- **Delta** 800-241-4141
- **United** 800-241-6522

BY TRAIN

Two **Amtrak** lines run through Texas: the Eagle from Chicago to San Antonio, with a Dallas to Houston connection; and the Sunset from Los Angeles to Orlando. The trains stop at 19 passenger terminals in the state: Alpine, Austin, Beaumont, Cleburne, College Station-Bryan, Corsicana, Dallas, Del Rio, El Paso, Fort Worth, Houston, Longview, Marshall McGregor, San Antonio, Sanderson, San Marcos, Taylor, Temple and Texarkana.

Accommodations include coach and sleeping facilities. There are lounge and dining cars. Outside North America, you can purchase a USA Railpass from travel agencies, which allows unlimited rail travel within specified dates.

For reservations and information inside the US, call 1-800-USA-RAIL or 1-800-872-7245 toll-free.

Down Mexico Way

Many visitors to Texas proceed onwards into or visit Mexico. This can be done at several border points, of which the main ones are El Paso, Eagle Pass, Laredo and Brownsville. For short visits within the border area, no special documents beyond proof of citizenship are required from US citizens; others must carry passports and the appropriate visas if required. If you're traveling deeper into the country or staying for longer than 72 hours, a Mexican tourist card is required. These cards, called the *forma migratoria turista* (FMT), are free from immigration officials at the border and also from Mexican consulates and Mexican government tourist offices.

Drivers must obtain automobile permits, valid for 180 days, when venturing beyond the border region.

These cost $15 from Mexican immigration officials on production of a tourist card.

It is mandatory to obtain Mexican insurance and highly advisable because in the event of an accident vehicles are usually impounded, regardless of fault. Sanborn's Mexican Insurance is a reliable company that specializes in this insurance. They have offices in most large border towns and also in San Antonio. At the border you will be given a temporary import permit after you show proof of ownership (photocopy of title will do) and the insurance policy. Keep these handy, as 12 miles (19 km) into Mexico, every car without Mexico tags is stopped at the border checkpoints.

For more information telephone 800-44-MEXICO or see www.visitmexico.com

BY BUS

Greyhound buses, tel: 800-229-9424; www.greyhound.com, connect Texas with all major US cities (major credit cards accepted.) Buses are always air-conditioned and there are toilets on board. Outside North America, contact your travel agent for an Ameripass, which allows unlimited bus travel within specified dates.

Specialist Tours

Gray Line tours are available in many Texas towns and cities. For specific information call 800-472-9546, Other companies include:
Adventure Tours
Tel: 800-638-9040.
Central West of Texas, 3426 W. Gilbert Road, Grand Prarie 75050, Tel: 972-399-1059.
Discover Houston Tours
P.O. Box 230183,º Houston 77223. Tel: 713-222-9255.
Idle Time Tours
P.O. Box 610423, Dallas. Tel: 817-790-7909.

Practical Tips

Business Hours

Offices: Mon–Fri 8am–5pm; **Banks**: Mon–Fri 9/10am–3/4pm (although most have drive-thru sections that stay open longer); **Retail shops**: Mon–Fri 10/11am–5/6pm , except in large shopping malls, when hours are extended to 8, 9 or 10pm and weekends. **Museums**: many are closed on Mondays.

Media

PRINT

Like many big American cities, Dallas and Houston have more than one daily newspaper, covering local, national and international news. There are also several weekly newspapers in most cities that cover local and, sometimes, state-wide news. Local newspapers include: *Dallas Morning News, El Paso Times, Fort Worth Star-Telegram, Galveston Daily News, Houston Chronicle, San Antonio Express-News* and *Waco Tribune-Herald*.

BROADCAST MEDIA

There are over 70 television stations and at least 550 AM and FM radio stations in Texas alone. Thanks to cable, satellite or pay television, programs from all over the world can be seen almost any hour of the day or night. The installation of cable in most hotels and motels and many homes means that how a particular station is found depends on where it appears on the cable to which they subscribe. Consult the newspaper for television listings. Radio listings are sometimes given in Sunday supplements of newspapers.

Telephones

To call from **city to city** in Texas, you must first find out the area code *(see box)*. The state's vast size requires that it be divided into different three-digit codes. The proliferation of fax machines and computers within recent years has resulted in more and more areas being re-assigned new area codes at a speed quicker than lightning, so don't be surprised if an area code has changed from the one currently published.

To call from **one area to another**, dial 1 before the three-digit area code and the local seven-digit telephone number. If calling from a pay phone, you must first insert a coin to connect with the operator. If you want to pay for the call with coins, a recorded voice will tell you how many to insert. Unless you have a credit card with the telephone company, your only other option is to call your party "collect" (reversing the charges).

Directory Assistance calls from pay telephones are free. However, to be connected to some of them you must first insert a coin, but as soon as you are connected with the operator it will be returned to you. To get the information operator dial 411, but to get an **information operator** in another city, dial 1+area code of the city+555-1212.

Local Dialing Codes

Abilene – 915
Amarillo – 806
Brownsville – 956
Corpus Christi – 361
Dallas – 214, 972
El Paso – 915
Fort Worth – 817
Galveston – 409
Houston – 713, 281
Laredo – 956
Lubbock – 806
Pecos – 915
San Antonio – 210
Waco – 254

For **local calls** from pay telephones which accept coins, insert a coin and dial the seven-digit local telephone number. There is no time limit for local calls. Many businesses have toll-free (no charge) telephone numbers; these are always prefaced with 800 rather than an area code.

There are **Western Union cablegram offices** in most cities. Look in the local telephone directory in the white pages (for major cities, there may be separate books for businesses and residences) under Western Union. Messages and money can be sent over the wires immediately. You must have positive identification, such as a driver's license, to receive money

Postal System

The postal system may be the only thing that is constant throughout Texas. First-class postage is the same anywhere in Texas, or in the US, and bills arrive just as quickly in tiny Cut-and-Shoot as they do in big-city Dallas. Post offices open at 7, 8 or 9am and usually close at 5pm, Mon–Fri. Many of them are open for at least a couple of hours on Saturday mornings, but they are all closed on Sunday.

There may also be coin-operated stamp machines that dispense stamps whether the office is open or not. Rates are usually listed nearby. There are US Post Office Information numbers in the phone book, or call 411 and ask the operator.

Visitors can receive mail at post offices if it is addressed to them, care of "General Delivery", followed by the city name and (very important) the zip code. You must pick up this mail in person within a week or two of its arrival and will be asked to show some form of valid personal identification.

Tourist Information

Information is available from various sources in Texas. Most cities have a Convention and Visitors' Bureau

(CVB), which will provide you with brochures and maps, while elsewhere you must rely on the local chamber of commerce. These are oriented toward business people, but the staff are usually happy to help, particularly in tourist areas.

Tourist Offices

Abilene, 1101 N. First St, TX 79601, tel: 915-676-2556; fax: 915-676-1630; www.abilene.com/visitors
Arlington, 1905 E. Randol Mill Road, tel: 817-265-7721; fax: 817-265-5640; www.arlington.org
Austin, 201 E. Second St, TX 78701, tel: 512-474-5171; fax: 512-583-7280; www.austintexas.org
Beaumont, 801 Main St, TX 77701, tel: 409-880-3749; fax: 409-880-3750; www.beaumontcvb.com
Corpus Christi, 1201 N. Shoreline Boulevard, TX 78401, tel: 361-881-1888; fax: 361-887-9023; www.corpuschristicvb.org
Dallas, 1201 Elm St, TX 75270, tel: 214-571-1000; fax: 214-571-1008; www.dallascvb.com
Denton, 414 Parkway, TX 76201, tel: 888-381-1818; www.discoverdenton.com
El Paso, 1 Civic Center Plaza, TX 79901, tel: 915-534-0696; fax: 915-534-0686; www.elpasocvb.com
Ennis, 2 E. Ennis Ave, TX 75119, tel: 972-878-4748; fax: 972-875-1018; www.visitennis.org
Fort Worth, 415 Throckmorton St, TX 76102, tel: 817-336-8791; fax: 817-336-3282; www.fortworth.com
Galveston Island, 2428 Seawall Boulevard, TX 77550, tel: 409-763-4311; fax: 409-770-0015; www.galvestoncvb.com
Granbury, 100 N. Crockett, TX 76048, tel: 800-950-2212; fax: 817-573-5789; www.granburytx.com
Grapevine, 1 Liberty Park Plaza., TX 76051, tel: 800-457-6338; fax: 817-410-3038; www.grapevinetexasusa.com
Houston, 901 Bagby, TX 77002, tel: 713-437-5200; fax: 713-227-6336; www.houston-guide.com

Laredo, 501 San Agustin, TX 78040, tel: 956-795-2200; fax: 956-795-2185; www.visitlaredo.com
Lubbock, 1301 Broadway, TX 79401, tel: 806-747-5232; fax: 806-747-1419; www.lubbocklegends.com
McKinney, 1650 W. Virginia, TX 75069, tel: 972-542-0163; fax: 888-649-8499; www.mckinneycvb.org
Midland, 109 N. Main, TX 79701, tel: 915-683-3381; fax: 915-682-9205; www.visitmidlandtx.com
Nacogdoches, 200 E. Main, TX 75961, tel: 936-564-7351; fax: 936-560-3920; www.visitnacogdoches.org
Odessa, 700 N. Grant St, TX 79761, tel: 915-333-7871; fax: 915-333-7858; www.odessacvb.com
Port Arthur, 3401 Cultural Center Drive, TX 77642, tel: 409-985-7822; fax: 409-985-5584; www.portarthurtexas.com
San Angelo, 500 Rio Concho Drive, TX 76903, tel: 915-655-4136; fax: 915-658-1110; www.sanangelo-tx.com
San Antonio, 203 S. St Mary's St, (2nd Floor), TX 78205, tel: 210-207-6700; fax: 210-207-6782; www.sanantoniocvb.com
San Marcos, 202 N. C.M. Allen Parkway, TX 78667, tel: 512-393-5900; fax: 512-393-5912; www.sanmarcostexas.com
South Padre Island, 600 Padre Boulevard, TX 78597, tel: 956-761-6433 or 800-SO-PADRE; fax: 956-761-9462; www.sopadre.com
Waco, 100 Washington Ave, TX 76702, tel: 254-750-5810; fax: 254-750-5801; www.wacocvb.com

Tourist Publications

Current information on hotels, and all kinds of events and cultural activities, can also be found in Texas periodicals. The Texas Department of Transportation, Box 149249, Austin, 78714, tel: 800-452-9292, publishes a monthly travel magazine, *Texas Highways*, at a moderate subscription fee. *Texas Monthly* is available at most newsstands.

Embassies in Texas

● **Australia** 5757 Woodway Drive, Houston, TX 77057, tel: 713-782-6009
● **Canada** 750 N. St Paul St, Suite 1700, Dallas, TX 75201, tel: 214-922-9806
● **United Kingdom** 2911 Turtle Creek Boulevard, Dallas, TX 75219, tel: 214-521-4090. Wells Fargo Plaza, (19th Floor), 1000 Louisiana Street, Suite 1900, Houston, TX 77002, tel: 713-659-6270

There are also magazines dedicated to a particular city, such as *D Magazine* in Dallas. Bookstores display a wide array of books about Texas, from the *Texas Almanac* – covering every conceivable subject – to comprehensive bed-and-breakfast listings and bicycling trip guides.

Security & Crime

As is the case in large cities all over the world, Dallas, Houston, El Paso, San Antonio, Austin and Corpus Christi have notoriously dangerous areas, especially if one is alone or if it is after dark. Always use common sense and survey your surroundings. Do not walk a long way after dark in strange or deserted parts of town. Keep a watchful eye on your belongings. Do not leave your car unlocked in parking lots, and never leave your children alone. Smaller towns in Texas have much lower crime rates, but use the same precautions everywhere as you would in a big city.

Hotels usually warn you that they will not guarantee the safety of belongings left in your hotel room. If you have any valuables, you may want to lock them in the hotel safe.

Tipping

Restaurant bills do not usually include a tip, unless you are in a group of five or more when a gratuity of 15 percent may be added to the total; otherwise tips of between 10 and 20 percent are expected. Unless the service is dreadful, you are obligated.

Fifteen percent is a good rule of thumb when tipping for any service, including taxi rides and haircuts, although some Texans have not got used to tipping barbers. The owner of a hair salon is usually not tipped. Bellhops and parking attendants expect a dollar, shoeshine dispensers more.

Etiquette

The key word here is "relaxed." Openness and natural friendliness rule. Don't be insulted – as new arrivals, surprisingly, sometimes are – when strangers smile broadly at you and ask how you are doing as you pass them in the street. You can expect almost everyone with whom you come into contact during the day to ask how you are feeling, where you come from, where you are going and, if you prove to be a foreigner, whether you are married, how many children you have, what your job is and why you are here. Or they may just ask how you're "doin'."

This is not inappropriate behavior, personally invasive or presumptuous, not even an attempt to begin a long, intimate conversation. It is a Texas custom, and it is natural friendliness and goodwill that prompts these genial greetings and enquiries from passers-by, waiters, and salespeople who suddenly become new Texas friends. Don't even be surprised at a congenial slap on the back to emphasize a point, or – particularly in South Texas – a friendly embrace in greeting.

One of the best things about Texas is the relaxed dress codes whether on city streets, at the shopping centre, at the symphony or theater, or in restaurants. Although some of the more expensive establishments in larger cities like Dallas and Houston require men to wear jackets and ties and women to have on dresses or dress pants, in most restaurants almost any attire is tolerated.

However, state regulations

require shoes to be worn in eating places, and even most country coffee shops and restaurants hang the sign "No Shirt, No Shoes, No Service" on the door.

In most places where parties wearing jeans and T-shirts happen to be seated next to couples in evening dresses and tuxedos, both groups feel perfectly comfortable. If there is a rule for dress, it may be to wear whatever feels good.

Health regulations prohibit all animals, except guide dogs, in public eating places in Texas.

Pests

Because much of Texas is in the open (that is, all its small and sprawling cities together occupy only a tiny portion of the state), anyone who spends much time exploring it has a good chance of coming into contact with a poisonous animal.

Avoidance has always been the best strategy against threatening pests. If you are walking in a field, for example, loose clothing discourages ticks and chiggers from finding a tight spot in which to embed themselves. Tall, thick boots usually protect against stinging ground insects and reptiles. Once bitten or stung, however, there are a few procedures that will ease your suffering. The most important thing to do is to find what got you and, if possible, get it (taking the pesky pest with you to a doctor will help determine the correct remedy).

Insects
Watch out for loose mounds of dirt in grassy areas, which could house

fireants. Once their house is disturbed (try and test the area with a long stick), they will swarm at great speed and can be all over your legs in no time at all. Be careful with children as they may not think fast enough to brush off the ants once attacked.

The bite or sting of a **spider**, **ant,** or **scorpion** is not usually fatal but it can cause a lot of pain and itching, and the area round it may swell. In most cases, discomfort gradually subsides. If extreme symptoms such as numbness, tingling, shooting pain, high temperature, low blood pressure, abdominal cramps, spasms, breathing difficulty, or problems focusing the eyes occur, see a physician at once. Remember that bringing the insect with you greatly aids the doctor.

Texans often call **chiggers** "red bugs". There is not much you can do for a chigger bite. A salve from the drugstore may help relieve the itching, but you will just have to wait for it to go away. The same is true of the bite of the **mosquito**, found by the million around water in low-lying areas.

Snakes
Never bother a snake. Most snakes in Texas are not harmful to people and only strike in self-defense; entering a snake's territory and standing too close can agitate it enough to strike.

Again, before fleeing in panic at least try to see what the snake looked like. A positive identification is extremely important for the physician making a treatment

decision. Do not attempt any first aid treatments such as freezing the limb, tourniquets, or the outdated cut-and-suck method. Instead, go to the emergency centre of the local hospital.

Coral snakes are abundant in Texas and because of their beauty and relatively small size they are frequently picked up by children. Be sure to discourage children from picking up strange animals.

Rattlesnakes and coral snakes have very different toxins, the toxin of the former attacking the nervous system and the latter primarily affecting the respiratory system. Treatment therefore consists of injecting very different antivenins, which makes identification extremely important. Snakes are not quite the omnipresent menace that strangers in Texas fear. They usually remain in fields or sand dunes and often hide under logs or in holes waiting to hunt at night or early in the morning. Your best bet for seeing one is to keep your eyes peeled for a "roadkill" squashed by a car while trying to make its way across a country road.

Rabies Carriers
Raccoons, skunks, bats, and **squirrels** can all be found in Texas, but should not be touched; they are potential carriers of rabies, which is easily transmitted to people.

In the Water
The **Portuguese man-of-war** are found in their hundreds on Padre Island. Washed ashore, their blue balloon-like forms with long tentacles continue to pulsate for a while. If you are stung by their tentacles, either on shore, or in the water where they are harder to avoid, you may develop rashes and red welts. A few sensitive victims go into shock or endure fever, cramps, and nausea. Some lifeguards treat these stings with meat tenderizer; others wash the area with sodium bicarbonate, boric acid, lemon juice, or alcohol. If symptoms are severe, you should see a physician.

Emergency Medical Services

Most cities have 24-hour pharmacies (often called drugstores) and minor emergency clinics, major emergency rooms at hospitals, and poison control centres. Look in the *Yellow Pages* or the inside cover of the telephone book. Or **dial 411** for telephone operator assistance.

If you need to call for help,

such as an ambulance or the police, many areas of Texas can gain access to the **emergency number 911** used in most parts of the country. A dispatcher will answer your call, provide immediate first-aid information if needed, and send help. **If in a non-911 area, dial 0** for the telephone operator.

Getting Around

On Arrival

There are three airports in Texas classified as international: Dallas-Fort Worth, George Bush Intercontinental in Houston, and San Antonio. The Dallas-Fort Worth International Airport, tel: 972-574-3197, is the world's second-busiest airport and the largest US airport. It is 18 miles (29 km) northwest of Dallas; about 30–45 minutes' driving time from the downtown area.

The George Bush Inter-continental Airport, tel: 713-230-3000, is 18 miles (29 km) north of Houston via the Eastex Freeway (US-59). Allow 30–35 minutes to get to downtown from the airport, depending on traffic.

The San Antonio International Airport is 8 miles (13 km) from downtown, about 20 minutes by car.

There are regular shuttle services from all airports. Taxi service is also available, but is usually expensive. Most major hotels provide courtesy shuttle service from the airport.

Public Transportation

BY BUS

All cities and most towns have some form of local bus service at very low rates. Contact the Chamber of Commerce for listings *(see pages 342–3)* or call the main office of the bus company listed in the telephone directory. Major cities like Dallas, Austin, San Antonio, and Houston offer other bus services well-suited to visitors, such as the Armadillo "trolleys" in Austin and Citran in Fort Worth.

BY TRAIN

There are 31 stations on the **Dallas Area Rapid Transit**, or DART, system (tel: 214-979-1111, www.dart.org). Each station has ticket machines with clear instructions for use. There are also special services for the disabled. For further information, tel: 214-515-7272.

The light rail connects at Union Station from which **Amtrak** trains connect Dallas with Chicago and Houston. The station is connected by pedestrian tunnel to the Hyatt Regency Hotel (beside Reunion Tower). For **Amtrak information** call 800-872-7245.

BY TAXI

Taxis can be a convenient way to get around cities. However, unlike those in major cities like New York and London, Texas taxis do not cruise around looking for people hailing them from the curb. To get a taxi, you must call the cab company *(see companies listed below* or look under Taxicabs in the *Yellow Pages* of the local telephone directory). Ask what the rates are, as they vary from city to city (but not from cab to cab). A 15 percent tip is appreciated if you are satisfied with the service provided, and especially if you need help with luggage.

Taxi Companies in Dallas
● **Executive Taxi Service**: 972-554-1212
● **Terminal Taxi Corp**: 214-678-9951
● **Yellow Cab**: 214-426-6262

Taxi Companies in Houston
● **Fiesta Cab**: 713-225-2666
● **Liberty Cab**: 713-695-6700
● **Square Deal Cab**: 713-659-7236
● **United Cab**: 713-699-0000
● **Yellow Cab**: 713-236-1111

Driving

The size and climate of Texas are good reasons to drive, since walking between attractions, even in a city, requires more time than

most people have for vacations and, much of the year, it is too hot to walk for pleasure.

US (Interstate) Highways 10, 20, 27, 30, 35, 37, 40 and 45 crisscross Texas, providing direct and relatively hazard-free routes to major cities. For anyone interested in a closer look, however, there are a variety of state highways and back roads (marked on the maps as FM or "Farm to Market", RM or "Ranch to Market", and RR or "Ranch Road") intertwined between all the major cities, smaller communities, and even ghost towns. Buy a map and plan a tour, but allow plenty of time to reach your destination since some of these Texas roads get quite winding and pot-holed. Some even become dirt roads.

Be aware, as well, that leaving the main track means fewer gas stations and convenience stores, some of which may be closed after dark or on a holiday.

However, if you remember to fill the tank and allow plenty of time to get where you're going, especially after dark, these secondary roads may prove the most enjoyable way to travel since you'll be able to enjoy the countryside without having to worry about heavy traffic.

The Texas Department of Transportation runs 12 information centers offering advice on trip planning, road conditions and other travel matters. For information call 800-452-9292.

Interstate Highways
Interstate highways are planned to bypass most towns, and they do get you to your destination fast, but when you are driving from Austin to Dallas or from San Antonio to El Paso, even fast can mean 4 to 10 hours. Along the interstates there are restrooms and roadside picnic areas, as well as food and petrol.

Highway Patrol and Hitchhiking
The Highway Patrol cruises these highways, not just monitoring speed limits but also looking for drivers in trouble. If you have any emergency that won't allow you to continue the trip, signal your distress by raising

the hood. Be sure to keep a current driver's license and a certificate proving you have liability insurance with you at all times because you will be required to show them to the law enforcement officer who stops your car for any reason. It is illegal to drive in Texas without these items.

Motorists are often warned that they are safer staying in the car with the doors locked until a patrol car stops to help, rather than leaving it and trying to hitchhike. Hitchhiking is not considered safe, whether you are on the giving or the receiving end. In some places in the US it is illegal.

Speed Limits

Speed limits for roads and highways are posted on white signs to the right, as are all other road

Car Rental

Cars can be rented in most cities. This is usually done at the local airport since much of the rental business is with customers who have arrived by air. Choose the best rate available from one of the side-by-side booths.

You must be at least 21 to rent a car. Credit cards are accepted, and by several companies they are required. Some agencies expect the car to be returned to them. If you want to drive to another city and fly on from there, be sure to inform the rental agent at the time you arrange the terms. There may be a charge to drop the car at their branch in another city.

The major car rental companies all have toll-free (800) numbers and are as follows:

- **Advantage**   777-5500
- **Alamo**   462-5266
- **Avis**   831-2847
- **Budget**   527-0700
- **Dollar**   800-4000
- **Hertz**   654-3131
- **National**   227-7368
- **Rent a Wreck**   535-1391
- **Thrifty**   367-2277

signs. Some roads are for one-way traffic only and are identified by a black and white sign with an arrow pointing in the permitted direction of travel. At an intersection where each corner has a red stop sign with a smaller sign below it which says "4-Way" or "All-Way," motorists must completely stop and then proceed across the intersection following the order in which they arrived at the stop.

The official highway speed limit is 55 mph (89 kph). Although everyone passes you, resist the temptation to accelerate. If caught in a "speed trap" by the Highway Patrol, whose black-and-white cruisers have radar, you will get a speeding ticket that has to be paid in a nearby (or sometimes not so near) town before continuing your trip.

The same advice should be followed when driving through towns and cities. Be sure to notice the white signs warning that, upon entering the town, you will be in a different "Speed Zone Ahead." Be prepared to slow to the lower speed you will soon see posted on upcoming white signs. Some very small Texas towns are notorious for catching and fining drivers who have not slowed down quickly enough from the highway speed to the in-town 30 mph (48 kph) speed limit. You may not notice the local (variously colored and lettered) police car parked surreptitiously in an alley until it is too late.

Pay attention to other drivers flashing their lights at you; probably either an accident or speed trap is ahead. Some Texas motorists ask the gas station attendants if there are Highway Patrol cars ahead but they cannot always be relied upon.

Seatbelts

A state law requires every passenger in a car to use a seatbelt and there are also requirements that small children and babies be secured in youth or infant seats which have been fitted into the car seat.

Where to Stay

Choosing a Hotel

Whatever your budget, you should be able to find a suitable place to spend the night in Texas. In addition to independently owned hotels and motels in every price range, even the many chains operating in Texas reach into some of its smallest towns.

At the expensive end of the scale there are Sheratons, Hiltons, Marriotts and Hyatt Regencies. A more moderately priced choice would be the Holiday Inns, La Quintas and Ramada Inns. Quality Inns, Howard Johnsons and Best Western motels are reasonable; the Motel 6, Days Inn, Rodeway Inn and Travelodge chains are relatively inexpensive.

Quaint and historic inns and other lodgings are the specialty of an association called **Historic Accommodations of Texas**, P.O. Box 203, Vanderpool, TX 78885, tel: 800-428-0368, www.hat.org. A free brochure lists the statewide membership.

Hotel Listings

Places are listed in alphabetical order by town, and the hotels listed alphabetically within each town.

ABILENE

Antilley Inn
6550 Highway 83, 79602
Tel: 915-695-3330;
fax: 915-695-9872.
52 units, with Continental breakfast served. **$**
Clarion Hotel
5403 South 1st, 79605
Tel: 915-695-2150;
fax: 915-698-6742.

Comprising 180 units; well-kept rooms at a good price, facilities for the disabled, heated indoor pool, whirlpool, saunas. **$$**

ALPINE

Antelope Lodge
2310 W. Highway 90, 79830
Tel: 915-837-2451; fax: 915-837-3881; www.antelopelodge.com
Rustic comfort in a valley setting; cottages with kitchenettes. **$**
The Corner House
801 E. Avenue E., 79830
Tel: 915-837-7161.
Garden with a fountain. Delicious home-baked breads. Five rooms. **$**
Fiesta Country Inn
1200 E. Highway 90, 79830
Tel: 915-837-2503.
Opposite the university with a pool, 15 rooms – some with kitchenettes – golf and tennis facilities nearby. **$**

AMARILLO

Holiday Inn Express
3411 I-40 West, 79109
Tel: 806-356-6800;
fax: 806-356-0401;
www.hiexpress.com.
Comfortable chain option with a heated pool and 97 rooms. **$$**
Travelodge West
2035 Paramount Drive, 79109
Tel: 806-353-3541 or 800-578-7878;
fax: 806-353-0201;
www.travelodgewest.com
100 rooms, pool and lots of restaurants nearby. **$**

AUSTIN

Austin Motel
1220 S. Congress Avenue, 78704
Tel: 512-441-1157;
www.austinmotel.com
Award-winning 1938 motel is conveniently located a few blocks south of Town Lake. Restaurant and laundromat, pool, whirlpool/spa, and video rental library. Weekly rates can be arranged; 41 units. **$$**

Brava House
1108 Blanco Street, 78703
Tel: 512-478-5034;
www.bravahouse.com
Classy, period bed-and-breakfast suites, centrally located. **$$**
Driskill Hotel
604 Brazos Street, 78701
Tel: 512-474-5911
or 800-252-9367;
fax: 512-474-2214;
www.driskillhotel.com
Historic hotel in a great downtown location. Workout facilities, bar and internet-wired TVs, 176 rooms and 12 suites. **$$$$**
Doubletree Guest Suites
303 W. 15th Street, 78701
Tel: 512-478-7000;
fax: 512-478-3562;
www.doubletreehotelaustin.com
All-suite hotel with 189 units. **$$$$**
Embassy Suites Downtown
300 S. Congress Avenue, 78704
Tel: 512-469-9000
or 800-362-2779;
fax: 512-480-9164.
www.embassysuites.com
Cooked-to-order breakfasts, and workout facilities. **$$–$$$$**
Four Seasons Hotel
98 San Jacinto Boulevard, 78701
Tel: 512-478-4500;
or 800-819-5053
fax: 512-478-3117;
www.fourseasons.com/austin
This four-star hotel has a restaurant with outdoor dining overlooking Town Lake. Most rooms have a lake view. On hike-and-bike trail. **$$$$**
Hilton Austin North
6000 Middle Fiskville Road, 78752
Tel: 512-451-5757 or 800-347-0330;
fax: 512-467-7644.
www.austinnorth.hilton.com
Fitness club; facilities for the disabled. **$$$**
Hyatt Regency on Town Lake
208 Barton Springs Road, 78704
Tel: 512-477-1234;
fax: 512-480-2069;
www.austin.hyatt.com
Excellent location on Town Lake's hike-and-bike trail. **$$$**
Lake Austin Spa Resort
1705 S. Quinlan Park Road, 78732

Price Categories

Price categories are based on the cost of a double room for one night in high season.
$$$$ = above $200
$$$ = $125–200
$$ = $50–125
$ = up to $50

Tel: 800-847-5637;
fax: 512-266-1572;
www.lakeaustin.com
All amenities including facilities for the disabled Interesting package deals. **$$$$**
Radisson Hotel on Town Lake
111 E. Cesar Chavez, 78701
Tel: 512-478-9611
or 800-333-3333;
fax: 512-473-8399;
www.radisson.com/austintx
Excellent downtown location on hike-and-bike trail. Fitness center and pool, 303 rooms and 99 suites. **$$$**
Days Inn Austin North
820 E. Anderson Lane, 78752
Tel: 512-835-4311;
fax: 512-835-1740;
www.daysinn.com
146 remodeled rooms, with a pool, and a golf course nearby. **$**
Renaissance Austin Hotel
9721 Arboretum Boulevard, 78759
Tel: 512-343-2626;
fax: 512-346-7953.
www.renaissancehotels.com
As well as a restaurant this hotel also has a pool, spa and workout facilities. Specialty shops and restaurants nearby. **$$$**

BANDERA

Bandera Lodge
1900 Highway 16 S., 78003
Tel: 830-796-3093;
fax: 830-796-3191.
This motel-lodge has 44 rooms and a picnic area on the Medina River. Restaurant, pool and nearby golf course. **$**

Holiday Apartments

Condominiums and beachfront/ bay front homes are available to rent in some areas, particularly on Galveston and South Padre islands. Check the *Yellow Pages* under "Realtors", or contact:
● **Century 21 Bay Reef Realty**
12200 FM 3005 Road, Galveston, 77554, tel: 409-737-2300 or 800-527-7333; www.bayreef.com
● **Sand 'n' Sea Pirates Beach**
13706 FM 3005 Road, Galveston,

77554, tel: 740-6400 or 800-880-2554, www.sandnsea.com
● **Island Services**
1700 Padre Boulevard, South Padre Island, 78597, tel: 956-761-2649 or 800-527-0294, www.island-services.com.
● **Padre Island Rentals**
3100 Padre Boulevard, South Padre Island, 78597, tel: 956-761-5512 or 800-926-6926, www.pirentals.com

COMFORT

Motor Inn at Comfort
I-10 and US 87
Tel: 830-995-3822;
www.shopcomfort.com
Small motel offering no-frills lodging. **$$**

CORPUS CHRISTI

Best Western Marina Grand Hotel
300 N. Shoreline Boulevard, 78401
Tel: 361-883-5111;
fax: 361-883-3686;
www.marinagrandhotel.com
Fully equipped, 11-story hotel across from the seawall, with bay and marina views. **$$–$$$**
Embassy Suites
4337 S. Padre Island Drive, 78411
Tel: 361-853-7899;
fax: 361-851-1310;
www.embassysuites.com
Restaurant, indoor pool, spa, workout facilities. **$$–$$$**
Fairfield Inn by Marriott
5217 Blanche Moore Drive, 78411
Tel: 361-985-8393;
fax: 361-985-8393;
www.fairfieldinn.com
Pool. Breakfast included. **$$**
Holiday Inn Emerald Beach
1102 S. Shoreline Boulevard, 78401
Tel: 361-883-5731, or 800-465-4329;
fax: 361-883-9079;
www.holidayinncorpus.com
This large (368-room) hotel has a private beach area, health club, two restaurants, indoor/outdoor pool,

free airport shuttle, free parking, a spa and golf course nearby. **$$$**
Villa del Sol
3938 Surfside Boulevard, 78402
Tel: 361-883-9748 or 800-242-3291;
fax: 361-883-7537;
www.villa-delsol.com
Situated on the beach. Whirlpool/ spa, kitchenettes, 2 pools and volleyball court, 200 units. **$$**

DALLAS

Aristocrat Hotel
1933 Main Street, 75201
Tel: 214-741-7700 or 800-231-4235;
fax: 214-939-3639;
www.holiday-inn.com
A national landmark with period charm, dating from 1925; 172 rooms. **$$$**
Atrium Suites Inn
215 E. Airport Freeway, Irving, 75062
Tel: 972-255-5500.
Near airport; indoor pool, 122 rooms. **$$**
Classic Motor Inn
9229 Carpenter Freeway, 75247
Tel: 214-631-6633;
fax: 214-631-6616.
Pool, sauna, exercise room. **$$**
Crescent Court
400 Crescent Court, 75201
Tel: 214-871-3200;
fax: 214-871-3272;
www.crescentcourt.com.
Elegantly furnished hotel with gardens, pool, spa, exercise room, renowned restaurants. **$$$$**
Days Inn Texas Stadium
2200 E. Airport Freeway,

Irving, 75062
Tel: 972-438-6666;
fax: 972-579-4902
Outdoor pool. Free transport to airport. **$$**
Embassy Suites – Airport South
4650 W. Airport Freeway, Irving, 75062
Tel: 972-790-0093;
fax: 972-790-4768;
www.esdfwsouth.com
Free transport to and from airport. Restaurants, pool, sauna and free breakfast included. **$$**
Embassy Suites – Love Field
Love Field, 3880 West Northwest Highway, 75220
Tel: 214-357-4500;
fax: 214-357-0683;
www.embassysuites.com
Garden atrium and complimentary cooked breakfast; 248 units. **$$$**
Embassy Suites – Market Center
2727 Stemmons Freeway, 75207
Tel: 214-630-5332;
fax: 214-631-3025;
www.embassysuites.com
Landscaped 9-story atrium, pool and laundromat. Complimentary cooked breakfast; 244 units. **$$$**
Fairmont Hotel
1717 North Akard, 75201
Tel: 214-720-2020;
fax: 214-720-5269;
www.fairmont.com
Lavish hotel in Arts District. Pool; 550 rooms. **$$$$**
Four Seasons Hotel and Resort
4150 N. MacArthur Boulevard, Irving, 75038
Tel: 972-717-0700;
fax: 972-717-2428;
www.fourseasons.com/dallas
Raquetball and squash courts. Pools and sauna; 357 rooms. **$$$$**
Harvey Hotel – Airport
4545 W. Carpenter Freeway, Irving, 75063
Tel: 972-929-4500;
fax: 972-929-0733;
www.harveyhotel-dfwairport.felcor.com
Shuttle from airport. Impressive atrium, restaurants, rooftop pool. **$$**
Harvey Hotel – Dallas
7815 LBJ Freeway, 75251
Tel: 972-960-7000;
fax: 972-788-4227.
Facilities for the disabled. With 313

units, whirlpool/spa, work-out
facilities. Just 5 minutes from
Galleria mall. **$$**

Holiday Inn
4440 W. Airport Freeway,
Irving, 75062
Tel: 972-399-1010
or 800-360-2242;
fax: 972-790-8476;
wwwholiday-inn.com/dfw-airports
Near the airport, biggest of the
chain in Texas. With pools and a
sauna. **$$$**

Hyatt Regency DFW Airport
International Parkway, 75261
Tel: 972-453-1234;
fax: 972-615-6825;
www.dfwairport.hyatt.com
Pool, sauna, racquetball, tennis,
golf, restaurants. **$$$$**

Hotel InterContinental
15201 Dallas Parkway,
Addison, 75001
Tel: 972-386-6000;
fax: 972-991-6937;
www.interconti.com
Located in north Dallas. With 530
rooms and a whirlpool/spa. **$$$**

The Mansion on Turtle Creek
2821 Turtle Creek Boulevard,
75219
Tel: 214-559-2100;
fax: 214-528-4187;
www.mansiononturtlecreek.com
Famously luxurious, hilltop haven
for the affluent. Pool, sauna, health
club, expensive restaurant. **$$$$**

Melrose Hotel
3015 Oak Lawn Avenue, 75219
Tel: 214-521-5151;
fax: 214-521-2470;
www.melrosehoteldallas.com
Classy, 75-year-old landmark built in
1924, 3 miles (5 km) from Love
Field airport. **$$$**

Ramada Limited
3447 E. Highway, I-30,
Mesquite, 75150
Tel: 972-270-4000;
fax: 972-681-5178;
www.ramada.com
Fifteen minutes from downtown.
$$

Hotel St Germain
2516 Maple Avenue, 75201
Tel: 214-871-2516;
fax: 214-871-0740.
Luxurious, in a Victorian former
home. Champagne bar. **$$$$**

Sheraton Dallas Brookhollow Hotel
1241 W. Mockingbird Lane, 75247
Tel: 214-630-7000;
fax: 214-640-9221;
www.starwood.com/sheraton
Near Love Field and Market Center.
Recently renovated. Pool,
restaurant, 348 rooms. **$$**

Sheraton Grand at DFW
4440 W. John Carpenter Freeway,
Irving, 75063
Tel: 972-929-8400;
fax: 972-929-4885;
www.starwood.com/sheraton
Whirlpool/spa and work-out
facilities. Interpreters. **$$$**

Stoneleigh Hotel
2927 Maple Avenue, 75201
Tel: 214-871-7111;
fax: 214-871-9379;
www.stoneleighhotel.com
European-style hotel. Pool, choice
of restaurants, 153 units. **$$$**

Wyndham Anatole Hotel
2201 Stemmons Freeway, 75207
Tel: 214-748-1200;
fax: 214-761-7520;
www.wyndham.com
27-floor hotel with 1,600 rooms.
Pool, seven restaurants, valuable
art on loan from Trammell Crow.
$$$

Wyndham Garden Market Center
2015 Market Center Boulevard,
75207
Tel: 214-741-7481;
fax: 214-747-6191.
Handy for business and leisure;
work-out facilities, 228 units. **$$$**

EL PASO & JUÁREZ

Best Western Airport Inn
7144 E. Gateway Boulevard, 79915
Tel: 915-779-7700;
fax: 915-772-1920;
www.bestwestern.com
165 clean rooms, heated pool and
a rose-filled courtyard. Airport
shuttle. **$**

Camino Real Paso del Norte
101 S. El Paso Street 79901
Tel: 915-534-3000;
fax: 915-534-3024;
www.caminoreal.com
Historic, highly rated
accommodations with 360 units.
Health club, and the classiest bar in

the city. International cuisine in the
Dome restaurant. **$$$**

Chase Suite Hotel by Woodfin
6791 Montana Avenue, 79925
Tel: 915-772-8000;
fax: 915-772-7254;
www.woodfinsuitehotels.com
Close to the airport (7 miles/11 km
from downtown), with
complimentary continental
breakfast. **$$–$$$**

Holiday Inn
Lincoln Av., Zona Pronaf,
Juárez, 32315;
Tel: 011-52656-6131310
or 915-892-7790;
www.holiday-inn.com
170 recently renovated units. Pool,
fitness center, restaurant and
cocktail lounge.

Price Categories

Price categories are based on
the cost of a double room for one
night in high season.
$$$$ = above $200
$$$ = $125–200
$$ = $50–125
$ = up to $50

FORT DAVIS

Indian Lodge
P.O. Box 1707, 79734
Tel: 915-426-3254;
www.tpwd.state.tx.us/park/indian
The only hotel/restaurant owned by
the state of Texas. Reservations
must be made far in advance. You
could always try just for lunch. **$$**

Hotel Limpia
On the town square, 100 Main
Street 79734
Tel: 915-426-3237;
fax: 915-426-3983.
www.hotellimpia.com
Historic restored hotel, built in
1912; period furnishings. With 39
non-smoking rooms, restaurant and
cocktail lounge. **$$**

Old Texas Inn
Main Street, 79734
Tel: 915-426-3118;
fax: 915-426-2368;
www.oldtexasinn.com
Cowboy-style hotel with old-fashioned
drugstore and soda fountain. **$$**

Prude Ranch
Highway 118 North, 79734
Tel: 915-426-3202;
fax: 915-426-4401;
www.prude-ranch.com
This old cattle ranch 6 miles (10 km) west of town is now a dude ranch with open-range horseback riding and a mountain resort. Cabins and motel units. Facilities include tennis courts and hot tub. **$$**

Stone Village Motel
Main Street, 79734
Tel: 915-426-3941;
fax: 915-426-2281;
www.stone-village.com
Mountain retreat close to Fort Davis National Historic Site. **$$**

FORT WORTH

Clarion Hotel
600 Commerce Street, 76102
Tel: 817-332-6900;
fax: 817-877-5440.
Downtown hotel with healthclub and four restaurants. **$$**

Days Inn Fort Worth West
8500 I-30 West at Las Vegas Trail, 76108
Tel: 817-246-4961;
fax: 817-246-0368;
www.daysinn.com
Disabled facilities and free breakfast; with 121 rooms. **$**

Hilton Arlington
2401 E. Lamar Boulevard, 76006
Tel: 817-640-3322;
fax: 817-633-1430;
www.hilton.com
Close to all local attractions. **$$**

Green Oaks Hotel
6901 W. Freeway, 76116
Tel: 817-738-7311;
fax: 817-737-4486;
www.greenoakshotel.com

Price Categories

Price categories are based on the cost of a double room for one night in high season.
$$$$ = above $200
$$$ = $125–200
$$ = $50–125
$ = up to $50

284 units, pools, sauna, spa, tennis courts. **$$**

La Quinta Inn West
7888 I-30 West, 76108
Tel: 817-246-5511;
fax: 817-246-8870;
www.lq.com
Complimentary breakfast; with 106 units. **$$**

Ramada Plaza
1701 Commerce Street (adjoining Water Gardens), 76102
Tel: 817-335-7000;
fax: 817-335-3333;
www.ramada.com
Pool, spa and restaurant. **$$$**

Renaissance Worthington Hotel
200 Main Street, 76102
Tel: 817-870-1000;
fax: 817-338-9176;
www.renaissancehotels.com
This imposing, modern, downtown hotel dominates Sundance Square, with adjoining mall, athletic club, pool, restaurants and sauna. There are 504 units. **$$$**

Sandpiper Airport Inn
4001 N. Main Street, 76106
Tel: 817-625-5531;
fax: 817-625-5531.
With 84 rooms, some with whirlpool baths. **$$**

Stockyards Hotel
109 E. Exchange Avenue, 76106
Tel: 817-625-6427 or
800-423-8471;
fax: 817-624-2571;
www.stockyardshotel.com
Choice of four decors – Victorian, Mountain Man, Cowboy or Native American. **$$**

FREDERICKSBURG

Dietzel Motel
909 W. Main (Jct 290W & 87N), 78624
Tel: 830-997-3330.
Twenty units, simple but well-maintained rooms 1 mile (1.6 km) west of the town center. **$**

Sunday House Inn
501 E. Main, 78624
Tel: 830-997-4484;
fax: 830-997-5607;
www.sundayhouseinnandsuites.com
German-American hotel with a pool and ethnic restaurant. **$$**

GALVESTON

Days Inn Galveston
6107 Broadway Street 77551
Tel: 409-740-2491;
fax: 409-740-6805;
www.daysinn.com
88 units and an outdoor pool. **$$**

Flagship Hotel
2501 Seawall Boulevard, 77550
Tel: 409-762-9000;
fax: 409-762-1619;
www.flagshiphotel.com
Nautically themed hotel on a pier stretching 1,000 ft (300 meters) out to sea. **$$$**

Gaido's Seaside Inn
3802 Seawall Boulevard, 77550
Tel: 409-762-9625;
fax: 409-765-9285;
www.gaidosoffalveston.com
With 104 motel-style units, many of which have a sea view. Also a tiered flower garden. **$$**

Hotel Galvez
2024 Seawall Boulevard, 77550
Tel: 409-765-7721;
fax: 409-765-5780;
wwwwyndham.com
Historic seafront hotel run by the Wyndham chain. Features a sauna and whirlpool and 231 units. **$$$**

Harbor View Inn
928 Ferry Road, 77550
Tel: 409-762-3311;
fax: 409-762-6264;
www.galveston.com/harborview
With 49 rooms. Close to ferry. Kitchenettes available. **$**

Moody Gardens Hotel
7 Hope Boulevard, 77554
Tel: 409-741-8484;
fax: 409-683-4936;
www.moodygardens.com
Impressive hotel in the Moody Gardens entertainment park. Surrounded by 242 acres (98 hectares) of gardens and pyramids. **$$$**

The Tremont House
2300 Ship's Mechanic Row, 77550
Tel: 409-763-0300;
fax: 409-763-1539;
www.wyndham.com
Historic, European-style hotel, near the Strand. Part of the Wyndham chain. 119 Victorian-style rooms. **$$**

HOUSTON

Best Western Park Place Suites
Astrodome, 1400 Old Spanish Trail
Tel: 713-796-1000;
fax: 713-796-8055;
www.bestwestern.com
Pool, sauna, exercise room,
restaurant, and 191 rooms. **$$**

Comfort Inn Brookhollow
4760 Sherwood Lane, 77092
Tel: 713-686-5525;
fax: 713-686-5365;
www.comfortinn.com
46 units, with outdoor pool and free
breakfast. **$$**

Courtyard by Marriott
3131 West Loop South, 77027
Tel: 713-961-1640;
fax: 713-439-0989;
www.courtyard.com
Whirlpool/spa and workout
facilities, near the Galleria. **$$**

Days Inn Astrodome
8500 Kirby Drive, 77054
Tel: 713-796-8383;
fax: 713-795-8453;
www.daysinn.com
With 129 units and outdoor pool. **$$**

Doubletree Hotel
at Allen Center, 400 Dallas Street,
77002
Tel: 713-759-0202;
fax: 713-759-1166;
www.doubletree.com
In the business district; 350 rooms
with floor-to-ceiling windows. **$$$**

Fairfield Inn Marriott
Near the Galleria, 3131 West Loop
South, 77027
Tel: 713-961-1690;
fax: 713-627-8434;
www.marriott.com
107 units and a whirlpool/spa. **$$**

Grant's Palm Court
8200 South Main Street, 77025
Tel: 713-668-8000;
fax: 713-668-7777;
www.palmcourtinn.com
Elvis Presley was once a guest at
this 1950s inn with 64 units, pool,
spa, and restaurant nearby. **$**

Hampton Inn I-10 East
828 Mercury Drive, 77013
Tel: 713-673-4200;
fax: 713-674-6913;
www.hampton-inn.com
90 rooms; outdoor pool;
complimentary breakfast. **$$**

Hilton Hobby Airport
8181 Airport Boulevard, 77061
Tel: 713-645-3000;
fax: 713-645-2251;
www.houstonhabbyairport.hilton.com
The Hobby has 305 units, some
with jacuzzis. On-site healthclub,
café and restaurant. **$$**

Holiday Inn NASA
1300 Nasa Road 1, 77058
Tel: 281-333-2500;
fax: 281-335-1578;
www.houston-nasa.holiday-inn.com
Across the street from NASA. Pool,
kids' playground, 224 rooms.
Complimentary underground tram
service to George Bush
International Airport. **$$**

Houston Airport Marriott
18700 Kennedy Boulevard, 77032
Tel: 281-443-2310;
fax: 281-443-5294;
www.marriott.com
7 floors; good business facilities;
revolving restaurant. **$$$**

The Houstonian Hotel, Club and Spa
111 North Post Oak Lane, 77024
Tel: 713-680-2626;
fax: 713-680-2992;
www.houstonian.com
291 rooms in wooded grounds.
Spa and pools; tennis and
racquetball courts, plus jogging
tracks. **$$$**

Hyatt Regency Houston
1200 Louisiana Street, 77002
Tel: 713-654-1234;
fax: 713-951-0934;
www.hyatt.com
Downtown hotel with 977 units.
Recent $15 million facelift. **$$$$**

Hyatt Regency Houston Airport
15747 JFK Boulevard, 77032
Tel: 281-987-1234;
fax: 281-590-8461;
www.hyatt.com
With 314 units, next to the airport.
$$$$

Lancaster Hotel
701 Texas Avenue, 77002
Tel: 713-228-9500;
fax: 713-223-4528;
www.lancaster.com
Luxurious hotel built in 1926,
located in the downtown theater
district; 84 rooms, each with VCR
and PC. **$$$$**

Marriott West Loop
by the Galleria, 1750 West Loop

South, 77027
Tel: 713-960-0111;
fax: 713-624-1560;
www.marriott.com
With 300 rooms on 13 floors.
Indoor pool, sauna, spa, restaurant.
$$$

St Regis
1919 Briar Oaks Lane, 77027
Tel: 713-840-7600;
fax: 713-840-8036;
www.starwood.com/stregis

Campgrounds

There are more than 200 state,
federal, or privately owned
campgrounds throughout Texas.
  For information on camping in
national parks, recreation areas,
forests and the 20-plus lakes
administered by the US Army
Corps of Engineers, you should
contact: **The National Park
Service**, Southwest Region, PO
Box 728, Santa Fe, New Mexico
87504.
  Around 70 Texas parks and
recreation areas managed by the
state allow camping within their
grounds. **Central Reservations**,
tel: 512-389-8900,
www.tpwd.state.tx.us can make
bookings for anywhere within the
state park system. A useful free
booklet, called *Texas Public
Campgrounds*, is available from
the **Travel and Information
Division, State Department of
Transportation**, PO Box 5064,
Austin, 78763.
  *RV and Camping Guide to
Texas*, the best list available of
private campgrounds, which
include about half the total
number of campgrounds in
Texas, is available free of charge
from the **Texas Association of
Campground Owners**,4621 S.
Cooper #131–104, Arlington
76017,
www.campingfriend.com/taco.
  In addition, **The Texas KOA
Kampground Owners
Association**, www.koa.com,
can provide a list of 20
member campgrounds around
the state.

Has 232 upscale units in River Oaks residential area. **$$$**

Sheraton Suites
Galleria, 2400 West Loop South, 77027
Tel: 713-586-2444;
fax: 713-586-2445;
www.sheratonsuiteshouston.com
There are 281 units, a pool, spa, exercise room and restaurant. **$$**

The Warwick
5701 S. Main Street, 77005
Tel: 713-526-1991;
fax: 713-526-0359;
www.warwickhotelhouston.com
Pool, sauna, exercise room and restaurant. European-style decor. **$$$**

The Westin Oaks
5011 Westheimer, 77056
Tel: 713-960-8100;
fax: 713-960-6554;
www.starwood.com/westin
Recently renovated; with 406 rooms on 21 floors in the Galleria. **$$$**

JEFFERSON

Hotel Jefferson
124 West Austin Street, 75657
Tel: 903-665-2631;
fax: 903-665-6222;
www.historicjeffersonhotel.com
Converted from an 1850s cotton warehouse in the historic downtown district; 23 rooms. **$$**

LAREDO

Family Garden Inn
5830 San Bernardo Avenue, 78041
Tel: 956-723-5300;
fax: 956-791-8842.
With 190 rooms on two floors. **$$**

La Hacienda Motor Hotel
4914 San Bernardo Avenue, 78041
Tel: 956-722-2441;
fax: 956-725-4532.
98 units, and live *tejano* music Tues–Sun nights. **$**

Loma Alta Motel
3915 San Bernardo Avenue, 78041
Tel: 956-726-1628;
fax: 956-724-4339
Reasonable facilities including for travelers with disabilities. Pool, 70 units. **$**

La Posada Hotel
1000 Zaragoza Street, 78040
Tel: 956-722-1701;
fax: 956-722-4758;
www.laposadahotel-laredo.com
Classic Mexican colonial-style hotel with 208 rooms. Within walking distance of the international bridge to Nuevo Laredo. **$$**

LUBBOCK

Days Inn – Texas Tech
2401 4th Street, 79415
Tel: 806-747-7111;
fax: 806-747-9749;
www.daysinn.com
90 units. At the university. **$**

Price Categories

Price categories are based on the cost of a double room for one night in high season.
$$$$ = above $200
$$$ = $125–200
$$ = $50–125
$ = up to $50

Inn of the South Plains
310 Avenue Q, 79415
Tel: 806-763-2861;
fax: 806-747-1020.
58 units. **$**

Lubbock Inn
3901 19th Street, 79410
Tel: 806-792-5181;
fax: 806-792-1319;
www.lubbockinn.com
Cocktail lounge, outdoor pool, laundry, 117 units. **$$**

MARATHON

The Gage Hotel
101 Hwy 90 West, 79842
Tel: 915-386-4205;
fax: 915-386-4510;
www.gagehotel.com
Split between a historic 1920s hotel, a courtyard-based annex and a restored 1900 house. Mexican and Southwestern cuisine. **$$–$$$$**

NACOGDOCHES

Econo Lodge
2020 N.W. Loop 224, Stallings, 75964
Tel: 936-569-0880;
fax: 936-569-0303;
www.econolodge.com
68 rooms. Free breakfast. **$**

Pine Creek Lodge
341 Pine Creek Road, 75964
Tel: 936-560-6282;
fax: 936-560-1675;
www.pinecreeklodge.com
17 rooms on a farm 10 miles (16 km) west of town. **$$$**

NEW BRAUNFELS

Hotel Faust
240 S. Seguin, 78130
Tel: 830-625-7791;
fax: 830-620-1530;
www.fausthotel.com
Historic landmark hotel with its own brew pub; 62 rooms. **$$**

Gruene Mansion Inn
1275 Gruene Road, 78130
Tel: 830-629-2641;
fax: 830-629-7375;
www.gruenemansioninn.com
Overlooking Guadalupe River, with 25 antique-furnished rooms in restored barns. The oldest dancehall in Texas is next door. **$$$**

Prince Solms Inn
295 East San Antonio Street, 78130
Tel: 830-625-9169;
www.princesolmsinn.com
1898 hotel with 12 rooms furnished with antiques. Fine restaurant and garden. **$$**

Schlitterbahn Waterpark Resort
305 W. Austin Street, 78130
Tel: 830-625-2351;
fax: 830-620-4873.
In the grounds of a 65-acre (26-hectare) waterpark; over 200 units. **$$**

PALACIOS

The Luther Hotel
409 South Bay Boulevard, 77465
Tel: 361-972-2312.
Historic 1903 hotel with 41 rooms and great views of the bay. **$$**

PORT ISABEL

Queen Isabel Inn
300 S. Garcia St, 78578
Tel: 956-943-1468;
fax: 956-943-3574;
www.queenisabelinn.com
National landmark property with
seven rooms; private and quiet.
Fully furnished kitchens. Beach gear
provided, fishing pier. **$$–$$$**

RIO-GRANDE VALLEY: HARLINGEN, McALLEN & BROWNSVILLE

Sun Valley Motor Hotel
1900 S. 77 Sunshine Strip,
Harlingen, 78550
Tel: 956-423-7222;
fax: 956-428-6394.
Sun Valley has 83 cottage-style
units, most with carports. Large
pool. Complimentary breakfast. **$**
**Rancho Viejo Resort and
Country Club**
US Highway 83 and Rancho Viejo
Drive , Brownsville, 78575
Tel: 956-350-4000
or 800-531-7400;
fax: 956-350-9681;
www.playrancho.com
Complete resort made up of 22
villas set on a golf course. **$$**
Renaissance Casa de Palmas Hotel
101 N. Main St, McAllen, 78501
Tel: 956-631-1101;
fax: 956-631-7934;
www.cascadepalmas.com
Spanish colonial-style hotel with
165 units, next to the Mexican
consulate. A national landmark-
preserved structure. **$$**
Microtel Inn
801 E. Expressway 83,
McAllen, 78501
Tel: 956-630-2727;
fax: 956-630-0666.
Outdoor pool; 102 units. **$**

ROCKPORT

Hunt's Court Motel
725 South Water St, 78382
Tel: 361-729-2273.
25 units; waterfront with fishing
pier. **$**

SAN ANTONIO

Bullis House Inn
621 Pierce Street, 78208
Tel: 210-233-9426;
fax: 210-299-1479;
www.bullishouseinn.com
Seven units. Spacious, fireplaces,
VCR, gardens, full kitchen adjacent,
near downtown, good value. **$$**
Clarion Hotel Airport
12828 US 281 North, 78216
Tel: 210-494-7600;
fax: 210-545-4314;
www.clarioninn.com
European-style hotel. Cooked
breakfast included. **$$$**
Crockett Hotel
320 Bonham, 78205
Tel: 210-225-6500 or 800-292-1050;
fax: 210-225-6251;
www.crocketthotel.com
Historic central hotel with 204 rooms
done in "Southwestern" style. **$$**
Days Inn Alamo-Riverwalk
902 E. Houston Street, 78205
Tel: 210-227-6233;
fax: 210-228-0901;
www.daysinn.com
Days has 50 units. One block from
Riverwalk and Alamo. **$$**
Fairmount Hotel
401 South Alamo, 78205
Tel: 210-224-8800;
fax: 210-475-0082;
www.wyndham.com
Part of the Wyndham group;
37 rooms and a well-known
restaurant, Polo's. **$$$**
La Mansion del Rio
112 College Street, 78205
Tel: 210-518-1000
or 800-292-7300;
fax: 210-226-0389;
www.amansion.com
Spanish mission architecture; 337
units, on quiet portion of Paseo del
Rio. Interpreters. **$$$**
Marriott Riverwalk
889 E. Market Street, 78205
Tel: 210-224-4555;
fax: 210-224-2754;
www.marriott.com
Heated pool, saunas, 500 rooms
on 30 floors. **$$$$**
The Historic Menger Hotel
204 Alamo Plaza, 78205
Tel: 210-223-4361 or 800-345-9285;
fax: 210-228-0022;

www.historicmenger.com
Revered 1859 structure next to the
Alamo, 350 rooms and spa/fitness
center. **$$$**
Hilton Palacio del Rio
200 South Alamo, 78205
Tel: 210-222-1400;
fax: 210-270-0761;
www.palaciodelrio.hilton.com
A fully equipped modern hotel with
Spanish touches, 481 units, on the
River Walk. **$$$**
Radisson Market Square
502 W. Durango, 78207
Tel: 210-224-7155;
fax: 210-224-9130;
www.radisson.com/sanantoniotx
Patio café, whirlpool/spa and work-
out facilities, 250 units. **$$$**
Super 8 Motel
3617 North Pan Am Expressway,
78219
Tel: 210-227-8888;
fax: 210-224-2098;
www.super8.com/sanantonio,tx
93 units. Outdoor pool; restaurant. **$**
Sheraton Gunter Hotel
205 E. Houston Street, 78205
Tel: 210-227-3241;
fax: 210-227-3299;
www.gunterhotel.com
Historic hotel built in 1909; 322
units. **$$–$$$**
Super 8 Motel Fiesta Texas
5319 Casa Bella & I-10, 78249
Tel: 210-696-6916;
fax: 210-696-4321;
www.super8.com/sanantonio,tx
71 units. Handy for Six Flags and
Sea World. **$**
Travelodge Suites
4934 NW Loop 410, 78229
Tel: 210-680-3351;
fax: 210-680-3709;
www.travelodge.com
With 201 units. Free "cookout"
every Wednesday in the summer.
$$

SOUTH PADRE ISLAND

Motel 6
4013 Padre Boulevard, 78597
Tel: 956-761-7911;
fax: 956-761-6339;
www.motel6.com
52 units. A mile (1.5 km) north of
downtown. **$**

Radisson Resort South Padre Island
500 Padre Boulevard, 78597
Tel: 956-761-6511;
fax: 956-761-1602;
www.radissonspi.com
With 190 beachfront units and lots of amenities. **$$**

VAN HORN

Best Western Inn of Van Horn
1705 W. Broadway, 79855
Tel: 915-283-2410;
fax: 915-283-2143;
www.bestwestern.com
Large family rooms and pool. **$$**

WACO

Lexington Inn
115 Jack Kultgen, 76706
Tel: 254-754-1266;
fax: 254-755-8612;
www.lexhotels.com
Near Baylor University. Work-out facilities, Continental breakfast. **$$**
La Quinta Inn
1110 S. 9th Street, 76706
Tel: 254-752-9741;
fax: 254-757-1600; www.lq.com
Close to university. **$$**
Waco Hilton
113 S. University Parks Drive, 76701
Tel: 254-754-8484;
fax: 254-752-2214;
www.waco.hilton.com
On the Brazos River Walk. Tennis, whirlpool. **$$**

Bed & Breakfast

Bed and breakfast rates in Texas are generally reasonable. In historic districts or towns there is not much of a distinction made between "bed and breakfast" and "historic inn," since they are much the same.

ABILENE

Bolin's Prairie House B&B
508 Mulberry Street,
Abilene, 79601
Tel: 915-675-5855;
fax: 915-677-4694;

www.abilenebedandbreakfast.com
Historic downtown home, with four rooms decorated with antiques. Good breakfast. **$**

AMARILLO

Auntie's House B&B
1712 S. Polk Street, 79102
Tel: 806-371-8054;
www.auntieshouse.com
Downtown historic home with period furnishings. Three rooms and a private cottage. **$$**

Price Categories

Price categories are based on the cost of a double room for one night in high season.
$$$$ = above $200
$$$ = $125–200
$$ = $50–125
$ = up to $50

AUSTIN

Woodburn House B&B
4401 Avenue D, 78751
Tel: 512-458-4335;
fax: 512-458-4319;
www.woodburnhouse.com
Charming Victorian house with wrap-around porches, gourmet breakfasts; fax/computer available. **$$**

BRENHAM

Ant Street Inn
107 W. Commerce, 77833
Tel: 979-836-7393
or 800-805-2600;
fax: 979-836-7595;
www.antstreetinn.com
Elegant B&B with stylish, high-ceilinged rooms. **$$**

DALLAS

Amelia's Place
1775 Young Street, 75201
Tel: 214-651-1775
Downtown B&B only one block from City Hall. **$$**

The Bingham House
800 S. Chestnut St, McKinney, 75069
Tel/fax: 972-529-1883;
www.binghamhouse.com
Friendly hosts Bill & Karen Lynch, history buffs, have decorated their 1883 home in charming period style. **$$**
Dowell House
1104 S. Tennessee Street, McKinney, 75069
Tel: 972-562-2456;
www.dowellhouse.com
This 1870 home doubled as haunted house in the 1973 movie *Benji*. **$$$**

DENTON

The Tudor Revival Redbud Inn
815 N. Locust Street, 76201
Tel: 940-565-6414;
fax: 940-565-6515.
This pleasant inn, as well as Magnolia House next door and Pecan House, are under the same ownership of heritage inns. **$$**

FORT DAVIS

Veranda Country Inn B&B
210 Court Avenue, 79734
Tel: 915-426-2233;
fax: 915-426-3839;
www.theveranda.com
Historic, country adobe home. 14 rooms with antique furnishings. Full breakfast. **$$**

FREDERICKSBURG

Fredericksburg Bed & Brew
245 E. Main Street, 78624
Tel: 830-997-1646;
fax: 830-997-8026;
www.yourbrewery.com
B&B with brew pub, *biergarten* and restaurant. 12 rooms with private bath. **$$**

GALVESTON

The Inn at 1816 Postoffice
1816 Postoffice Street, 77550
Tel: 409-765-9444 or 888-558-9444

Restored Victorian residence in heart of historic East End district. **$$–$$$**

GRANBURY

Dabney House B&B
106 South Jones Street, 76048
Tel: 817-579-1260.
Five rooms in a 1907 house with private bath; full breakfast. **$$**

Oak Tree Farm B&B
6415 Carmichael Court, 76049
Tel: 817-326-5595.
Five rooms with private baths. Gourmet breakfast. Country setting, walking trails. **$$**

HOUSTON

McLachlan Farm B&B
24907 Hardy Road, Spring, 77383
Tel: 281-350-2400;
fax: 281-350-1011;
www.macfarm.com
1911 farmhouse six rooms in quiet country setting. **$$**

Sara's Bed & Breakfast Inn
941 Heights Boulevard, 77008
Tel: 713-868-1130;
fax: 713-868-3284;
www.saras.com
Victorian mansion with 12 rooms; no children under 12. **$$**

JEFFERSON

Old Mulberry Inn B&B
209 Jefferson Street, 75657
Tel: 903-665-1445
or 800-263-5319;
www.oldmulberryinn.com
Louisiana-style house located in the historic district. Five distinctly decorated rooms. **$$**

Pride House
409 E. Broadway, 75657
Tel: 903-665-2675;
fax: 903-665-3901;
www.jeffersontexas.com
Stately Victorian mansion with princely interiors. Ten rooms. **$$**

NEW BRAUNFELS

Historic Kuebler-Waldrip Haus & Danville Schoolhouse B&B
1620 Hueco Springs Loop, 78132
Tel: 830-625-8300
or 800-299-8372;
www.kueblerwaldrip.com
Consists of an 1847 wine merchant's house and a relocated old school, with 10 rooms. Full country breakfast and nearby water recreation. **$$–$$$**

Karbach Haus B&B
487 W. San Antonio Street, 78130
Tel: 830-625-2131;
fax: 830-629-1126.
Six spacious rooms. German-style breakfast. Spa, gardens. **$$–$$$**

PALACIOS

Moonlight Bay B&B
506 S. Bay Boulevard, 77465
Tel: 361-972-22
fax: 361-972-0463;
www.moonlightbaybb.com
Eight rooms with indoor/outdoor verandas, bay views, casual elegance, gourmet breakfast. **$$**

ROCKPORT

Hoopes' House
417 N. Broadway, 78382
Tel: 361-729-8424.
Restored Victorian house with eight ensuite rooms, swimming pool and hot tub.

SAN ANTONIO

Beckmann Inn & Carriage House
222 E. Guenther St, 78204
Tel: 210-229-1449;
fax: 210-229-1061;
www.beckmanninn.com
Victorian home in King William's historic district. River Walk and Alamo both within walking distance. Full breakfast. **$$–$$$**

Ogé Inn Riverwalk
209 Washington St, 78204
Tel: 210-223-2353;
fax: 210-226-5812;

Useful Contacts

For information and bookings at many of Texas' B&Bs, you can contact:
Bed & Breakfast Texas Style, 701 Honeysuckle Lane, College Station, 77845; tel: 979-696-9222 or 800-899-4538; fax: 979-696-9444; e-mail: info@bnbtexasstyle.com

www.ogeinn.com
An 1857 antebellum mansion with exquisite antiques. **$$$–$$$$**

Yellow Rose B&B
229 Madison Street, 78204
Tel: 210-229-9903;
fax: 210-229-1691;
www.ayellowrose.com
Five units with antiques. In King William Historic District, within walking distance to downtown and River Walk. **$$$**

SAN MARCOS

Crystal River Inn
326 W. Hopkins, 78666
Tel: 512-396-3739;
fax: 512-353-3248;
www.crystalriverinn.com
12 rooms in an 1883 inn. Gourmet breakfast, antiques, courtyard and rose garden. **$$–$$$**

SOUTH PADRE ISLAND

Moonraker B&B
107 E. Marisol 78597
Tel: 956-761-2206;
www.moonrakerbb.com
Three units on the beach; fishing, close to restaurants. **$$**

UVALDE

Casa de Leona B&B
1149 Pearsall Highway 140, 78802
Tel/fax: 830-278-8550.
Fishing, fountains, antiques, luxury. Gourmet breakfasts. **$$**

Price Categories

Price categories are based on the cost of a double room for one night in high season.
$$$$ = above $200
$$$ = $125–200
$$ = $50–125
$ = up to $50

Where to Eat

WIMBERLEY

Homestead Cottages B&B
105 Scudder Lane at Ranch Road 12, 78676
Tel: 512-847-8788
or 800-918-8788;
fax: 512-847-1110
www.homestead-tx.com
16 cottages, on swimmable Cypress Creek. Decks, hot tub, fireplaces, catered meals. $$

What to Eat

Don't plan on dieting while in Texas: Texans love their food, and a visit here wouldn't be complete without sampling a good portion of it. Tex-Mex food has become synonymous with the state, and it's not all fire-breathingly hot, so even the most wary should give it a try.

Another Texas staple is the barbecue – usually huge chunks of beef (but sometimes pork and sausage) that are cooked slowly for hours over special wood such as hickory or mesquite to add the distinctive flavor. One of the state's celebrated barbecue joints is The Salt Lick at Driftwood, tel: 512-858-4959, www.saltlickbbq.com, 13 miles (20 km) west of Austin in the Hill Country.

The state dish of Texas is chili con carne, and you'll find it in abundance throughout the state. On average, some 15 chili competitions are held each month.

The "runner-up" to the state dish must surely be chicken-fried steak, an inexpensive steak covered with batter and fried, usually served with gravy and found on most Texas menus. And you mustn't forget to try pecan pie.

Restaurant Listings

In most big cities you can find almost every type of restaurant, from Thai and nouvelle cuisine, through traditional Texas dishes, to the usual run of nationwide fast-food chains. In small towns, you basically have two choices: the local Dairy Queen or some good ol', down-home cookin' "like Mama used to make". Experiment and enjoy. The listings below focus on the larger cities.

AUSTIN

Amaya's Taco Village
5405 N. I-35, Capital Plaza
Tel: 512-458-2531
Mexican. $

Chez Nous
510 Neches Street
Tel: 512-473-2413
French. $$

Chuy's
1728 Barton Spring Road
Tel: 512-474-4452
Light-hearted Tex-Mex: one of three Chuy's in town. $

The County Line on the Hill
6500 West Bee Caves Road
Tel: 512-327-1742
Classic, acclaimed Texas-pit BBQ.
$$

East Side Café
2113 Manor Road
Tel: 512-476-5858
Continental, vegetarian; patio.
$

Fonda San Miguel
2330 West North Loop Boulevard
Tel: 512-459-4121
Colonial, indoor patio. Gourmet Mexican influences. $$

The Granite Café
2905 San Gabriel Street
Tel: 512-472-6483
Southwestern gourmet; music. University nearby. $$

Green Mesquite Barbeque & More
1400 Barton Springs Road
Tel: 512-479-0485
Good food, live music. $

Hudson's on the Bend
3509 Ranch Road, 620
Tel: 512-266-1369
Classy, Continental cuisine, especially game. $$$

Jeffrey's Restaurant and Bar
1204 West Lynn Street
Tel: 512-477-5584
Award-winning restaurant with international cuisine. $$$

Manuel's
310 Congress Avenue
Tel: 512-472-7555
Bustling Mexican. $

Mother's Café & Garden
4215 Duval Street
Tel: 512-451-3994
Enclosed garden patio, vegetarian food a specialty, popular with locals. $

The Old Pecan Street Café
310 E. 6th Street
Tel: 512-478-2491
Charming, historic café with full menu. **$**

Shanghai River
2700 W. Anderson Lane
Tel: 512-458-9598
Bountiful Chinese buffet. **$**

Shoreline Grill San Jacinto Center
98 San Jacinto Boulevard
Tel: 512-477-3300
Top-rated steak/seafood restaurant at the Four Seasons Hotel. **$$**

Taj Palace
6700 Middle Fiskville Road
Tel: 512-452-9959
Close to airport, Indian cuisine. Lunch buffet **$**; ethnic Indian. **$$**

Threadgill's
6416 Lamar Boulevard
Tel: 512-451-5440
301 W. Riverside Drive
Tel: 512-472-9304
Texas roadhouse café in two locations. Southern cuisine, Cajun, vegetarian. **$**

Z-Tejas
1110 6th Street
Tel: 512-478-5355
9400 A. Arboretum Boulevard
Tel: 512-346-3506
Creative spicy cuisine. **$$**

DALLAS

Adolphus Hotel French Room
1321 Commerce Street
Tel: 214-742-8200
Arguably the best French cuisine in town. **$$$**

L'Ancestral
4514 Travis Street
Tel: 214-528-1081
Beautifully decorated "French country inn"; classic French cuisine. **$$$**

Avanti
1445 Ross Avenue
Tel: 214-965-0055
Mediterranean cuisine. Charming for lunch, surrounded by fountains and waterfall. **$$**

Baby Doe's Matchless Mine
3205 Harry Hines Boulevard, Market Center
Tel: 214-871-7310

This replica Colorado mine is a haven for steak. set high atop a hill overlooking the city's skyline. **$$**

Beau Nash
Hotel Cresent Court
Tel: 214-871-3240
International cuisine served in elegant surroundings, with live jazz on weekends. **$$$**

Bob's Steak and Chop House
4300 Lemmon Avenue
Tel: 214-528-9446
Upscale steakhouse; oversized portions. **$$$**

Café Capri
15107 Addison Rd at Beltline
Tel: 972-960-8686
Stylish atmosphere, with excellent seafood and a live harpist. **$$$**

Café Izmir
3711 Greenville Avenue
Tel: 214-826-7788
Plentiful Middle Eastern food. **$$**

Café Pacific
24 Highland Park Village
Tel: 214-526-1170
Great seafood. **$$$**

Casa Dominguez
2408 Cedar Springs at Fairmont
Tel: 214-871-9787
Good Tex-Mex food since 1963. **$$**

Cock and Bull Wine Bar & Restaurant
6330 Gaston Avenue
Tel: 214-841-9111
Bistro-type food, pâté, pastas s anddelicious fish. **$$**

Coffee Haus
numerous branches
Bagels, classy sandwiches, to-die-for desserts. **$**

Daddy Jack's Wood Grill
2723 Elm Street, Deep Ellum
Tel: 214-653-3949
Lobster, shrimp, wood-grilled steaks, rack of lamb, chicken. **$$**

Dakotas
600 N. Akard Street
Tel: 214-740-4001

Price Categories

Price categories, based on the cost of a meal for one person without drinks, are:
$$$ = over $30
$$ = $15–30
$ = under $15.

Seafood, wild game and poultry in appealing surroundings. **$$$**

Deep Sushi
2624 Elm Street, Deep Ellum
Tel: 214-651-1177
Japanese bar/restaurant. **$$**

Del Frisco's Double Eagle Steakhouse
5251 Spring Valley Road
Tel: 972-490-9000
Fine steaks. **$$$**

Dick's Last Resort
1701 N. Market Street in the West End
Tel: 214-747-0001
Fun-loving waiters and sturdy buffet. Music every night; rousing gospel singers Sunday lunchtimes. **$$**

Eccolo Ristorante and Enoteca
4900 McKinney Avenue at Monticello
Tel: 214-521-3560
Well-regarded restaurant and wine bar, featuring regional Italian dishes. **$$$**

Fogo de Chao
4300 Belt Line Road, Addison
Tel: 972-503-7300
Meat-oriented Brazilian restaurant. **$$$**

Joe's Crab Shack
3855 Beltline
Tel: 972-247-1010
Lively scene and crabs, crabs, crabs. **$$**

Korea House Restaurant
2598 Royal Lane
Tel: 972-243-0434
Classy Korean cuisine. **$$$**

Lombardi's
311 N. Market Street
Tel: 214-747-0322
Italian provincial cuisine in casual surroundings in the West End. **$$**

Lone Star Oyster Bar
3707 Greenville Avenue
Tel: 214-827-3013
Cozy pub, topless oysters and cold beer. Cheap! **$**

The Mansion on Turtle Creek
2821 Turtle Creek Boulevard
Tel: 214-559-2100
Award-winning American nouvelle cuisine. **$$$**

St Martin's Wine Bistro
3020 Greenville Avenue
Tel: 214-826-0940
Romantic dining, French cuisine, fine wine selections. **$$$**

Drinking

For a state with such a robust reputation for hearty living, it may come as a surprise to learn that about one-fifth of the 254 counties choose to be "dry," banning all alcoholic beverages. This rarely presents a problem for would-be drinkers, who merely drive a mile or two to a neighboring county where anything goes.

Three brands of **beer** brewed in the state qualify as "famous" – Pearl, Lone Star and Shiner. Arguments often ensue among locals as to which is best.

Texas **wines** have also acquired an excellent reputation over the years, and many will be found on menus throughout the state.

Tequila may well be the most popular liquor consumed, due to the proximity of Mexico, where it is made in vast quantities. Tequila-based margaritas are probably drunk in Texas more than anywhere else in the US.

Recently, the **micro-brewery** concept has taken hold, with the Belgian-style Celis from Austin having established a statewide reputation. Many "brewpubs" have decent food. Drinking-based places to try include:
Bitter End Bistro and Brewpub, 311 Colorado Street, Austin, tel: 512-478-2337.
Flying Saucer Draught Emporium, 111 E. 4th Street, Fort Worth, tel: 817-336-7468. Massive range of draught beers.
Ginger Man, 5607 Morningside Drive, Houston, tel: 713-526-2770. First pub in a chain with venues also in Austin and Dallas. Loads of beers.

Momo's Pasta
3312 Knox
Tel: 214-521-3009
Good neighborhood Italian restaurant. **$$**
Newport's Seafood
703 McKinney, West End Avenue
Tel: 214-954-0220
Top-notch seafood in a restored

turn-of-the-20th-century brewery. **$$$**
Pierre's by the Lake
3430 Shorecrest Dr.
Tel: 214-358-2379
Lobsters, crabcakes, live piano music Tues–Sat. **$$$**
Sal's Pizza
2525 Wycliff, Market Center Avenue
Tel: 214-522-1828
Quaint Italian restaurant that won a vote for best Italian food in Dallas. **$**
Tolbert's Texas Chili Parlor
350 N. St Paul
Tel: 214-953-1353
Regional cuisine and hamburgers have been served here since the 1960s. **$**
Trail Dust Steak House
10841 Composite Drive
Tel: 214-357-3862
Live country music every night of the week. Five venues in Dallas/Fort Worth area. **$$**
Uncle Julio's
4125 Lemmon Avenue
Tel: 214-520-6620
Local papers call this the best Tex-Mex in town. **$**
Watel's
2719 McKinney Avenue
Tel: 214-720-0323
French bistro established in the 1980s. **$$$**
Wilhoite's
432 S. Main Street, Grapevine
Tel: 817-481-7511
Fun food in a famous building in a famous hamlet. **$$**

EL PASO/JUÁREZ

Billy Crews
1200 Country Club Road, Santa Teresa
Tel: 505-589-2071
Famous steak- and seafood-house, since the 1950s. Just into New Mexico. **$$$**
Forti's Mexican Elder
321 E. Chelsea Street
Tel: 915-772-0066
Steak, seafood and famous chicken *salpicon.* **$$**
H&H Car Wash & Coffee Shop
701 E. Yandell Drive
Tel: 915-533-1144

Chorizo burritos or *carne picada* are the favorites on the menu here while you sit back and watch the waterworks. **$**
Kentucky Club
629 Avenîda Juárez
1930s bar, inimitable margaritas. **$**
Leo's Mexican Food
5103 Montana Avenue
Tel: 915-566-4972
Family fare. **$**

FORT WORTH

Al's
1001 NE. Green Oaks Boulevard, Arlington Tel: 817-275-8918
Local hamburger favorite for 30 years. **$**
Billy Miner's Saloon
150 W. 3rd Street, downtown
Tel: 817-877-3301
Big burgers in rustic setting entices all types. **$**
Café Ashton
610 Main Street
Tel: 817-332-0100
Well-rated, New American-style restaurant in the Ashton Hotel. **$$$**
Cattlemen's Steak House
2458 N. Main St, Stockyards
Tel: 817-624-3945
The cowboys' choice. **$$**
Costa Azul
1521 N. Main St
Tel: 817-624-0506
Another stockyard favorite, this time for Mexican food. **$**
Flying Saucer Draught Emporium
111 E. 4th Street, downtown
Tel: 817-336-7468
"Rib-sticking" German fare says one of the local weeklies. Vast selection of beers. **$$**
Humperdink's
700 Six Flags Drive., Arlington
Tel: 817-640-8553
Sports bar and brew pub (the Big Horn Brewing Company). **$$**
J&J Oyster Bar
612 N. University Drive
Tel: 817-335-2756
An old favorite. **$$**
Joe T Garcia's
2201 N. Commerce Street
Tel: 817-626-4356
Informal Tex-Mex spot with family-style dinners and no menu. **$**

Kimbell Art Museum Buffet
3333 Camp Bowie Boulevard
Tel: 817-332-8451
The setting is delightful and the
salads and sandwiches enticing. **$**

La Madeleine
2101 N. Collins Street, Arlington
Tel: 817-461-3534
Great breakfasts at this charming
French bakery. **$**

Massey's
1805 8th Ave
Tel: 817-921-5582
Sooner or later you'll have to try
Texas' ubiquitous chicken fried
steak, so why not here? **$**

Paris Coffee Shop
704 W. Magnolia Avenue
Tel: 817-335-2041
Old-time atmosphere. Great pies. **$**

The Parthenon
401 N. Henderson Street
Tel: 817-810-0800
Pasitio, *dolmades* and the *baklava*
are all excellent in this spacious
Greek/Mediterranean place. **$$**

Reata
312 Houston Street
Tel: 817-336-1009
Relocated restaurant, big steaks,
high-class cowboy cooking. **$$$**

Riscky's BBQ
300 Main Street
Tel: 817-877-3306
Legendary BBQ from a family chain
at this and other locations.
Sandwiches, etc, in baskets labeled
"for the lighter appetite" but in
Texas that's a relative term. **$$**

The Tandoor
532 Fielder North Plaza, Arlington
Tel: 817-261-6604
Good Indian spot for lunch as well
as dinner where you should leave
room for dessert. **$$**

GALVESTON

Clary's
8509 Teichman Road, off I-45
Tel: 409-740-0771
Longtime family-owned seafood
haven. **$$$**

Fisherman's Wharf
Pier 22 adj. the Elissa
Tel: 409-765-5708
Patio dining overlooking the
port. **$$**

Miller's Landing
Seawall & 19th St
Tel: 409-763-8777
Overlooks the Gulf; seafood,
steaks. **$$**

Ocean Grill Restaurant
2227 Seawall Boulevard
Tel: 409-762-7100
On the water, mesquite-grilled
seafood. **$$**

The Original Mexican Café
1401 Market Street
Tel: 409-762-6001
Dispensing Mexican food for 80
years. **$**

HOUSTON

Annemarie's Old Heidelberg
1810 Fountainview Drive
Tel: 713-781-3581
German cuisine, piano bar, dancing.
Romantic. **$$$**

Barry's Pizza & Italian Diner
6003 Richmond Avenue
Tel: 713-266-8692. **$$**

Benihana of Tokyo
9707 Westheimer
Tel: 713-789-4962
Also at 1318 Louisiana Street
Tel: 713-659-8231
Communal dining; sushi. **$$**

Billy Blues Bar & Grill
6025 Richmond Avenue near
Fountainview
Tel: 713-266-9294
Five-story saxophone as
landmark, BBQ and live blues.
$$

The Bombay Palace
4100 Westheimer Road
Tel: 713-960-8472
One of the renowned worldwide
chain. **$$**

The Brownstone
2736 Virginia Street
Tel: 713-520-5666
Long-established favorite.
Elegant surroundings, opulently
decorated. Top-notch food, too.
$$$

Dave and Buster's
6010 Richmond Avenue
Tel: 713-952-2233
Pool hall and grub. **$**

Dessert Gallery
3200 Kirby Drive
Tel: 713-522-9999

Sara Brook's sexy desserts
plus furniture as art; open late
on weekends; lunch specials.
$

Dimassi's
5064 Richmond Avenue
Tel: 713-439-7481
Middle Eastern cuisine. **$**

Doneraki
2836 Fulton
Tel: 713-224-2509
Authentic Mexican food, live
mariachis (Mexican street
musicians). **$**

Golden Room Restaurant
1209 Montrose Boulevard
Tel: 713-524-9614
Tasty Thai food. **$**

Goode Company Bar-B-Q
5109 Kirby Drive
Tel: 713-522-2530
Also at 8911 Katy Freeway
Said to be best barbecue place in
the city. **$$**

The Great Caruso Dinner Theater
10001 Westheimer Road
Tel: 713-780-4900
Steaks, pasta, vegetarian food.
Plus Broadway shows. **$$$**

This Is It
207 Gray Street
Tel: 713-659-1608
Funny name but tasty soulfood.
$

Kim Son
2001 Jefferson Street
Tel: 713-222-2461
Vietnamese. **$**

Kirby Drive Grille
8111 Kirby Drive
Tel: 713-790-1900
Casual bistro; American food.
$

Marina Bar & Grill
3000 Nasa Road, in Nassau Bay
Marina
Tel: 281-333-9300
Fresh seafood, grilled steaks; view
over water. **$$**

Price Categories

Price categories, based on the
cost of a meal for one person
without drinks, are:
$$$ = over $30
$$ = $15–30
$ = under $15.

Price Categories

Price categories, based on the cost of a meal for one person without drinks, are:
$$$ = over $30
$$ = $15–30
$ = under $15.

Maxim's
3755 Richmond Avenue at Timmons
Tel: 713-877-8899
French cuisine, piano bar. **$$$**

McGonigel's Mucky Duck
2425 Norfolk Street
Tel: 713-528-5999
As Irish as its name. Pub grub. **$**

Ousie's Table
3939 San Felipe Street
Tel: 713-528-2264
Cozy ranch house with own herb garden. American cuisine. **$$**

Pappadeaux Seafood Kitchen
6015 Westheimer Road
Tel: 713-782-6310
One of eight favored local Cajun spots. **$$**

Rainbow Lodge
1 Birdsall Street near Memorial Park
Tel: 713-861-8666
Upscale fishing lodge with classy decor, lovely gardens, seafood and wild game. **$$$**

Rotisserie for Beef & Bird
2200 Wilcrest Drive
Tel: 713-977-9524
American colonial cuisine, wild game, good wine list. **$$$**

Sammy's Lebanese Restaurant
5825 Richmond Drive
Tel: 713-780-0065
Falafel, taboule, hummus. **$**

Vincent's Rotisserie
2701 W. Dallas Street
Tel: 713-528-4313
Spit-roasted chicken, various meats and seafood. **$$**

SAN ANTONIO

Asian Kitchen
1739 SW Loop 410
Tel: 210-673-0662

Chinese restaurant with attached fish market. **$**

Boudro's
421 E. Commerce Street, on the River Walk
Tel: 210-224-8484
Ribs, seafood; don't miss the smoked shrimp enchiladas. Barge dinners possible. **$$**

Cactus Flower Café
711 E. Riverwalk
Tel: 210-224-4555
Part of the Marriott Hotel. Tortilla soup, prime rib, sandwiches. **$$**

County Line
111 W. Crockett Street, on the River Walk
Tel: 210-229-1941
BBQ. Party barges organised **$$**

Crumpets Restaurant & Bakery
3920 Harry Wurzbach Road
Tel: 210-821-5454
Long-established restaurant, popular Sunday brunch. **$$**

Fatso's Sports Garden
1704 Bandera Road
Tel: 210-432-0121
Huge TVs for sports fans. **$**

La Fogata
2427 Vance Jackson
Tel: 210-340-1337
Mexican; nationally recognized among the best. **$$**

Guenther House
129 E. Guenther Street
Tel: 210-227-1061
Century-old store, restaurant and museum; roof garden. **$$**

Hung Fong
3624 Broadway Street
Tel: 210-822-9211
Favorite Chinese location, in business for 60 years. **$$**

Jailhouse Café
1126 W. Commerce
Tel: 210-223-7033
Varied, many plaudits for the chicken fried steak. **$$**

Magic Time Machine
902 NE Loop 410
Tel: 210-828-1470
Theme park restaurant aimed at children. **$$**

Mama's Café
2442 Nacogdoches
Tel: 210-826-8303
Home-style food, nice atmosphere. **$**

Maverick Café
6868 San Pedro Avenue at Oblate
Tel: 210-822-9611
Chinese/Mexican. **$**

Mi Tierra Café & Bakery
218 Produce Row in Market Square
Tel: 210-225-1262
Colorful, festive, time-honored restaurant with a bakery. **$**

Michelino's
521 Riverwalk
Tel: 210-223-2939
Italian country kitchen, pasta, pizza, fabulous desserts. **$$**

Los Patios
2015 NE Loop 410 at Starcrest Drive
Tel: 210-655-6171
Tex-Mex and Southwestern in twin garden restaurant by the river. **$$**

Republic of Texas
526 Riverwalk at Commerce Street Bridge
Tel: 210-226-6256
Enormous steaks, Mexican dishes, margaritas. **$$**

Texas Land & Cattle Steakhouse
60 Ne Loop 410 at McCullough
Tel: 210-342-4477
Authentic ranch house, stone fireplaces, covered patio, mesquite grill. **$$**

Thai Orchid
9921 I-10 West
Tel: 210-691-8424
Typical Thai, vegetarian, seafood. **$**

Tokyo Steak House
9405 San Pedro
Tel: 210-341-4461
Sushi bar, steaks, lobster. **$$**

Tower of the Americas
222 Hemisphere Plaza
Tel: 210-223-3101
Spectacular views from the revolving tower and some classy food. **$$$**

Culture

Music & Dance

The **Dallas/Fort Worth** cultural calendar is crowded with events. The **Morton H. Myerson Symphony Center** in the burgeoning arts district is the home of the **Dallas Symphony Orchestra**, tel: 214-871-4000, and the **Dallas Opera**, tel: 214-443-1000, which performs between November and February.

The **Performing Arts Center** at 5th and Walnut Streets, tel: 972-205-2780, is the home of the **Garland Civic Theatre** and the **Garland Symphony**.

Further performing arts listings include:
● **The Fort Worth/Dallas Ballet**, tel: 817-763-0207
● **Dallas' Black Dance Theatre**, tel: 214-871-2376
● **The Fort Worth Symphony**, tel: 817-921-2676
● **The Dallas Chamber Orchestra**, tel: 214-321-1411
● **The Greater Dallas Youth Orchestra**, tel: 214-528-7747

On the lighter side are the regular events staged at the **Smirnoff Music Centre**, tel: 214-421-1111, in Dallas' Fair Park and the series of **Dallas Summer Musicals**, tel: 214-691-7200, also at Fair Park.

In Houston, the spectacular **Wortham Theater Center**, situated northeast of downtown, is home to the **Houston Ballet**, tel: 713-523-6300, and **Houston Grand Opera**, tel: 713-546-0246, as well as a variety of other activities. Nearby is **Jones Hall**, home to the **Houston Symphony**, tel: 713-224-7575, and the **Society for the Performing Arts**, tel: 713-227-5134, which presents world-class orchestras, dance companies and solo artists.

Houston's **Rice University** has its share of cultural activities with music and drama performances at the **Hermann Park** amphitheater in summer, tel: 713-520-3292, and other venues, including the university's **Hamman Hall**.

It's also well worth making the relatively short trip to **Galveston** for a performance at the glorious **Grand 1894 Opera House**, tel: 800-821-1894, www.thegrand.com, whose stage has been graced by everyone from Sarah Bernhardt to the Marx Brothers.

As befits a college town, **Austin** is also rich in classical music events, with regular performances by the **Austin Symphony Orchestra**, tel: 512-476-6064, and the **Austin Chamber Music Center**, tel: 512-454-7562.

Theater

Notable theater events in **Dallas** include the **Shakespeare in the Park Festival**, tel: 800-433-5747, held in Fort Worth's Trinity Park in July and August. Also worth a visit is the **Dallas Children's Theater**, tel: 214-978-0110.

Houston's **Wortham Theater Center** is the centerpiece of the city's compact Theater District, which also includes the 50-year-old award-winning **Alley Theatre**, tel: 713-228-8421, www.alleytheatre.org, which has earned a national reputation for original drama.

Broadway shows are regularly presented at the downtown Music Hall on Bagby Street in Houston by **Theatre Under the Stars**, tel: 713-558-2600.

Nightlife

DALLAS/FORT WORTH

Much of Dallas' liveliest nightlife, including clubs, bars, theaters and restaurants is centered around Greenville Avenue, from the LBJ Freeway down to Ross Avenue, and Deep Ellum, the former industrial neighborhood in the 3500 block of Elm just east of the central

Expressway. In Fort Worth, head for the stockyards area, where the **White Elephant Saloon** and **Booger Red's Saloon** along E. Exchange Avenue are among the spots offering live entertainment.

Other nightspots in Dallas/Fort Worth include:
Billy Bob's Texas, Fort Worth Stockyards, tel: 817-624-7117, www.billybobstexas.com. The world's biggest honky tonk. Country stars, 40 bars, slot machines, BBQ, dance lessons and (real) bulls to ride Fri–Sat.
The Aardvark, 2905 W. Berry Street, Fort Worth, tel: 817-926-1512.
Circle Spur, Holiday Inn, 4440 W. Airport Freeway, tel: 972-399-1010. Offers Country and Western dancing.
Country 2000, 10580 Stemmons Freeway, tel: 214-654-9595. The top-rated dance club. Enormous floor. Dance lessons. Open Wed–Sun.
Club Dada, 2720 Elm Street, Dallas, tel: 214-744-3232. Rock and pop.
Dallas Alley, West End Marketplace, tel: 214-720-0170. One admission price gets you into seven nightclubs.
Deep Ellum, Elm Street, Dallas, tel: 214-748-4332. Has clubs, restaurants and "underground" music.
Humperdink's, 4959 N. O'Connor, Las Colinas, tel: 972-717-5515. The world's tallest bar, has DJs and karaoke nightly.
Poor David's Pub, 1924 Greenville Avenue, Dallas, tel: 214-821-9891. Folk and country.
Sambuca Jazz Café, 2618 Elm, tel: 214-744-0820. Top-notch food.
Sundance Square, tel: 817-255-5700, www.sundancesquare.com. Downtown Fort Worth has numerous restaurants, some outdoors with music.
White Elephant Saloon, 106 E. Exchange Ave, Forth Worth Stockyards, tel: 817-624-1887, www.whiteelephantsaloon.com. Old West saloon with nightly entertainment.
The Pour House Sports Grill, 209 W. 5th St, Fort Worth, tel: 817-335-2575.

HOUSTON

Houston's nightlife is centered upon **Richmond Avenue**, north of the Southwest Freeway and west of US-610, a short walk from the Galleria. Among the dozens of clubs featuring rock 'n' roll, blues or Country and Western music, the best-known are **Billy Blue's Bar & Grill** and **Trail Dust Steak House**, both on the Richmond Avenue itself. There are dance halls in the gay district of Montrose, with such lively clubs as **Pacific Street**, tel: 713-523-0213, and **South Beach**, tel: 713-529-7623.

SAN ANTONIO

Most of the city's best nightlife can be found near the river, with dancing nightly at the **Republic of Texas Nightclub**, 526 Riverwalk, tel: 210-226-6256, and rowdy sing-alongs taking place at **Durty Nelly's Irish Pub** in the Hilton Palacio, which claims to hand out one ton of peanuts each week. The **Rivercenter Comedy Club**, tel: 210-229-1420 is a showcase for old and new performers.

Half-an-hour's drive away at New Braunfels is century-old **Gruene Hall**, tel: 830-629-5077, www.gruenehall.com, the oldest dance hall in Texas, where Lyle Lovett and Hank Ketchum began their careers.

AUSTIN

In this city of a mere 656,000 inhabitants, there are more than 100 live music venues, justifying Austin's boast of being "the music capital of America". East 6th Street downtown is the main area.

For blues, try:
Antone's, tel: 512-320-8424.
Joe's Generic Bar, tel: 512-480-0171.
Ego's, tel: 512-474-7091, on nearby Congress Avenue.

Rock and pop fill the air at:
Fat Tuesday, tel: 512-492-9545.
Country and western can be found at:

Broken Spoke, 512-442-6189.
Variety at:
The 311 Club, tel: 512-477-1630.
Maggie Mae's, tel: 512-478-8541.
And jazz at:
Jazz on 6th Street, tel: 512-479-0474.
Pete's Peanut Bar & Piano Emporium, tel: 512-472-7383, where customers sing along.

These listings, of course, merely scratch the surface of what's available, because music venues are spread all over town.

Highly recommended is the veteran **Threadgill's**, tel: 512-451-5440, where diners share long tables and stomp their feet to a never-ending stream of live Country and Western groups.

The **Austin Convention & Visitors Bureau** distributes a free folder (also on-line at www.austin360.com), *101 Musical Things To Do*, which includes telephone numbers and listings for such seasonal events as **Jerry Jeff Walker's Annual Birthday Party**, (March), tel: 512-477-0036, and the summer outdoor **concert series in Zilker Park**, tel: 512-499-6700.

Festivals

Dallas Arts District is the home of several free outdoor festivals held throughout the year. Visitors can enjoy the **Imagination Celebration** (a children's arts festival in April), the **Jazz Concert Series** in May, the Latin Jazz Festival in June and the Dallas **Dance Festival** in September.

Houston's ethnic celebrations include a Greek festival, a Chicano festival and an Asian-American festival, all held in October.

JANUARY

Cotton Bowl Classic. Major college football game nationally televised, Dallas. Tel: 214-634-7525.
International Boat, Sport & Travel Show, Houston. Tel: 713-526-6361.
Janis Joplin Birthday Bash, Port Arthur. Tel: 800-235-7822.

Livestock Show and Rodeo, Fort Worth. Tel: 817-877-2400.
Texas Citrus Fiesta. Celebrates the Ruby Red Grapefruit etc, Mission. Tel: 956-585-9724.

FEBRUARY

Charro Days with traditional Mexican rodeo, Brownsville. Tel: 956-542-4245.
Livestock Show and Rodeo, Houston. Big in every sense. Tel: 713-791-9000.
Mardi Gras celebrations, Galveston, tel: 888-425-4753. Port Arthur, tel: 800-235-7822. Jefferson, tel: 903-665-2672.
Southwestern Livestock Show and Rodeo, El Paso. Tel: 915-532-1401.
Washington's Birthday Celebration, Laredo, Tel: 956-722-0589.

MARCH

Easter Fires Pageant. Celebrates the Easter Bunny and religious traditions, Fredericksburg. Tel: 830-997-6523.
Oysterfest. Celebrates the state's oyster industry, Fulton. Tel: 361-729-2388.
Rattlesnake Roundup. Hunts, tours, demos. Sweetwater. Tel: 915-235-5488.
St Patrick's Day Festival, Dublin. Tel: 254-445-3422. Also at Shamrock, tel: 806-256-2501, and San Antonio, tel: 210-497-1131.
Stock Show and Rodeo, San Angelo. Tel: 915-653-7785. Also at Mercedes in Rio Grande Valley, tel: 956-565-2456.
Star of Texas Fair and Rodeo, Austin, Tel: 512-919-3000.

APRIL

Arts and Jazz Festival, Denton. Tel: 940-565-0931, www.dentonjazzfest.com
Bluebonnet Trail Spring Celebration, Highland Lakes. Tel: 888-336-4748, www.visitennis.com

Buffalo Bayou Regatta. Texas' largest canoe race, Houston. Tel: 713-752-0314.

Fiesta San Antonio. Celebrated for more than a century. Tel: 210-227-5191, www.fiesta-sa.org.

Germanfest. Polkas, strudel, sausage, etc, at Muenster. Tel: 940-759-2227.

Houston International Festival. Music, theater, food. Tel: 713-654-8808, www.ifest.org.

Scarborough Faire. Three weeks of jousting, eating, juggling, dancing, living chess games, folkcraft, etc. in Waxahachie. Tel: 972-938-1888.

Worldfest. International film festival, Houston. Tel: 713-965-9955.

Texas. Musical pageant of Panhandle history, nightly thru August 23, Palo Duro Canyon. Tel: 806-655-2181, www.epictexas.com.

Texas Folklife Festival. Food, music and many ethnic activities, San Antonio. For information, tel: 210-452-2224.

Texas High School Rodeo Finals. Abilene Tel: 915-676-2556

Viva El Paso! Outdoor musical drama Thurs–Sat thru Aug, El Paso. Tel: 915-565-6900.

Watermelon Thump. Arts and crafts, beer garden, melon judging and World Championship Seed Spitting Contest, Luling. Tel: 830-875-3214.

Arts Listings

In Dallas, a service called Dallas Artsline, tel: 214-522-2659, offers a complete listing of arts events, as do local tourist offices.

Comprehensive listings for scores of nightclubs – rock, country, jazz, blues, Latino, Caribbean etc – along with dance venues, coffee houses, piano bars and sports bars can be found in the Friday edition of the Dallas Morning News.

Tickets for a wide variety of theater, dance music and other performances are available through Ticketmaster, tel: 214-373-8000. Half-price tickets to some events on the day of the performance may be available. Call tel: 214-696-HALF OR 972-263-1061 for further information. For schedules consult local paper listings.

MAY

Columbus Live Oak Festival. Historic homes, arts and crafts, antiques, performances. Tel: 979-732-6090.

Cinco de Mayo celebrations at San Marcos, tel: 512-353-8482, and at Goliad, tel: 361-645-3563.

Flying Day. Vintage aircraft fly overhead. Galveston. Tel: 409-740-7722.

Historic Homes Tour, Galveston Island, tel: 409-765-7834

Historical Pilgrimage. Period costumes, tours of old homes, Jefferson. Tel: 903-665-2672.

Mayfest. Family festival beside the Trinity River, Fort Worth. Tel: 817-332-1055.

JULY

Great Texas Balloon Race. Competing hot air champions, Longview. Tel: 903-237-4000.

Freedom Festival. Honors American Independence, Houston. Tel: 713-621-8600.

Harambee African American Arts Festival. Arts and crafts, dancing, food, reggae, Houston. Tel: 713-524-1079.

Houston Shakespeare Festival. Free nightly in Hermann Park. Tel: 713-743-3003.

Texas International Fishing Tournament, South Padre Island. Tel: 956-943-8438.

West of the Pecos Rodeo, Pecos. Tel: 432-940-4777.

SEPTEMBER

East Texas State Fair, Tyler. Livestock, exhibits, arts and crafts etc. Tel: 903-597-2501, www.statefairtyler.com

Egyptian Festival, St Mark's Coptic Church, Houston. Tel: 713-669-0311.

Festa Italiana, Houston. Tel: 713-524-4222, www.houstonitalianfestival.com

Fiesta Patrias. Hispanic celebration of Mexican independence, Houston. Tel: 713-926-2636.

Pioneer Days. Stockyards, Forth Worth. Tel: 817-626-7921.

Grapefest. Annual wine celebration at Grapevine, near Dallas. Tel: 817-410-3185.

National Championship Indian Pow Wow. Tribes from all parts of the US attend, Grand Prairie. Tel: 972-647-2331.

State Fair of Texas, Dallas. Tel: 214-565-9931, www.bigtex.com. Runs until mid-October.

Texas Forest Festival, Lufkin. Arm wrestling, lumberjacks etc. Tel: 936-634-6305.

JUNE

Chisholm Trail Round Up and Pow Wow, Fort Worth. Tel: 817-625-7005.

Dog Days of Summer, Denton. Hundreds of dogs, parading, in costume, in contest. Tel: 888-381-1818.

Frontier Days & Rodeo Celebration (100th anniversary, 1999) Van Horn. Tel: 915-283-2682.

Juneteenth. Celebrates emancipation of Texas African-Americans, Richmond. Tel: 281-342-1256.

AUGUST

Gillespie County Fair, Fredericksburg. Annually since 1888. Tel: 830-997-2359.

Hotter 'n Hell Hundred Bike Ride. Thousands of peddlers, Wichita Falls. Tel: 940-322-3223, www.hh100.org

Houston International Jazz Festival. Outdoors. International groups. Tel: 713-839-7000.

Peach and Melon Festival, De Leon. Annually since 1916. Tel: 254-893-6600.

Washington County Fair, the state's oldest. Brenham. Tel: 888-273-6426, www.brenhamtexas.com.

OCTOBER

Autumn Trails, Winnsboro. Fall foliage celebration with dancing, domino tournament, chili cookoff etc. Tel: 903-342-3666.
CavOILcade, Port Arthur. Parade, fishing tournament, pet show and more. For further information about this celebration of oil, tel: 498-983-1009.
East Texas Yamboree, Gilmer. Bike ride, yam pie contest, fiddlers, antique car show. Tel: 903-843-2413, www.yamboree.com.

Greek Festival. For information, tel: 713-526-5377; **Asian American Festival,** 713-861-8270, and **Festival Chicano,** tel: 713-222-2783, all in Houston.
Halloween on Sixth Street, Austin. Characters and costumes. Tel: 512-478-0098 or 800-926-2282.
International Chili Championship, Terlingua. Tel: 210-887-8827.
Oktoberfest, German heritage festival, Fredericksburg. Tel: 830-997-4810.
Seafair, Rockport. Seafood, gumbo cookoff, music, arts and crafts, anything-that-floats boat race, crab contest, etc. For information, tel: 361-729-6445 or 800-242-0071.
Texas Renaissance Festival, Plantersville, Houston. Tel: 800-458-3435.

NOVEMBER

Gathering of the Clans, Salado. Highland games, piping, drumming, sheepdogs, and haggis. Tel: 254-947-5040.
International Quilt Festival, Houston. Tel: 713-781-6864.
Regional Christmas Lighting, Hill Country. For information, tel: 830-997-6523.
Wonderland of Lights, Marshall. Downtown is all illuminated. Tel: 903-935-7868.

DECEMBER

Campfire Christmas, Richmond. At George Ranch Historical Park. Feasts and hayrides. Tel: 281-343-0218.
Christmas Candelight Tour, Jefferson. A tour of charming homes, plus choral music, handbell ringers, brass bands, trolley rides. Tel: 903-665-2672.
Dickens on the Strand, Galveston. Victorian-clad performers, choirs, handbell ringers, puppets etc. Tel: 409-765-7834.
Fantasy of Lights, Wichita Falls. Thousands of colored lights, lifesize storybook characters, animated scenes on MSU campus. Tel: 940-322-1212.
Fiestas de las Luminarias, San Antonio. Riverside pageant. Tel: 210-227-4262.
Weihnachten, Fredericksburg. Christmas celebrations with a German spin. For information, tel: 830-997-6523.

Activities for Children

The following attractions are particularly appealing to children: **Houston's Space Center**, 1601 Nasa Road, tel: 281-244-2100, is one of the biggest family attractions with its interactive exhibits, IMAX films about being an astronaut (shown on a screen five stories high), a moon rock display and behind-the-scenes tour by tram. Another giant screen can be found in the **Wortham IMAX Theatre** at the **Museum of Natural Science**, which also includes a planetarium and a butterfly garden.

Houston has a **Children's Museum** (1500 Binz Street) with hands-on exhibits and mock-ups of ethnic villages.

Six Flags AstroWorld Houston and its nearby **WaterWorld** are huge theme parks near the Astrodome, the former a 75-acre (30-ha) amusement park, with over 100 rides, and the latter offering slides and a river for inner-tube riders.

The Dallas area has a variety of amusement parks, including the major **Six Flags Over Texas** and **Hurricane Harbor**, a family park featuring a plunging raft ride, whirlpools, wave pools, rain tunnels, a sandy beach and shops. Both of these are in Arlington. **The Sandy Lake Amusement Park** in Carrollton features paddle boats, miniature golf and a giant swimming pool.

San Antonio has two theme parks: **Sea World of Texas**, 10500 Sea World Drive off Loop 1604, tel: 210-523-3611, a 250-acre (100-ha) park with killer whales, a shark-infested coral reef and a park with waterslides and exotic birds; and **Six Flags Fiesta Texas**, I-10 West & Loop 1604, 800-473-4378. with all the familiar attractions.

The **Austin Visitors & Convention Bureau**, tel: 800-926-2282, will send you on request a free brochure, *101 Things for Kids*, with information about activities such as watching the peacocks in **Mayfield Park**, shopping in a tiny grocery store in the **Children's Museum**, taking a miniature train ride in **Zilker Park,** or trying computer animation at the **Dougherty Arts Center**.

Sport

Participant Sports

WATERSPORTS

There is canoeing, tubing, and rafting on the Guadalupe River in Gruene. Contact the Gruene River Company, tel: 830-625-2800 the Rockin R River Rides in New Braunfels, tel: 830-629-9999. These activities are also available on the Rio Grande. Contact Texas River Expeditions, tel: 800-839-7283, www.texasriver.com or Far Flung Adventures, tel: 800-359-4183, www.farflungcom. Be sure to ask about the three-day gourmet raft trips with chef Francois Maeder of Crumpets Restaurant tel: 210-821-5454) in San Antonio – an excellent adventure.

CYCLING

Bike tour companies include **Planet Earth Adventures**, tel: 800-923-4453, www.planetearthadventures.com which has a reputation for well-organized multiday cycle tours of the Davis Mountains, Hill Country and Bandera. Contact a local bike shop for information.

GOLF

There are many golf courses in Dallas, including:
Bridlewood Golf Club, 4000 W. Windsor Road, tel: 972-355-4800. Lakes and a meandering creek thread through this 7,000-yard (6,400-meter) course.
Hyatt Bear Creek Golf and Racquet Club, Dallas/Fort Worth airport, tel: 972-615-6800. Trees line the fairways of two 18-hole courses.

Hawks Creek Golf Club, 6520 White Settlement Rd, Fort Worth, tel: 817-738-8402.
Gulch at Granbury, 25 miles (40 km) southwest of Fort Worth, Hwy 377, tel: 817-579-1515. Family park with mini-golf course, batting cages, practice range, picnic area.
Hank Haney Golf, 8787 Park Lane at Abrams, tel: 214-341-9600. Illuminated four-hole course, mini courses, driving range and teaching facility.
There are a number of courses in Irving, including:
Four Seasons Resort and Club, 4150 N. MacArthur Boulevard, tel: 972-717-0700.
Hackberry Creek Country Club, 1901 Royal Lane, tel: 972-869-9364
L.B. Houston Municipal Golf Course, 11223 Luna Rd, tel: 214-670-6322.
Twin Wells Golf Course, 2000 E. Shady Grove Rd, tel: 972-438-4340.
Riverchase Golf Course, 700 Riverchase Dr, tel: 214-462-8281.
And, at San Antonio:
Hyatt Regency Hill Country Golf Club, 9800 Hyatt Resort Dr, designed by Arthur Hill, tel: 210-520-4040.
Westin La Cantera Golf Club, 16641 La Cantera Parkway, designed by Tom Weiskopf and home of the Westin Texas Open each September, tel: 210-558-4653.
The Quarry Golf Club, 444 E. Basse Road, designed by Keith Foster, tel: 210-824-4500.

TENNIS

There are about 300 athletic fields and more than 250 public tennis courts in Dallas. Call **Dallas Parks General Information**, tel: 214-670-4100, for details.

HORSEBACK RIDING

Horseback Riding can be found near downtown San Antonio in **Bracken-ridge Park** at 840 E. Mulberry. Also try **Fredricksburg Western Adventures** 830-644-2770, who

Who Plays Where

Dallas Cowboys play football in Texas Stadium, Irving, tel: 972-554-6368.
Dallas Stars play hockey, Sept–April, at the American Airlines Center, tel: 214-273-5200, www.americanairlinescenter.com
Texas Rangers play baseball April–October in The Ballpark at Arlington, tel: 817-273-5100.
Dallas Sidekicks play soccer in Reunion Arena, tel: 214-939-2800.
Dallas Burn play soccer in Reunion Arena, tel: 214-979-0303.
Dallas Mavericks play basketball at the American Airlines Center *(see above)*.
Mesquite Championship Rodeo, tel: 972-285-8777. Weekends, April–Oct.
Houston Astros play baseball at Houston Astros Ballpark, tel: 713-627-8767.
San Antonio Missions play baseball at Nelson Wolff Stadium, tel: 210-625-7275.
San Antonio Spurs play basketball at the Alamodome, tel: 210-207-3663.

offer guided and unguided trail rides, camera tours and ranch experiences of real cowboy life. Other centers include:
Skyline Ranch, 1801 E. Wheatland Road, Dallas, tel: 972-224-8055
Texas Lil's Dude Ranch, 1125 S. Mulkey Lane, Justin, tel: 817-430-0192
Wagon Wheel Ranch, 816 Ruth Wall Road, Grapevine, tel: 817-481-8284

Spectator Sports

Horse Racing
Retama Park, 1-35N Selma, Texas (just north of San Antonio), tel: 210-651-7000.

Rodeo
San Antonio Stock Show and Rodeo. Two weeks of events in early February. Ttel: 210-225-5851.

Shopping

Where to Shop

Dallas

Dallas boasts that it has more shopping centers per capita than any other US city.

Not only is it home to the internationally recognized specialty store **Neiman-Marcus** and the retail giant **J.C. Penney**, but it is also the site of America's oldest shopping center, **Highland Park Village** (Preston Road at Mockingbird Lane) where Victor Costa, internationally known for copying the designs of Paris couturiers, has a boutique. Avant-garde designer Todd Oldham is a Dallas native.

Most of the major names in retailing are represented in Dallas, many in the four-level **Galleria** (LBJ Freeway & Dallas Parkway), with 200 stores in a dramatic glass atrium supplemented by an ice rink and a Westin hotel. Other huge malls include **NorthPark Center** (Northwest Hwy at N. Central Expressway).

Fort Worth

Sundance Square, Main and **Houston streets** in downtown Fort Worth, is fun to visit with its collection of shops, restaurants, and museums set among red-brick sidewalks and charming courtyards. **Love Field Antique Mall**, tel: 214-357-6500, behind the Mobil station at the entrance to Dallas' Love Field airport, has 350 shops in addition to a collection of classic cars. As with everything else, there are many different specialties: The Englishman's Antiques, 15304 Midway Rd, Dallas, tel: 214-980-0107, has a vast array of Staffordshire pottery, Welsh dressers and other European

furniture. The **Stockyards Antique Mall**, 1332 Main St, Fort Worth, invites you to tour scores of shops in an 1890s hotel.

Houston

There are more than 30 malls in the Houston area, a city where shopping is taken very seriously. In the city's southwest section, **Rice Village** was one of the earliest shopping districts and it still draws the crowds today with more than 300 stores ranging from familiar names to fashionable designer boutiques and funky mom-and-pop shops. There are also art and craft galleries and spas. Even bigger is the **Post Oak-Galleria** area uptown, which sports most of the big-name stores – including Neiman-Marcus, Tiffany, Hermes, Marshall Fields, Saks Fifth Avenue – and claims to draw 10,000 visitors per day.

Three blocks east, the Highland Village Shopping Center also features upscale stores. For hard-to-find antiques and arty treasures, check out **The Heights**, whose streets (between 11th and 19th) are lined with Victorian structures and Craftsmen-style bungalows. Western wear is purveyed by **Rick's Ranchwear** (5085 Westheimer) and **Cavender's Boot City**, which has 11 separate locations in Houston alone. Call 800-256-9190 for nearest store.

Austin

Austin's biggest mall, **Highland Mall**, is at 6001 Airport Boulevard, tel: 512-451-2920, www.highlandmall.com, but there are also numerous little specialty stores, such as the **Turquoise Trading Post**, Burnet Road at Koenig, which displays a large selection of Native American jewelry, including Zuni fetishes, Navaho Kachina dolls, medicine wheels and dreamcatchers. The more macabre-minded will enjoy the selection of skulls, hides and trophy mounts available at the **Corner Shoppe**, 5900 Lamar Street.

Clothing Chart

This table compares American, Continental and British clothing sizes. It's always advisable to try clothes on before buying as sizes can vary.

Women's Dresses/Suits

American	Continental	British
6	38/34N	8/30
8	40/36N	10/32
10	42/38N	12/34
12	44/40N	14/36
14	46/42N	16/38
16	48/44N	18/40

Women's Shoes

American	Continental	British
4.5	36	3
5.5	37	4
6.5	38	5
7.5	40	6
8.5	41	7
9.5	42	8
10.5	43	9

Men's Suits

American	Continental	British
34	44	34
–	46	36
38	48	38
–	50	40
42	52	42
–	54	44
46	56	46

Men's Shirts

American	Continental	British
14.0	36	14.0
14.5	37	14.5
15.0	38	15.5
15.5	39	15.5
16.0	40	16.0
16.5	41	16.5
17.0	42	17.0

Men's Shoes

American	Continental	British
6.5	–	6
7.5	40	7
8.5	41	8
9.5	42	9
10.5	43	10
11.5	44	11

As befits a college town – and state capital – Austin is proud of its literary leanings, pointing out that not only does it house branches of the big bookstore chains, such as **Borders** and **Barnes & Noble**, but also many independents, among them Congress Avenue Booksellers, Half Price Books – which deals in used books and music – and stores specializing in African-American literature: Folktales and Mitchie's Fine Black Art Gallery & Bookstore.

San Antonio

Visitors to San Antonio's **North Star Mall** (Loop 410 between San Pedro and MacCullough) are invited to begin their browsing with a visit to the information booth to pick up a free shopping bag and a coupon booklet offering discounts at many of the 200 stores. These include such big names as Saks Fifth Avenue, Marshall Field's, Guess, Williams-Sonoma and Gap.

There are other malls, of which the most attractive architecturally is **Rivercenter**, 849 E. Commerce, adjoining the restaurants and IMAX theater in the heart of downtown. **La Villita**, the recreated Mexican village on the site of the original town, and **El Mercado** (514 W. Commerce) both offer specialty shops with Mexican arts and crafts.

Shop Listings

AUSTIN

Capitol Saddlery, 1614 Lavaca Street, tel: 512-478-9309. Leather goods.
Tesoro's Trading Company, 209 Congress Avenue, tel: 512-479-8377.
Texas Custom Boots, 2525 S. Lamar Boulevard, tel: 512-442-0926.
Texas Hatters, 5003 Overpass Road, Buda, tel: 512-441-4287. Clients include Bob Dylan, Willie Nelson and Burt Reynolds.

DALLAS

Highland Park Village, at Preston and Mockingbird, tel: 214-559-2740. The oldest of Dallas' many shopping centers and malls. With boutiques like Polo/Ralph Lauren, Guy Laroche and the swankiest Sanger-Harris in town, Highland Park claims to be Dallas' answer to Los Angeles' Rodeo Drive.
Neiman-Marcus, 1618 Main, tel: 214-741-6911. There are several Neiman-Marcus stores around town at various shopping malls, but this is the legendary original.
Hat Brands, 601 Marion Drive in Garland, tel: 972-494-0511. Here you can get a good western hat for a very reasonable price.

EL PASO

Cowtown Boot Company, 11401 Gateway Boulevard W., tel: 915-593-2929. Boots of all kinds.
Tony Lama Factory Store, 7156 Gateway Boulevard E., tel: 915-772-4327. An outlet for these famous boots.

FORT WORTH

Justin Boot Company Outlet Store, 717 W. Vickery Boulevard, tel: 817-654-3103. Boots, belts, jackets, wallets.
Luskey/Ryon's Western Wear, 2601 N. Main Street, tel: 817-625-2391. Carries Tony Lama and Justin boots, among others.

HOUSTON

Eagle Dancer "The American Indian Store", 159 South Gulf Freeway at FM 518, League City 77573, tel: 281-332-6028.
The Galleria, 5075 Westheimer, tel: 713-621-1907. A three-story shopping mall with two hotels, a skating rink, 19 restaurants, 4 movie theaters, and expensive stores such as Neiman-Marcus, Laura Ashley, Gucci, Gumps of San Francisco, Mark Cross, Tiffany & Co., Alfred Dunhill, Cartier and Fred Joaillier of Paris.
Stelzig's of Texas Western Store, 3123 Post Oak Boulevard, tel: 713-629-7779. Another good western store; even sells saddle blankets.
Paul Wheeler Boot Company, 4115 Willowbend Boulevard, tel: 713-665-0224. Custom-made boots that are popular with the Houston oil-rich.

Where to Find Western Wear

Western wear is, of course, a big seller in these parts with 28 shops and restaurants located in renovated hog and sheep pens at **Stockyards Station** (140 E Exchange Ave, **Fort Worth**). More western paraphernalia is available in the shops at **Southfork Ranch** (3700 Hogge Rd, Parker, tel: 972-442-7800), location of the TV-famous Ewing Ranch.

Boot fanciers often prefer to go directly to the **Justin Boot Company Factory Outlet Store** in Fort Worth at 717 W. Vickery Boulevard, tel: 817-654-3103.

Factory stores have become a major phenomenon, situated outside almost every big town. Sometimes they are grouped together in malls, each offering different merchandise. Often they stand alone and are enormous. Several chains exist with branches spread over the state. **Justin Boots and Cowboy Outfitters**, which claims to be the world's largest western store, is headquartered in Justin, but in addition to Fort Worth also has branches in Dallas and Denton – tel: 800-677-2668. A rival, **Cavender's Boot City**, 2019 West SW. Loop, Tyler, TX 75701, has stores in Austin, San Antonio, Dallas and Houston, tel: 800-256-9190.

JUÁREZ (MEXICO, BORDER)

Centro Commercial ProNaF, off 16 de Septiembre, east of downtown. A government-run center featuring Centro Artesanal, which offers items like Oaxacan pottery.
El Mercado Juárez, near downtown at 16 de Septiembre No. 103. This is the main city market.
Mercado Cuauhtenoc, one block off 16 de Septiembre between La Presidencia (City Hall) and Our Lady of Guadalupe Cathedral. A smaller version of El Mercado Juárez.

NUEVO LAREDO (MEXICO, BORDER)

El Mercado, 300 Avenida Guerrero. This is the main marketplace.
Marti's, 2923 Calle Victoria and Guerrero, tel: 011-52-871-23337. Famous for first-quality Mexican crafts.

SAN ANTONIO

Dillard's, at Alamo Plaza and Commerce, tel: 210-227-4343. One of San Antonio's most popular department stores. Also located at various shopping malls.
Kallison's Western Wear, 123 S. Flores, tel: 210-222-1364. Cowboy gear for all the family.
La Tienda, 123 Alamo Plaza, tel: 210-222-1588. Mexican imports.
Lucchese Boot Co., 255 E. Basse Road, tel: 210-828-9419. Founded in 1883 by Italian immigrant Sam Lucchese.

Further Reading

GENERAL

1001 Texas Place Names by Fred Tarpley (University of Texas Press, 1988)
A Personal Country by A.C. Greene (Texas A & M Press, 1979)
Backroads of Texas by Ed Syers (Gulf Publishing, 1988)
The Best of the Old West by Ron Butler (Texas Monthly Press, 1983)
Cattle Kings of Texas by C.K. Douglas (Cecil Baugh, Dallas, 1939)
The Chisholm Trail by Wayne Gard (University of Oklahoma Press, 1954)
Cow People by J. Frank Dobie (Little, Brown & Co., 1964)
The Cowboy Encyclopedia by Richard W. Slatta (ABC-CLIO, 1994)
Encyclopedia of the American West, eds. Charles Phillips and Alan Axelrod (Simon & Schuster, 1996)
Food Festivals of Texas (e-book) by Bob Carter (Falcon Publishing)
A Guide to the Lone Star State, WPA guide; revised edition edited by Harry Hansen (Hastings House, 1970)
How Come It's Called That? by Virginia Madison & Hallie Stillwell (October House, 1958)
Journey Through Texas by Frederick Law Olmsted (1860: republished 1969 by Burt Franklin, NY)
Kinky Friedman's Guide to Texas Etiquette: Or How to Get to Heaven or Hell Without Going Through Dallas-Fort Worth by Kinky Friedman (Cliff Street Books, 2001)
Life on the King Ranch by Frank Goodwyn (Texas A & M University Press, 1993)
The Longhorns by J. Frank Dobie (Bramhall House, 1961)
A New Handbook of Texas (Texas State Historical Association, 1996)

Smithsonian Guide to Texas and the Arkansas River Valley by Alice Gordon (Stewart, Tabori & Chang, 1998)
The Texas Coast by Robert R. Rafferty (Texas Monthly Press, 1986)
Texas Rangers by Stephen Hardin, Richard Hook (Osprey, 2000)
Texas Wines & Wineries by Frank Giordano (Texas Monthly Press, 1984)
They Called Them Greasers by Arnoldo De Leon (University of Texas Press, 1983)
Twelve Years in the Saddle with the Texas Rangers by W.J.L. Sullivan (University of Nebraska Press, 2001)
Where Texas meets the Sea by Brian Wooley (Pressworks, Dallas, 1985)

HISTORY & CURRENT AFFAIRS

Austin: Old and New: A Map Guide to the Heart of the City (Treaty Oak Press, 1984)
Cowboy Culture: A Saga of Five Centuries by David Dary (Avon Press, 1982)
Early Times in Texas by J.C. Duval (Stock-Vaughn Co., 1892)
The Galveston That Was by Howard Barnstone (MacMillan, 1966)
The German Texans by Glen E. Lich (Institute of Texas Cultures, 1981)
The Great Galveston Disaster by Paul Lester (Pelican, 2000)
Gone to Texas: A History of the State by Randolph B. Campbell (Oxford University Press, 2003)
The Handbook of Waco and McLennan County, Texas, edited by Dayton Kelley (Texian Press, 1972)
Historic Austin: A Collection of Walking/Driving Tours (Heritage Society, 1981)
Houston: A History by David G. McComb (Univ. of Texas Press, 1981)
The Illustrated History of America's Great Department Stores by Robert Hendrickson (Stein & Day, 1979)

Lone Star: A History of Texas and the Texans by T.R. Fehrenbach (Da Capo Press, 2000)
The Men Who Wear the Star: The Story of the Texas Rangers by C.M. Robinson (Modern Library, 2001)
North Toward Home by Willie Morris (Delta, 1976)
Oil in Texas: The Gusher Age 1845–1945 by Diana Davids Olien and Roger M. Oliens (University of Texas Press, 2002)
People & Places in the Texas Past by June Rayfield Welch (GLA Press, 1974)
Sam Houston's Texas pictures and text by Sue Flanagan (University of Texas Press, 1964)
San Antonio. A Historical and Pictorial Guide by Charles Ramsdall (University of Texas Press, 1976)

Texas: 1876, edited by Robert S. Gray. (Cordovan Press, 1974)
Texas: A Bicentennial History by Joe B. Frantz (W.W. Norton & Co., 1976)
The Texas Almanac (Dallas Morning News)
The Years of Lyndon Johnson: The Path to Power by Robert A. Caro (Vintage, 1983)

ART & ARCHITECTURE

Center: A Journal for Architecture in America (Center for the Study of American Architecture).
Harwell Hamilton Harris by Lisa Germany Austin (Center for American Architecture, 1985)
Talking with Texas Writers by Patrick Bennett (Texas A & M Press, 1980)

Texas Catalog: Historic American Buildings Survey by Paul Goeldner (Trinity University Press, 1974)
Texas Museums: A Guide-book by Ron and Paula Tyler (University of Texas Press, 1983)

NATURAL HISTORY

The Explorer's Texas: The Lands and Waters by Del Weniger (Eakin 1984)
A Field Guide to the Birds of Texas by Roger Tory Peterson (Houghton Mifflin Company, 1963)
The Guadalupe Mountains of Texas by Alan Tennant (University of Texas Press, 1980)
Roadside Geology of Texas by Robert Sheldon (Mountain Press, 1979)

Armchair Travel

Movies/Videos
Many of the state's major towns and cities have established their own Film Commissions, as the state has grown increasingly popular with moviemakers. Almost everybody has seen a movie with Texas as its main location. If not, here are a few to see:
The Alamo, 1960.
All the Pretty Horses, 2000.
The Best Little Whorehouse in Texas, 1982.
Big Country, 1982, starring Charlton Heston, Gregory Peck, Burl Ives and Jean Simmons.
Blood Simple, a 1984 Coen brothers film.
Bonnie & Clyde, 1967, starring Warren Beatty and Faye Dunaway.
Born on the Fourth of July, a 1989 Oliver Stone film starring Tom Cruise.
Dancer, Texas Pop. 81, 1998.
Giant (Elizabeth Taylor, Rock Hudson, James Dean), shot at Marfa in the Trans-Pecos region in 1956.
Happy, Texas, 1999.
Honeysuckle Rose, 1980, with Willie Nelson.

The Last Picture Show, a Peter Bogdanovich film written by Texan Larry McMurtry.
Letter from Waco, 1996, documentary.
The Newton Boys, 1998.
Paris, Texas, a 1984 Wim Wenders film.
The Positively True Adventure of the Allegedly Texas Cheerleading Mom, a Michael Ritchie film, 1993.
Texas Rangers, 2001.
Texasville, 1990, another Bogdanovich film.
The Trip to Bountiful, 1985.
Two for Texas, 1998.
Urban Cowboy, which proved to be the (temporary) downfall of John Travolta in 1980.

Television
Notable television series that have presented a view (sometimes greatly exaggerated) of Texas life, past and present:
Austin Stories, 1997.
Dallas, 1978–91.
Houston Knights, 1987–8.
King of the Hill, 1996–.
Lonesome Dove, 1989 (plus sequels *Return To Lonesome*

Dove, Streets of Laredo and *Lonesome Dove: The Series*.
Tales of the Texas Rangers, 1958–9.
The Texan, 1958–60.
Walker, Texas Ranger, 1993–.

Discography
The following are considered to be among the best of recorded Texas music available.
Buddy Holly, *Buddy Holly: From The Original Master Tapes* (MCA)
Lightning Hopkins, *Texas Blues* (Arhoolie)
Blind Lemon Jefferson, *King of the Country Blues* (Yazoo)
Willie Nelson, *Red-Headed Stranger* (Columbia)
Roy Orbison, *The Legends: Roy Orbison* (CBS Special Products)
Big Mama Thornton, *Hound Dog: The Peacock Records* (MCA)
Stevie Ray Vaughan & Double Trouble, *Couldn't Stand the Weather* (Epic)
T-Bone Walker, *The Complete Imperial Recordings* (EMI)
Various artists, *Tejano Roots/Raíces Tejanas* (Arhoolie)
Various artists, *Texas Music Vols. 1, 2 & 3* (Rhino)

Texas Weather by George W. Bomar (University of Texas Press, 1983)

Touring Texas Gardens by Jessie Gunn Stephens (Republic of Texas Press, 2002)

Wildflowers of Texas: A Field Guide by Geyata Ajilvsgi (Shearer Publishing, 1984)

The 200 titles in the acclaimed *Insight Guide* series cover every continent, with many books covering major cities and regions in the US.

There are also over 100 *Pocket Guides*, designed to assist the traveler with a limited amount of time to spend in a destination. The carefully planned one-day itineraries written by a local resident make a location easily accessible, and each book contains an easy-to-use full-size pull-out map.

In addition, more than 80 *Compact Guides* offer the traveler a highly portable encyclopedic travel guide packed with carefully cross-referenced text, photographs and maps.

Other *Insight Guides* that highlight destinations in this region include:

Insight Guide: *Arizona and the Grand Canyon*. This dramatic land of sweeping vistas, gaping canyons, abundant wildlife and whitewater rivers is a visual feast for the intrepid traveler.

Insight Guide: *New Orleans*. Founded by the French, conquered by the Spanish, this colorful city lies to the north of the Caribbean Sea. We bring to life the home of jazz and the wonderful Mardi Gras.

Insight Guide: *USA on the Road*. By documenting travels along five trans-American routes, our writers and photographers have created a realistic portrait of the places, peoples and history of the USA.

We do our best to ensure the information in our books is as accurate and up-to-date as possible. The books are updated on a regular basis, using local contacts, who painstakingly add, amend and correct as required. However, some mistakes and omissions are inevitable and we are ultimately reliant on our readers to put us in the picture.

We would welcome your feedback on any details related to your experiences using the book "on the road". Maybe we recommended a hotel that you liked (or another that you didn't), as well as interesting new attractions, or facts and figures you have found out about the country itself. The more details you can give us (particularly with regard to addresses, e-mails and telephone numbers), the better.

We will acknowledge all contributions, and we'll offer an Insight Guide to the best letters received.

Please write to us at:
Insight Guides
PO Box 7910
London SE1 1WE
United Kingdom
Or send e-mail to:
insight@apaguide.co.uk

ART & PHOTO CREDITS

American Friends Service
Committee 67
Austin Chamber of Commerce 91
Bruce Bernstein, Courtesy of
Princeton Library, NJ 24/25, 29,
30L&R, 38
Carolyn Brown/Image Bank 124T
Christopher B. Kuhn 329
Dave G Houser 4BL, 16/17, 21, 62,
96/97, 101, 108/109, 110/111,
118, 174, 213, 255, 268
David Redfern/Redferns 175T
D.W Hamilton/Image Bank 40
Eleanor S Morris 137, 147, 153,
186, 225T, 238T, 247
Frank Whitney/Image Bank 303
Grant V Faint/Image Bank 14
Harald Sund/Image Bank 48, 286T
Index Stock 208T, 258
Jack Hollingsworth 1, 2/3, 4BR,
6/7, 8/9, 12/13, 19, 20, 22, 33,
39, 43, 46/47, 54, 56/57, 71, 72,
74, 75, 76/77, 79, 80, 81, 82, 83,
84, 86, 88/89, 90, 98, 103, 104,
116/117, 119, 121T, 121, 122,
124, 125, 127, 128, 130, 131,
133T, 133, 134, 136, 138, 140,
141T, 144, 154, 159, 163, 167,
183, 184T, 187, 188, 189, 190R,
191, 192L, 193, 194, 200/201,
203, 205T, 205, 207, 208, 209,
210, 216/217, 219, 221, 228T,
230/231, 235, 239, 241, 242,
243, 244, 277, 279, 281, 287,
291, 292, 296, 297, 300, 302,
307, 308, 310T, 310, 313, 314,
328, 329T, 330
Jan Butchofsky-Houser 5B, 187T,
301T
Joseph Savant/Image Bank 123
Joel Glenn/Image Bank 265
Kathy Adams Clark/KAC
Productions 147T, 149T, 173,
221T, 246T, 251T, 282, 291T, 333
Kenneth Breisch back cover bottom,
63, 148R, 149, 160L, 192, 233,
237, 253, 284, 285, 322, 332
Laurence Parent 2B, 35, 68, 100R,
145, 156, 158, 161T, 223, 228,

248, 254, 272, 273, 283, 288,
301, 304, 305, 316/317, 319,
325, 326, 332T, 334
Nancy Boghossian Keeler 161
Neiman-Marcus 126
Paul Vozdic/Rex Features 274T
Peter Gottschling/KAC 28, 34, 254T
Peter Newark's American Pictures
26, 41, 42, 44, 73L&R, 164, 260T,
260, 275
Rankin Harvey/Houserstock 55,
135, 141, 150, 206, 211, 309,
312, 314T
Rex Features 52, 95, 128T, 222
Rex Features/Sipa Press 50L, 50R
Robert Fried 18, 65, 99, 196
Robert & Linda Mitchell 10/11,
32, 51, 70, 105, 112, 134T, 155,
158T, 165, 170, 171, 172T, 175,
176, 180/181, 182, 185, 197,
227, 249, 263, 269, 270T, 283T,
293, 298T, 306, 311, 315
The Ronald Grant Archive 278T
Ruben Guzman 58, 60, 93, 100L,
102, 226, 242, 246, 250,
251L&R, 252
Russell Thompson/Archive Photos
166
Spectrum Colour Library 4/5, 274
Texas Highway Department back
flap bottom, 31, 64, 94, 129,
148L, 151, 152, 218, 225, 259,
261, 318, 331
Texas Tourist Development Agency
(Michael Murphy) front flap bottom,
36/37, 66, 92, 142/143, 157,
162, 168/169, 190L, 240, 245,
262, 266/267, 276, 280, 289,
323, 327, 335 (Richard Reynolds)

Cartographic Editor **Zoë Goodwin**
Design Consultants
Carlotta Junger, Graham Mitchener
Picture Research **Hilary Genin**

front flap top, spine, back cover left
& center, back flap top, 53, 59, 61,
106/107, 139, 195, 229, 238,
256/257, 271, 294/295, 324
(Henry Seawell) 160R
Tony Stone Worldwide 49, 78, 85
Topham/ImageWorks 27
Topham Picturepoint 306T, 325T
Wesley Bucxe/Rex 274T
William D Adams back cover right,
23, 45, 87, 151T, 165T, 177, 202,
212, 224, 232, 264, 299, 334T, 336

Picture Spreads

Pages 178–179
Top row, L–R; Dave G Houser,
Rankin Harvey, Eleanor S Morris,
Robert & Linda Mitchell: *Center row,
L–R*; Robert & Linda Mitchell,
William D Adams: *Bottom row, L–R*;
Robert & Linda Mitchell, Jack
Hollingsworth, Jack Hollingsworth
Pages 198–199
Top row, L–R; Laurence Parent,
Robert & Linda Mitchell, Jack
Hollingsworth, Robert & Linda
Mitchell: *Center row, L–R*; Dave G
Houser, Dave G Houser
Bottom row, L–R; Robert & Linda
Mitchell, Dave G Houser, Dave G
Houser, Robert & Linda Mitchell
Pages 214–215
Top row, L–R; NASA, Southern
Photos, Topham Picturepoint,
Robert & Linda Mitchell: *Bottom
row, L–R*; NASA, Fred Mawer, NASA,
NASA, NASA
Pages 294–295
Top row; All Robert & Linda
Mitchell: *Center row*; Spectrum
Colour Library *Bottom row, L–R*;
Kathy Adams Clark, Robert & Linda
Mitchell, Robert & Linda Mitchell,
Topham Picturepoint

Maps Colourmap Scanning Ltd
© 2003 Apa Publications GmbH & Co.
Verlag KG, Singapore.

Index

Numbers in italics refer to photographs

A
B
C
D
E
G
H
I
J
a
b
c
d
e
f
g
h
i
j
l

INSIGHT GUIDES

The world's largest collection of visual travel guides & maps

A range of guides and maps to meet every travel need

Insight Guides

This classic series gives you the complete picture of a destination through expert, well written and informative text and stunning photography. Each book is an ideal background information and travel planner, serves as an on-the-spot companion – and is a superb visual souvenir of a trip. **Nearly 200 titles.**

Insight Pocket Guides

focus on the best choices for places to see and things to do, picked by our local correspondents. They are ideal for visitors new to a destination. To help readers follow the routes easily, the books contain full-size pull-out maps. **125 titles.**

Insight Maps

are designed to complement the guides. They provide full mapping of major cities, regions and countries, and their laminated finish makes them easy to fold and gives them durability. **133 titles.**

Insight Compact Guides

are convenient, comprehensive reference books, modestly priced. The text, photographs and maps are all carefully cross-referenced, making the books ideal for on-the-spot use when in a destination. **133 titles.**

Different travellers have different needs. Since 1970, Insight Guides has been meeting these needs with a range of practical and stimulating guidebooks and maps

INSIGHT GUIDES

The classic series that puts you in the picture

Alaska
Amazon Wildlife
American Southwest
Amsterdam
Argentina
Arizona & Grand Canyon
Asia's Best Hotels & Resorts
Asia, East
Asia, Southeast
Australia
Austria
Bahamas
Bali
Baltic States
Bangkok
Barbados
Barcelona
Beijing
Belgium
Belize
Berlin
Bermuda
Boston
Brazil
Brittany
Brussels
Buenos Aires
Burgundy
Burma (Myanmar)
Cairo
California
California, Southern
Canada
Caribbean
Caribbean Cruises
Channel Islands
Chicago
Chile
China
Colorado
Continental Europe
Corsica
Costa Rica
Crete
Croatia
Cuba
Cyprus
Czech & Slovak Republic
Delhi, Jaipur & Agra
Denmark

Dominican Rep. & Haiti
Dublin
East African Wildlife
Eastern Europe
Ecuador
Edinburgh
Egypt
England
Finland
Florence
Florida
France
France, Southwest
French Riviera
Gambia & Senegal
Germany
Glasgow
Gran Canaria
Great Britain
Great Gardens of Britain
 & Ireland
Great Railway Journeys
 of Europe
Greece
Greek Islands
Guatemala, Belize
 & Yucatán
Hawaii
Hong Kong
Hungary
Iceland
India
India, South
Indonesia
Ireland
Israel
Istanbul
Italy
Italy, Northern
Italy, Southern
Jamaica
Japan
Jerusalem
Jordan
Kenya
Korea
Laos & Cambodia
Las Vegas
Lisbon
London

Los Angeles
Madeira
Madrid
Malaysia
Mallorca & Ibiza
Malta
Mauritius Réunion
 & Seychelles
Mediterranean Cruises
Melbourne
Mexico
Miami
Montreal
Morocco
Moscow
Namibia
Nepal
Netherlands
New England
New Mexico
New Orleans
New York City
New York State
New Zealand
Nile
Normandy
North American &
 Alaskan Cruises
Norway
Oman & The UAE
Oxford
Pacific Northwest
Pakistan
Paris
Peru
Philadelphia
Philippines
Poland
Portugal
Prague
Provence
Puerto Rico
Rajasthan

Rio de Janeiro
Rome
Russia
St Petersburg
San Francisco
Sardinia
Scandinavia
Scotland
Seattle
Shanghai
Sicily
Singapore
South Africa
South America
Spain
Spain, Northern
Spain, Southern
Sri Lanka
Sweden
Switzerland
Sydney
Syria & Lebanon
Taiwan
Tanzania & Zanzibar
Tenerife
Texas
Thailand
Tokyo
Trinidad & Tobago
Tunisia
Turkey
Tuscany
Umbria
USA: The New South
USA: On The Road
USA: Western States
US National Parks: West
Venezuela
Venice
Vienna
Vietnam
Wales
Walt Disney World/Orlando

INSIGHT GUIDES

*The world's largest collection of
visual travel guides & maps*